MW00635009

Nebraska's Living Water:
20th-Century Assemblies of God

Compiled and Written by

Elisabeth James Lemp and Glenn W. Gohr

Foreword by

James D. Wilkins, Robert L. Nazarenus, and Dwight A. Sandoz

NEBRASKA'S LIVING WATER:
20TH-CENTURY ASSEMBLIES OF GOD

Compiled and Written by
Elisabeth James Lemp and Glenn W. Gohr

The Nebraska District Council of the Assemblies of God
P.O. Box 1965
Grand Island, Nebraska 68802

Cover artwork and windmill drawings by Reggie Roepke

Cover layout by Zach Dyer Design, LLC.

Scripture taken from the HOLY BIBLE, KING JAMES VERSION, is in public domain in the United States.

ISBN: 978-1-934635-66-7

Printed in the United States of America

Table of Contents

Foreword

How well I remember studying history while in high school. Perhaps the word "studying" is a misnomer. Studying history was not my favorite pastime, but as my friends and associates began to become a part of history, it started to take on more meaning. That is true as it relates to this great movement known as the Assemblies of God, and more particularly regarding the Nebraska District Council of the Assemblies of God.

In this book you will read stories — lots of stories. There are stories about the early days of pioneering churches. There are stories about people who at great personal sacrifice made a lasting contribution to the Nebraska District and ultimately to the Kingdom of God. There are references to district events, church events, struggles and victories, and perhaps your story is in these pages. Stories are important! Stories tell us who we are and in a sense contribute to making us what we are.

Knowing our history can give us a point of view that otherwise would be foreign to us. Times change, people say, and never has that been truer. Our history can help us put things in perspective and assist us in keeping things in perspective. Every young person has had to endure tales from elders about the horrific financial times they endured. Sometimes there is a tendency to dismiss those stories about the past because of preoccupation with our own struggles. The fact is that every generation does make unique sacrifices which will become a part of history. The "present struggler" should not become weary of reading history while making history. Knowledge of what went before can be an encouragement to one's spirit while expanding the possibility of being courageous in present-day hardships. It can produce a challenge to emulate what was good in the past and make it relevant to the present. It may also be a safeguard against repeating past mistakes. So read history. Read this history! It tells us where we have been. Like it or not, it made us what we are and brought us to where we are. Our history is significant.

This history of the Nebraska District Council would not have come into being were it not for the determined effort of Elisabeth Lemp. She has spent long months — yes, years in calling, reviewing what other historians had put down as being important, collecting photos and documents, and editing. This has been a task of gigantic proportions. The final compilation and editing of this chronicle was delayed because of a tragic auto accident that disabled Elisabeth for many months and took the life of her husband. At this writing she is still in recovery mode but with unflagging zeal has continued the push for the conclusion f this project. She deserves our profound admiration, appreciation, and gratitude. Pastor Joe Masten and Faith Tyson were involved with the project from the very beginning. They too have earned our sincere thanks.

Elisabeth's hope is that for some of those reading this history, it will provide a time to remember and rejoice. And for the ones who are younger, that it will provide a time for reflection to see who we are — to review accounts of dedication and faith, and to impart impetus for effectively carrying on the mission God has called us to. These hopes also reflect the desire of our district leadership.

Read this history with gratitude for those who have gone before you and with appreciation for the great things that God has done and will do through *you*.

~ James D. Wilkins
Former Nebraska District Superintendent and Pastor

Foreword (Cont.)

It is my privilege and joy to recommend this record of the rich history of the Nebraska District Council of the Assemblies of God. Page after page is a reminder that those of us who are ministers, members and adherents, owe a huge debt to those who have laid the strong foundation for this great Fellowship.

Serving this great district for over seventeen years, as district superintendent, I had a wonderful opportunity to feel the heartbeat and see firsthand the development of the Nebraska Assemblies of God. Truly, God birthed and blessed this movement by His Holy Spirit.

The testimonies of God's call, anointing, power and glory are sure to be a blessing to those who take this journey back in time. My prayer is that you will be inspired to release greater faith and commitment to fulfilling the Great Commission given by the One who has called us from darkness into His marvelous light.

Special thanks to Elisabeth Lemp, Joe Masten, and Faith Tyson for their dedicated tenacity to research, compile and publish this book.

Until the Author and Finisher of our Faith closes the curtain of history, as we know it, may each of us joyfully continue working in the Church that Jesus is building. To Him be all glory and praise!

~ Robert L. Nazarenus
District Superintendent (Retired)

Some truly great stories of faith and courage are found in the history of the churches and the people who led them in the Nebraska District of the Assemblies of God. Men and women sacrificed and worked to see churches and ministries built across the state. Pastors and lay leaders joined hands and hearts in labor for the kingdom. Their labor transformed lives, homes and communities and changed the destiny of thousands of people. Leaders emerged from these churches and ministries that you will read about in these pages and they have spanned the globe. Great pastors, teachers, evangelists and missionaries have been sent from Nebraska and traveled this nation and the world telling the good news of Jesus Christ.

History is a great teacher, and there are many lessons to be learned as you read about the journey of faithful men and women launching and building ministry in Nebraska. Lessons of endurance, faith, patience, and sacrifice are recorded in this work. Genuine giants who loved and led congregations into spiritual and numerical growth worked tirelessly to preach Jesus Christ as Savior, Healer, Baptizer and Soon Coming King. Lay leaders found places of ministry and worked with diligence to fulfill the Great Commission. Small and large communities became launching places of dynamic ministry. You will find messages of hope, strength, and courage that will bring a connection to the past and inspiration for the future. My prayer is for you to discover fresh insights that bring direction and courage as you read about God's working through the lives of the people who served the Lord and His church in Nebraska.

~ Dwight A. Sandoz
District Superintendent

Acknowledgements

Much thanks and appreciation belongs to others, and I know it is impossible to mention them all. First, however, I would like to say thank you to Joe Masten for his concern to preserve the testimonies of God‘s goodness and miraculous love for the Nebraska Assemblies of God. His continual support, advice, and time spent in encouraging me have helped make these pages possible. Words are inadequate to express gratitude for his guidance.

Second, I owe recognition to the Flower Pentecostal Heritage Center in Springfield, Missouri, for their years of preserving historical records. Wayne Warner, former director, and Darrin Rodgers, director of the Flower Pentecostal Heritage Center, and especially Glenn Gohr, who has helped me continually and immensely. Without his assistance, there would be little information on the early years. I appreciate the resources made available to us, and to Glenn, for his knowledge, advice, research, and editorial help.

Third, thanks for Dennis and Faith Tyson‘s continuing efforts to prepare a viable and completed document. Faith did a tremendous job of putting together history of the churches which responded with information. That was a big job in itself. Dennis also helped with editing. The time and input they have given to these pages have made this product feasible!

Fourth, I am grateful for the never-ending support of my husband, Harold, who did proofreading of everything that came across my desk and or from my printer. His ceaseless reading, and the words: "I just couldn‘t put it down until I was finished," became my motivation and encouragement.

Fifth, I am grateful to my parents, Harold and Marie James, and all the other "Pentecostal pioneer preachers." These great people of God paved the way for me to enjoy the wonderful fellowship I have with my Lord, and other believers — Believers in many denominations that I value and love so much! — Christians in other houses of worship to pray with!

Oh, how grateful I am for the faithfulness of these brave pioneers in bringing the Pentecostal message along with the gospel.

Thanks also go to Mike Converse and the Lexington Assembly of God — and your secretary, for help with the computer and printing projects along the way, such as, but not limited to, copying the pictures we received, which made it possible to return the original pictures to their owners. Mike, your teaching has been invaluable and will be appreciated for years to come — your patience in answering the computer questions that stumped me has been awesome. Thanks for your graciousness.

I am grateful to the administration of the Nebraska Assemblies of God District Office, under the administration of Robert Nazarenus, for giving me access to important resources and documents located in the district office. I must say a big thank you, for with those materials to work from, these pages came into existence!

Dwight Sandoz and Terry Brown, your office continued to supply materials and support. I am so grateful for all your help. Appreciation to you and your office, especially the secretaries for working towards the final completion, will be appreciated by the people.

And so with the guidance from the Nebraska Assemblies of God District Office, and all those involved — the Flower Pentecostal Heritage Center; Joe Masten; Dennis and Faith Tyson, and each of you that personally contributed stories or data, we have these pages of our history. For this is the history of the Nebraska Assemblies of God people. These pages are your story!

Most importantly, I must give credit to the Holy Spirit for His guidance, inspiration, and help. Praise the Lord! "For the Lord is good, his mercy is everlasting, and his truth endureth to all generations" (Psalm 100:5).

~ Elisabeth James Lemp

Preface

At my Mother's graveside in May 1995, Jim Wilkins, former Nebraska District Superintendent, said to me, "Marie James was the last of that era of Pentecostal pioneers in Nebraska."

When I told my sister, the late Lena Mae Leach, this statement, we both said, "We must document as much of Mother and Daddy's history as we can remember."

The time for asking questions was past — that was gone. Only what we could remember or find written could we keep. Then the questions began, first about the camps that were loved so much, and then about other aspects of their ministry in Nebraska, South Dakota, and Kansas. My mother and dad were just one example of the many pioneer preachers in the early days of Pentecost in Nebraska. What other stories could we find? What should we include in this manuscript? And on the questions came.... And so it was that these pages became written form, far beyond our parents' history.

The information in this book includes gathered data and compiled stories of the great works of our mighty God in the twentieth century of the Nebraska Assemblies of God — stories showing us "Jesus Christ is the same yesterday, today, and forever" (Hebrews 13:8). These are narratives of people that loved God and the full gospel message.

We've endeavored to keep as close to the original writings as possible. For example, from the Nebraska District Council minutes, in some decades they used mostly Brother and Sister instead of first names; other decades only initials before the last name were used. Full names have been inserted as needed for clarification. Many times during these last years, I've asked, "Why me, Lord?" There are others more qualified, more knowledgeable, and more experienced in writing than me. I have no answer!

It was my desire that we include history of our great state, and of the twentieth century that's gone. Through these stories and pictures, there are glimpses into past times, including common means of travel which have become obsolete, different methods of communication, and other aspects of life. Thus, we have little snips of wonderful historical information.

Most of these words are written by others. My part was to compile them. As much as possible, I continued to keep to the original spelling, abbreviations, etc. I'm awed and grateful for the big God we serve, for blessing us with such a great body of believers, and allowing us to record a few of the happenings of the last century and more!

I look forward to the amazing stories that will come from the 21st century. Great is our God and greatly to be praised!

~ Elisabeth James Lemp

Preface (Cont.)

It has been a privilege to be part of this wonderful project outlining the history of the Nebraska District of the Assemblies of God, from its earliest beginnings up until modern days. As Elisabeth has expressed, after her mother's passing, she felt an urgency to record the testimonies of many of the early church planters, evangelists, pastors, and missionaries, who have been a part of building the Nebraska District to make it what it is today. This took a lot of hard work and dedication. And for a project like this to be completed, it takes a vision. Elisabeth had a vision in her mind's eye and ran with it (Habakkuk 2:2). She never gave up on the goal!

Then it took others to join in with the task. She has offered acknowledgements to many of the people who took a special interest in this project. Although originally this was Elisabeth's project, I have been a part of this project from the beginning. I remember during the summer of 1995 that Elisabeth came to the Assemblies of God Archives [later renamed the Flower Pentecostal Heritage Center] in Springfield and needed assistance with photographs and other historical materials. I helped her on the spot and then continued to provide her with testimonies of Nebraska people as well as additional photographs and information I was able to locate over time. We continued communications by letter and phone as well as yearly (and sometimes more often) visits.

When the time came, I volunteered to fact check and edit the manuscript once it was in its first draft form (Dennis Tyson also later helped with editing). Then when it came time to publish, I did my best to double check facts, edit, write, and put the manuscript into a good format to be published as a book. I'm grateful to persons such as Joe Masten and Terry Brown, and my friend John Hall, who each offered personal assistance to me. It is difficult to work on a project from long distance, but I believe this has been accomplished.

As the Bible says, one plants and one waters, but God gives the increase (I Corinthians 3:7). There are so many individuals who provided testimonies (either personally or by having them written down as an article). Anyone with an Assemblies of God connection to Nebraska has a part in the making of this book.

I bless the Lord for Elisabeth Lemp, who is like a second mom to me now after all these years. She has exhibited a Christlike spirit and attitude in all that she does. I'm also thankful for my wife, Marion, for her patience, love, and understanding as I pursued this huge project.

I pray that you, the reader, will be inspired by the wonderful testimonies from long ago up through the end of the 20th century. This book chronicles the moving of the Holy Spirit in Nebraska beginning in the 1890s and up through the founding of the Nebraska District of the Assemblies of God. It also covers the first 80 years of the Nebraska District (1919-1999). It will be up to others to write the history of the coming years and decades as we all strive in the 21st century to fulfill the Great Commission to spread the gospel through word and deed (Matthew 28:19-20).

~ Glenn W. Gohr

Addendum

By the summer of 2008, Elisabeth Lemp was in the process of finalizing this manuscript. On June 16th she shut off her computer and said to herself: "I'm almost done!" However, on the very next day, June 17, 2008, she and her husband, Harold, were involved in a terrible car accident. Both were in critical condition and not expected to live. After two months of being under hospital care, Harold was called home to heaven on August 27, 2008. Now almost two years have passed since the accident. Elisabeth underwent several surgeries over the next year. At the end of January 2010 she was able to move into a house with her daughter, Nancy, at Ridgedale, Missouri.

Chapter 1: Introduction

"But whosoever drinketh of the water that I shall give him shall never thirst; but the water that I shall give him shall be in him a well of water springing up into everlasting life." (John 4:14 KJV)

You are about to embark on an amazing adventure into the Nebraska State history of the Assemblies of God. It is a journey that promises to be filled with faith-building excitement as you traverse the many twists and turns along the way!

This great literary adventure would not have been possible without the diligent work and dedication of my dear friend, Elisabeth Lemp. From inception to completion she "waded" through document after document, photo after photo and wasn't afraid to "get her feet wet" so to speak. With her faithful husband, Harold, by her side, supporting her, encouraging her, and driving her to various meetings, she dove in with a sincere passion for the preservation of our wonderful history. Countless hours were lovingly spent piecing together this incredible historical journal to be passed on and enjoyed by many generations!

"LIVING WATER" … You are probably asking yourself, "What is the spiritual or historical significance of such a name!" Glad you asked!

Step back in time to the 1800s when the pioneers moved westward with great visions of a new land and new opportunities. As they arrived at the Nebraska Territory, their hopes and dreams were met with the stark reality of hundreds of miles of dry prairie. In fact, it was commonly known as the "Great American Desert." Nebraska's climate was very arid, and raising a crop was difficult at best. Rain was sporadic and rarely enough to sustain the life of crops.

Often the rivers in central and southern Nebraska, such as the North Platte and Republican would simply dry up completely during summer months, leaving no water to sustain life. This was a real dilemma since water was the primary source of survival in this "new land."

But one day … everything changed! It was discovered that Nebraska was situated directly over the Ogallala Aquifer … the largest underground fresh water ocean in the world. All that was needed now was to access this massive resource of life-sustaining water to change the landscape and life of every creature within its borders! In many parts of the state this "liquid gold" lay only six feet under the surface!

Life changed in Nebraska. Suddenly, there was water in abundance! Windmills sprang up across the horizon, pumping this "life-giving water" to a parched and dry land. Water for drinking; water for livestock; water for irrigating crops — an endless source of LIFE-giving water! The future of the State of Nebraska was changed FOREVER! No longer were its residents dependent on the occasional rain! The treasure hidden beneath the barren surface would allow Nebraska to go from desolate wasteland, to one of the world's leaders in agriculture!

But back to your question … "What does that have to do with this book?"
The spiritual climate of the day was also mirrored in the arid Nebraska weather.

Nebraska was in a "spiritual drought." Souls were dry and parched after decades of little or no "spiritual rain." People lacked hope, purpose, and vision … even life. But then … then, the "LIVING WATER" came! Jesus Himself, through the power of His Holy Spirit began to flow and even flood across the state. From the populated eastern cities, to the rural farmlands of central Nebraska and on northward into the Sand Hills, the LIVING WATER" flowed unabated … refreshing and renewing each dried up soul as "It" stretched across the state!

Just as windmills were used to carry the physical water across the land, spiritual encounters with the Holy Spirit began to "spring up" in individuals and groups, pumping "LIVING WATER" into communities, towns and rural areas!

As you "float" through page after page of this amazing history, you will be encouraged and uplifted by stories of home prayer meetings, traveling evangelists, and pioneering pastors being used by God as conduits or perhaps "spiritual windmills" to take this water to a thirsty people.

Nebraskans responded by drinking deeply. Soon churches were being planted; Men and women were being called into ministry, and the Nebraska Assemblies of God was birthed and began to grow and flourish just as the surrounding terrain was growing and flourishing in the presence of life-giving water!

Your heart and spirit will thrill as you get swept up in the current of the accounts of numerous miracles, camp meetings, revivals and personal testimonies from these pioneers and later generations. From Nebraska, God has raised an amazing number of leaders per capita to serve not only within the Nebraska District, but also nationally within the leadership of the General Council of the AG as well as missionaries around the world! What an incredible display of God's provision from such meager beginnings!

The "LIVING WATER" of God runs deep and abundantly and it is with grateful and humble hearts that we acknowledge His hand in shaping the Assemblies of God in the great State of Nebraska!

So Thank You Elisabeth for blessing us with such a wonderful memoir of our spiritual heritage in … "NEBRASKA'S LIVING WATER!"

Now, sit back and enjoy the journey! And to Jesus Christ be all the glory! Amen!

~ Rev. Joe Masten
Lexington, NE

Chapter 2: Holiness and Divine Healing Influences (Pre-1900)

***"... he was wounded for our transgressions, he was bruised for our iniquities: the chastisement of our peace was upon him; and with his stripes we are healed."* (Isaiah 53:5 KJV)**

Historical Background

This history would never have been necessary except for prophecy fulfilled. Joel had promised an outpouring of the Spirit which was fulfilled on the day of Pentecost. Upon that momentous occasion Peter declared that, "In the last days will I pour out my Spirit upon all flesh." The fulfillment of this prophecy has culminated, in part, in the formation of our District.

The Holy Spirit continued to be poured out upon hungry hearts through the centuries following Pentecost, even in the darkest hours of Church history. Tertullian described tongues as being prevalent in the church in his days. Irenaeus, who lived between A. D. 130 and 202 wrote. "In like manner we do also hear many brethren in the church, who possess prophetic gifts, and who in the Spirit speak all kinds of languages." ... Also in the 16th century, Louis Bertrand, a missionary to the Indians, "was miraculously endowed with the gift of tongues." In 1731, John Knox reported an account of "speaking in tongues" among the Jansenists of France. Some writers state the phenomenon was found in the early revivals in America.

As the 19th century progressed many reports are available of this experience. In Florida about 1854, "Elder S. G. Mathewson spoke in tongues and Elder Edwin Burnham interpreted the same." Robert Boyd wrote that he attended the Moody revival in Great Britain in 1873, and, "When I got to the room of the YMCA I found the meeting on fire. The young men were speaking in tongues and prophesying." ... Henry Ness of Seattle wrote that in 1892 the Spirit was poured out in a Swedish Missions church in Minnesota, "This spiritual revival began in 1892 and continued many years. There were many remarkable healings, ... the power of God would fall, people dropping to the floor and speaking in other tongues as the Spirit gave them utterance."

Mrs. Woodworth-Etter recounted several instances in her meetings during the 1890's in which people were slain under the power of God and spoke in tongues. She later testified that she had the like experience but did not place any doctrinal significance upon it until she later heard the preaching of the experience as for all believers. This seemed to be true of all those who received prior to the present century. The recipients seemed to have either considered it a sign to themselves or a gracious impartation which was not available to every believer.

(Rev. A. M. Alber, Mrs. L. E. King, and Rev. S. K. Biffle Jr., *The 50th Anniversary Book 1917-1967 of the Nebraska District of the Assemblies of God.*)

The following pages contain the history, personal stories, testimonies, and data of Nebraska people who drank from the Holy Spirit's living water beginning as early as the 1890s and who continued to drink of the living water in each generation throughout the 20th century.

The Testimony of B. H. Irwin from Tecumseh, Nebraska

This is my old home. I lived in this town fifteen years, and in this county nearly thirty years. I practiced law in this town for eight years. Here I spent my boyhood, was converted, regenerated, sanctified wholly and ordained to preach the gospel. Here I had to resign my pastorate for preaching full salvation. Here I held my first holiness meeting, and it was from this place that the Lord thrust me out into the evangelistic work.

I found that Bro. Corson, who lives near here, had lost the precious grace of entire sanctification, and the joy of his salvation had leaked out of his heart.

It would seem that in these troublous times there are many things to try the faith of God‘s elect, but let the saints of God claim 1 Peter 1:7, I am living in this promise to-day.

With tearful, drooping eyes, and a faraway, longing look on this 13th of October, 1896, I am patiently and yet expectantly and lovingly waiting for my coming Lord. I confidently expect to live until he comes. Oh, how blessed it will be to be "caught up together with them in the clouds, to meet the Lord in the air; and so shall we ever be with the Lord."

But, blessed be God, I was permitted to remain with Bro. Corson and pray with him until he found the blessing of sanctification again; and when I left him he was seeking the two-fold baptism of Jesus. May the Holy Ghost fall on him "as on us at the beginning," and may the fire that fell from heaven in Elijah‘s day fall on Bro. Corson.

Father and Mother Thompson, blessed saints of God; and Sister Cook, faithful in entertaining holiness preachers and supporting holiness meetings; and Brother and Sister Vetter, and Sister Vandervert and Sister Nina Blake, I found on the up-grade, hungering and thirsting after holiness. Father Thompson said that since he had become too feeble to get out as he used to the Lord just moved in to abide with him for ever. Hallelujah!

(B. H. Irwin, "The Testimony of B. H. Irwin from Tecumseh, Nebraska," *The Way of Faith* (a holiness paper that ran from 1895 to 1930), edited by J. M. Pike, Columbia, SC, November 4, 1896.)

(B. H. Irwin later founded the Fire Baptized Holiness Association of America in 1898.)

John Alexander Dowie and His Influence

An early mention of Pentecostals in the State of Nebraska may be found in the *Leaves of Healing*, a paper published by John Alexander Dowie who was a strong proponent of divine healing at the turn of the century.

Found in *Leaves of Healing* volumes from 1897 and 1898 are testimonies of healing by Nebraskans. Also in the column "Obeying God in Baptism" are names of Nebraskans that joyfully followed their Lord in the ordinance of believers‘ baptism by triune immersion.

By 1901 (*Leaves of Healing* Vol. 8, No. 25, April 13, 1909) there was a church at Auburn, Nebraska with Charles A. Hoy as elder in charge and wife Susan R. Hoy assisting. By 1905 there were workers in Cambridge, Falls City, Fremont, Inman and South Omaha.

Here is what the *Dictionary of Pentecostal and Charismatic Movements*, Stanley M. Burgess and Gary B. McGee, eds., says about John Alexander Dowie:

> John Alexander Dowie became a strong proponent of divine healing at the turn of the 20th century and established Zion City, Illinois, as a religious community.
>
> Intensely evangelistic, Dowie stressed consecration and holiness and welcomed participation from blacks and women. The primary focus of his work, however, was healing. In the 1890‘s, he started a publication, Leaves of Healing, and opened a divine healing home in Chicago. In 1895, Dowie organized his followers into the Christian Catholic Church.

Dowie's end-time expectations, his message of divine healing, and his restorationist vision made him an important forerunner of Pentecostalism. Many of his followers accepted Pentecostal views; some became prominent leaders in a movement that regarded itself as an end-time restoration. Most Pentecostal leaders with roots in Zion affiliated with the Assemblies of God. Some, however, more committed to a thorough going restorationism, moved on into Oneness Pentecostalism.

Agnes Ozman, a Nebraska girl who spoke in Tongues at Topeka on January 1, 1901

Mrs. Agnes N. Ozman LaBerge was the first person to speak in tongues at Bethel College [Charles Parham's Bible School] in Topeka, Kansas. The following account is taken from "History of the Pentecostal Movement from January 1, 1901" that she sent to Bro. [J. R.] Bell, February 28, 1922 (published in What God Hath Wrought: Life and Work of Mrs. Agnes N. O. LaBerge, *Chicago: Herald Publishing Co., [1920?], and "Where the Latter Rain First Fell: The First One to Speak in Tongues" by Miss Agnes Ozman, Missionary, Gospel Tabernacle, Lincoln, Nebraska, taken from the* Latter Rain Evangel, *January 1909.*

I was born in Albany, Green County, Wisconsin, on September 15, 1870, on my father's 33rd birthday. In the next spring when yet in long dresses, we went in a covered wagon overland to Nebraska. We arrived in Lincoln on the 4th of July, 1871 and went south and a little west for about 24 miles. My father took a homestead in Highland, Gage County, Nebraska where we lived until after I was 15 years old, and then moved on another farm two miles west of Cortland until after mother's death. There were six of us children.

How much sacrifice people do make to obtain an earthly home and how much more by the grace of God and power of God upon us and with the burden for souls the followers of Jesus go through for Him. Thank God, His grace is sufficient. My parents endured great trials, lived in a dugout, and I well remember when my father drove an ox team and we went through poverty.

We all went to church and Sunday school at the Star school house some 22 miles away. Mother had us all stay in during preaching. My brother, Roscoe, felt mother was hard on the boys for not letting them go up as some other boys did to play when meetings were held at Cortland, Nebr. But later in life said mother was right. She also taught them never to play keeps. And in later years said honesty was planted in his heart through mother's teaching and training. Blessed be God. My father sent us older children to the city to school at Beatrice, Nebraska. I sat behind a colored girl one term and she said she became a Christian because I was good to her. I heard of a colored woman who could not read, and of a blind man, and oh! how happy I was to read the Bible to them, and to do this for Jesus. It will make every boy and girl very happy to do good to others. We each worked at home and enjoyed helping with the duties about the home. Our parents read the Bible to us and taught us to pray. From my earliest remembrance I loved to hear about the Lord and wanted to follow Jesus. At family prayer I learned to bring my sins to Jesus and to know He forgave me. I do not remember when I was first forgiven of my sins. I thank God for the call of God to the children's hearts. The Bible says: "For whosoever shall call upon the name of the Lord shall be saved." Acts 2:21. "These things have I written unto you that believe on the Son of God, that ye may know that ye have eternal life, and that ye may believe on the name of the Son of God." 1 John 5:13.

"Remember now thy Creator in the days of thy youth, while the evil days come not; nor the years draw nigh when thou shalt say, I have no pleasure in them." Ecclesiastes 12:1. We have learned we can teach the children that they can know that Jesus forgives them their sins, for the Bible says He does. "I write unto little children because your sins are forgiven you for His name's sake." 1 John 2:12.

It did me so much good when these verses were pointed out to me later in life. And we can also tell them God will give them power over sin and self here and now. I believe I should have lived a continuous victorious life much sooner in life if I had these portions of Scripture pointed out to me earlier in life.

After coming to Christ and repenting, asking God to forgive us our sins, He does, and we receive forgiveness of sins, and the cleansing of our hearts as we yield ourselves to Him. We see by teachings of the Bible that God does give victory over sin. "If we confess our sins, He is faithful and just to forgive us our sins and to cleanse us from all unrighteousness." I John 1:9 ...

And God does give the fulfillment of promise of His Spirit to the children also now as it is given later in this book. "And it shall come to pass in the last days, saith God, I will pour out of my Spirit upon all flesh, and your sons and your daughters shall prophesy, and your young men shall see visions, and your old men shall dream dreams." Acts 2:17 ...

When I was 18 years old my mother died at the age of 48. (The light of healing through Jesus alone was not brought to us yet.) My heart sorrowed, as also all of us six children and my father, after her death. Nobody told us Jesus bore our sorrow and carried our grief, Isa. 55:3.... In the winter of 1890, I was taken with the grippe and pneumonia and became very ill. My folks called doctors, Mr. and Mrs. Starr and Dr. Harris. Some of them said I might live four more hours. My folks asked prayers for me and sent for the Methodist preacher, Bro. Stewart and wife, came quietly to me and prayed, asking God to spare my life, for he told God he believed I had a greater work to do, and that praying felt like God heard it. I had a wonderful experience, it seemed that I traveled the way to heaven, and oh! it was a taste of glory, and I just got there and came back. My oldest sister, Elizabeth, prayed, wringing her hands over the cook stove, asking God to heal me. I improved very fast. The doctors said it was marvelous the way I lived ...

That spring I prayed all night once for my oldest brother, Edmond, and he came back to the Lord when at Pickrell, Nebr. My heart has believed the promise in Acts 16:30, 31, "What must I do to be saved? Believe on the Lord Jesus Christ, and thou shalt be saved, and thy house." So I believe yet for all our household to be saved.

I had joined the Y.W.C.A. and Sisters White and Sibbly gave us lessons from the Bible. As we studied the Bible with them they gave us verses on different subjects and the Scriptures were opened up to us all in a wonderful way. The subject of assurance was made so clear that no one need to doubt about God accepting them and saving them, washing away every sin as in St. John 10:9, "I am the door; by me if any man enter in, he shall be saved, and shall go in and out and find pasture." "And let him that is athirst come." "And whosoever will, let him take of the water of life freely." Rev. 22:17 ...

My father married again and as the way was opened for me to go to Bible School, I went to St. Paul, Minn., to C. Horton's Bible School, 1892 to 93 ... In 1894, I went to New York City to A. B. Simpson's Bible School....

I went back to Nebraska. At the request and provision of my oldest sister, Elizabeth, I stopped at Alexander Dowie's Divine healing home. I had him pray for me, for I had chills and night sweats. And as soon as he prayed he said, "She is touched or she is healed," and I was delivered, I have never had that since. Bless God. He declared the Word in power at that time ...

I spent some time in missionary work at Kansas City and called on a sick woman. She became very bad and the doctors called the family, saying she was dying. She looked up and asked me to lay my hands on her and pray. I did so as Mark 16:18, "They shall lay hands on the sick, and they shall recover." She was healed and said she felt like electricity go through her...

The Bible School was opened at Bethel College in the fall of 1901 in October. I asked the Lord to give me the fare if it was His will for me to go there and one sister gave me $5.00 and soon after she gave me the same amount again and I felt assured it was from the hand of God. I with a number of others went from Kansas City. We studied the Bible, attended a mission in the city of Topeka and did some visiting in homes...

My heart became hungry for the baptism of the Holy Ghost. I wanted the promise of the Father more than ever I did food or to sleep. On New Year's night, January 1, 1901 near eleven o'clock, I asked that prayer be offered for me and hands be laid on me to fulfill all scripture, that I might receive the baptism which my whole heart longed to have. There as I was praying I remembered in the Bible hands were laid on believers as on me and prayer was offered for me; I began to talk in tongues and had great joy and was filled with glory. After this fulfillment of promise as in Acts 19:1 to 6, others in the school became hungry for this outpouring and three days after the baptism of the Holy Ghost came in me, He was received by twelve others and they each one spoke in tongues. Some had the interpretation also and when the language was spoken it was translated in English and was all edifying. I did not know that I would talk with tongues when I received the Baptism, but as soon as I did on that night I spoke in tongues and I knew I had received the promise of the Father, fulfilled. Blessed be God! Hallelujah! Bless the Lord! Amen...

On Jan. 2, Bro. Parham and some of us students went down town Topeka to a mission. As we worshipped the Lord I offered prayer in English and then prayed in another language in tongues. A Bohemian who was present said I spoke his language and he understood what was said. And some months later when at a school house with others holding a meeting, and through the power of the Spirit I spoke in tongues another Bohemian understood me. Bless God. And since others have understood other languages...

In 1911 Agnes Ozman married Philemon M. LaBerge in Arkansas, who was also a preacher and Christian worker, and later together they joined the General Council of the Assemblies of God. They had one child, a daughter, Naomi Dorcas. In 1925, they moved to California where her husband died in 1929. Still feeling the call to missionary work, she later moved into Los Angles and was active in missions until her death in 1937.

"Stones Folly" at Topeka, Kansas, circa 1901

Agnes Ozman LaBerge, 1937

John Alexander Dowie

Chapter 3: Early Revival Influences (1900-1915)

"In the last days, God says, „I will pour out my Spirit on all people…" **(Acts 2:17a NIV)**

Speaking in Tongues at Lincoln, Nebraska in 1906

Amid the flurry of the world-renowned Azusa Street Revival at Los Angeles which began in April 1906, we find the Spirit was moving in Nebraska through tongues and interpretation and other manifestations as well.

> *"For to one is given, by the Spirit, the word of wisdom; to another the word of knowledge, by the same Spirit; To another faith by the same Spirit; to another the gifts of healing by the same Spirit; To another the working of miracles; to another prophecy; to another discerning of spirits; to another divers kinds of tongues; to another the interpretation of tongues."* (I Corinthians 12:8-10)

LINCOLN, Neb. Dec. 4. — Claiming that after long prayer she has received the "gift of tongues" promised to believers in the 12th chapter of I Corinthians, Mrs. G. C. Shumate, 826 N. Sixteenth St., was shaken with a strange power at a revival meeting and began to speak rapidly in a language that no one could understand.

The services, under the leadership of Evangelist C. F. Ladd, Mendota, Ill., had been going on for two weeks at the little meeting house of the First Advent church. The church seats hardly 100 people, but prayers had been offered for the gift of tongues with unflagging hope

Mrs. Shumate is unable to explain her wonderful gift. She firmly believes that it comes from God.

"That evening I could hardly wait until the evangelist had finished," said Mrs. Shumate. "A strange feeling came over me, and I rushed to the altar and fell in a swoon while something seemed to be grasping my throat. Then came the rush of words. I don't attempt to explain it. I only know that it is an answer to my prayers for weeks."

Only two words could Mrs. Shumate translate. "Eflen", she says means "amen," and "Lassen" means "Jesus."

It was not until Lazarus A. Mallek, a Persian who had been a missionary to south Russia, heard the strange language, that it was identified. Mallek speaks 10 languages.

"It is the language of the Kalmucks, a nomadic tribe of Caucasia," he said. "The tribe lives in the government of Atravropol, east of the Sea of Azof. The word "eflen" does mean 'amen' and "lasen" means 'God or God as revealed to man.'"

The gift of tongues has also come upon Mr. Reeder at the meeting. He speaks a strange language very slowly. Up to this time it has not been identified.

("Nebraska Woman Gets the 'Gift of Tongues,'" *Los Angeles Herald*, December 4, 1906, p. 6.)

History of the Christian Evangel
By Glenn W. Gohr

The* Christian Evangel *was the forerunner of what we know today as* the Pentecostal Evangel. *The magazine went through several name changes and locations. As a point of reference, here follows a list of those changes.

July 1913 — *Christian Evangel* founded at Plainfield, Indiana (a suburb of Indianapolis) by J. Roswell Flower (editor) assisted by his wife, Alice Reynolds Flower. (Vol. 1 #1 was dated July 19, 1913.)

April 1914 — *Christian Evangel* authorized as the official voice of the Assemblies of God at the First General Council held at Hot Springs, Arkansas.

July 1914 — *Christian Evangel* first published at Findlay, Ohio, where the first headquarters of the Assemblies of God was located. The headquarters, a Bible school, and printing plant were housed in facilities owned by Rev. T. K. Leonard. (First issue at Findlay was dated July 11, 1914.)

March 1915 — Name changed to *Weekly Evangel* after AG headquarters moved from Findlay, Ohio to St. Louis, Missouri. Name change requested by the post office because of another religious magazine, *The Christian Evangelist*, was also being published in St. Louis. (Name change effective March 13, 1915.)

June 1918 — Name changed back to *Christian Evangel* when the Gospel Publishing House moved from St. Louis to Springfield, Missouri. (Name change and location effective with June 1, 1918 issue.)

Sept. 1919 — Name changed to *Pentecostal Evangel* to better describe the magazine's Pentecostal outlook at a time when the initial evidence controversy was in full swing. (Name change was approved at the General Council meeting in September and became effective with the Oct. 18, 1919 issue.) The name has remained *Pentecostal Evangel* ever since.

Can Prayer Change the Weather?

The following report was written by Rev. A. A. Boddy of England after he made a trip to America and visited for a time in Nebraska in July of 1914. He includes an interesting description of a windmill and the farmhouse where he stayed. He also gives an insight into early church life and a marvelous testimony of answered prayer.

A Nebraska homestead on the plains. The white wooden farmhouse embowered in its copse of trees. The high skeleton frame in the yard, carrying the rotary wind-wheel which, with every breeze, brings up water from the deep well for the cattle and man. A great barn, a round "Silo," of 150 tons capacity. Shelter for buggies and horses (over 20 of these). These are the farm-buildings where I was staying.

The hot sun was "wilting" the corn. The roads were deep in fine dust, the thermometer generally about 100 degrees in the shade, and there was cry for rain.

The Christian farmer living and working here is an earnest brother. a group of like-minded ones had come out from the local Mennonites, a Puritan Church, once very earnest, but now in some places only formal, even worldly, and often opposed to the "Latter Rain" teaching.

My farmer friend has a large family of grown-up sons, all converted but one. Also two daughters, who are most useful in the culinary and lactic departments. One had been for a time to the Moody Bible Institute at Chicago and hopes one day to go to Africa as a Missionary.

It was most interesting to sit between the hired man from Tennessee and the head of the house (and his haus-frau). The home was bi-lingual. One daughter said they didn't speak either very good German or good English.

The little church at which I was to speak stood at a cross road, and along the four roads came buggies, sometimes with sedate "sisters" sitting under the leather hoods, and light-limbed horses stepping along easily. But then came speeding along also farmers' automobiles, some overflowing with family life, and others with fewer occupants.

The whole congregation seemed to arrive thus, scarcely anyone on foot. As I walked from "Pleasant View" I could reckon what the congregation would be by the number of horses hitched up, and the motor cars in the "Kirkgarth."

The Services were very simple. They didn't wait for preacher or minister. Some sister would speak out, "Say, let's sing 49" and hymn followed hymn. Then a few earnest prayers. Generally one long prayer in German also (it took me back to Mulheim Conference). I heard two brethren one night talking in French, but they all understood English.

"I now introduce Brother Boedy, of England" ("Boddy," I suggested correctionally). They had an appreciating hunger for the Word, and seemed disappointed if I concluded before two hours were up. Then came the "altar-call" and individual prayer for needy ones. Fans fluttered all over the congregation during the sermon, the brothers took off their coats, and then their waistcoats came off also. The thermometer surely was over 100 degrees. I should certainly have succumbed to sleep once or twice if I had not been preaching and fighting with the hosts of black flies who went for the perspiring preacher from England.

The Nebraska plains were burning hot, the corn was wilting, the farmers were longing for rain, but it didn't come.

I suggested a special time of prayer for rain. The farmer friend told us how he had rebuked an old soldier at the depot. One old man had been telling another, "What d' ye think the Methodist folks at Colton have been doing? Why, praying for rain, right outside their church by the woods; a-shouting and a-hollerin', too. I call 'em fools, I do." The Christian farmer had asked him if he had never read of Elijah in the Bible. He had prayed, and it rained not for three years and six months. He prayed again, and the rain fell. "What we want," he said, "is more prayer, and not to scoff at folk for praying."

So, at the Monday afternoon service, before I commenced the subject announced, I suggested a special time of prayer for rain, and emphasized the need, not so much for prayer as the prayer of FAITH. Then I spoke of Elijah near the top of Carmel, and his faith before the smallest cloud appeared. Six times "There is nothing" made no difference to him. I told them how in England, at a Convention held in a large tent near London, the rain poured down ceaselessly one morning, and we wanted no one to be kept away from the afternoon meeting. One of the ministers "Waved the flag of victory" by faith over the rain, and claimed, in the name of the Lord, that the rain should cease. Before we got up from our knees a beam of sunlight broke through the clouds right down into our midst, and we had a fine afternoon and a good attendance, and we publicly thanked the Lord for this swift answer to our prayer.

So, these earnest Mennonites joined in the prayer of faith. The heavens were as brass and the sun blistered around. But when about two hours later we closed the meeting, there came a distant muttering of thunder, and in the distance a cloud much bigger than a man's hand. "Yonder is our encouragement to our faith," I said to Bro. Rediger. "Why," he said, "it's almost 'sight' now."

We came back to the evening meeting. The farmhouse was "60 rods" up the road. Clouds were now gathering, and about halfway through my address, the heavy patter of tropical rain drops was heard. Then a terrific downpour. The horses outside were patiently standing, and the warm water floods seemed to do them no harm, and the motor cars and buggies were getting a thorough washing. But crashes of thunder were drawing nearer, and vivid flashes almost constantly lit up the night, which was dark now, as well as hot.

It was my last address, and I was making an appeal and depicting the great Judgment Throne. The lightning came nearer, the peals of thunder were incessant. Then came an appalling crash, and flash, and scent of burning. It was a wonder there was no panic. We committed one another to the Lord, and sang some trustful hymns and choruses. That tremendous blinding flash had been just over us and had actually killed one of the poor horses outside the church. It was lying dead on its side, its neighbor was standing beside it, but there was no stampede.

The rain did much good, and we saw a wonderful answer to prayer. The death of the horse was sad, and a great loss to a dear German brother, but some of us felt it was meant also as an endorsement of the appeal to be ready for the Judgment Throne.

There was a backslidden soul present, for whom special secret prayer had been made, and who seemed hardened against God. Here seemed to come God's personal call through the nearness of death, and we pray it may not go unheeded. With death at the very door, I reminded them that Martin Luther had turned to the Lord in such a thunderstorm, when his comrade was killed by a flash of lightning at his side as they sheltered beneath a tree.

Like Ahab and Elijah there was difficulty in getting home. The waterflood stopped some. A little company had to stay all night in the chapel because of the present rain, and the hours of continuous lightning flashes and bolts.

Next morning, before leaving the neighborhood, I went back to the chapel yard. There lay the dead horse. They were just about to bury it out of sight, and I took a snapshot. Two or three brothers were with me, and I asked one to cut some hair from the horse, which I placed in an envelope as a reminder of a very solemn incident. Yes, God answers prayer, and can even change the weather, or by solemn circumstance back home the word of His servant. I shall not forget that last night in Nebraska. [Monday, July 27, 1914]

(Rev. A. A. Boddy, "Can Prayer Change the Weather?" *Confidence* [Sunderland, England], September 1914, pp. 165-167.)

Pentecost Among the Mennonites at Milford, Nebraska

Milford, Nebraska, June 28, 1915.

At the age of fourteen years the Spirit of God dealt with me, showing me my lost condition, but I hardened my heart and would not yield to God until four years later, when I was twice brought face to face with death. I gave my heart to God, and as I fully yielded to Him He saved me, and joy and peace filled my soul.

I walked in this blessed state for some time, but after passing through severe trials and not having the proper teaching how to go on with God, I lost out. In this miserable state my heart continually longed for the peace and joy that had once filled my life. I was most miserable, living this up and down life, and knew that I was not pleasing to God, although I continued to go on in this way for many years.

About fifteen years ago, sanctification as a second work of grace was being taught here, and although feeling my great need for more of God, as I searched the Word, I was convinced that there was no such experience to be found in the Bible, but I saw that God‘s word taught salvation in Christ and when a person was saved he was fully saved from sin, and that it depended upon his remaining in Christ and under the blood to keep the experience, as Jesus said in John 15:16: "If a man abide not in Me, he is cast forth as a branch." Also we find in Revelation the second chapter that the Ephesian Church had left their first love and were told to do their first works over again, not to get a second work of grace. This was very clear to me, and when Bro. Schrock came to us a year ago last spring and the Lord began to deal with us, I humbled myself before Him, and when I confessed to God, He fully restored me to my first love, and the blood of Christ once again cleansed me from all sin.

Although being mightily blest of God, I still felt a great lack in my life and the need of the power of the Holy Ghost, and while looking to God and searching the Word I found there was a second experience for the believer the gift of the Holy Ghost, but did not know how this was obtained until Bro. Van Loon came and preached the Word to us, saying we could be baptized in the Holy Ghost the same as the apostles were on the day of Pentecost, Acts 2:4. And after going down before God and humbling my heart, on the fourth day of June, God‘s power came upon me and I fell to the floor. God wonderfully dealt with me, shaking me under His mighty power, and after a time the power took hold of my jaws and tongue and in a short time I spoke in a language I never learned. Tongue can not tell how wonderful all this was, what unutterable joy filled my soul. Oh, what peace and satisfaction this was, to know the Holy Ghost had come to abide. Since the Comforter has come my soul is satisfied and the joy of the Lord is with me day by day. God‘s will and Word has been revealed unto me as it never has been before, and Jesus is becoming most real and precious.

I must say that every one needs the power of the Holy Ghost in their lives. He makes Jesus so real and satisfies to the uttermost.

I thank God that He not only baptized me, but eight others in my family, including Jesse, the youngest, age nineteen years; also my wife, and they all spoke in tongues as the Spirit gave them utterance. All glory and praise unto His name. I shall never cease to praise Him for His goodness and mercy to me. Amen.

(John S. Miller, "Nine in One Family Baptized in the Holy Ghost," *The Gospel Witness* [Los Angeles, California], Vol. I, No. IV, [1915?], pp. 2-3.)

Testimony of Rev. Silas Miller of Milford, Nebraska

Here is the testimony of Rev. Silas Miller of Milford, Nebraska, who received the Pentecostal baptism on May 30, 1915. He reports on a mighty moved of God in Nebraska just one year after the founding of the Assemblies of God.

Oh, that men would praise the Lord for his goodness, and for his wonderful works to the children of men! Psalm 107:8. It is with a grateful heart that I give my testimony for what the Lord had done for me. After years of empty profession, He gloriously saved me in the month of February, 1905. Soon after I was saved I felt a call for active Christian service and yielded myself wholly to God, to live for His glory and the up-building of His cause. A few years later I entered the ministry and about this time the Lord began to deal with me, creating within me a great hunger for more of Him. I had seen, heard and read much of the second work of grace theory, but always felt that was not what I wanted. I read everything I could get in regard to the Holy Spirit and His office work. All this time I realized I was growing in the grace of God, and getting stronger in Him, and received many precious experiences, and many definite blessings from God, but only after a time to feel the hungry heart again crying out for more of God.

A few years ago I began to hear and read of the Pentecostal outpouring all over the earth. I watched this closely, and came in contact with people that had received the baptism in the Holy Ghost with the speaking in other tongues as the evidence. I at once saw that they had something that I did not have and God revealed to me that this was for me and that it was what my heart was hungering for. On the evening of May twenty-ninth God began to pour out His Spirit upon his people here, and on Sunday morning May thirtieth, as I humbled myself before the Lord, the power of God came on me and soon I was speaking in a language I had never learned as the evidence that the Holy Ghost had come and was speaking through me, the same as on the day of Pentecost, and also the same as the house of Cornelius and at Ephesus. Since that day my heart is satisfied, the hunger is stilled. All glory to God for what He has done.

Many people say, when asked to seek the baptism in the Holy Ghost, "Why should I throw away what God has done for me." I would say that it is not necessary to throw away what God has done for you, but humble yourself anew at Jesus feet and tarry before Him, until he baptizes you with the Holy Ghost and speaks through you in other tongues as the evidence.

After years of earnest prayer and waiting on God, for Him to manifest Himself the power has at last began to fall. Souls, that nothing else could move, have now been brought down by the power of God, and have been gloriously saved and filled with the Spirit. Fifty-three have now received the baptism in the Holy Ghost with the evidence of speaking in other tongues, and twenty-four have been saved through the blood of Jesus. God seems to be stirring the people for a great distance from here. Two sisters have come quite a distance to the meetings and both have received the Holy Ghost, and have gone home to tell others what God has done for them. They report of other hungry hearts where they are.

Beloved I believe we are just entering upon a great awakening, and if God's people keep true and in the Spirit, our blessed Lord will reveal Himself in power and great glory. Pray for the dear saints here, that each one may go on with God and be kept unto the coming of the Lord.

(Silas J. Miller, "Personal Testimony of Pastor Silas J. Miller," *The Gospel Witness* [Los Angeles, California], Vol. I, No. IV, [1915?], p. 2.)

Revival in Kansas and Nebraska

When this simple Gospel is preached, God is able to work. Sinners are saved, souls that are in bondage and under the law are gloriously set free, believers who are hungry for God are filled with the Holy Ghost and speak in tongues. If the preaching of this simple Gospel was only a matter of establishing a doctrine and no results follow it would be evident that God would not confirm it, but when souls get through to God and receive their heart's desire and the glory of God shines in their face it is seen a proof that God does confirm it. This we have seen ever since we came in contact with the Pentecostal movement. We seen it again during the recent REVIVAL IN KANSAS AND NEBRASKA where many souls were saved and baptized in the Holy Ghost. Many who were in bondage saw their liberty in Christ and were gloriously set free and are now praising God for His wonderful works.

... In Nebraska where the opposition is not so strong God is working in a much mightier way. The ministers and the people were hungry for more of God. They had been praying for years to get deeper into God. As soon as the Truth was preached to them the power fell and sinners were saved and believers baptized in the Holy Ghost. The remarkable feature of this revival is that God is sweeping in almost entire families. A family of five belonging to the Evangelical church were all baptized in the Spirit, another family of eleven were all filled with the Holy Ghost except two, also a family of nine were all filled except two, one of these was saved just previous to her baptism. A week ago the Lord began to deal in a definite way with a large family, every member which was unsaved. One of the younger boys was first saved and immediately afterwards he was filled with the Holy Ghost, and a great burden came upon him for the rest of the family. Five other members of the family including the father have since been gloriously saved and four of these have received the Holy Ghost.

People from other churches have been coming to these meetings. A sister from the German Methodist church came from a distance of two hundred miles. She had been seeking for the Holy Ghost a long time and was very hungry; God baptized her in the third service after she came. Another sister was sent here from a distance of fifty miles to investigate the work to see if it be of God. The power fell on her in the first meeting and a few days later she was filled with the Holy Ghost. She returned home to declare the glad tidings and we trust that many in that assembly will receive the like precious gift of the Holy Ghost. God is still working in this community saving sinners and baptizing believers in the Holy Ghost. May God have a people in this place that will be firmly established in the simple Gospel of Jesus Christ and grow up into Him in all things.

(A. D. Guth, "A Life of Victory and Power," *The Gospel Witness* [Los Angeles, California], Vol. I, No. IV, [1915?], pp. 6-7.)

Chapter 4: Harold Allen to Norman Correll

"Teach them to your children, talking about them when you sit at home and when you walk along the road, when you lie down and when you get up. Write them on the doorframes of your houses and on your gates, so that your days and the days of your children may be many in the land that the Lord swore to give your forefathers, as many as the days that the heavens are above the earth."
(Deuteronomy 11:19-21 NIV)

Allen, Harold	Blair, Charles	Cave, Mary
Anderson, Chester	Buffum, Herbert	Comstock, George
Argue, Dave	Carmichael, Adele	Correll, Norman
Birdwell, Robert	Carmichael, George	

The next section of the book includes testimonies from a sampling of people in Nebraska's 20th-century Pentecostal history, divided into three chapters (A-C; D-K; and L-Z). Some testimonies are from the early 1900s, and others are reflections from contemporary people. These are memories worth repeating.

Allen, Harold E.

I was saved in 1924 and in 1925 attended a camp meeting in McCook, Nebraska, where Brother Harris was Pastor and Brother T. K Leonard was the camp meeting speaker. This was a wonderful experience….

My first ministry began in 1936. It began, when a dear friend of mine, Brother Alva Kite, was holding a meeting in Ogallala, Nebraska. Since we were good friends and from the same church, he wanted me to help him in the meeting. I led the singing, helped at the altar, and preached some. The meeting ended with the church calling him to be their Pastor. Brother Alber was the District Superintendent at that time.

My first Pastorate was in 1937 at Oberlin, Kansas. After leaving Oberlin a first time, LoRee [my wife] and I returned to Oberlin in 1943. It was during this time that we visited and enjoyed several special meetings in McCook.

In 1970, we became Pastors in Wallace, NE. We were pastors there for five years. (Rev. Harold E. Allen, 1998).

Harold Allen received a certificate and was honored for fifty years of continuous service to the Assemblies of God in 1988.

Anderson, Chester and Lura

Chester Anderson, the 7th of eight sons, was born to Mr. and Mrs. George Anderson of Mariaville, Nebraska on the 17th day of February, 1896. He had lived the happy, busy, carefree life of a normal boy until the age of ten. He was summoned to the bedside of his dying mother. She had called each of the sons to give them precious last words of assurance, guidance and a whispered goodbye. Placing a feeble hand on a boyish shoulder, to Chester she gently said, "Now Chester, you be a good boy, live for God, and do something for Him." Soon she had slipped away inside the portals of Heaven--leaving behind a saddened father and eight motherless boys to feed, clothe and to establish a home and future for. He was kept busy with the farm work and household tasks. In 1910, George wed Melissa Maddoux, giving him a partner and some help in raising the boy.

Chester attended a country school, helped with the farm work, and played baseball. He loved to sing and play musical instruments.

In the fall of 1917, Brother Harvey, a stern man of God, conducted Full Gospel meetings in the old schoolhouse. People gathered in to hear his stirring messages of repentance, the Baptism of the Holy Ghost with the Bible evidence of speaking in other tongues, Baptism by immersion, divine healing by prayer and anointing with oil, and the Second Coming of Christ. Some people were convicted and gave their hearts to God. Others scoffed, jeered and threatened the preacher and those who favored his doctrine.

One evening, as Brother Harvey gave the altar call, Chester felt that tugging at his heart strings, sadness for his sins, and he could hear again his mother‘s last whispers. Stepping out from the crowd composed of his former schoolmates, neighbors, members of the baseball team and those who had danced to his music; he walked to an old recitation bench and gave his heart to God. Lura, too, felt she needed that peace and gave her heart to God also.

Gene, a brother of Chester‘s, and Effie, Lura‘s sister, were attending the meetings also. They too felt the call to wash their souls in the blood of the Saviour and they found peace in their hearts. They all received the Holy Spirit just as those who were in the Upper Room.

Brother Harvey told Chester he felt God had a work for him to do. But Chester loved the farm and the sacrifice and struggle looked great. He thought using his music for God would be enough....

Jesus became even more precious after the death of their little baby boy and they endeavored to do more for him--soothing and healing some of the wounds on their hearts. They traveled to schoolhouses and small towns such as Burton and Burke, Nebraska; and Lucas, Wewela, and Clearfield, South Dakota with Brother Gene or alone, giving their testimonies and singing God‘s praises. They endured many long miles of snow and mud in old cars with broken windows, poor tires, and hesitant motors. Gas came high due to meager means. They risked washouts, condemned bridges and straying livestock hurrying with the Gospel message.

Chester and Gene felt that preaching the Gospel became more necessary while they made a living from their farms also. On the 24th day of August, 1920, Vance was born—partially filling little Verlin‘s place in their home ... Also to this union was born Garlen, Loris, Cressel, Bobbie, and Darlene. Crops failed to give an abundant living but food enough to feed hungry mouths. Patches gave longer life to much worn garments and feet were wrapped in newspaper to make the cold walks to school more endurable. Many chores were to be done alone as their parents journeyed with the Gospel....

Lester Dye, Gus Adamson, and Raymond Davis, newly converted young men, asked for the Gospel to be taken to Anoka. The revival began on January 12, 1934. Crowds filled the cement block building while many stood on the outside--some hungry for God, yet some curious, reluctant, or defiant. The roof had leaked and the water had frozen on the ceiling and walls. When a wood stove was started, steam formed and you could hardly see from one end of the building to the other.

Meanwhile, at the age of twelve, Garlen was ill with a ruptured appendix, but God restored his health. There was scarcely money enough for food and gas to drive to services. Darlene, ill with pneumonia, was nursed back to health in the poorly heated building where the Gospel was being preached....

Discouragement came, due to the lull in the progress of saving souls. Dry seasons, dust storms, grasshoppers, poor crops and debts began to cut Chester away from the farm. Sadly he parted with his few possessions and moved his family to Anoka. More time and effort was spent in proclaiming the Gospel.

In the fall of 1934, a camp meeting was held at the point where the Niobrara and Keyapaha Rivers meet. The people newly saved and older people in God attended the services enjoying the messages from God and the power that fell. Wonderful joy and peace flooded their hearts as they fellowshipped together.

Chester felt the burden to carry the Gospel further. He built a house trailer to provide living quarters while carrying the Gospel. He took the Word to Meek, Dorsey, and Scottville.

One night God gave Chester a dream to build a portable tabernacle. With God's blue print as a guide, the tabernacle was carefully built. The tabernacle was set up in Butte, Lynch (South Dakota), and O'Neill where more names were written in the Book of Life.

Without the help of those who had found God, it would have been impossible to proclaim the Gospel to so many places. Tithes, offerings, food, and clothing were given as God laid the burden on the hearts of His children. Vance has said the people in Butte sacrificed so their pastor, Chester, could take the gospel to other areas.

The burden led to the towns of Monowi, Wood, Newport, Wagner, Delmont, Lake Andes, Ravinnia, Herrick, Gregory, Bonesteel, St Charles (SD), and Spencer. People arrived at the crossroads of life. Some decisions were made to follow the Lord, others turned Him away.

In 1944 while visiting in the Anderson home, God showed Mariesther Wuest, a girl in her teens that was a high school convert in the Lake Andes, South Dakota meeting, an old store building where he wanted Chester to preach. Chester asked her if she could recognize the building. She felt she could, so they started driving the main streets of towns. The building was located in Ewing. After long hours of hard work, the building was made in condition for services. (August 12, 1944 services began, according to Ileen Lee, Ewing, Nebraska) Living quarters in the back were crowded, too warm or cold. The heavy load put Chester's health in a critical state. Lura carried the load the best she could and others helped keep the regular services going. Russell was just a toddler. Vance was serving his country. His absence was deeply felt at this time. Chester became disheartened because his poor health making it impossible to be active in God's service.

From November until Easter, Chester was absent from his duties as Pastor and Evangelist. Soon he was busy again traveling to Clearwater, Jamison, Wausa, Brockaburg, Atkinson, Amelia, Page, Niobrara, Bloomfield, Verdel, Center and Orchard. Many decisions were made and problems solved because God visited someone in the night hours.

Churches were built in Butte, Ewing and Jamison where people may worship God and hear His Word. In recent years, Chester and Lura had been putting much time, prayer, money and effort into the work at Niobrara. The tabernacle has been made into a permanent place of worship for the Indian folk and others nearby.

(Ilene Anderson, "A Glimpse into Past Years," February 1962; and Vance Anderson's writings, 1997.)

The Andersons were used by God to bring the Pentecostal message to the Nebraska/South Dakota border towns in the 1920s and for many more years. Their musical ministry drew large crowds and played a large part in the revivals of the 1920s and '30s in that area.

Argue, Dave

I came to Nebraska in December of 1970. After living briefly in Grand Island, I moved with my wife Rogene (Christensen) of Holdrege, Nebraska, to Lincoln to begin work at the University of Nebraska. At that time, the Lord had raised up a powerful revival which was a direct offshoot of the Jesus people revival of the late '60s and early '70s. The running back Joe Orduna and other collegians formed the nucleus of an extremely powerful move of God's Spirit that attracted upwards of 250 people to weekly meetings in the student union on campus.

Out of that ministry contact and groups developed on up to twelve campuses throughout the state of Nebraska, and out of the five and a half years that I was state director for campus ministries, we could count 30 persons who ended up entering full time vocational ministry.

The campus ministry was supported by the churches of Nebraska very faithfully. Out of campus ministries we did summer bookstores at the camp grounds in Lexington, seminars across the state and special evangelistic outreaches to the campuses in Chadron, Kearney, Omaha, Lincoln, Milford, Crete, Peru, Wayne State, and others.

When campus ministries began in Nebraska, we were one of perhaps twelve other full-time campus ministers in the nation and our program was considered by many to be a leader in state wide development and support.

(DaveArgue, 1998).

Birdwell, J. Robert

J. Robert Birdwell, pastor of the Christian Life Fellowship, in Lincoln, is senior chaplain of Lincoln Chaplaincy Corps.

The corps, a cooperative effort of the Lincoln Police and Fire Departments, is made up of 24 active-duty chaplains who are on call to do follow-up work for the two city departments.

Much of the work referred to the corps involves domestic difficulties, needs of senior citizens, child abuse, drug addicts, suicide attempts, bereaved individuals and families, sex offenders, and missing persons.

Many of the chaplains are ministers of the Lincoln area and all serve on a volunteer basis. In a month‘s time, most chaplains give 24 hours or more to police and fire department referrals.

As the senior chaplain, Pastor Birdwell supervises the new chaplains and takes them through a training period. His enthusiasm for the chaplaincy work is well known.

In a recent Lincoln newspaper story, "Profiles of Lincoln Police," Chaplain Birdwell‘s work with the corps was highlighted. Police and fire departments of other cities have become interested.

Brother Birdwell came to Lincoln in 1958 to pastor the Havelock Assembly, now the Christian Life Fellowship. In recent years, besides the pastoral and chaplaincy work, Chaplain Birdwell has been actively engaged in ministry to refugees from Vietnam and Thailand. His interest has taken him to refugee camps abroad. He also has served on the state board of the Parent Teacher Association.

His wife, Twila, an accomplished musician, assists the chaplain.

("Lincoln Pastor is Senior Police Chaplain," *Pentecostal Evangel*, July 22, 1984, p 27.)

Blair, Charles E. Blair

Here follows a narrative about Rev. Charles Blair in Nebraska. During 1942 and 1943 Charles E. Blair was Nebraska's D-CAP. Blair later pastored Calvary Temple in Denver, Colorado.

"... Money, however, continued a problem. Right away I had to buy an overcoat, the first one I‘d ever needed. Laundry was another expense I hadn‘t reckoned on: shirts and underwear I could do myself, but sheets had to go out, and in smoky Minneapolis it seemed my light beige suit was always at the cleaners. Then winter began in earnest: for the first time in my life I needed gloves, overshoes, a scarf. (Charles was from Oklahoma.)

In December I met the man who was to affect everything that happened afterwards. He was the Reverend A. M. Alber, a huge, white-haired bear of a man, as tall as my father and third again his weight, who was Superintendent of the Assemblies of God churches for the Nebraska District. Two of my roommates,[at North Central] Carlyle Beebe and Paul Wagner, were from Nebraska and Reverend Alber stopped by our room whenever he came to lecture at the school. He would ease his giant frame on to one of our small desk chairs, his shock of hair gleaming like a Minnesota snowfall in the light of the study lamp, and encourage us to hold fast to our dreams.

As the long winter gave way to a breath catching Northern spring, I became part of a team serving country churches, as at Southwestern. I preached in a gentler, less passionate manner now, modeling myself after Dr. Linquist at the Minneapolis Gospel Tabernacle. But I was still a raw, untrained speaker who knew little about the Bible and less about the world.

How then could I explain what happened each time I stood up to deliver one of these stumbling sermons? The small congregation would be made up of hard-muscled no-nonsense people whose grandparents had cleared these Northern forests and to whom an inexperienced 19-year-old boy had nothing, in a natural way, to teach. But as I opened my mouth to speak, something bigger, stronger, better than myself took over. I forgot where I was and who I was, forgot everything except the incredible love of God for each person in that place. And these farmers and woodsmen and shopkeepers wept, and called out Jesus' name, and came forward to give Him their lives. I knew it wasn't my word, and yet I also knew that I was somehow meant to be doing what I was doing.

How then was I to get the necessary ordination? The cost of living in Minneapolis was simply too high for me. At the beginning of May the last month's meal ticket had to be purchased. May 1 arrived and I didn't have the money. With a heart as heavy as the day I first entered the lobby, I went to Mrs. Ketter's office to tell her I would not be able to complete even this year at North Central.

I had a standing offer of a full-time job at the Minneapolis Penney's. What other choice was there? ... In Minneapolis I could stay with a student who lived in town and work at Penney's until I had saved enough to go back to school.

Packing my suitcase was easy, saying goodbye to friends like Tim Hollingsworth, Carlyle Beebe, and Paul Wagner was not. We sat about the room, my last night in the dorm, making elaborate plans for reunions that each of us knew in his heart would never be held. I looked up to see Reverend Alber's large bulk filling the doorway. "What's this they tell me downstairs? You're leaving North Central, Charles?"

I explained about the meal ticket. He knew I'd been living from one financial crisis to the next.

"How do you feel about it?" he asked. "Leaving school to go to work?"

"It should be okay," I said with what I trusted was nonchalance. "I mean, I like the store and--" The treacherous tears that all my life had betrayed my feelings pricked the back of my eyes.

The other students looked away, feeling my embarrassment, but Reverend Alber continued to stare at me, a curious, scrutinizing gaze. "What do you want to do, more than anything on earth?" he asked.

"To preach," I said instantly, not even stopping to think.

Still he continued to study me. "If you want to preach," he said at last, "I can find a platform for you right now in Nebraska. I"m setting up the District summer program and I could use a youth speaker."

It was as though the sun had burst through an overcast sky. The Assemblies of God at that time required only the "equivalent" of three years Bible training before a candidate could be considered for ordination. The experience I would gain as a preacher to youth groups, besides being the thing I longed to do, would mean I was still moving toward my goal of one day becoming a minister.

At the end of the week I drove with Reverend Alber to Burton, Nebraska, then to other camp meetings around the state. At these summer gatherings ministers from nearby towns would be present. Some would invite me back to speak to the young people of their home churches that fall, and in this way I gradually established a year-round itinerant ministry.

My favorite times were car trips with Reverend Alber. On these long drives across the sand hills of Nebraska he shaped my career, as he did for scores of young men before and since. Don't speak in abstractions, he'd tell me. Talk about things you really know. Don't spend money on dating;

there'll be time to meet girls and find a wife later. Use every penny you can save to do two things. Travel to increase your knowledge of the world. And buy books. Every week read a least one book from cover to cover.

For the next two years I followed his advice scrupulously. Next to the hours on my knees beside my bed each night, the time I spent reading now became my favorite part of the day. Usually I would be housed with the pastor of the church where I was holding youth meetings. I would ask permission to browse through his library, spending blissful mornings feeling my narrow horizons expand.

I also haunted secondhand bookstores, using my share of the "love offerings" collected at each service to start a library of my own. As I read I would look up words I did not know in the dictionary, then work them into my talks. In the households where I stayed there was no place to practice my sermons. So I would go out in the fields, stand on a rise of ground, and inform a startled herd of cattle that supercilious attitudes could only lead to unprecedented problems.

Through 1940 and 1941 I traveled the length and breadth of Nebraska, learning from the pastors, living with their bighearted families. I remember that I was reading a collection of sermons in Bayard, in the extreme west of the state one Sunday afternoon in early December, 1941, when the pastor burst into the study. "Charles, we're at war!"

I ran with him to the kitchen where his wife and Bob Teague, the handsome darkhaired young pianist who now traveled with me, were bent over a round-topped Crosley radio. For a long time we listened to the bewildering news. Where was Pearl Harbor? Why would the Japanese bomb it?

Since I had turned 21 in September, I had to go home at once to register for the draft. I hitched a number of rides down to Cherokee, Oklahoma, where my parents were currently living. In Cherokee, they had found a tiny, pastorless church into which they poured all the passion of their new faith. After a long day climbing poles and stringing wires, Dad did repairs on the neglected building and gave it the fresh coat of paint he would never have squandered on the place he lived in, while Mother delivered the Sunday messages that drew a growing congregation...

It was April before I heard from the draft board. I'd applied for the Chaplaincy Corps and I tore open the official government envelope eagerly. My application had been denied. Instead, since I had listed my occupation as "youth evangelist" I'd been classified 4-F--exempt from service. Bob had received the same classification two weeks earlier. I returned to Cherokee to try this time to enlist as a Chaplain's assistant but was again turned down.

The Assemblies of God held their annual [April, 1942] statewide meeting to elect officers. When I arrived Reverend Alber took me aside.

"Charles," he said, "I've put your name up for state president of Christ's Ambassadors." This was the young people's organization.

"But I'm not ordained." The president had to be a duly certified Assemblies of God minister.

"You're scheduled to be examined by the state elders this afternoon." he went on. He felt confident, he said, that my experience speaking throughout the state these past two years, plus the study I was doing on my own, would convince the elders that I was qualified for ordination.

I did not share his optimism and my legs would scarcely carry me into the church building in Grand Island, on the banks of the Platte, where the 1942 convention was being held. For two hours the state officers questioned me about my schooling, my beliefs, my commitment to Christ. Apparently they were satisfied, because the following day when Reverend Vogler from the national headquarters in Springfield Missouri, arrived in Grand Island, I was sitting at the front of the church with eight other young men awaiting ordination.

Mr. Vogler preached a sermon emphasizing the life-committing step we were about to take. Then one by one we stepped forward to kneel at the railing. Mr. Vogler for the national church and Mr. Alber for Nebraska District stepped down from the platform to lay their hands on our heads. The words in Reverend Alber‘s rich bass were brief:

"Charles Blair, we now ordain you into the full-time ministry of the Lord."

But for me, they were the marching orders that would govern the rest of my life. The knowledge that I, the most unlikely person on earth, had been set aside to serve God with all my strength, was so overwhelming that when next day as Reverend Alber had predicted, I was elected state president of Christ‘s Ambassadors, I was scarcely aware of the proceedings.

It was the start of the busiest year I‘d ever spent. As president I was expected to visit every one of the scores of local youth groups across the state, and in addition represent Nebraska around the country. The war, however, made any kind of travel difficult. Train and bus seats, when they could be had, needed to be booked weeks ahead. I had known how to drive ever since the out-station work at Southwestern, and occasionally I would borrow a car to get to a meeting. This also meant, though, using the other person‘s precious gas coupons.

"Why don‘t you get a car of your own?" Reverend Alber asked me one day in July. "Ministers get an extra gas ration, you know."

A car of my own! In my daydreams this was no trustworthy old second hand Model-A, but a sleek new sports model. It was only a dream though--until that conversation with Reverend Alber. If I was to do my job and not be a constant drain on other people‘s gas allotment, why, I‘d have to have a car! As for that sensible Model-A, to my secret delight I found that secondhand cars just weren‘t available. Anyone with any kind of car in 1942 was hanging on to it. I went before the ration board in Lincoln, Nebraska, where I stayed between trips with a family named Throne, and applied for a new-car permit.

It came through almost at once. With the government form in my hand I almost ran to the automobile showroom. And there stood my car in the window: a Chevrolet "fast-back" built like a torpedo, the rear end swooping to a streamlined point. It was bright red.

I knew I should talk over such a major purchase with all kinds of people, especially Reverend Alber who was putting up the down payment. But I had no more ability to resist that car than a moth can resist a floodlight, and from then on Bob Teague and I traveled in style.

Army bases had sprung up around the state and now that we had transportation we volunteered our services to the chaplains. The men seemed to enjoy the meetings we held, but I was painfully aware that a lot of these guys were going to be killed somewhere overseas while I was driving around Nebraska in a flashy red car.

Men our age in civilian clothes, in fact, had become rarities. It took Bob and me a while to perceive one result. All we knew was that by July there had stopped being an extra bedroom in any pastor‘s home in Nebraska. Wherever we went, the parsonage was being repainted or a great aunt had just arrived from Montana. Instead, we‘d be placed with "one of our finest families." They were fine folks, indeed, kind, hospitable, feasting us with enormous meals that included a month‘s ration of butter, meat and sugar.

It was August before it dawned on us how very many unmarried girls lived in these households. Bob and I were terror struck. With the car payments and gasoline, plus the books I was buying, I didn‘t have enough to take a girl for an ice cream soda, let alone get serious. Besides, the daughters of the "finest families" were such pale, solemn young women. Following Reverend Alber‘s advice, I had not so much as spoken with a girl, outside a group, for more than two years. That didn‘t stop me from thinking about them. My fantasy girl, in addition to being a Christian, was brilliant and beautiful, with the wardrobe of a fashion model and the figure of a movie star.

Toward the end of August, Bob and I drove out to Lexington, Nebraska, near the center of the state, where a week-long camp meeting was to climax the summer season. The campground was several miles out of town in a field beside some train tracks, and Bob and I gratefully set up a sleeping tent, far from the ministrations of the finest families. Out first job, as often, was to help erect the meeting place. Lexington was located on the main line of the Railroad; every quarter hour, it seemed, a train would thunder past. As I sawed planks for benches, I wondered how we'd ever make ourselves heard during the meetings.

After the first day, we simply stopped trying. All singing and preaching would halt while the train lumbered by, 200, 250 freight cars at a time in that flat country, while black smoke poured through the open sides of our temporary building. Still it was the best meeting of the summer, with hundreds of families camping in tents across the fields. Thursday was Christ's Ambassadors Day, with representatives of local chapters from all over the state attending. I gave the evening address and afterwards stood outside greeting people. It was the night of the August full moon, the train tracks glowed silver.

And it was then I saw her, standing in the cluster of people waiting to shake hands, the moon making a halo of her light brown hair. She was maybe five-foot-three with a trim, athletic figure and a pixie face set off with a touch of lipstick. I could not see the color of her eyes in the moonlight; I only knew she was the most beautiful girl I had ever seen.

The most out of reach too. Everything about her--her clothes, her hair, some indefinable air of self-assurance--spoke of privilege and wealth, and I gazed at her with the same kind of awe I felt for the moon itself. After an age, we were face to face. And at that moment a freight train thundered abreast of us ..."

(Charles E. Blair; with John and Elizabeth Sherrill, *The Man Who Could Do No Wrong* (Chosen Books, Inc., a division of Baker Book House Company, 1981). *Reprinted by permission.)*

Alice (Kersey) Farley and Herbert Buffum

Alice Kersey (who later became Mrs. A. R. Farley) was in Holdrege, Nebraska in 1919 when Aimee Semple McPherson was there. Alice was a traveling evangelist and traveled quite a bit with Herbert Buffum, who was a well-known songwriter, musician, and evangelist. Most of Alice's meetings or main place of residence was in Kansas, but at least this once she was in Nebraska. She was an important figure.

(Taken from a letter January 8, 1997, by Glenn Gohr, Assemblies of God Archives Assistant; and an October 11, 1919 letter from Alice Kersey's ministerial file.)

Lillie and Herbert Buffum, Early Evangelists

Herbert Buffum was an evangelist for over 40 years, bringing the Pentecostal message to north-central Kansas and south-central Nebraska in the early part of the twentieth century. It was said a wagon pulled by a horse, was his means of transportation.

On one visit to Nebraska, Rev. Buffum dedicated Ruth Palmer King at Franklin, Nebraska in 1916.

As well as evangelizing the central plains, Herbert Buffum is remembered for the many songs he wrote. One of the best loved was "I'm Going Through." Another favorite was "I'm Going Higher Some Day." Rev. Buffum estimated he wrote upwards of ten thousand, and many hundreds were published.

When Herbert Buffum died in 1939, the Los Angeles Times published this tribute in the editorial section: "He who writes the songs of a nation, it has been said, has done more for the people than he who makes its laws. What Stephen Foster did for American folklore, Herbert Buffum did for its homely religious sentiment; he expressed it in simple musical strains that all could understand.

"His death is a loss to the cause of evangelism in which for 40 years he was an earnest worker. His best legacy to humanity is the number of hymns he left behind him."

His wife, Lillie, worked with her husband in the evangelistic field and then several years alone. Lillie was a veteran of over fifty years' labor for the Lord. She was remembered for the many poems she wrote. Later in her life, she traveled and recited her poems often with musical background. What a thrill it was to hear that fiery little lady's "Bible in Rhyme."

(Herbert Buffum, Jr., compiler, "Above the Shadows.")

Carmichael, Adele

In about 1919 some people from Perry, Iowa, held a tent meeting in Scottsbluff, Nebraska. and three Baptist Carmichael boys received the Baptism of the Holy Spirit. In 1919-20 the Assemblies started a Bible School in Auburn, Nebraska. The three Carmichael brothers came to the Bible School and so did I from Des Moines, Iowa.

I fell in love with Richard Carmichael and we were married in 1923. The following year, 1924, Richard and I came out to visit his parents in Scottsbluff. We rented an old school building and had a series of meetings. Many were saved and among them was a banker who helped buy ground and build a church. For there were so many saved, they needed a Pentecostal church. A few years later we came again to visit my husband's parents and I preached for the pastor, Brother Albers. He was working and the church was not supporting him. I preached on tithing and took an offering for him, and he never went to work Monday morning.

We also held meetings in other Nebraska towns. I was the evangelist and my husband was the musician. He finally became a good preacher and pastor. He passed away in 1960. I am 95 years old and still teaching Bible classes. I have been ordained 80 years. (1997) In Him, Adele Carmichael.

(Adele F. Carmichael shared the above testimony in a letter written in 1997.)

Richard and Adele Carmichael were the parents of musician, composer, and conductor, Ralph Carmichael.

Carmichael, George

It was in a sod house on a cattle ranch in western Nebraska that George Carmichael was born. It was due to the influence and power of their grandmother's life, Brother Carmichael says, that four boys and a girl from his family entered the ministry.

On one occasion while he was away herding sheep, his mother and brothers were converted in a Methodist revival. When he returned he found the home filled with joy. On his own empty life the happiness of the others grated discordantly, and he left home to escape it. Through the months and years that followed, however, he was gripped constantly with conviction, and at last, in a tent meeting, he surrendered his life to God.

With a desire to witness for Christ, he started out with a case of tracts, and from one ranch house to another he took his testimony. God blessed his efforts. Later, when he heard the Pentecostal message he began to seek for the Baptism in the Spirit, and, after several months of tarrying, he received it in Granite City, Illinois.

With his brother, George Carmichael attended a Bible School in Auburn, Nebraska. After that he went to Southern California Bible College. He studied at a Baptist Seminary in Los Angeles and later at Pacific College.

After a time on the evangelistic field, he pastored in Fullerton, California. From there Brother and Sister Carmichael came to Springfield to become a vital part of Central Bible Institute (C.B.I.) this year.

(*C.B.I. Cup*, 1941.)

Cave, Mary

It was October 17, 1949, when I, Mary Cave, accepted the Lord Jesus Christ as my Saviour. I was twenty-four years old at the time.

Many events led up to this most important day in my life. As I came to realize, He had been dealing with me for months. In my mind's eye I could see as in a panoramic view with a road winding down through it, just how He had been drawing me ever closer to Him.

My husband Harold and I had lost a baby boy at birth a few months before this and I had gone through months in bed and the hospital trying to keep from miscarrying, but we lost him anyway. It was when I was at death's door in the hospital and in one of those old style oxygen tents that I felt the conviction of my sins. It was like great waves of the ocean washing over me. I knew that if I died, I would not go to heaven. I felt an urgency to "make things right" with some people I had wronged, and I requested paper, pen and envelopes so I would write some short letters. The nurses offered to write these for me as I was very weak, but I just had to do it myself. (Incidentally, I never received even one reply to those letters, and I did ask for their forgiveness. Later, when I encountered them I asked if they got a letter from me, and, of course, they did. All of them didn't think it was important they answer; they all knew I was very ill and attributed it to that. They disregarded my confession as, "Why it was nothing—forget it." I assured them that it was very important to me.)

Finally, after weeks in bed after the loss of our little one, I could walk again, but one thing let to another and I never lost the urgent feeling that I needed "something." Not getting what I needed in the church I had attended all my life, I went looking and ended up in the Assembly of God Church in Chappell, Nebraska.

The Sunday School lesson on the seventeenth of October, 1949, was about Salvation. Everyone in the class of Young Marrieds seemed to be saved and on their way to heaven. I asked, "How do you know when you are saved? What happened?"

The teacher of the class asked each one to give his testimony of what his experience of salvation was like. All were very different, but I was not daunted. In the church service afterward, the congregation stood and sang a song I had never heard--"Oh, For a Heart Whiter Than Snow." (I have never seen that song in any other hymnal.) Something marvelous came over me and I trembled from head to foot as the tears ran down my face. My heart, which had felt so heavy and scarred with sin, felt all at once clean and white without a blemish. I knew that the Lord had forgiven me all my sins. My heart was filled with a love for everyone and the whole world looked different.

I know when and where I received salvation, and I know it is real.

("Chappell," 1998.)

George and Katie Comstock

Here are James Nicholson's Remembrances of George and Katie Comstock evangelizing in Nebraska and Iowa.

I was 20 days old when my mother died in October 1918 with the flu — which killed 548,000 in the United States and 20 million in the world. My father, William Nicholson, gave me to George and Katie Comstock — my mother's parents — to rear, on one stipulation: he would never take me away from them, but only if I carried his name all of my life, which I have done.

God ordered my steps. I grew up in a Pentecostal minister's home. All of my life I've seen what God can do!

Grandpa Comstock received the Holy Spirit in Sister Woodworth-Etter's meetings. Prior to that experience he and Grandma were Salvation Army officers. Then he began to preach tent crusades in Nebraska, out of Sioux City, Iowa. He started 13 Assemblies of God churches in that area.

When Sister Etter went to Sioux City for meetings, my grandfather invited her to our home. This was before Grandma's infilling of the Spirit. George got places for other members of Sister Etter's party to stay but told Grandma that Sister Etter would stay at our house.

At breakfast the next morning, Sister Etter came into the dining area and suddenly began to praise God. "Oh, Lord, thank you for the dear wife who has prepared a great meal. Bless her, oh Lord!"

When they looked at Grandma, she was sobbing and weeping. God is so good. This is how Grandma was filled with the Spirit.

One Sunday my Uncle Stanley Comstock took an unsaved friend to our church in Sioux City. He said to the friend, "No matter what anyone does in our church, keep your eyes on my mother. She never does wrong."

But that service was especially ordained, for it was then that the power of the Holy Spirit hit her. She started to walk around, bending over, up and down, crying out, "Oh, Jesus, Jesus, Jesus!"

When Uncle and his friend saw this, Uncle said, "Come on, let's leave here and go home!" "No way," the friend said, "I wouldn't miss this for anything." Grandma was filled! The Holy Spirit did a great work in her heart.

When I was about 4 or 5 I remember Grandpa taking us and his tent equipment to Macy, Nebraska (an Indian Reservation town). On the trip, Grandma asked Grandpa, "Dear, where will we put up the tent when we get to Macy?"

Grandpa answered, "Well, it's been on my mind and I think we'll put it on the Pow Wow grounds."

"But Dear," Grandma answered, "all those Indians with all their drums and all the noise. You won't be heard at all."

Grandpa answered, "Well dear, I know that, but that is where the people will be."

So powerful were the results that the Pow-Wow closed, and many were saved and healed.

Grandpa Comstock always had an "Evangelistic Party" in his meetings. Not the kind we are familiar with today but people who had been saved in prior meetings and who came to help. Grandma had a five-sided military tent in which she prepared the meals daily.

We slept in tents. My own cot wore out, so Grandpa repaired it by pulling two sacks from the end, and that was my bed. Nice back-breaker in the middle where it came together. But I lived through it.

Church after church was started in N.E. Nebraska and still going strong today. Heaven will reveal just how effective and solid they were.

Grandpa would attend the Assembly on Myrtle Street in Sioux City if he was not preaching. Sometimes evangelists would make crude remarks. I'd listen to my Grandfather say, after those kinds of remarks, "no, that's not Bible!" I always wondered what Grandpa meant when he said that. In my teen years I went to a service, and the speaker roared out with a pretty heavy remark. Suddenly I said to myself, "No, that's not bible." Then I knew what my Grandpa was saying. It had to be Bible!

(James Nicholson, "The Experience of George and Katie Comstock," *Assemblies of God Heritage*, Spring, 1998.)

James Nicholson has been a missionary to Cuba, as well as pastoring and evangelizing in the United States.

Correll, Norman and Norma (Shoff)

Norman Correll and I were married in Bassett, Nebraska, July 9, 1946. Joylene Sue was born at Columbus, Nebraska, and Brian Leigh was born at Bassett.

We were traveling evangelists four and one-half years and then we moved to Grand Island for over two years. Norman was the State Youth director for our Assembly of God churches of the Nebraska District.

In 1958, we went as Missionaries to Mbeya, Tanzania, East Africa, and after a furlough we returned to Arusha, Tanzania and spent one term there, a total of eight and one-half years as missionaries.

We returned to Springfield, Missouri in 1966. Norm took a position at our General Council Headquarters until 1975, then we made preparations to go to Brussels, Belgium, where Norm was Dean of Education for International Correspondence Institute.

We returned to Springfield in 1979. Norm again took the position in the Division of Foreign Missions at our General Headquarters.

(Norma Correll, "Norma (Shoff) Correll." In *Iceland to Nebraska: The Olafur Hallgrimson*

Family, by Margaret L. Sybrant. N.p: N.p., the author, 1985, p. H-15.)

Chapter 5: Lester Dickinson to Irene Kisser

***"He is like a tree planted by streams of water, which yields its fruit in season and whose leaf does not wither. Whatever he does prospers."* (Psalm 1:3 NIV)**

Dickinson, Lester
Dixon, Howard
Eckley, Mrs. Edwin
Evans, Walter
Foster, E. R.
Greene, Howard
Hall, Wayne
Hallgrimson, Olafur
Harvey, H. L.
Hawley, George
Heinze, B. C.
James, Marie
Johnson, Mel
King, Clyde
Kisser, Irene

Dickinson, Lester

As I look back over the past my heart is filled with praises to Him who has directed my steps. As a child the words of the song, "God Leads His Dear Children Along" thrilled my heart, but today they have a new and deeper meaning.

It was my privilege to be reared in a Christian home.... To my heart comes great rejoicing when I think how good the Lord was in saving me when I was so young.... As a young boy I attended meetings of every kind, in the School houses, in cottage prayer meetings. It seemed I spent the early years of my life going to some church service most every night. Attending cottage prayer meetings, I saw our father lying on the floor under the power of the Holy Spirit by the hour. After seven years of praying and waiting on the Lord the Lord filled him with the Spirit as he was praying alone out in his field.... Our father set about to evangelize his community (the Girard Community north west of Buffalo, Oklahoma) by personal involvement.

Our mother was also a very devout Christian. My first introduction to the Pentecostal experience of someone speaking in another language came from our mother. There was a cottage prayer meeting in our home. I was possibly three years old, (1913) the hour was very late and I was asleep on the couch along the west wall of our living room. Our mother was kneeling beside the couch. I awakened for a moment or so, just long enough to hear her speaking in Tongues. I never doubted the experience, because our mother had received.

When I was fifteen, my godly father passed away, leaving mother and me alone. (My brothers and sisters had married and established homes of their own.) ... A few years after my conversion the Lord wonderfully filled me with the precious Holy Spirit. Soon after this experience I began to feel the Lord was laying His hand upon my life for some special service. But several years went by, and still I was on the farm....

In the fall of 1929, I attended Southwestern Bible School in Enid, Okla., completing that term in the spring of 1930. Mother moved with me to Enid while I was in school.

May 4, 1933 I was married to Myrtle Rexroat. We lived on the farm for a time, but not too long after our marriage, we began to definitely feel the Lord had a ministry for us. We had no particular place to go, but soon the Lord opened a door and we held a short revival meeting. We thought surely other doors would open in the immediate future. However, God kept us waiting for some time.... We became despondent and were ready to go back to the farm. God permitted sickness to come upon my body and for some time I was unable to do anything. This test seemed quite severe at the time, but afterwards we could see how God was leading us in mysterious ways, His wonders to perform.

At Christmas time of 1934 Cleo Hink a young lady from the Girard church was home for the holidays, she and a co-worker were pastoring in Nebraska. (Beaver City) She said, Why don't you write our District Superintendent, Brother A. M. Alber, he might be able to assist you in getting started into the ministry. We wrote a letter, assisted by Myrtle's brother, Silas Rexroat, to Brother Alber. Brother Alber responded by telling us he had an opening for a pastor in Aurora, Nebraska, and could we be there the following Sunday. We immediately responded by telling him we could not make it for that Sunday, but would be there the following Sunday. We had no idea what the place was like or anything, but we had been praying for an open door and this was the only one open....

(A. M. Alber wrote in a letter of November 7, 1974 — "I received a typewritten letter from him (Bro. Dickinson) asking if there was a church in Nebraska needing a pastor. I generally filed such letters for later reference, but this one I put in my coat pocket and carried it with me for some time and on occasion would take it out and read it again and decided that it was a very well written letter.)

"So in the course of time the work in Aurora opened up and I wrote the Dickinsons about it telling them it was not an easy place to go to at that time for there had been a great division in the church. However they came and assumed the pastorate. Under the circumstances they did very well and I am sure went through a very strenuous time for them although they lived up to the occasion."

... The 10th of February 1935 we (Myrtle and Lester Dickinson) left Oklahoma for a long trip away from home, 400 miles. We packed our few belongings into the model A Ford and left Oklahoma. We arrived in Aurora, Nebraska, February 11th and went to the home Brother Alber had directed us to, the Elmer Schlegel home. Sister Schlegel came to the door, I told her who I was, she looked at me very skeptical and unfriendly like. I had never been accustomed to that typc trcatmcnt. Thcrc was nothing clsc for us to do, as we were a long ways from home. These people didn't really want us to stay with them, but we had no choice. She finally asked us in the house, and when Brother Schlegel came home, he was no happier to see us than she was. They gave us a room in their house, which we were very appreciative. We had our first service in our very first pastorate February 12, 1935.

We found some very discouraged, disappointed people. Their pastor who had led them into Pentecost and been their spiritual leader went bad morally. I could see then the reason for Sister Schlegel being hesitant to accept us, one preacher had disappointed them and were all preachers alike?

We made our home with the Schlegels and with another family for six weeks before they would trust us with enough to rent us a house for $6.00 per month. This was our first open door, but what a large room it led us into. Paul said, "A great door is open unto me." This was our great door. We saw people saved in that church that would have made everything worth while, but that was not the end. During those twenty months we were in Aurora, we received in support an average of $16.00 per month.

... October 1936 we accepted a call to pastor the church in Ord, Nebraska. This was a promotion as the congregation was larger and the support much better.... We pastored this wonderful group of people for the next three years ... During our time in Ord the greatest thing that had happened to our family up until this time, our son Gary was born December 1938.

My first involvement in District work was during the C. A. Convention in Hastings in the fall of 1937, I was elected to serve as the Secretary-Treasurer of the C. A. Department of the District. In November of 1939, I was elected as C. A. President and S. S. Director. I was the first full time Director of this Department in Nebraska.

In June of 1940, we moved to Chappell, Nebraska and became the pastor of the church in this little western town. The following five years were some of the happiest years of my life. We had a number of farmers and ranchers in our church, so we had the opportunity of going to the country real often....The people of that little town were so very friendly and the people treated us so very royally. The church did well those five years. We completed a very beautiful brick veneered church. I did not remain as C. A. President after the election in 194l, but I was the Sectional Presbyter of that section for a short time.

During the State Camp meeting in Lexington in 1941, I was asked by the Brethren to be the Secretary-Treasurer of the Nebraska District Council. Brother Roy Barnes had resigned and was moving to California. This was a very high honor, I was not only to serve the District, but was also, by virtue of this office a General Presbyter of the General Council. I served in this capacity for the following ten years.

April 2, 1945, we loaded our personal belongings into our car and started for Lincoln, Nebraska, where we had accepted the pastorate of First Assembly in the Capitol City . The first few months in Lincoln were very frustrating to me, the large city with life totally different than we had every known was a little difficult to become accustomed to. Gary was frightened by the vastness of the city. Myrtle loved Lincoln. In spite of the different life, we found we were in the will of the Lord and this took care of the frustration.... We saw people saved and filled with the Holy Spirit."

(Lester W. Dickinson, "District Family and Nebraska District," (from personal writings); and "God Leads," *Christ Ambassadors Herald*, May 1941, p. 12.)

In 1985, Lester W. Dickinson was honored for fifty years of continuous service to the Assemblies of God. Lester Dickinson was superintendent of the Nebraska District from 1951 to 1975.

Dixon, Howard

Reverend Gene Anderson received permission from my parents, Elmer and Sarah Dixon, to begin services in 1933 in Wewela in the vacant Gunsil Store Building. This also included an invitation to attend the services.

We went each evening and my mother responded immediately to the anointed preaching. The second night she responded again and received a vision and a great experience as she was filled with the Holy Spirit.

We attended services each week and in over a years time, all five members of our family accepted the Lord and were filled with the Holy Spirit Baptism. This was a strange religion to us, but the Bible taught it, and others believed and received; so we wanted it too.

At the close of the revival meeting a church was started and F. E. [Gene] Anderson was our beloved pastor for eight years. Most of the people in the church lived in Nebraska since Wewela was only one mile into South Dakota. Together the farmers and ranchers from Nebraska worshiped with the farmers and ranchers from South Dakota in this small border town.

A water baptismal service was held at the John Myers' pond on July 28, 1935. Fifty-five persons were baptized in water. A large crowd was in attendance. For me, this was a very definite statement of faith in the presence of my neighbors and friends.

I was called to the ministry and in September 1938, went to North Central Bible College in Minneapolis, Minnesota.

(Howard Dixon, "Wewela, South Dakota," 1997.)

Howard Dixon pastored in Nebraska.

Eckley, Mrs. Edwin

... at the age of thirteen. There was a change in my life. I read my Bible more. I read about people being baptized in the Holy Spirit, and it worried me. I asked my mother what it meant, and she told me that when the preacher baptized me in water and said he baptized me in the name of the Father, Son and Holy Spirit, that was being baptized in the Holy Spirit. I was not satisfied, but did not say anything more. I lived this way for about two years and then went back into sin, and was worse than ever. For 18 years I was sick in soul and body. I would see the faults of professing Christians and think I was as good as they. I just let it go at that and did not realize how fast I was on my way to hell.

I was sick and miserable all the time. There was always a doctor's bill to pay. I had bowel trouble, gall-stones, dyspepsia, catarrh of head, throat and lungs. I had been deaf in one ear for six years. Three years after my marriage, the birth of our child left me in a terrible condition. I suffered so at times I wished for death, and then I fear I was not saved. As I look back, now I can see the pain of soul was worse than the body. Two running sores came on my breasts which we thought cancers. The least jar from walking would cause sharp, cutting pains to go through them, and the odor from them was terrible. None of the many remedies we tried availed and it ran into heart trouble. I would wake up in the night panting and fighting for breath, and some days almost died.

Before Jesus came to my rescue I read novels, because I was too poorly to do anything but read. Oh, it makes my heart shudder when I think what a state I was in. I would read the novels through the day, but when a spell came on I would put down the novel, and take the Bible in my hand. I feared I would die. I found no comfort, but cried to God for mercy and help. Oh, praise God! Help was coming. Meetings were being held in the Union church west of Springview, Nebr. Glory to Jesus! Praise His name forever! I didn't feel able to go to the meetings and was not interested. My husband's father went one night and next morning seemed so excited about it that my interest was aroused. He told us we had better go. So I got ready and went just to see what kind of foolishness it was. When I got there, I found it was different from anything I had ever witnessed. I could just feel the power of God there that night.

As the minister gave out the truth, I could see Jesus dying upon the cross for my sins. Praise His Name! Joy and peace flowed into my soul as our brother told of the sick woman of the Bible touching the hem of Jesus' garment. Oh, how happy and full of joy I was! The love in my heart would just cry out praises to Jesus. I went home that night and burned up all my novels--about fifty of them. This blessed joy and peace continued until June; then Jesus came in His wonderful power and glory, baptizing me in the Holy Spirit, and I spoke and sang in tongues.

My joy became deeper than before, and the last of all the diseases I ever had were healed. I could now hear some out of my deaf ear, which has since been nearly restored. The next morning when I arose, there was not so much as an inflamed place left of those two cancers on my breast, and they stayed healed, too. That was two years ago this month and they are perfectly well yet. It took me six months to make things right with all the precious people I had spoken mean to and done wrong to in many ways when I was my old rebellious self. Praise God! He has taken those sins away from me as far as the east is from the west and will remember them against me no more.

My husband and little daughter were both saved in the same meetings. For two years the Lord has been our Savor, Baptizer, Cleanser, Physician, and our Refuge. Oh, what a change in our lives! How different this wonderful new life from the old sinful life, and how much happier the new home than the old one! Jesus has changed everything by coming into our home to stay and rule.

Mrs. Edwin Eckley, Ainsworth, Nebr.

("Testimony of Mrs. Edwin Eckley, Ainworth, Nebraska," *Word and Work,* July 1920, p. 5.)

Word and Work *is a Pentecostal paper that was published in Framingham, Massachusetts. Most of the people connected with this paper were Assemblies of God.*

Evans, Walter

There are many fond memories of Brother Evans, the black evangelist. In the 1930's and the 1940's, he drove a black car. At each place he stayed, he'd spend time, washing and polishing his car. As he traveled across Nebraska sharing his music, he stayed with pastors and their families sharing the love of Jesus. Walter Evans was licensed with the Nebraska District.

Many recalled that before Bro. Evans played his guitar, he'd take a white handkerchief out of his pocket and lay it on a chair. He'd then place one foot on the handkerchief, and putting his guitar on his knee would sing. Some of the favorites were "We Are All God's Children" and " I'm Just An Irishman Turned Inside-Out."

At the Lexington Camp, Brother Evans played the drums in the orchestra. He liked to spend time in Lexington and stayed with some of the ministers that pastored there. He's remembered for saying, "I'd rather wear out for the Lord than rust out for the devil!" When Howard Dixon was pastoring at Westerville about 1950, Bro. Evans was sitting at the drums on the platform ready for the music at the end of the service. Bro. Dixon emphatically stated something about your sins making you black in the face—when Bro. Evans interrupted with a big OH! OH!

In 1944, he stayed with the Clyde Kings in Alliance. During this period of our history, it was common to hear sermons about women's dress (sometimes called "Clothes Line Preaching). Sister Ruth King recalls hearing Brother Evans preach, "When my shoes have holes in them, I don't wear them!!"

Sister King also remembered Brother Evans giving gifts, and she still has a set of ice tea spoons he gave her. He'd sing songs about Heaven and would question, "I wonder what they are doing up in heaven now?"

Several men, who were boys growing up in the parsonages across Nebraska, recall Brother Evans telling tales of his serving in the Spanish/American War.

(Collective remembrances of Brother Evans, the Black Evangelist.)

Foster, E. R.

Rev. E. R. Foster (Kathy's Great Uncle) began preaching when in his teens, over 50 years ago. He is known affectionately by his family as "Uncle Ralph." He is Kathy's great Uncle, brother to Sister Kathleen Fisher. You will thrill and be blessed as you read a few pioneer experiences of faith on these following pages.

Prove to Me you're a Sinner! One of the incidents that helped bring the Revival in Aurora was the following. A certain woman of the town, a woman in disrepute, came to the Tent one night. Everyone had left but she remained praying at the altar. Uncle Ralph began praying with her and then asked, "My Sister, what is burdening your heart?" She replied, "I'm having trouble believing there really is a God." "Why is that?" asked Uncle Ralph. "Well, for one thing, my Pastor and brother drink together in the basement of his home. Also, I have made a serious mistake (2 illegitimate children) but none of the church people or pastor seem to want to help me back to God. The Church members pass on the other side of the street to avoid me when I come that way."

After praying with her for awhile, Brother Foster said, "Little lady, you're the very kind of woman that Jesus came to save. If you can prove to me that you're a sinner, I can prove to you that you have a Saviour, and His name is Jesus! Well she was gloriously saved and filled with the Holy Spirit and became that NEW CREATURE in Christ.

She could not do enough for the Lord from then on. She sang in the choir, witnessed on the streets and was on fire for the Lord. However, eyebrows were raised and several Church people came to Brother Foster saying, "Brother Foster, you don't know what kind of a person she is! "Well," answered Uncle Ralph, "I don't know what kind of a person she has been, but I know what kind of a person she is now since she has met Jesus." Her testimony stirred the town and the revival was on!

Take the Tent Down! One of the early experience of Brother Foster was in Aurora, Nebraska. Here they pitched a Tent and began meetings. No one in the area had ever heard of the Pentecostal outpouring. When the meeting got in full swing, many received the Holy Ghost Baptism and the Revival fires were burning! Some of the Town people got irritated and among them was a lawyer who came out one night to visit the meetings. During the service, he arose and said, "I have held every administrative office in this city, and I declare unto you that nothing has ever gone on in town like this, and I assure you it will not be allowed to continue." But as Brother Foster often says, "He didn't know who he was dealing with." As the scripture states in Acts 5:38-39 Gamaliel said: "Refrain from these men, and let them alone; for if this counsel or this work be of men, it will come to naught; but if it be of God, ye cannot overthrow it; lest happily ye be found even to Fight against God."

Well, the city Fathers met, passed a resolution the Tent must come down, and had the Police serve this to Uncle Ralph! "Out of courtesy to you," he said, "you will be allowed one more night's service." Next morning, Brother E. W. White (District Supt. of Assemblies of God) and Brother Foster drove to Lincoln, Nebraska to see Attorney General Swanson. They presented him with a list of hundreds of Christian names petitioning him that the tent remain up in Aurora. "We want these meetings to continue," they said. "Aurora needs this revival." The Attorney General gave them some good advice. "If the city council is determined for you to close down and stop the meetings, it would be wise to take the tent down but go on with the meetings!"

Well, they came back to Aurora, and with Petition in hand, visited the Mayor of Aurora. "Oh," he said rather timidly, "We really didn't mean for you to stop the meetings--just quiet it down a little." Uncle Ralph said, "Your Honor, one of the constitutional rights of this country is the freedom to worship God according to the dictates of one's own conscience." "But Sir," answered the Mayor. "I hear folks are out there rolling in the straw." "Well," answered Uncle Ralph, "I don't know so much about that, but even if it were to be true, with the freedom our country allows, one could worship God standing on their head if they thought it would bring them closer to God." Well, the old Mayor agreed and from that time on, there was no harassment of the Tent meeting and the Revival grew bigger and bigger until the whole countryside was ablaze with Revival Fires! So the old tent stood its ground and a Church was established!

Money Left Over for the Tithe! Brother and Sister Foster pastored one of their first Churches in 1929 at Grand Island, Nebraska. They lived in the Church basement for the work's sake as the Church was small and still struggling. There was little money in those days. Depression and unemployment was high. On this particular Sunday, the snow was falling and it became a terrible winter snow storm piling up many feet. Not too many were in the service that Sunday as Uncle Ralph climbed the steps into the sanctuary. Sister Foster remained in the basement as she was not feeling too well, expecting their second child. While downstairs, she counted the bills owed by them. It came to $207.50. When Uncle Ralph came down after service, she handed him the list and said, "Honey, we must have $207.50 before we can even eat." Uncle Ralph threw $7.50 on the table and said laughingly, "Well, here's the offering this morning. All we need now is $200.00." Sister Foster began to cry. What are we going to do? she thought. Later there came a knock on the door. That afternoon a dear Sister, Sister Hanchet, had come through that blowing snow storm with some money. "Brother Foster," she said, "some relatives left me some money and I felt like you should have the Tithe." They accepted it with gratitude, thinking it perhaps to be $10.00 or $20.00. After she left, they opened the envelope to find $220.50. So with that morning's offering, plus Sister Hanchet's tithe, they had enough to pay off all the bills owed, plus money for the Lord's tithe! Thus making the answer to Prayer, Right to the Penny!

Just a Note of Interest! Mrs. Opal Whiley [Wiley], Sister Foster's mother, was with that first group of believers who took the message of the Holy Ghost Baptism to the State of Texas. They were known as the "Parham Party." It was Sister Whiley that prayed with Brother Seymore [Seymour] to receive the Baptism in the Holy Ghost before he left for California and the old Azusa Street Church where a short time later he did receive the Holy Ghost Baptism. The restoration of the Holy Ghost Baptism, that was practically unknown during the middle ages, date back to Brother Seymore on Azusa Street, Los Angeles, California. This great Spirit outpouring continues with greater force year after year...

(David & Kathy Walker, "Remembrance of Reverend E. R. Foster," *Spanning The Tide,"* pp. 39, 44-49.)

The following information is from a letter Glenn Gohr wrote to Elisabeth Lemp.

E. R. "Ralph" Foster and also Opal Stauffer Wiley were early preachers in Nebraska. (Opal's granddaughter, Kathleen Stafford, remembers that her grandmother also ministered in Nebraska at one point.)

Opal Stauffer Wiley was at Bethel Bible School at Topeka, KS on January 1, 1901 when the Holy Spirit was poured forth. She was one of those, along with Agnes Ozman, who received the baptism of the Holy Spirit on that day. Opal later traveled with Charles F. Parham in evangelistic meetings in Kansas, Missouri, and Texas... Opal's daughter was Jo Ellen Wiley who married E. R. Foster. Opal married Efton B. Wiley. Efton B. Wiley, Opal (Stauffer), and their 2 children, Jo Ellen and Philip Wiley, all attended the First General Council at Hot Springs, Arkansas, April 2-12, 1914. That shows one Nebraska connection to Hot Springs!

Greene, Howard

Making melody and harmony is the ministry which God has given our Brother Howard Greene--ministry which really began many years ago on a farm in Nebraska, when a seven-year old boy took his first piano lesson.

While herding his father's 22,000 sheep in the field one day, young Howard felt God speaking to him. He knelt and had a real experience with God; promising to give his talent to God's service.

With this in mind, the young man turned his face toward the Bible Training School at Angelus Temple....

While in charge of an Assembly at Santa Ana, Brother Greene studied for two years at Fullerton College, later earning his degree from La Verne College.

After graduating from college, Brother Greene taught in Anaheim. While teaching there and also caring for the work at Wood Lake, California, he attended night school and summer school for two years at the University of Southern California. During this period of time he built a tabernacle at Wood Lake.

During the year '39-'40 he directed the Orange County Symphony Orchestra. Last year he also conducted a 200-piece orchestra composed of the best talent in the Orange County public school orchestras.

This year Brother and Sister Green have added their talent and effort to C.B.I.'s staff.

(*CBI Cup*, 1941.)

Hall, Wayne and Hazel

Sister Hall related her infilling with the Holy Spirit in the 1930's. She was a young girl staying with her aunt. A pastor from Westerville held prayer meetings in her aunt's home where Sister Hall prayed to receive the baptism. After much prayer and asking, she turned to the pastor and said, "I've done everything and I'm still not filled." He then told her, "Just lift your hands and praise the Lord for everything He has done for you. Praise Him for what He's given you."

It wasn't long before Hazel was slain in the Spirit and fell backwards on her aunt's floor speaking in another language! Later they asked her, "How did it feel to fall on the floor?" "Just like falling on my feather bed!" she replied.

Hazel went to Bible School in Enid, OK from 1936 to 1939, graduating in three years. When Hazel left Bible School, she felt a call to the rural areas of Nebraska. She knew there were good people in the ranch country that didn't have church available to them. When Hazel was a girl growing up, she never got to go to church, and oh, how she wanted to! After Bible School, she wanted to take the Gospel and more of God's Word to these rural areas.

Upon arriving back in Nebraska, Hazel went to live with an aunt. This was about half way between Atkinson and Burwell in ranch country. This is where she met Wayne Hall. When there was a need for a preacher in one of the little churches, Hazel's aunt suggested they let Hazel preach. Hazel received $5.00 per week. She preached on Sundays then during the week she visited the ranches and would tell the people in their homes about the Baptism in the Holy Spirit. Wayne got saved in a ranch home....

The first time Wayne heard about the Baptism in the Holy Spirit and speaking in tongues was in the school house where his family was attending a revival meeting. The evangelist didn't give a positive message. The visiting preacher was not pleased with "those people who talked in tongues"! This man didn't approve at all. This disapproving sermon about speaking in other tongues was Wayne's introduction to Pentecost and it raised a lot of questions for the young man.

On the way home, Wayne began to question his dad. "What was the visiting preacher talking about? Doesn't everyone use their tongue to talk?" This seemed rather amusing to him! "What does this all mean?" (The year was 1940)

Wayne's dad replied, "We'll ask Hazel?" And then Hazel was once again privileged to explain the precious infilling of the Holy Spirit.

During the war years when most of the men were in the armed forces, Hazel held meetings in many rural areas. Anne Brill of Scottsbluff was her co-worker. Since the men were serving their country and weren't able to go out as ministers, more women served the Lord. Hazel was happy to share her love of God's Word...

In 1941, Wayne went to Central Bible Institute in Springfield, Missouri. He was drafted into the army in 1942 and served in the Air Force. After his discharge in 1946, he returned to C.B.I. and graduated in 1948. It was while he was on leave in 1944 Wayne asked Hazel to marry him. The Halls returned to North Carolina. Hazel worked in a linen factory while Wayne worked as a mechanic in the Air Force.

("Interview with Hazel Hall," Tahlequah, Oklahoma, June 23, 1997.)

Hazel Hall was the first director of the Girls Kids Kamp, Carlyle Beebe was the D-CAP at the time. Hazel Hall also was the state director of the WMC.

In 1994, Hazel received a certificate for 50 years of continuous service to the Assemblies of God.

Hallgrimson, Olafur and Skulina

In 1891, Olafur and Skulina Hallgrimson boarded a vessel for the United States. They came to Long Pine, Nebraska, July 15, 1891, settling close to Skulina's relatives.

In Iceland the main church was Lutheran, but because of poor means of travel, I doubt that our folks ever went to church. A minister would come to the home when a child was born and baptize them.

In 1904, they accepted Christ as their personal Saviour. In the family book , Iceland to Nebraska, a daughter, Freda, tells about where the folks got saved. It was in a school house revival. "Rev. E. E. Dillon, a Sunday School Missionary came and told the folks that he was holding revival services in the Willow Grove School House and invited them to come. The school house was about four or five miles from the home place, but the folks started going to the services about every night. Dad drove a team and a wagon, and we kids would sit on the straw and cover up with blankets as some nights were cold. During these services, my parents and five or six of us kids went to the altar. We all attended the services at Willow Grove after that...

There definitely was a change in the whole family life. Dad started the family altar and would read one or two chapters from the Bible, and then we all knelt down for prayer. Sometimes he would call on one or two of us kids to pray, and he would pray and he really prayed for his family and others. Down through the years we have seen God's answer to our parent's prayers. God will not fail us if we really trust in him."

What a change there was in their lives and in our home. 2 Corinthians 5:17 Therefore if any man be in Christ, he is a new creature; old things are passed away, behold, all things are become new. In 1915 they became affiliated with the Pentecostal Assemblies of God.

I faintly remember the Harvey revival in the school house, but I do remember my brother, Balder (George), taking the folks to Burwell (1919). This was before there was much of a road through the Sand Hills. From Burwell, the folks took a train to Holdrege to attend a few nights of Aimee Simple McPherson Revival. That is where they both received their Baptism of the Holy Spirit. They came home with the wonderful "Blessings of the Lord" in their hearts.

From then on, there were different ministers and evangelists that came and held revival meetings in the area. The folks always had room to keep those preachers even with a large family at home. I remember them having prayer meetings in our front room, and people tarrying for the Baptism.

The Wilson Evangelistic party that my sister, Lillie, traveled with held revivals in South Dakota and Nebraska. From there on, churches sprang up along the south border of South Dakota and northern Nebraska from Newport to Valentine--a church in almost every town. Then churches were organized like in Bassett, Ainsworth and Burton and people from the smaller places attended those churches.

Lillie and Rose, my sisters, went to a camp meeting in Riverton, Nebraska, where they received their Baptism. The next summer Rose, Lillie, Berger, my brother, his wife, Pearl, and I went to a camp meeting in Scottsbluff where Berger, Pearl and I received our baptism. Lillie and the Wilsons visited Sophia, my sister, during the Christmas vacation (1930) shortly after Glenn, her husband, passed away. They prayed with her, and that was when she got her Baptism.

The first pastor of the Burton Assembly of God Church, Harold James, would tell of Olafur Hallgrimson's faith. "A horrible storm was coming! The crops were going to be ruined! Grandpa Hallgrimson stood by the field and prayed! and there wasn't any damage to his field! The crop was spared! There was income for the coming year!"

(Viola Hallgrimson, "Memories of My Parents, Olafur and Skulina Hallgrimson," 1995.)

Descendents of Olafur and Skulina Hallgrimson who went into Assemblies of God ministry include: daughters, Rose, Viola, and Lilly (Blakkolb); grandchildren, Don Shoff, Nolan Blakkolb, Norma Shoff Correll, Joy Blakkolb Spain, Wanda Hallgrimson Sommers; great-grandchildren, Brent Shoff, Brian Correll, Tim Shoff, Kirk Spain, and Kriste Spain Belete. Also, others served in ministry in different denominations.

Harvey, H. L.

H. L. Harvey, a Methodist minister, received the Baptism of the Holy Spirit in 1916 in Springview, Nebraska, and was ejected from his position as pastor. As a result of this event, a miracle took place as far as the Anderson Family was concerned.

Brother Harvey traveled southeast, crossing the Niobrara River at the Karnes Crossing and continued southeast to Mariaville, Nebraska. Mariaville consisted of a country store, post office, and a school house across the road. He got permission to use the school house to hold revival services.

Chester and Lura (Anderson) were a newly married couple who lived three miles east. As the meetings progressed, people began to get saved. This included Chester and Lura, Gene, Chester's brother and his wife Effie, also several of Lura's family (Armstrong).

One evening, as the schoolhouse filled with people, outside word was sent to Brother Harvey that he had a phone call at the store. After several minutes, Chester and Gene felt something was wrong. They went outside to check and were told that when Brother Harvey stepped outside, men grabbed him, threw a blanket over him, put him in a model "T" Ford. They drove him to Newport, which was about 12 miles away. They instructed him to get on the next train and not come back or they would kill him.

Soon after this in 1918, Chester and Lura lost their first child at five weeks of age. They wanted Brother Harvey to preach the funeral. Chester went to each of the men, who were neighbors, that had taken Brother Harvey away and got permission for him to come back for the funeral, with the understanding that he would leave following the funeral. In later years, Vance (son of Chester and Lura) has been called to the area to conduct the funerals of the spouses of those involved in the kidnapping....

(V. Anderson, "Kidnapping of H. L Harvey" (Chester and Lura Anderson Family History), 1997.)

Hawley, George

We have just received word from Mrs. Luella Hawley of Auburn, Nebraska, that her husband, George W. Hawley, went to be with the Lord on July 27. Brother Hawley was one of the superannuated ministers of the General Council. It will be remembered by some that the Council school was first located at Auburn, Nebraska, and Brother Hawley was greatly interested in this school proposition.

Brother Hawley passed away at a ripe age, 80 years, 10 months, and 15 days....

("George Hawley Homegoing," *Pentecostal Evangel,* August 20, 1932, p. 15.)

Heinze, Rev. & Mrs. B. C.

In the summer of 1934, I transferred my 1926 ordination credentials to the General Council of the Assemblies of God. (About 1936) We received a call from a circuit of churches at Pender, Thurston and Emerson, Nebraska, which was accepted. This gave us a very busy schedule with services in all of these places every Sunday and other services during the week. This left us only one night open each week and that was Monday.

Then some folks from Allen, Nebraska came to our service one Sunday night. After the service, they approached us and asked if it would be possible to come and give them one service a week, to which I replied that we had only one night open a week. They pleaded with us and told us that they would be so happy if we would come on Monday nights, and if we would, they would have the electricity reconnected to their building. They would also secure a piano. So until school was out that spring, we continued going there on Monday nights.

That spring, we resigned from the three churches and made preparations to put on an all-summer tent meeting in Allen. What did we live in? A small tent, and it was not too good, for when it rained, it strained the rain and we would go inside the old building for shelter. We went there with no promise of any financial help from anyone (we never have demanded financial help from the District of General Council or anyone else). We had some pretty hard going financially in reestablishing the church. One week our only fare was tomatoes and bread. . However, the Lord laid it upon the hearts of some of the people at the end of the week and we were better supplied with our daily needs. We labored at Allen that summer in the tent meeting until fall when school would start. God sent along E. J. Dewey, for the Lord had directed him to come to us. In a few days, we received a call from the church at Burwell, Nebraska. Brother and Sister Dewey remained to care for the services and when we accepted the call to Burwell,

In accepting the call to the Burwell church (which was unanimous), we found that there was disharmony among the members, even so much that I could not get the Board together for a Board meeting. Sister Heinze and I took the matter before the Lord and asked him to help us with this situation. Then I finally was able to get the Board together and dealt with them. God came down and manifested Himself and restitution was made among the Board members and the Church as well, and God began to move. Our attendance increased so that in that little church we had attendances of close to 200. In a special drive, it reached over 200.

The church was having a hard time to take care of their current obligations. The Pastor was given all the tithes and very little came in for current expenses. In the meantime, Evangelist Wesley Goodwin and wife came to conduct special meetings for us. God laid it upon his heart to stress tithing. People got under conviction and came to the altar and pledged their tithes as well as themselves to the service of God. I've never seen a time like it. Some wept like they were sinners. After a couple of weeks, I called the Board members together and told them I would set myself, if they so desired, on a stipulated salary and the rest would go into the church treasury for needed expenses. This was entirely new to them, and the response was that they said to me, "If you are willing to do that, we surely should be willing!" God blessed, and we saw the work of the church go forward. Real unity and blessing of the Lord prevailed. Several have entered the ministry from that church. Herman Rhode, now Minnesota District superintendent, who also entered Bible School when we pastored there, and then the other three Rhodes, are in the ministry: George, who is a District official of North Dakota; Irvin, an official of the Montana District; and Clarence is pastoring the last I heard, I believe out west. Herman Thiemann is now the Administrator at Hillcrest Children's Home and formerly District Secretary of the Wyoming District. I understand there are others from that church who are in the ministry today....

The years that we ministered in Nebraska finally ended up with some more responsibilities when I was elected by the District Council to the office of Sectional Presbyter of the Assemblies of God. I was also asked to edit and publish the "Nebraska Pentecostal Fellowship" which had a good circulation. A. M. Alber was District Superintendent of Nebraska at that time. We found it a joy to work with him. My section covered an area up to the South Dakota border to the north. Fellowship meetings at that time (1937-38) were well attended. Many times we used to be at the morning service which began around 10:00 a.m. There were afternoon and evening services. God came down and blest. People were not in any hurry to have it over with; they stayed until they met with God in a real way.

I had been troubled with chronic appendicitis at times for a number of years. The last time I'd had an attack, was at Burwell. When I felt some better, I went to a doctor and he said, "The next time you have an attack, call me at once and I will operate on you for free. The only charge will be the room in the hospital." (Which at that time was not very much.) A few days later we started on a trip to visit our parents in Northwestern Minnesota. The first day we went as far as Centerville, South Dakota, where Sister Heinze's sister lived. When we arrived at her sister's place, I sat down in an easy chair in the living room, and later on Sister Heinze came and sat down on the arm of the chair. At that time, I felt another attack coming on. We were about 50 miles from the closest hospital, and I didn't have any hospitalization at that time. In fact, we had never heard of anything like that then. I told Sister Heinze it looked like our trip was over with and I cried out, "God help us!" Sister Heinze joined in with me. Then she went out in the kitchen to her sister. The Lord dismissed the whole matter from our minds until the next day when I said to Sister Heinze, "Say, I haven't had another attack of appendicitis!" It was gone, and to this day, I have not had another attack. Praise the Lord! That was in the later 1930's

We returned from visiting our parents, friends, and some relatives and continued in our ministry until the last part of 1938 at Burwell.

(*The Pioneer Preachers: The Life and Ministry of Rev. and Mrs. B. C. Heinze* [Watertown, SD?: B. C. Heinze, 197?].)

James, Marie (Bantel)

In July of 1937, we went to Gordon, Nebraska. Brother Alber, our District Superintendent, asked us if we would go and hold a tent meeting since there were a few saints there who wanted a full gospel work and had been praying that God would send someone to start one. We felt it was God's will for us to go.

A little two-wheel trailer carried all our belongings. Upon our arrival in Gordon, we were able to rent a furnished apartment and held services in our home until we began the meeting in the tent.

In a few days, the children all came down with the whooping cough and our five month old baby, Elisabeth, had it especially hard. One day we thought she had choked to death. I pleaded with God that if He wanted to take her, I was willing, but not to let her choke to death. We praise God that she never had another choking spell, nor ever "whooped" after that. But she was completely healed two and half weeks after coming down with this dreaded disease. It was a mighty testimony to the Christians and helped them to believe and trust God for healing.

After October, Bro. James had no work and we had to trust for all our needs. It was marvelous how God answered prayer and moved on even the unsaved. (Edward recalled he and his dad were allowed to sweep the coal dust out of the railroad coal cars and carry it home in buckets. Along with the corn cobs given by farmers to start the fire, this coal dust was a long-lasting, warm heat.)

Opposition was strong, but we reached hungry hearts. In November, the District put up a portable tabernacle where we held services for the next several years.

One time we were so hungry for meat and an evangelist we scarcely knew stopped and gave us a large mess of beefsteak. We wept like babies to know that God cared for us.

The first winter was very hard as the congregation was small and it was a real struggle to make ends meet, with rent, fuel and groceries to pay for. There were times that our baby had only skim milk to drink. But when it seemed the very darkest, God marvelously intervened by burdening the pastor and congregation of a neighboring church for our needs. The farmers brought generous supplies of meat, eggs, butter, flour and other delicious foods. I've often thought of their kindness and thanked God for their faithfulness. This church and pastor were also a real help by attending our services from time to time.

After about a year, God saved several farm and ranch families who had a real vision and desire to see our needs supplied and did so many kind and extra things for us, taking into great consideration our precious children.

The second winter we were there Brother James held prayer meetings in the Marshall home about ten miles from town every Friday night. We were unable to buy a license or gas for the car so he walked even though he didn't have an overcoat or overshoes. (Lena Mae remembered there were also holes in the soles of his shoes, and he would line them with newspapers! In the cold winter nights she was so afraid her daddy would freeze to death. His dedication and sacrifice to Jesus made a lasting impression upon Lena Mae.) Brother James would stay all night and return the next morning.

One time while he was there a fire was miraculously put out that had a good start in their upstairs. For sometime they were smelling smoke and looked everywhere but upstairs. Finally Brother James discovered it. A gallon of water was all they had on hand as the supply tank was empty due to no wind to run the windmill. Brother James took this water and went as far up the stairway as possible because of the smoke being so bad. Praying in the Name of the Lord, he threw the water against the flames and then continued to pray in other tongues. The fire was extinguished and the people were convinced that the Pentecostal Power was real. These people became some of our most faithful saints. A dear elderly grandmother in the home gave money for the car license and also to buy gas.

After a summer and winter in the furnished apartment, we asked God to give us a place near the edge of town, where we could have a garden, yard and place for chickens. We learned that just such a place was for rent by a railroad man, who was retiring and moving to Chadron. When we made inquiry, they were quick to inform us that they did not want to rent to anyone with children. But we kept praying!

Several weeks went by and we believed God for that place. One evening the man came to see us and asked us if we would promise to make the children be careful about the house, yard, trees etc. This we were happy to do as we felt that children should be taught to be careful.

Here (at this house on the edge of Gordon in the late '30's during the Great Depression) is where God helped us to have a miracle garden that became a testimony far and wide. When the grasshoppers moved into town, the gardens were devoured. They moved into ours, but after a day of prayer and fasting, we knelt in the garden and rebuked them in the name of the Lord. The grasshoppers did no further damage. The running water at this house was used to keep the vegetables growing. God was so good that we canned nearly 500 quarts of delicious vegetables. It was a real joy to write to Brother and Sister Alber and ask them to bring 50 quart jars as we wanted to give them the tithe of all we canned....

The Thanksgiving services were especially blessed and owned of God's divine presence. As we look back over the years, we raise our hearts in praise and say, "Great Is His Faithfulness!"

(Marie James: "Memories of Pioneering the Work at Gordon.")

Harold and Marie James pioneered churches in Nebraska and South Dakota and also pastored in Kansas. In 1982, both Harold and Marie James received recognition for fifty years of continuous service to the Assemblies of God.

Johnson, Mel and Barb

We are both natives of Chappell, Nebraska where we grew up on our family's farms. The Assembly of God Church has been involved in periods of powerful Revival down through the years. I was privileged as a boy to be a part of revival services where people were saved, filled with the Holy Spirit, Gift Ministry, and various signs and wonders as spoken of in the Bible. One such revival took place when I was 5 years old. (1944) During the evening altar service people were dancing in the Spirit, lying prostrate under the power of the Holy Spirit, praying at the altars, and being prayed for by Pastor Lester Dickinson and Evangelist. During this time I was setting close to the front observing this when I saw a vision of an angel or the Lord walking across the Platform in a shining white robe. This experience was shared with my parents and grand-mother Davis while driving home from church that evening. I asked if they had seen Jesus during the altar service. My Mother wisely counseled me, "No, but we sensed His presence so we knew He was there." I said, "I saw Him, He was walking across the front of the platform in a shining white robe." My life has never been the same.

It was shortly after that time that I was riding with my Dad on a load of railroad ties when the mules that were pulling the wagon suddenly stopped, causing the ties on which we were sitting to fall forward on the mules. They then lunged forward as I fell under the steel wheel of the wagon and was ran over. My Dad picked me up and carried me to the house because I could not walk. My parents had prayer for me and then began to clean me up to take me to the doctor. In a few minutes I came walking out of the bedroom completely well. The Lord had healed me. Praise The Lord!

My Dad went into the Army January 7, 1945, and we moved to Mineral Wells, Texas where he was stationed for a couple of years. While my family was driving on a busy highway near Wichita, Kansas, I fell out of the car which was going 60 MPH into the oncoming traffic. The driver that returned me to my family said, "He rolled into a little ball, came to a stop, got up and ran in the opposite direction as fast as he could go." I thought I was going in the same direction as my folks' car, and that I needed to catch them. I only had scratched and bruises but no broken bones or concussion. My parents took me to an Assemblies of God Minister to have him pray for me and he said after praying, "God has something special for this boy. He should have been run over by an oncoming car and killed, but he is fine now, Praise the Lord!" I guess I was too mischievous as a boy to have time to die.

I had the privilege of attending one of the first boys' camps in Lexington back when they had to put up tents for all the campers. I stayed in a tent with numerous boys including Dale Lesher from Thedford, who was not saved at the time. He was some older than me and did he ever give his pastor, Erwin Rohde, a tough time. It rained about every night and we had to put our suitcases on our army folding cots to keep them from getting wet. We went bare footed most of the time because there was water everywhere. I remember climbing up the center tent pole one night when our counselor was out, and when he came back, he couldn't find me. Was he ever in a panic. Finally the boys shined their flashlights on me. I was hanging on for dear life and afraid to come down for fear of what my counselor would do. Everybody had a big laugh at the "monkey" when I finally did come down.

A few years later at a Kid's Kamp I went to the altar to pray about getting along with my sisters better and was filled with the Baptism of the Holy Spirit. I was flat on my back speaking in tongues for several hours. When I "came to," everybody was gone but Brother Clyde Buck who was still there praying with me. WOW, what a powerful experience that was for a 10 year old boy.

While a junior in high school, the Lord began to deal with me about becoming involved in full time ministry. During my senior year the Lord powerfully called me into the ministry at a Sunday evening service while I was praying during the altar service

Barb and I were married and moved to Minneapolis, Minnesota, to attend North Central Bible College in the fall of 1957. I graduated with a B.S. degree in Pastoral Theology & Missions in 1961. I worked my way through college in four years with the help of Barb, my wife. a License to Preach credential was given from the Minnesota District upon entering full time ministry. Barb also shares this call and works whole heartedly in the Lord's work also. We've been involved in church work together for 37 great years.

Our first church taken in January of 1962 was a small District work in Central City, Nebraska, with 12 people the first couple months. We served there and worked a part time job in a grocery store for 3 1/2 years. I was granted an Ordination in 1964 at the District Council in McCook. The church in Central City grew to an attendance of 45 people.

We accepted a call to Norfolk in 1964. While pastoring there, we struggled to maintain a steady attendance because there was such a turnover in the church, with 45 people moving to other cities, during our first year there. God was faithful to provide each need in unique ways: special gifts, a sales job with commission, and the church people sacrificing in giving tithes and offerings. In spite of the exodus of people the attendance did not go down much since we were able with God's help to get people who had been a part of the church some years back to begin to return to the church.

We were blessed by the Lord in Norfolk with a powerful Revival Campaign with Evangelist Dale Seeber, a friend of mine, who I went to school with in Chappell. We were encouraged to fast and pray before the campaign started by the evangelist, and we faithfully did just that. The Revival services started right off with powerful things happening. People were being saved, healed, going down under the power of the Holy Spirit, filled with the Baptism of the Holy Spirit, delivered from bondage, etc. Rick, our son, was having serious ear problems and could not hear very well. He was prayed for and instantly healed. He could hear the evangelist whisper while standing behind him. He has never had ear problems since.

Evelyn Jenkinson was in the hospital with severe back problems and pain that couldn't be controlled. The Doctors told her she may be in a wheel chair the rest of her life. She finally persuaded the Doctor to let her come to church Sunday evening and was prayed for. She went down under the Power of God and writhed on the hard tile floor like a snake. She was miraculously healed. The Doctor called her Monday morning at home demanding that she get back to the hospital or she could be paralyzed. She returned to testify to the team of 4 doctors that God had healed her. They quizzed and tested her in amazement. One doctor a young specialist, became angry and stomped out of the room saying, "You will be back here in a wheel chair in a few weeks unless you let us do surgery on your back." She had no surgery and never had back trouble again even though a year later she fell on the ice under a parked car and had to be pulled out by a friend, but she was still well and strong.

Mert Fisher had her little grand-daughter with her in a service and she went down under the power of God while standing at her seat. She hit her head on the pew like a crack of a hammer but was not harmed. The little girl told her unsaved grand-father about it when they got home. She said, "Granddad you should have been at church tonight. Grand-ma fell down and hit her head on the pew, and it never even hurt."

Praise God for what He did in the lives of the people and in my life as well. I became a believer in the miracle power of God and His signs and wonders that He does when we obey His direction as revealed by the Holy Spirit.

During August of 1968 we accepted a call from Bethel Assembly in Thedford. The church was running around 55 in attendance at the time but it was a very healthy church of stable ranch families and business people. We were asked by the Youth Department to sponsor a group of 13 young people called AIMER'S to Venezuela for three weeks. We were able to lead 300 plus people to decisions for Christ as the team worked with missionaries in Puerto Ordaz. I was elected Sandhills Section Youth Rep. Barb and I directed one week of the three weeks of Kid's Kamps at Lexington. I earned a private pilot's license and flew many hours in church and District related business.

Cathy Andersen a North Central Bible College graduate was asked by the church to do her summer intern work at Thedford and worked with the Youth Program of the church for 3 months. She was then asked to stay as the church's first full time Youth Pastor where she served for 2 years. During this time many high school kids were saved and a great youth revival began. a large percentage of the High School became born again Christians and were filled with the Holy Spirit. Kid's were saved on the buses to and from ball games and gift ministry was taking place on the buses also. It was a glorious time. The church grew to a full capacity of 125 to 135 people each Sunday. Land was purchased north of the church with a small house for Pastor Cathy and for a future addition for a church building. We were active in various community leadership groups which afforded open doors for ministry. I was a member of the Service Club and served in each of the offices over a period of years. God enabled us to see people from 45 to 55 miles around become involved in the church for which we Praise The Lord.

We were not aware of it at the beginning of our ministry in Thedford but the "Latter Rain" movement had a strong negative influence on the church and as a result "gift ministry" from the people had about ceased in the Church. Not knowing of this fear we encourage Biblical gift ministry in the services. Several again, began to be used by the Holy Spirit in messages in tongues, interpretation, prophecy, etc. Ron Blauvelt told me after we had been at the church for several years, that he had not seen this in the church for many years.

People's faith began to grow in great ways as people were saved, filled with the Holy Spirit Baptism, healed, and delivered in glorious ways. Ruth Blauvelt was diagnosed with uterine cancer and a biopsy was taken which verified what the doctors thought. She was scheduled for surgery on a Monday morning at the North Platte Hospital. She was very upset of course and asked the church to pray for her. We had a special time of prayer and anointed her with oil during the Sunday evening service. We sensed the mighty power of God in a special way that night. She went to the hospital early Monday morning. Barb and I were there to pray with her and Forrest, her husband, before she went into surgery. In about half an hour, the doctors came out to report that no surgery was necessary because upon taking another biopsy before surgery they could find no cancer and were quite puzzled. We were made to rejoice and Praise The Lord for His grace and healing power. She was healed by the Lord and has never had another sign of cancer since.

We accepted a call from Bridgeport Assembly and moved there September 1, 1978. Cathy Anderson was asked to be the Youth Pastor as a step of faith and obedience by the church. She came on staff along with us in 1978. She got a job and received one offering a month from the church. There were around 25 people in attendance the first few months and it was very challenging for us. We became involved in several home Bible Study groups that had been started as a result of a Lowell Lundstrom crusade held there earlier. Most of these new Christians soon began to come to the church regularly and became members. Within 6 months Cathy was able to work full time for the church as a result of church growth and financial strength. She began reaching many teens in the school and community with Jesus' saving grace. She was able to see a steadily growing youth group of 35--40 kids each week.

People began to get saved in the church and then go out and bring their family members to church to be saved or recommitted to Jesus. Young couples began to get saved and became a part of the church. Many of these couples had been in the drug and party world. It was amazing what the Lord was doing to change lives in Jesus' name. The church grew to a high of around 150 people in attendance at the regular services.

A severe agricultural crunch occurred in 1983 that affected the church also and we lost five families that year because they lost their farms and moved elsewhere. Cathy resigned in 1984 and moved back to Wisconsin her home state. She had made a powerful impact for Christ on the entire Bridgeport area among the youth and adults.

After a time of in depth study and prayer, Rick and Kenya Johnson (our son) were invited to be the Associate & Youth Pastor in November of 1984 and served with us for 11 great years. The youth program continued to grow in strength and many of the kid's parents got saved, joined the church, and became leaders.

Kathy Bartholomew had returned home from California after having a severe Diabetic seizure which caused her to completely loose her memory, her ability to read, write, etc. She did not even know who she was until a reporter began to help her after seeing her setting on a street corner with her dog. This reporter was doing a story on street people and became compelled to help her. She finally traced her family to Bridgeport and helped her return home. Kenya, our Youth Pastor's wife, began helping her in various ways and she began to know Jesus and grow in the ways of the Lord. A true miracle of healing took place during one of our Sunday evening services. We were praying for a variety of different needs, and I had ask different people to lead in prayer for a specific need. Dwain Riddle was praying for his grand-daughter Bethany, a teenager, who had just been diagnosed as a diabetic. He was praying with great conviction and began to speak in tongues as he was praying. During his prayer Kathy fell face forward with a thud on the floor and laid there motionless. I looked at her as did Kenya and Ardis Stewart, a nurses aid, and we wondered what to do. I motioned for them to stay where they were for a little bit because I sensed that God was doing something in her life. In a few moments I motioned them to go help her because she was starting to move a little. They helped her up and asked if she was feeling faint or what. She indicated she was feeling fine. We dismissed the service in a few minutes. I asked Kenya and Ardis to take her home, tell her father what had happened, and to check her blood sugar because she was diabetic. They did this and her blood sugar was normal, so they went home.

Kathy [Bartholomew] called Kenya about 30 minutes later and asked her to come over to her house because she needed to talk. When she got over there, Kathy told her what had happened to her at church but made her promise not to send her to a mental hospital. She told her that when she was praying at church she saw the hands and feet of a man coming towards her, and when he touched her it seemed like something exploded in her stomach and that was when she fell down. She then saw people going up into heaven, everybody was going up in the air it seemed. Then she looked and not everybody was going up just some of the people. Kenya [Johnson] told her that she didn't need to go to a mental hospital. What she saw was a vision from God about Jesus coming to take the true Christians up to heaven with him. This is what we call the Rapture. The next day Kathy called Kenya again and said something strange is happening. She didn't need insulin this morning and feels better than she had for many years. She used to take large doses of insulin twice a day for 21 years and now doesn't need it at all.

Kathy is a Veteran and called her doctor who told her to get to Cheyenne to the hospital the next day for a check-up. They could find nothing wrong after many tests. She was told to go home, but to check her blood sugar every day because the diabetic condition would return. Nobody has ever been cured of diabetes, they said. She has the doctors dumbfounded because she has never needed to take insulin again in four years now. She is also beginning to remember some things and has begun to learn to read, write, and do math again with the help of a teacher. God is continuing to do great things in her life as she grows like a baby Christian.

We served the Lord in Bridgeport at the New Life Assembly for 17 successful years and many truly miraculous things were done by our wonderful Lord.

Pastor Rick and Kenya [Johnson] accepted a call from Broken Bow Assembly in September of 1995 to be their Senior Pastor.

The Lord began dealing with me in prayer early in the mornings about becoming involved at the Camp Grounds in Lexington. I told Barb and Rick about it and we just left it at that. Pastor Bob Nazarenus told me on one occasion when I was at the District Office that we need to pray because Joe Masten the Camp Director was wanting to get back into the pastorate sometime. I considered talking to him then about what the Lord was impressing upon me about Camp, but didn't feel it was the right time. A few months later Pastor Bob was in Bridgeport before the District Tour Dinner in Alliance and we were planning the up-coming Presbyter's meeting. He again said that we needed to pray because Joe was talking about pastoring again. I said, "Pastor Bob, I need to share something with you. The Lord has been dealing with me about becoming involved at the Camp for several months." He said, in a shocked way, "That is interesting, but you know I can't fire Joe." "Yes, I know that and that's not what I'm saying. It is just what the Lord has been impressing upon me. I don't know what it all means at this time." As Pastor Bob left my office he said, "We will have to pray about this."

It was about a month later in November that he called me about the Camp and said, "Joe is looking at the church in Thedford so you better pack your bags." I said, "I don't know if I should have talked to you about this or not." Barb and I began to pray and talk it over. Barb wasn't sure she wanted to go. About one week later Pastor Bob called to let us know Joe Masten had accepted the call to go to Thedford, and he wanted to know how soon we could move to Lexington. I told him that I'd be more comfortable if the Presbyters were brought into the loop of this on a conference call before an appointment is made, so that was done. Pastor Bob announced Joe's resignation and the need of a new Camp Director. After some discussion, he asked me to take the position and there was a unanimous vote given.

Barb and I then drove to Grand Island to go over job descriptions, expectations, etc. It was amazing because the Lord had impressed upon me four to five months earlier a list of things that I wrote down about the Camp. The things Pastor Bob gave me were about the same as my list. We stopped at Lexington on our way home and looked at the Camp and house, but we were still in a spin mentally about the whole thing. Barb was in tears about the house as we drove to Broken Bow to talk this over with Rick and Kenya our son and daughter-in-law. I told her just to be patient and the Lord will work that out just in His way. When Pastor Bob called the next day for our decision, "I told him yes, but the house is a mess." He said, "Yes I know. We'll make that the number one priority and remodel it completely." We accepted the position in the middle of November and moved on December 11, 1995 to Lexington, Nebraska. We stayed in the Youth Director's cabin for several months while we remodeled the house and conducted Retreats that were scheduled. WOW! What a way to get started as the Camp Development Director.

Our job entails managing and developing the Camp in a variety of ways: financially, physically, and activities at the camp. Our duties also include supervising the District Construction Corps and promoting the General Council Foundation in the District. This move also enables me to serve the District better as Secretary-Treasurer.

Barb and I are now involved in week-end ministry in various churches across the District. We are enjoying this ministry immensely. It is a new type of ministry for us in that it enables us to minister more as an evangelist and bring the Lord's healing to a large variety of people. We have three lovely children who have their own families, and eight grand-children.

It is truly a joy to serve the Lord each day as well as His wonderful people in the Nebraska District.

(Mel and Barb Johnson, "History of Ministerial Service of K. M. (Mel) & Barbara Johnson," 1998.)

Barb Johnson has served as sectional WM representative. Mel Johnson has served the Nebraska District as sectional youth representative, assistant youth & C.E. director for the District, sectional presbyter and Secretary-Treasurer of the District. Mel is currently Camp Development Director of the A/G Camp and Conference Center. Their son Rick is an Assemblies of God pastor.

King, Clyde

It was winter, cold sifted in around the windows of the little Coburg Community Church and the window panes chattered to the wind as a faithful little flivver chugged to a standstill at the front door--Sis. Stella Howard, with Rose and Viola Hallgrimson, had come to 'turn loose' a revival.

1933 and '34 were hard years. The Depression was no respecter of persons, nor places, and it came to the Coburg Community along with the rest. The shifting of sand makes strange patterns sometimes and God is able to bring beautiful blessings from strange situations. Such is the story of Coburg, King and Christ.

In those depression days entertainment was at a premium and there was no lack of crowds when word got around that some ladies were preaching at the church.

Clyde King was one of many young persons living in the community at that time and his mother took an active part in the Sunday School work as teacher and superintendent. However there was no pastor, no parsonage and no finances. The King's home was only about 1 1/2 miles from the church and the family went to every service.

Hardships were the order of the meeting with the response about as poor as the heat from the wood and coal stove--that roasted you on one side and froze you on the other--but those 150 persons continued to be fired upon by the faithful Sis. Howard and sung to by the girls.

After preaching for about a month, with no converts, it must have seemed that there was no use, but God does not always move according to our time table. Seventeen year old Clyde King was being convicted of his need of God, but he told himself, he wasn't too bad and one night on the way to church he even spoke this thought aloud to his mother. "Sure, I know I need God but others need Him worse than I do." A wise Mother chose her words with care and said, "Yes son, but you must get right with God regardless of what others do." Those words might have made the difference between one soul and hundreds.

There was nothing unusual about the day that Clyde King was saved except that God uses every turn in the wheel of circumstances to bring Glory to His Name.

Sis Howard walked into the rooms that Rose and Viola Hallgrimson shared with the new faith that they were putting in God to supply their need. Quite an experience for anyone. "I have an opportunity to see my brother in Wakefield and so I will be gone over Sunday. You girls know how to carry on and I will be praying for you."

That Sunday as Rose preached she used a familiar passage from the book of the Revelation concerning the coming of the Lord. There was no special anointing upon the message but at the last God took hold of His messenger and the Sword of the Spirit cut to the heart of another country boy.

The music played an altar call and with the call of God upon his heart, Clyde made his way down the aisle. It seemed the old gas lights burned brighter and everything looked better after he had made peace with his soul.

It was some time after Clyde's conversion before a real break was seen, but one by one folks began to melt before the Lord and the revival fires began to burn.

At the close of the meeting some fifty to sixty persons were baptized in the Middle Loup River during two different service. It pays to seek God and have revival. May a hunger for a move of God sweep over us again in this our present generation.

(Harold Mintle, "Clyde King's Conversion," *Nebraska Fellowship,* August 1957, p. 9; September 1957, p. 4.)

Kisser, Irene

In Southern Illinois, the church we were to pastor was run down; a new building was just started, so Joseph, my husband, began work on it. Verna and Evelyn, my daughters, were in high school and also worked after school at a drive-in restaurant until 11 p.m. I was concerned because they came home so late; and the pressures of the church, building, and the family caused me to again go into a bad siege of depression. About all I did besides cry was the family laundry each week. I always had written my parents regularly; so when I quit they became worried.

We heard that Oral Roberts was to be in Scottsbluff for a healing crusade. My brother, Clarence sent for us, asking us to move to Scottsbluff, including $300. So we did (yes, another change of school for the children). We attended the crusade and I went through the healing line and felt a lot better. We rented a house and Joseph assisted in the church and worked at Sash and Door cabinet shop. Our children got in with Christian young people and were seemingly contented, but also concerned about their Mother. That spring Verna graduated from high school with honors.

In the fall, we were ready to take another pastorate, although I was not feeling completely well. In the mornings when I awoke, I just did not want to face the day. At night I cried myself to sleep. Joseph was very good to me and talked and prayed with me again and again. It is very hard for anyone to know what to do for a person in such a condition if they have never experienced depression themselves.

Verna was in Bible College now and Evelyn had gone to summer school and was teaching in a country school. So just four of the children were at home.

I finally decided to go to a hospital in Colorado Springs; and if necessary, I would have shock treatments. The doctor advised me to be admitted for six weeks. They gave these treatments twice a week. I was there for two weeks, receiving four treatments. Prayers had been offered continually by churches, friends and relatives for my deliverance. After two weeks, I was determined to go home and trust the Lord to help me from then on. The doctor granted my request and released me, telling Joseph that I had strong faith in God, and with the four treatments I would make it; and I did after fighting this depression for about five years. I had determined in my mind and heart to defeat this in the name of Jesus, and Praise God deliverance came. Twenty years have gone by and I haven‘t had such a depressed feeling since ...

One spring Joseph and I attended a Ministers‘ Institute in Helena, Montana, where I got very sick and it was hard for me to breathe. I was again hospitalized and saints prayed and in a couple of days I was dismissed. We returned to our home in Montana a couple of hundred miles away. Now we had this extra expense, and no insurance; but we trusted God to supply the need. After a week passed, we received a letter in the mail with a $100 check from the Helena church and pastor saying that God had impressed them to do this for us because of the unexpected expense. We Praise the Lord for again and again supplying our needs.

Later when moving back to Nebraska, a doctor advised to have heart surgery. I replied that I had never had surgery, even for tonsils or appendix, and now have heart surgery? I said I would not. Another time I was desperate and when I couldn‘t get my breath was rushed to a hospital. After an hour or so, deliverance came. One day I asked one of our sons-in-law if he were in my place if he would have open-heart surgery? He answered that if it would help, he sure would.

After I decided to have it done, I wrote twenty letters to different prayer warriors, asking them to pray for me. A Bassett doctor made the arrangements with one of the best heart surgeons in Denver, Colorado, and we traveled five hundred miles to Denver (1971). I went with strong faith that all would go well. While in the doctor‘s office I told him that we could not afford such a surgery and I trusted after his thorough examination that I wouldn‘t need surgery. He said, “And what if you do?” He also quoted from Psalm 91. I was admitted in the hospital on Tuesday and the following Monday had my surgery ...

I was also praying that I wouldn‘t need my heart valve replaced; and I didn‘t for which I praised the Lord. One main valve was closed with scar tissues all around it ... I got along wonderfully and the doctor said it was a phenomena--my recovering so quickly. I was in the hospital three weeks ... After I was dismissed, Joseph took me to Scottsbluff and Gering where I recuperated for four weeks. When the four weeks were up Marjorie happened to be in Western Nebraska, because of her job; so she took me home to Bassett. It was two more months before I could do much. Anna Belle and family were living in Bassett at that time and she helped out, and Verna came from Milford and stayed several days too.

The surgery and hospital care cost several thousand dollars; but God undertook for us. The insurance, we so miraculously took out just before my surgery, covered most of it; and the Nebraska churches, friends and loved ones sent gifts in offerings, so we only had to pay $600. God cares for His own!

It has been eight years this month since my heart surgery and I haven‘t been in a hospital once since that time. God is so good and we Praise Him.

(Irene Kisser, “A Backward Glance: Praise God!” from *Irene Kisser's Testimony of Healing*, pp. 10-16.)

Irene was born in a sod house in North Dakota. The Kirschman family later lived at Scottsbluff, Nebraska. Irene's daughter, Verna, is the wife of Jim Wilkins, former Nebraska superintendent. Daughter Evelyn (Kisser) Albin is involved in MAPS work. Marjorie (Kisser) Stahly lives in Milford. Son, Melvin is a pastor. Daughter, Berniece Geer is a pastor's wife.

Daughter, Anna Belle Groseclose is a missionary to Suriname, South America. At least twelve grandchildren are in the ministry or are worship leaders. Grandson, Bartley Wilkins pastors in Omaha.

Wayne and Hazel Hall

Harold James family at Nebraska Camp

Brother Walter Evans at Burton, NE, Feb. 14, 1943

James children with water

Unit 2: Memories Worth Repeating

Chapter 6: Lena Mae Leach to Lawrence Wilkins

***"Who forgives all your sins and heals all your diseases."* (Psalm 103:3 NIV)**

Leach, Lena Mae	Nichols, Lynn	Wehrli, Kevin
Leach, Roscoe	Shirley, Bede	Wilkins, Jim
Lee, Ileen	Steinle Sisters	Wilkins, Lawrence
Lemp, Elisabeth	Turner, Delbert	
Loutzenhiser, Esther	Wagoner, Paul	

Leach, Lena Mae (James)

"The call of God led my parents, Harold and Marie James, from the farm in Lucas, South Dakota to Burton, Nebraska; there they pastored the new congregation that formed from the great 1930 and '31 revival. Even before moving to Burton in the fall of 1931, Mother and Dad traveled from the farm in South Dakota to Burton each night for several weeks for the revival services. Each evening before the people arrived, Mother placed me on a blanket behind the piano. Apparently I had my bottle and toys and would eventually go to sleep. When the folks moved to Burton, one lady asked my mother about their baby (me). The lady never realized I was behind the piano during those weeks of meetings.

One night in the old white church in Burton where services were held I sang a solo when I was only two or three years old. Lena Bantel, my Mother's mother, was in the service. Grandma Bantel, as everyone called her would have been about seventy years old, very well known and loved by all since she had served this frontier area for over forty years as a nurse and midwife. When I finished my solo, Grandma Bantel stood up and said, "Doesn't that sound just like the voice of an angel?"

In 1937, our family moved to Gordon, Nebraska. Mother and Dad's deep concern for us three children was very evident. In spite of depression years and our meager income, my parents found a way for me to take seven piano lessons. That must have been a great sacrifice for them. I had wanted piano lessons for so long, and finally at age 7 — 7 lessons — perfect! In those lessons I learned the basic concepts of reading music and beginning piano skills. That knowledge carried me through the next four years when lessons were not affordable. On my own I practiced the piano for hours at a time. People gave me piano books and along with hymn books, I taught myself, thus acquiring a measure of fluency. The art of improvisation fascinated me to no end. At district meetings I watched pianists play with such grace and beauty, their fingers flying up and down the keyboard. I listened to Rudy Atwood, Old Fashioned Revival Hour radio pianist and determined I was going to improvise like him. Those years of not being able to formally take lessons turned out for good, although as a child I thought they were wasted. Later, through the grace of God, I wrote a piano course on improvisation and taught my method to many students in America as well as in overseas missions.

Mother and Dad's personal sacrifice for God's work and for their children made an unforgettable impression upon me. Their love and joy in serving Jesus motivated us to such an extent that I never thought about being poor. As one of about thirty third graders, we were excitedly planning the Valentine's Day party. The teacher asked "would one of you children volunteer your mother to make homemade ice cream for our party?" My hand shot up and I said "my mother will be glad to make a freezer of ice cream for us." "That's wonderful Lena Mae, thank you so much". When I arrived home from school, I excitedly told my parents about volunteering a gallon freezer of ice cream for my class party. I have no idea where they got money to buy the ingredients although farmers gave us eggs and cream. We didn't even have gas money to drive the car with the big freezer of delicious pink ice cream to the school. So my big brother, Edward, came to my rescue. He pulled that load of ice cream, packed in ice in our little red wagon to the school, a distance of about two miles. We were rich indeed with love of God, family and friends.

In 1940, we moved to Westerville where the parsonage was a tiny house directly across from the Assembly of God church and a one-room school. One block to the north was a general store and one block to the east was the high school. Mother always had a way of making a run-down cottage into a delightful home. This place was no exception. Walls were papered or painted. Clean curtains on the windows and new linoleum on the floors made the home clean and attractive. The one little bedroom went to mother and dad while a part of an old back porch was made into a bedroom for Edward with the screens covered in the winter time for a little more warmth, and cardboard covering what walls were there. Elisabeth and I slept on the couch that made into a bed in the living room.

The Westerville congregation was mostly farmers. They were hard working people who depended on their crops for income; on gardens for vegetables; on cows for milk, cream and meat; on hogs for market income or meat; and chickens for eggs or meat. To a great extent their existence was self-contained. As pastors, my parents received tithes from sales of their crops, hogs, cattle, chicken and eggs. Very often tithes were paid by the farmers in dairy produce, garden products and meat that they themselves butchered.

Electricity had not come to that rural area so before each evening service, deacons lit the gas lamps. I recall this process included cleaning the entire lamp, pumping air pressure, and adjusting the mantle. In our home we used kerosene lamps with a wick, not as bright as the gas lamps but sufficient. The most memorable Sunday night service in Westerville was December 7, 1941. Earlier that day everyone's radio broadcast the devastating news of the Pearl Harbor attack. The church service was mostly prayer for our nation, president, military forces and families who suffered such tragic losses. Several of the young men of that congregation, even though they qualified for farm deferment, later were drafted for military duty.

Because of my parents' farm background, they quickly bonded with the families of this rural community. One evangelist was critical of the men who seemed to sleep through every service. Not my Dad! He praised the men for coming to church after long, hard days of field work. Their sleeping didn't bother my father! "They need their rest" was my Dad's quick reply. He loved and admired those farmers for coming to church in spite of their exhaustion.

Mother and Dad led the church in buying a nicer parsonage. In this new house Elisabeth and I shared a pretty blue bedroom. While living in the new parsonage, electricity came to Westerville.

After my seven piano lessons at Gordon, the family could not afford more. Time and again I asked God to supply the money for more lessons. When I learned about the annual county music contest, I prayed even more. I could not enter the piano solo division without a teacher's guidance. When dress shoes were needed, my Father had made a way for new "high-heels," and it was Mother who insisted we pay the 50 cent lesson fee to a teacher in Ansley, a nearby town. Finally at last when I was 12 years old, I could take a few lessons to prepare for the big music contest! I was so excited! I shall always be thankful for my parents' great sacrifice in helping me get a music education.

The Ansley teacher was so strict, striking my hands with her pencil so that I would get correct time. It seemed that she had to correct not only time, but notes, my hand and body position, everything having to do with my playing the piano. I could hardly hold back the tears, but my determination to play in the contest helped me endure this demanding teacher.

Many weeks before the contest I was given a piano piece entitled "At the Donneybrook Fair" by John Prindle Scott. "This will be your contest piece" announced Mrs. Cain, my teacher. "Oh but I want to play the "minute Waltz" I responded. The student before me was playing that selection as I arrived for my lesson and I immediately fell in love with this Chopin number. "No," she sharply answered. "The Minute Waltz is much too hard for you. If you practice very diligently, in a few years you will be able to play it." Although I said nothing, I had a plan.

My plan was to learn "At the Donneybrook Fair" so well in the next week that Mrs. Cain would be surprised allowing me also to learn the "Minute Waltz," I shared my strategy with no one but started practicing several hours each day. Since Elisabeth and I slept in the small living room just outside my parents small bedroom, they permitted me to start daily practice at 6:00 A.M. It was dark and winter time, but I was delighted with their willingness. Each night before falling asleep, I conditioned my mind to wake shortly before six o'clock so I could begin playing at 6:00 A.M. The plan worked well. One morning mother called from the bedroom. "Lena Mae what are you doing?" "Just practicing mother," I answered softly. "Lena Mae, do you know what time it is?" dad asked. "I think about 6 o'clock," I answered. In a stern voice Dad continued, "it is 1:30 in the middle of the night, Lena Mae, and we must all get our sleep." "Okay Daddy" I softly said as I slipped back into bed. I had no idea that it was so early in the morning! From then on, my parents let me use the alarm clock!

Because I practiced so many hours, I thought Mrs. Cain would be surprised and would allow me to work on my beloved "Minute Waltz"! She complimented me on my progress with the Scott piece and then said, "If you keep up the good work, 'At the Donneybrook Fair' should be in good shape for the contest." "What about the 'Minute Waltz'?" I shyly asked. "Just as I told you, you will be ready for it in a few more years!" she sternly replied. There was no reasoning, her word was final. Again the tears started to flow, but with the same determination to learn the "Minute Waltz" at that very moment I determined to master the Scott number. By contest time the piece was learned perfectly! I received the highest rating "superior" and was also selected as the one instrumental soloist to play for the county school graduation. That was a special honor! I admit Mrs. Cain chose the right selection, and because of extra practice "At the Donneybrook Fair" was ready for the graduation performance.

Shortly after my performance at the county graduation program it was necessary to stop piano lessons. Our family budget could not stretch enough to cover the 50 cent lesson fee. From earliest childhood until I was fourteen, I had few formal lessons. This seemed like wasted time, but God turned it for good. During those years I developed my skills of improvisation and began teaching that concept when I was a freshman in Central Bible Institute.

With gratitude, I have often thought about my piano teacher, Mrs. Cain. Even though we could afford only a few lessons, her training was invaluable in preparing me for teaching music on the mission field, in churches and in colleges here in America. In spite of her strict teaching style, she laid the foundation for my work at universities as teacher and as a performer in classical and sacred music in the United States and abroad. Of course this included playing the "Minute Waltz"!

(Lena Mae James Leach, "A Musician Remembers Growing up During the Great Depression," *A Pioneering Pastor's Home,* 1996.)

Dr. Lena Mae James Leach served as pianist for Sermons In Song *and then* Revivaltime.

While the Leaches were in the Netherlands, Lena Mae directed choirs, taught piano and music, gave concerts with the choirs as well as performing herself. She also taught in Assemblies of God colleges in the United States and was Director of Music for Valley Forge Christian College.

Leach, Roscoe L.

Lena Mae and I came to Nebraska in 1954. Our first pastorate was in Norfolk. The church was a basement church with a flat roof. We had a total of 7 people when we arrived as our congregation. I later learned that the District had considered closing this work but when the Presbyters heard that we might come they said, "Let them come, they can't hurt anything." Our Presbyter was B. F. Correll who was the pastor at South Sioux City. What a great privilege to come under his supervision.

Wanting to get acquainted with the presbyter we invited him and Sister Correll to speak on a Wednesday evening and asked them to come for dinner before the service. Our furniture was all hand-me-down. Some of it was Salvation Army reject. Our kitchen table was in this class. It leaned like the tower of Pizza ... so much that you could only fill a coffee cup 3/4 full or it would run over the low side of the cup. Well we did have a set of 4 matched dinnerware. Some of you would remember the "in style" color avocado. There was only one small problem with the set...we had broken off a handle on one of the cups. Well that was all right because if you kept your thumb sort of under the cup you would support it just fine. No problem ... just be sure that one of us got the cup and not either Brother or Sister Correll.

You are way ahead of the story ... Alas Brother Correll somehow got the cup but without the special instruction on how to use the cup. On his second sip the handle separated from the cup and fell straight down. When it hit the table, there was an atomic explosion of coffee which struck Brother Correll and also made contact with the ceiling. The fall-out began. In the stunned silence that only this kind of a moment holds the coffee on the ceiling began to slowly shower down on us. Well so much for impressing your presbyter.

The church slowly grew and we learned to trust the Lord for his provision. We did not have enough money for gas for the car so I began to walk from street to street witnessing and doing a canvass in search of people who would come to the church. Many doors were shut in my face. Sometimes people were friendly but did not come to visit us in church. As far as we could tell no one ever came to church from all of the days of visitation. One thing that can be learned from this is that we need to do what we can and God will build His Church, for each week we would be surprised as new people came to hear the gospel.

With a new baby, Stephen, we needed enough money to take care of a baby and our own needs. The offerings just didn't meet all of the family needs. I remember two different occasions when I went out to look for work in the mornings. One time I spent the morning leading a druggist to the Lord. When I came home in the afternoon, Lena Mae said, "Look at this mail." There was a letter from a friend in California with enough money to last us a month. Another similar experience happened after a striking couple had visited the church on a Sunday Morning. He worked for the railroad as inspector ... traveling throughout the Mid-West. Well they only came the one Sunday because his work took them away. That week I went out to look for part-time work and again spent the morning witnessing. But that afternoon, we had a letter from this couple which said, "... since we have no home church at this time, we have asked the Lord to let us help promising struggling works. The work that we have been supporting in Iowa is doing well now and after visiting you last Sunday, we will be sending you our tithes until the Lord directs us otherwise." Well we received a check every two weeks until we left Norfolk and accepted the church in Aurora. The week that we were going to leave we got a letter from this wonderful couple that they would not be sending their tithe to us any longer.

Another beautiful lesson was learned while we were at Norfolk. Since finances were so scarce, we were not always able to attend all of the District events and even had to miss some of the sectional events. Well there was a special day long event planned by the District, and we did so want to attend ... but alas there were no funds. Then just a couple of days before the event, we received a call from Bro. and Sis.[Wayne] Hall. They told us that the Lord had spoken to them about us, and that they wanted to pay for our trip and stay at this very special event. How good to know that we do after all serve the Lord of the harvest. Is it any wonder then that with such mentors, Lena Mae and I have always had such joy in helping others in ministry ... especially young pastors in pioneer or hard places?

After the ministry in Norfolk the Lord led us to Aurora. This was certainly a new challenge. We were there for several years and how precious these dear people were. The Lord continued to grow us in ministry in preparation for later challenges. It was during this time that we saw many miracles of healing. The Lord helped us develop a plan for the future which started with the sale of the parsonage and would later include the building of a new parsonage and later a church. We were able to build the new parsonage, but other pastors who followed us saw the completion of this vision with the building of the new church.

Following our pastorate at Aurora, we were elected to serve as the Nebraska D-CAP following the ministry of Norm Correll. These were days of great blessing in our personal ministry. I was able to preach in many District Youth Camps, Conventions and Retreats throughout the country. This was during the time when we also had full-time Christian Education Directors. Lena Mae began her ministry in District music at this time. She later served in three other districts as District Music Director. Because of these Nebraska days of experimenting and training, she served on the National Assemblies of God Music Committee on several occasions.

During our time as the D-CAP, we also helped in the family camps. I ran the snack shop several years. This was a joyous time and the Nebraska Camp/Conference Center has continued to be a focal point for God's blessing and call to the wonderful people of the state.

One last camp story. We had finished the camp season, and it was the last day of Family Camp. It was the great missionary Sunday Afternoon service. Lena Mae and I were planning a short week vacation. Finances were better for this young family who now had three boys to take care of for the Lord. We had saved $100.00 for this vacation. What fun we were going to have. Then the missionary service. The power of the Lord was so evident ... the missionary message so powerful. And now it was time for the offering. Because of the care of the three little Leaches, we were seated near the back of the old tabernacle. The offering started at the front. The Lord spoke to my heart to give the $100.00. I began to bargain with the Lord ... $25.00 for the offering and we'll cut back on our vacation ... the plates were about half-way to us ... $50.00 for missions and we'll camp and stay a couple less days ... the plates are now just a couple of rows away ... $75.00 for missions ... $25.00 for us and just two days by the lake in a tent ... the plate is coming down our row.... Lena Mae pokes me in the ribs, hard, and says in a quite whisper ... stop arguing and give the $100.00. What the Holy Spirit was having a hard time accomplishing, my little darling did with a poke in the ribs.

Well I'd like to tell you that my response was all joy and glory ... wrong. I was angry, pouty and upset. I said to Lena Mae, "Let's get the boys to bed." So off to the cabin we disappeared. I continued to pout in the dark, and sometime later we heard a soft call from outside the cabins. "Brother and Sister Leach, are you there?" Outside were Brother and Sister Paul Sherman. They said they had looked for us following the service and wanted us to have a hamburger with them. Still pouting my answer was, "We've got the boys down and can't come out." "Well can you come to the door for a minute?" Can you imagine the shame I felt when they told us that their church in Thedford was sending them to Yellowstone Park and wanted them to take the Leaches with them for an all expense paid vacation. We "men-of God" are sometimes so puny. My darling wife never said a word or refereed to my sad behavior. She just allowed her golden silence to thunder around me. How thankful I have been for the precious wife that the Lord gave to me.

(Roscoe L. Leach, "Memories," 1997.

Dr. Roscoe Leach served as D-CAP for Nebraska from 1957 to 1961. The Leaches were missionaries to the Netherlands and established a Bible school in the Hague. Roscoe (Bud) taught at Trinity Bible College and Valley Forge Christian College as well as pastoring in Nebraska, Kansas, California, Ohio and Virginia.

Lee, Ileen

In the mid-thirty's, I became a sickly child. I never asked my mother what was the matter with me when the doctor said I needed bed rest or when my hair began to fall out when it was washed. When my hair began to grow again it was coming in pure white above my forehead. I looked in the mirror and wondered, "Would it all be white?" My mother's tears came down her cheeks as she helped me dress. I tried to be brave and still did not ask.

My father had his first heart attack and died when I was five years of age. I saw the struggle my mother had trying to raise and provide for her last four children. I was the youngest. The older eight were already away from home. Time went on and I often suffered a severe pain in my chest. It felt like a knife plunging through and someone twisting it. I told no one. I was tired of being sick!

In 1946, my mother became very ill and told me, "My chest feels like a knife plunging through and someone twisting it!" You can believe my eyes opened wide and my whole being became alert. After her three day illness, her death and funeral, I went to the doctor in Tilden. I asked for a complete physical. His findings were a valve closing in my heart, hence such great pain. No cure (no heart surgery those days).

My husband was overseas in W.W. II, having been sent there to serve during the Battle of the Bulge and beyond. I decided not to tell Phil as he needed all his strength and peace of mind to survive. Neither did I tell any of my family. Pity, I didn't need. Help, they couldn't give. I did apply to the Red Cross for my husband's return home because of the circumstances. The request was rejected. When I had a very bad attack, the doctor, himself, stopped at the Red Cross and applied for Phil's return. It was immediately accepted. The Chaplain broke the news to my husband. The Army flew him home.

We wept together and felt alone without anyone who would really care. We decided to build a small trailer-house and go to Washington State. Land was available there for veterans to homestead. No one would be bothered by our troubles and when life was over for me, Phil would let the family know. However, God had different plans.

Brother Chester Anderson held a few services in the Clearwater, Nebraska town hall. We were invited by my brother, Leslie, to attend. He had become a peculiar person (Pentecostal), but to be kind we went. Oh my, how they did ruin our familiar hymns! They played and sang so fast (no longer a funeral dirge) and they clapped their hands! Oh my! They even prayed aloud! How could God ever hear such a mixture of voices and petitions? We did like the people though. They were so friendly and happy. I noticed too that no one had to be begged to stand up and 'testify' or lead song service.

Well, that was over. We had fulfilled our obligation to my brother. He had invited us and we had gone. But then a few months later, Brother Anderson brought the tabernacle to Clearwater. He met us on the street and gave us a personal invitation. We went.

We began attending the services which started January 30, 1947. The portable tabernacle was built by Brother Anderson several years before. The sawdust floor became the "Sawdust Trail" for us.

During one service he began to preach on being Born Again and what was sin! Now, I had held all sorts of offices in the formal church we attended. Besides that we were "faithful givers." We made sure we had money for the offering (a dollar was enough we thought). I had never robbed a bank or killed anyone. I was definitely "heaven bound"! What a surprise when I suddenly knew, I was a sinner. Tears started tumbling down my cheeks. I knew I needed to go to the altar.

I looked up at my husband and there he stood dry-eyed. I had a very stupid thought, "If he is not going to the altar, then neither am I. I don't want my home broken up by religion." I dried my tears. Somehow I did not take into account that on Judgment Day, I would stand alone. As the altar call was given, Philip leaned down and asked, "Do you want to go to the altar?" "Do you?" I asked. He started down the aisle as he answered, "I have to." I followed.

A few weeks later the sermon was preached on healing. I know Jesus healed when He was on earth, but I didn't know He would do it for me. Phil and I discussed it at home and searched the scriptures. Everywhere His Promise stood out. We would try it! Not telling anyone what I was being prayed for, I went to the altar for healing. I didn't want anyone telling me, "you're healed, just believe," and all the time the pain was hard to bear. I do not know exactly when God healed me, but two or three days later I realized, "Hey, I have no pain! Thank you, Jesus! Thank you, Jesus!"

Both of us, Philip and I, were filled with the Holy Spirit the same year as we gave our lives to Christ. 1947 was a wonderful year!

It has been more than 50 years since God did "surgery" on my heart and all the physicals since show a good strong healthy heart.

(Ileen Lee, "Personal Testimony of Ileen Lee, Ewing, Nebraska," 1997.)

Lemp, Elisabeth

In 1978, my dad, Harold James, a retired Assemblies of God minister, was serving in the Henderson, Nebraska community as chaplain in the nursing home. My parents were pioneer pastors in Nebraska, Kansas, and South Dakota. Our family legacy is one of prayer. It is with praise and thanksgiving we remember.

In the late winter of 1978, my son, Chuck went on a skiing trip with several of his high school friends to Colorado. When he came home, he was in a lot of pain. A tumble down a snow covered mountain resulted in a torn up knee. We immediately took him to our family doctor who at once sent him to an orthopedic surgeon in Omaha.

The diagnosis was torn ligaments requiring surgery. However, that Friday afternoon the surgeon continued with his explanation by saying, "I don't have a bed for you in the hospital or I'd operate this afternoon, so come back on Sunday, and I'll operate Monday morning."

With those words in our ears, we returned home. It was then I called my seventy-nine year old dad who had walked many years with his Lord. "Daddy," I said when he answered the phone, "Chuck has been hurt."

"I know!" he responded. But how? I thought, we hadn't called you. How could you know? Daddy," I continued. "Chuck has to have surgery on his knee Monday morning."

"No he won't!" Dad exclaimed. "I've already prayed through on it. He will not have surgery on his knee!"

After I finished talking to Dad, Chuck took the phone and talked to his grandpa. Grandpa then prayed for Chuck's knee. While Grandpa was praying, Chuck stated, "I felt my injured knee tingling like thousands of tiny stitches were putting things back together. It felt like a small current of electricity. This was the impression in my spirit."

Monday morning in that Omaha hospital, as the surgeon came into the waiting room, he addressed my husband and I with the words, "Well that didn't take long! Your son's knee was much better than on Friday. I only put a cast on the leg to help with the healing. No surgery required!"

When shown by the Holy Spirit the need, even before we told Dad of the injury, he prayed. Because a grandfather walked and talked with God and was obedient in intercessory prayer for his grandson, surgery wasn‘t necessary.

(Elisabeth James Lemp and Charles “Chuck” Lemp, “A Grandfather’s Prayers,” 1978.)

Loutzenhiser, Esther

My folks had moved to Utah shortly after I was born in 1922. My father was working in a mine. After over two years, in 1924, my mother became very homesick for her mother and sister who lived at Bridgeport, Nebraska. The very next year, after we moved back, Rev. Irl Walker came to Bridgeport with his tent in August, 1925. *[see report of Rev. Irl Walker regarding Bridgeport in the churches section.]*

At that time, my father was working the railroad in Northport, and that was where our home was. My mother was lying in bed after my baby brother‘s birth. My dad would come to see her after work. But one night after he had visited a short time, he looked at his watch and said, “Oh, there‘s a preacher uptown with his tent, and I would like to hear him.” Mom was a bit miffed to think he would leave her, but when she got to go, she was the first person to receive the Holy Spirit Baptism during those meetings in Bridgeport.

Several people from Bayard attended the meetings there with Brother Walker. One lady who sang in the choir caught Grandma‘s attention. Grandma had known that lady before and Grandma could see such a beautiful change in her life that she realized there was something about this religion. So my whole family got saved and church became a prime factor in our lives.

We have often thanked the Lord that we left the mining village in Utah. I am thankful too, because my aunt Bernice (Burry) Paine was saved then, and she and her husband were the first pastors in Minatare, Nebraska.

(Esther Loutzenhiser, “Memories,” 1998.)

Nichols, Lynn and Nila

Lynn and Nila Nichols write (1998), “My, Lynn‘s, family (Carl Nichols) was saved in maybe the first revival meetings that came to Bayard. It‘s always been a mystery how the Lord sought us out clear out in the country, and brought us into His family.

Nila and I met in Bible School in Seattle and were married after graduation from there. After a brief time in Montana, we came to Hartington to begin our pastoring in 1943. We pastored at: Hartington, Laurel, Wood Lake, Pender, Bassett, Columbus and Broken Bow. We have no big story to tell except a lot of gratitude to God for His Faithfulness and Love and Provisions through the years.

(Lynn and Nila Nichols, “God’s Faithfulness.”)

Lynn S. Nichols was honored with a certificate of fifty years of continuous service to the Assemblies of God in 1996.

Nichols Family Sod House

Here is some additional information about Carl Nichols (father of Lynn) and family.

Located about seven miles northwest of here, a three-roomed sod house was the home of Mr. and Mrs. Carl Nichols and their 12 children. Mrs. Nichols, who lives in Bayard, says her late husband built it in 1913 or 1914. Its three-foot thick walls are still sturdy for the most part.

Mrs. Nichols recalls that feeding 12 children wasn‘t easy. She notes that for 11 straight years during the depression the family harvested no crops. “On the 11th year we had a beautiful crop, but about half of it was ruined by hail one day and the other half was lost exactly a week later by another hail storm,” she remembers.

Also located on the place is an eight-sided wooden granary Nichols built.

(“Sod House was Home for 12 Children,” *Angora Star-Herald*, Sunday May 11, 1969.)

Shirley, Bede

In the summer of 1924 an evangelist, Florence Kletzing, came to Scottsbluff and conducted gospel meetings in an old school house. Word soon got around of the interesting meetings going on every night. One night Lawrence ventured close to the school house and came home with reports of good singing and music and many people there. The next night Vera went with him and they went inside. The very first night Vera responded to the invitation to accept Christ as Saviour.

When she told her parents [Bede and Ida Shirley] of her experience of having accepted Christ, her dad became quite upset and thought she had suffered a nervous breakdown. He forbid her to go again and had her confined to bed for several days. This seemed to aggravate her all the more as she cried and prayed that her folks also might come to know Christ as she did. To some extent it seems that Vera shared her dad's philosophy of life, that if a little is good, a lot ought to be better. At least he was at times accused of this.

After Vera had received a little taste of the blessings of God that night when she has responded to the invitation to accept Christ as Saviour, she now wanted her whole family to share in this wonderful experience. She prayed for them in the best way she knew and shared with them her experience in the Lord.

It was not long before the whole family came to know the Lord. But it seems that for a time at least, her dad had some reservations, thinking it was over emotional. His spiritual experience it seems was a bit like the story Jesus told about seed that fell on good ground and started to grow, but later on was choked by the thorns, thistles and weeds of human reasoning. But the other members of the family were like seed that fell on good ground and brought forth a bountiful harvest. Dad made a new commitment on his life to Christ later on, and then lived for the Lord until he was called home. This religious experience brought about a great change in their way of life. Church and other related Christian activities became the "in thing" for the whole family.

Dad's ol' fiddle that was used for so many years in the dance hall now became a violin, and he often played in the church orchestra. Though Dad didn't preach, he was a great help in getting churches started in communities where they lived in following years. (Torrinton, Wyoming and Ronan, Montana) It seems they were one of the first families to become associated with the new church in Scottsbluff, then in the process of being started.

(Clarence Strom, "Shirley Family in Scottsbluff: The story of the Shirley family of Bede LeRoy and Ida Jemimah Shirley, Orvia Shirley Strom's Mom and Dad.")

Lawrence and Vera mentioned in the narrative are Orvia (Shirley) Strom's brother and sister.

Steinle Sisters

Here is a narrative about Evangelists Hannah and Frieda Steinle at Walthill, Nebraska in 1933.

Hannah, the oldest daughter, of Henry and Rose Steinle had been converted in the Mennonite Brethren church at the age of 13 in Dorrance, Kansas. After being filled with the Holy Spirit, she felt God calling her to preach the gospel. One month before she turned 18, Hannah began teaching in a country school near her hometown of Dorrance. In the summer months, she would play the piano for camp meetings and revival services.

Launching out in faith, Hannah Steinle and her sister Mary began evangelizing the Midwest in January 1929. Hannah played the piano and did all the preaching, and Mary led the singing. They traveled to various places in Kansas, Colorado, Iowa, Missouri, and Nebraska....

After Mary became the wife of A. R. Sorenson in 1931, Hannah was joined in the ministry by her sister Frieda. Frieda played the autoharp and was a very gifted singer. She continued to minister with Hannah until about 1935 when she married Leonard Palmer [born in Franklin, Nebraska]. In the meantime Hannah was married to Max Johnson in 1934. The three of them traveled together for a short time.

An interesting occurrence happened at one of the Steinles' meetings in 1933. During a late tent meeting in Walthill, Nebraska, where C. F. Cox was pastor, a number of people remained to be filled with the Spirit. Frieda was praying with the seekers. Someone turned the fire siren on and people started running for safety. A man was preparing to turn a water hose into the tent. Someone stopped him, but of course, that broke up the meeting.

A newspaper story claimed that the Pentecostals did everything but hang from the tent ropes by their toes! This was the best advertising they could have asked for, and the crowds began flocking to the meetings which lasted for 6 weeks. As many as one thousand people gathered for the services that Sunday night. At the conclusion of the revival, more than 100 people were saved, with the converts being baptized in the Big Muddy River near Walthill....

(Glenn Gohr, "Musical Evangelists in the Midwest," *Assemblies of God Heritage*, Winter 1988-89, p. 15.)

The above mentioned article in the newspaper closes with this paragraph: "Village authorities called upon those in charge Tuesday morning and obtained a promise that the meetings will close hereafter at 11 p.m., and the people of the west and central parts of town are wondering why they didn't call out the fireman long ago."

Turner, R. Delbert

In the summer of 1946, I had just graduated from Southern California College. Having heard of the wonderful camp meetings in Nebraska, and the fact that my wife Joyce had come from Nebraska, we decided to come to the Nebraska District camp meeting. We arrived by train.

The main speaker that year, if I remember correctly, was Arthur Arnold and the spiritual tide was high. Some months later we became pastors of the church at Hershey.

Work was always underway for the improvement of the camp grounds. New cabins were being constructed usually by pastors and church people. Brother [M. F.] Brandt, the District Superintendent in the late "40's", enlisted the pastors and anyone he could get for the ongoing project. Many times we had the task of tearing down abandoned military barracks and hauling the used lumber to the campgrounds for use in building additions to the campgrounds.

During my years in the office of District C. A. President, 1952 to '55, I saw lots of action at the District youth camps. In those years there was a small lake within hiking distance of the campgrounds. On several mornings during the youth camp, campers could join a hike to this lake. A breakfast of bacon and eggs was cooked over an open fire. The fragrance of the cooking and the fire was wonderful. I remember the young ministers in those years who so enthusiastically gave a helping hand making these activities lots of fun. Among those frying the eggs and bacon were Norman Correll, vice president, and Loren Triplett, secretary-treasurer. The lake experience ended after some good fun and a devotional before the hike back to the campgrounds.

In 1953, the C.A.'s of the District purchased a home for the D-CAP in Grand Island. Having the D-CAP office near the District Superintendent's office strengthened the District C. A. program. Brother Dickinson was the District Superintendent at that time and gave great encouragement and support. We often traveled to sectional meetings together. We were able to consult together easily. The D-CAP office had not been permanently located until then.

(R. Delbert Turner, "R. Delbert Turner Remembers Nebraska," 1998.)

R. Delbert Turner was Nebraska D-CAP from 1952 to 1955.

Wagoner, Paul

Paul Wagner shares his memories of the revival at Clearfield, South Dakota, during September and October, 1932.

In the year 1931, two school teachers, Luella and Lovern Heitman came to teach the North and South Star Prairie schools. They were both vivacious, out going, and took a real interest in the people who lived in this rural community.

(All though we were not aware of it, I am sure they were also praying for many of us. One reason I think this is true is that I decided to quit smoking even though I had not yet accepted the Lord as my Saviour.)

During the summer of 1931 or '32, they asked me if I wanted to go with them to Meadville, Nebraska to a baptismal service. A large number of people were there and it seemed as I look back to be more like a Camp Meeting. The testimony service was interesting to me, but I could not understand how each one that got up to testify would start with the words, "I'm so glad I am saved!"

In my mind, it seemed that they could not be saved until they were in Heaven. So when I was asked after the service, "How did you like the service?"

I answered, "How can they know they are saved, they're still here aren't they?"

Only one person made any sense to me, perhaps because he didn't use the "I know I'm saved," statement in his testimony. He was a visiting Methodist pastor.

In the fall of 1932, when the Heitman sisters came back for a second term of school they brought along a preacher by the name of Chester Beebe. I don't remember the details, but they managed to rent the dance hall at Clearfield, South Dakota where they preceded to hold a service each night.

Apparently word got around and soon the building was packed with people. There was an altar which was a bridge plank with some pop bottle kegs holding it up. Some were even going down to this altar.

For some reason, we didn't hear about the meetings right away. Three weeks after they started, my brother-in-law, who was a well driller, stopped at our home and stayed all night with us. He told us all that was happening at the meetings. He even told who was sitting on the front row and was entering into the services by raising his hands, etc.

I remember Dad, Mom and three of us children going to the service the next night. I don't remember my Dad going after that. However, we children, ages 19, 16 and 12 continued to go. The conviction was strong. It was as if someone had a rope tied to your heart and was pulling on it. I wanted to go forward and give myself to the Lord, but the peer pressure was great then even as it is now.

October 6, 1932 we were sitting on our bridge plank, backless seats. The Chet Anderson Family, who were very musical, were there from Butte, Nebraska. Chet did the preaching that night. When the altar call was given, and after singing a number of verses of Just As I Am and Softly and Tenderly Jesus Is Calling, Brother Chester Beebe came back to the row where Darrel, others, and I were sitting. He touched Darrel on the shoulder, and asked him if he didn't want to step out into the isle. Darrel, who was four years older than myself, stepped out into the isle, and I was right behind him. Darrel had suffered some traumatic things in his life and felt the guilt of sin very heavy. I think it was after 12 o'clock when he finally arose from the altar of prayer a changed and forgiven man.

One day after our conversion, I remember we were hauling straw for bedding the cattle. The ground was covered with snow and Darrel made the remark to me, "When God washed our sins away, he made us whiter than the driven snow."

This revival was a supernatural, divine intervention of God into a community whose inclinations were constantly filled with evil desires. In a period of six weeks one hundred and fourteen (114) people accepted Christ as their Saviour. In this group were bootleggers, gamblers, plus every other type of sinner. All of us heathen in one sense. Of this one hundred fourteen who were saved, seven prepared for and went into the ministry. Three of us were pastors and one was a missionary to Upper Volta.

The church at Clearfield did not remain for long, because of the drought years when grasshoppers blackened the skies like huge dark clouds, literally blocking out the sun before eating almost everything in sight. These hostile conditions made it necessary for most of these people to move to Washington, Oregon and California. But wherever the people from the Clearfield, South Dakota Revival of 1932 went, they became assets to the churches of the communities to which they moved God had gloriously saved them!

(Paul Wagoner, "Revival Spills Over into South Dakota, or was it South Dakota into Nebraska?" 1997.)

Paul Wagner has pastored churches in Nebraska and Colorado.

Wehrli, Kevin

Here is a testimony from Kevin's wife, Angela, about his conversion experience.

Kevin was born and raised in Nebraska and lived there until he was 20. That is when God came into his life and set him on the road that he walks today.

Kevin came from a family where none of them ever darkened the doors of any church. Some of the family suffered with alcoholism. Kevin didn't even know who Jesus was. All he knew was that He had something to do with Christmas.

At the age of 20, he was dating a girl in Lexington. Her parents went to the Assembly of God church there. They asked him if he went to church, and he said he did. So they invited him to church and he went (just to impress them). As he walked in, there was a man *praising* God and speaking in other tongues. He thought, "He must know Gods language." Little did he know how close he was. He couldn't tell you who the preacher was or what he preached on, but a retired minister, Rev. Wayne Hall, came and introduced himself.

Kevin went home thinking nothing of the service until late that night. The Holy Spirit started working in Kevin's life. He was under such conviction he couldn't wait until morning. The next morning was a dark cloudy day, and was getting ready to rain. He went down to the park to use the pay phone to call Bro. Hall. You see he didn't want his family to know he was calling a preacher, or they would think he was crazy. He asked Bro. Hall if he could come and talk to him. On his way over he had planned out everything he was going to say, but when the door opened it all left and Kevin stood there crying and said, "I don't know why I'm here." Bro. Hall did, and took him in, and lead him to the Lord. When he left Bro. Hall's home, the sun was shining and a 20 year old skipped home. He remembered thinking to himself, "I don't know what has happened, but I've been changed inside."

Shortly after that Kevin moved to Oklahoma where he met his wife, [Angela], and they started attending the First Assembly of God in Woodward. It was there at one of the services, in the altar, that Kevin saw a man that had somehow worked his way up under the piano and was speaking in tongues. All Kevin said was "God do that to me." And it was done! He was gloriously filled with the Spirit.

In 1989, God called Kevin to load up his family, sell his business (that God had given to him), and go to Waxahachie, Texas and attend Southwestern Assemblies of God College. He had also been called into the ministry at that time. After attending 3 years, his father-in-law was killed in an accident, and he felt that they needed to go back to Oklahoma to help out the family.

While in Texas, he had received his license to preach. Beaver, Oklahoma was looking for a pastor, and Rev. Paul Sharpe asked if Kevin would like to fill in while they were looking. Kevin accepted, and after about two months, became the pastor. From there, he went to Allen, Oklahoma where he received his ordination. He was ordained at the 1994 Oklahoma District Council. Sometime during all of this that happened, Bro. Hall had moved to Oklahoma and was present at the ordination service. Today Kevin, his wife, and their two children live at Prague, Oklahoma, where he is the minister. He is serving God and expecting a mighty outpouring of the Holy Spirit.

Angela writes "Kevin is a great man of prayer and solely depends on God, and coming from the lifestyle that he was raised in is quite a miracle in itself."

(Angela Wehrli, "Kevin Wehrli's Conversion in Lexington, Nebraska," 1998.)

Wilkins, Jim

It was during the early years of pioneer ministry in Kearney of Lawrence and Nina Wilkins their son, Jim, was attending Central Bible Institute (now C.B.C.). Jim graduated in 1958. Two weeks out of college Jim accepted the pastorate at Fairbury. (Prior pastors at Fairbury were Harold Mintle, Loren Triplett, and F. D. McClellan.) Jim married Verna Kisser on September 2, 1958. They lived in the basement of the church during the time they pastored there.

During the C.A. Convention (Youth Convention) in 1961, Jim was elected as the District C.A. President (D-CAP). He officially took office in January, 1962 and moved to Grand Island where the district office is located. By then the family had grown to four. Jim and Verna were the proud parents of two boys, Brenton and Bryan. They lived in the little two-bedroom youth parsonage at 1028 South Sycamore in G. I. There was no central district office building at that time. The District Superintendent had his office in the district parsonage, and the youth director had his own office--a room that had been added to the side of the garage at the South Sycamore location. Even though the little room was cold and drafty in the winter it served as the office and print shop for the D-CAP. In those days there were no office secretaries. All the officers were their own secretary. Even the camp posters were printed by the D-CAP on a small offset press in the little office. During Jim's years as D-CAP the portfolio of State Sunday School Director was added to his responsibilities. That brought the Youth Camp, Teen Camps, and Kids Kamps under his direction. Some of the camp and convention speakers included Howard Cummings, Derald Musgrove, Forrest Arnold, Hilton Griswold, Little Jimmy Snow, C. M. Ward, and David Wilkerson. Nearly a thousand people were in attendance at the Convention when David Wilkerson was the speaker. As far as is known that was the largest Youth Convention in Nebraska up to that time.

Jim's fondest memories of his D-CAP years are of the revivals that took place during the summer camps. The services frequently continued into the early hours of the morning. Young people who had been revived would often go to the cabins and bring other kids back to the Tabernacle in the middle of the night to get right with God. Many young lives were touched and numerous young people ended up in gospel ministry.

Jim and Verna stayed with the D-CAP job until the late summer of 1966 at which time they responded to the call to become the pastor at the Milford Assembly. The tenure in Milford was for about eight years and nine months; then Jim was elected as the District Superintendent (1975) after the resignation of Brother Dickinson. Once again the Wilkins family moved back to Grand Island. By now there were four children: Brenton, Bryan, Bartley and Becky.

(Jim Wilkins: "Memories of Jim Wilkins," 1997.)

Jim Wilkins was Nebraska D-CAP from 1962 to 1966 and superintendent of the Nebraska District from 1975 to 1987.

Wilkins, Lawrence

Throughout most of his Christian life my dad, Lawrence Wilkins, was known as Brother Wilkins. Ministers were rarely called by their first name in those days. A few minister friends did call him by his initials, (L. E.) He grew up on a ranch near Burton, Nebraska.

It was in 1931 that a great revival broke out in Burton. The Anderson brothers, Chet and Gene, were tools God used. The Anderson families were very musical and that attracted a lot of people to the Camp Meetings which were held in Burton Park. The Anderson brothers were also good revival preachers. Many turned to the Lord at the meetings in the park. The Wilkins family was not among them, but Lawrence and his brother, Duane, did attend a couple of meetings out of curiosity.

Later in the Fall [1931] another revivalist, Reverend C. E. Thurmond, came to Burton and held services in a little white church that was then called "The White Church." Thurmond was a tell-it-like-it-is kind of preacher and through his ministry many people were convicted of their sin and turned to Christ. Harold and Marie James were the first pastors of what became the Burton Assemblies of God church.

Among the many converts during the Thurmond meeting was the Jim Wilkins family. Two of Jim's children entered full-time ministry. Lawrence and Velma responded to the call of God and traveled together holding evangelistic meetings. Eventually, Velma married Mervin Peck and they entered pastoral ministry. Lawrence met Nina Lavachek while in South Dakota and they too got married and entered pastoral ministry. As of this writing (1997) there have now been three generations of the Wilkins family involved in full-time ministry in the Assemblies of God: Lawrence, his son, Jim (named after his grandfather), and Jim's youngest son, Bartley, better known as Pastor Bart.

Churches in Nebraska that were pastored by Lawrence Wilkins were Beaver City, Pawnee City, Ord, Dalton, Lexington, Kearney, and North Platte First Assembly. It was while the Wilkins were still in Lexington that Frank Sobotka held a tent revival in Kearney. Following the meeting it was decided that a church should be planted and Lawrence submitted to the call of God to become the founding pastor. He rented an upstairs area over the J. M. McDonald store on the main downtown street of Kearney. Six or seven people showed up for the first service in the early Fall of 1954. God began to move among that small group. Additional people soon became a part of the fledgling fellowship even though they had to climb a long stairway to the meeting room and endure the cold unheated Sunday school rooms. It soon became evident that a church building was needed so Pastor Wilkins and one of the members, Herman Kehl, began the building project at the corner of 28th and Avenue H. In May of 1958, the building was dedicated.

People continued to be saved in the regular services. One of those was Monte Standage who remains a faithful member of the congregation which is now known as New Life Assembly. Lawrence and Nina continued in pastoral ministry in Kearney for 17 years and saw good results. While still pastoring in Kearney, Brother Wilkins was elected to the office of Secretary/Treasurer of the Nebraska District. He managed the dual role of pastor and district leader even after moving to

Brother Wilkins concluded his ministry in Hastings. Pastor Dale Harmon invited him to come and serve as a minister of visitation and minister to the senior citizens of the congregation. L. E. continued in that position until the time of his death.

(Jim Wilkins, "Personal information about Lawrence (L. E.) Wilkins," 1997; Verna Wilkins, "An interview of Nina Wilkins," 1997.)

In 1984, Lawrence E. Wilkins was recognized for fifty years of continuous service to the Assemblies of God. L. E. and Nina Wilkins were the parents of Jim Wilkins, former superintendent of the Nebraska District. Bart Wilkins, a grandson is a Nebraska pastor.

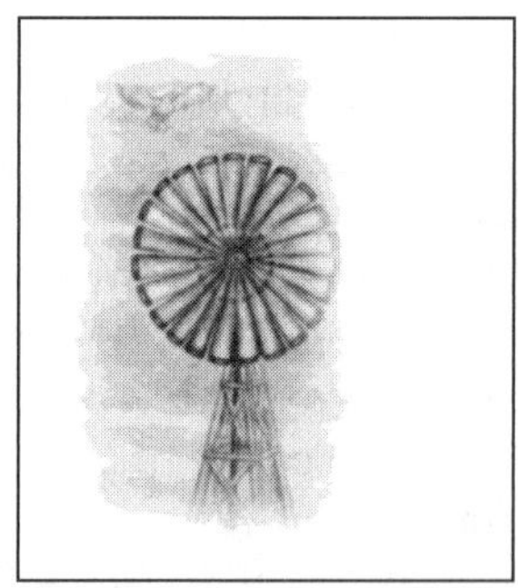

Chapter 7: Ainsworth through Bellevue

***"But you will receive power when the Holy Spirit comes on you; and you will be my witnesses."*
(Acts 1:8 NIV)**

This next section of the book includes history and reports from churches across the state. They are listed alphabetically and divided up between six different chapters. The pastoral listings and histories only cover through 1999 since this is a book on growth in the 20th century. An asterisk denotes the church histories (compiled by Faith Tyson from church and district records) to separate them from other testimonies. Records on the early churches is incomplete. Some congregations are very old, such as the church at Ainsworth, and others are relatively new. Be blessed as you read about how communities experience the move of God.

*Ainsworth—Assembly of God, 1915

The Assemblies of God in Ainsworth had its beginning in revival meetings conducted in Keya Paha County in the year of 1915 by Hermon Harvey who preached the Baptism of the Holy Spirit.... Later the same year Rev. Harvey and a number of families, who were converted as a result of his ministry, came to Ainsworth and began services in an unused store building and later in the building which became the parsonage at 220 West Dawes.

The church was known as the Pentecostal Church until 1920 when the congregation became affiliated with the Assemblies of God under the leadership of Rev. C. E. Thurmond. In about 1928 Pastor Thurmond and the congregation built a basement church at the corner of Dawes and Woodward Streets. This basement church was used until 1944 at which time the congregation under the leadership of Pastor Don W. Throne built a structure over the existing basement. In 1965, a new sanctuary was built at the corner of Second and Pine Street under the leadership of Rev. J. M. Peck. A new parsonage was purchased at 830 East Zero in 1978.

The list of pastors includes: Hermon Harvey, Rev. Moore, C. E. Thurmond, M. F. Brandt, Rev. Brown, Sisters Hink and Watson, Don Throne, Paul Cook, B. H Armes, J. M. Peck, Elmer Craver, Clyde King, Robert Wine, Leonard Herrman, Bob Rudichar, Dan St. Clair, John Gale, and Ralph Russo.

Maria Woodworth-Etter at Ainsworth, Nebraska

The Opera House at Ainsworth in which the meetings were held was crowded; the preaching of the Word was accompanied by the Power of God falling in their midst, so that several fell out of their seats onto the floor. The altar was crowded with seekers, and other people got saved, and others baptized with the Holy Ghost, from the start of the meetings till the finish ...

("Revivals at Ainsworth, Nebr. And Muncie, Indiana." In *Marvels and Miracles God Wrought in The Ministry for Forty-five Years*, by Mrs. M. B. Woodworth-Etter. Indianapolis: the author, 1922, pp. 366-367.)

Evangelist J. C. Timmons at Ainsworth, 1918

I was permitted the wonderful privilege of going with Sister Woodworth-Etter to the Ainsworth meeting in October, 1918. We were met by Pastor Harvey, who had rented a very large hotel to accommodate the people who came from a distance, but it was full from the first and rooms had to be secured in other parts of town.

The largest auditorium was secured to hold the meetings in, and it was filled from the start. God poured out His Spirit from the first meeting. Many said to me: "When Sister Etter walks into the meeting we feel the very presence of God; surely she is walking with him as the prophets of old, and as she talks we see the glow of the heavenly light around her." I have known Sister Etter nearly thirty years and have attended many of her meetings.

Through the prayer of faith God healed many, and many others were saved and baptized in the Holy Spirit. The meetings were growing in numbers, interest and conviction, when the influenza broke out and the city officials decided to close the meetings on account of contagion.

The day our meetings closed from thirteen to fourteen were taken with influenza. As I went with Sister Etter from room to room praying for them I hear her tell them not to fear, but believe and be true to God and not one would die. God undertook and not one died. Some of them had come from one hundred to two hundred miles in autos and they started home next morning in a storm, but God kept every one of them safe through it all.

Two or three times during the meetings word had come to pray for a young sister. Brother Harvey and I went and prayed for her. She had a high fever and every symptom of influenza, being unconscious. A few minutes after we prayed the fever left and she was completely healed. There were many other wonderful healings and manifestations of God's power.

(J. C. Timmons, "Report by Evangelist." In *Marvels and Miracles God Wrought in The Ministry for Forty-five Years,* by Mrs. M. B. Woodworth-Etter. Indianapolis: the author, 1922, p. 367.)

Hermon L. Harvey at Ainsworth, 1918

Sister Woodworth-Etter and workers opened the Convention in the Opera House here on Sept. 28. The Convention was to continue until Oct. 17th, but on Oct. 9th all public meetings were ordered closed on account of the Influenza. The meeting was just getting well under way. We thank God for what was already accomplished. Had the work been allowed to go on we believe it would have been a great meeting. Great good has been done as it is. The work has come to be looked upon with great favor in this new field. The large audiences were held with a wonderful grip and gave the closest attention to the strong messages of our dear sister now more than 74 years old. The singing of the "heavenly choir" impressed the people deeply.

There have been conversions, baptisms in the Holy Spirit and healings of incurable diseases, we do not know how many. The last night was the most wonderful of all. The sick flocked to the platform to be prayed for; some very remarkable cases were two women with inward goiters, a young woman with heart disease, and a trained nurse from Kansas with an incurable case of Bright's Disease. All of these were immediately healed when hands were laid on them; and their faces, their testimonies and their demonstrations of the new life and freedom from soreness and pain were wonderful. The women with the goiters threw back their heads and twisted their necks in a way impossible before being prayed for. The young women with the heart trouble paced the platform, shouted and praised God for her healing, wept and laughed for joy, and after embracing her weeping husband, went to her sister who quickly came to the altar and was saved. The trained nurse told how she had been examined in the best hospitals in the land by the best physicians and was given up as a hopeless case, but now after the prayer of faith had been offered for her, not a symptom of the dreadful disease remained .

The number attending the convention from different states was large and increasing when the meeting so suddenly closed. We had rented and fitted up a large hotel a half block from the Opera House for the convention. More than forty double beds were furnished, and meals for all who came. No one was charged anything and all expenses were met by the free-will offerings. We are sure God is pleased with the "faith method" of providing for the people at these conventions.

(Pastor Hermon L. Harvey, "Report of Sister Etter's Meeting at Ainsworth, Nebraska," *Christian Evangel*, November 16, 1918, p. 13.)

Ainsworth Revival, 1932

Leland R. Faith closed a revival at Ainsworth last month. In the four weeks fifty-three were saved and three received the Holy Spirit. We have a Christ Ambassador class here of thirty three charter members. Pentecost is sweeping this part of the country.

(*Nebraska Pentecostal Fellowship,* Vol. 1:1, March, 1932.)

*Albion—New Life Assembly of God, 1979

The first Sunday service of the new congregation in Albion was held August 19, 1979, in the living room of the Cal Sunderland home. Seven weeks later on September 30, 1979 Rev. and Mrs. James Bunch were installed as the first pastor of New Life Assembly of God. Sunday school attendance on that day numbered twenty-four. In late September of 1979, the storefront at 215 South Fourth Street belonging to E. E. Cleveland was acquired for the sum to $50 per month. This became the meeting place of the church for the next year. God was moving and the church continued to grow.

In August 1980, at the celebration of the church's first anniversary, the Women's Ministries of the Nebraska District presented the church with $2000 for their building fund which brought the total to approximately $2700....

... With the recommendation of District Superintendent Jim Wilkins, Rev. Larry Cooper candidated and was voted in with a 100% vote of approval. The Cooper family moved to Albion in June of 1981. The first service in the new facility at 11th and Columbia took place on March 28, 1982.

Rev. and Mrs. Joe Masten became the third pastor of Albion in August of 1983.

A new facility was built on Highway 39, during the time that Richard Bartz was the pastor. The first service was held on April 17, 1988. The old church building on 11th Street became a parsonage and the Bartz family moved in May of 1988. The dedication service with about 97 people in attendance was held April 1989. It has been such a blessing to the congregation and the community.

The list of pastors includes: James Bunch, Larry Cooper, Joe Masten, Richard Bartz, David French, Neal Sweet, Barry Johnson, and Rich Greaff.

*Alliance—Calvary Assembly of God, 1930

The Alliance Assembly of God had its beginning under the ministry of Rev. Claude Thurmond. Services were held in a home and later the group rented a small church at 3rd and Sweetwater Streets.

In October 1941 Rev. and Mrs. Clyde King came as pastors. The church still owned no property, but met in an old one-room church building on the main east-west road in town.... An old large wood heater stood near the middle of the room.... One cold wintry Sunday night Pastor King had to preach with his overcoat on. There was no parsonage so the Kings lived in rented apartments.... The house they were living in was sold. After a desperate search for housing the Kings moved into two rooms of a house with a lady and her daughter. The house had no water or bathroom.... One day a real estate man appeared at the King's door. He told them they were eligible for one of the new houses being built in town. But it would be several months before it would be finished. They were thrilled to move into this house after enduring the hardships they experienced. The lot at 824 Missouri Avenue was also purchased in anticipation of a new church building.

Rev. and Mrs. C. A. Beebe came as pastors in 1944, and during their ministry negotiations were completed with the War Assets Administration to buy one of the chapels at the Alliance Army Base. The structure was moved to the lot on Missouri Avenue and was remodeled and improved over the years.

During Pastor Porter's ministry a new church was built, and in July 1981 dedication services were held for Calvary Assembly of God. Later an addition was added in order to accommodate the Christian education needs.

The list of pastors includes: Claude Thurmond, Clyde King, C. A. Beebe, H. J. Blakkolb, B. F. Correll, R. W. Denny, Willis Dewey, Don Ziegler, E. M. Herrmann, Paul Wheeler, Hugh Campbell, Robert Porter, Terry Brown, Donald Owen, Michael Carl, and Michael Schaaf.

*Atkinson—West Holt Assembly of God, 1986

The list of pastors includes Mike Carl and Donald Bade Jr.

Auburn, Nebraska, 1913

(Auburn, Nebraska was one of the earliest places of Pentecostal revival in Nebraska. The Christian Evangel *published several articles which report on some of these early meetings at Auburn).*

Within a few days nine received the baptism with great joy. Some were also saved and healed and some backsliders came home to God. A mob threatened to tear the tent down, saying we hypnotized the people. The people crowded around the tent fifteen deep outside and when the altar call was given they even crowded on the rostrum to see God work. One young woman, very rich came ten miles to see the fun, as she said afterwards. She stood on the seat passing remarks and kept all around her laughing. When she went home she could not eat or sleep. In the next few days she came back and went to the altar and confessed publicly what she had said about us. She then fell like dead under the power of God. The Lord told her what she must do. She took off her ring (she did not remember having done so afterwards) as she was engaged to a rich man and she has given him up for the Lord. God has called her and she said she must go to the field.

(Mrs. Fannie Reif, "Early Revivals at Auburn, Nebraska," *Christian Evangel,* August 30, 1913, p. 8.)

L. A. Dieffenwirth at Auburn, 1915

God is blessing us in the work here. The homes where we have meetings will not hold the crowds. Souls are getting to God. Two have been baptized with the Holy Ghost and three saved this month. We are trying to raise money to build a house of worship. The assembly is small and there is not much of this world's goods. We should be glad if anyone feels led to send us help. It will be gratefully received. L. A. Dieffenwierth, pastor.

(L. A. Dieffenwierth, "Auburn, Nebraska," *The Christian Evangel,* 1915, April 10, p. 2.)

*Auburn—Assembly of God, 1966

Calvary Assembly of God began in Auburn in September 1966. The Lord laid the burden for a church in this town upon the hearts of the Kenneth Thee family, who were at the time pastoring a church in Whitewater, Wisconsin. They stepped out in faith and moved to Auburn without living quarters or a job. They were able to find a house to rent their first day in Auburn.

Services were held in the Thee home for the first two and a half years. In November of 1968 two lots and a small house were purchased at 1312 11th Street. The house was remodeled into a church by the pastor and congregation. The first service was held on April 20, 1968 … Charter membership certificates were given to ten people.

In January of 1971 the congregation leased the Baptist church located at 11th and M Streets for their services. Rev. and Mrs. Grant Rowell and daughters assumed duties as new pastors of the church on July 11, 1971. The Sunday school roll was twenty-six.

Rev. and Mrs. Kenny Dickinson and Kerrie came to pastor the church in December 1972. The young congregation was blessed through their ministry of nearly six years. The rented church building was purchased and officially became Calvary Assembly of God.

The list of pastors includes: Kenneth Thee, G. C. Rowell, Kenney Dickinson, Dennis Romine, Skip Stanley, Curtis Dunning, Sammy McKay, Mike Christian, and Scott Osenbaugh.

*Aurora—Assembly of God, 1931

... In the 1930s a group of people from the Assembly of God church in Grand Island, held services in a tent in Aurora for five weeks with great momentum.... The crowds came, many standing on the outside looking in. There were sightseers criticizing, some throwing eggs and threatening to cut the tent ropes. Nevertheless the people kept coming and many were saved and filled with the Holy Spirit.

Converts were added nightly as Evangelists Wyat and Foster ministered with power and authority and without fear. Many were slain in the spirit on the sawdust floor at the altar.

One evening just before the service began Brother Foster was handed a document prepared by the city fathers which read: "Out of courtesy to you, you may keep your tent up for tonight's service only, but tomorrow the tent must come down." In a few moments a petition was circulated through the audience and signed by practically everyone present. The petition stated the revival was meeting a need in the community, which had never been met before and asked the mayor and council to reconsider. This was presented to the mayor. As a result the officials allowed the meeting to continue.

The meetings continued in a local theater throughout the winter months with Reverend Wyat. In the spring the people built the Aurora Gospel Tabernacle. This was a convenient and roomy building located on 13th and K streets....

In a large three story building in Aurora, a Bible school was established. Youth came from far and near to prepare for ministry. They held services in various locations throughout the state and into Iowa.... This Bible School wasn't in existence very long however.

On January 3, 1939 a deed was signed between Louis G. Bald and the Assembly of God church for $100 ... for the north ½ of lots 1, 2, and 3, in block 12 of the Ellsworth addition, city of Aurora....

On July 31, 1944 the Assembly of God church paid $50.00 to Harold Bald as full payment on… the land on which the Evangelical German Church stood. On May 22, 1957 the church purchased the south ½ of lots, 1, 2, and 3 of block #12 for $2,350.00.... A beautiful brick parsonage was built under the direction of Pastor Roscoe Leach and was dedicated by Superintendent Lester Dickenson.

… The Lord provided mild weather and Brother Sauer worked and directed the building of a beautiful brick building ... Superintendent Lester Dickinson dedicated the church building to the Lord...

Pastors include L. W. Dickinson, Fred Stackling, H. W. Lebsack, Elmer Swick, Charles F. Cox, J. M. Cummings, Egon Kirschman, Roscoe Leach, George Clarke, Floyd Sauer, Bob Nazarenus, Howard Rice, Ron Murray, Gerald Veicht, James Ettwein, and James Garfield.

Bassett, Nebraska, 1932

February the 28th we closed an eight weeks revival at Bassett assisted by Brother Lester H. Sheets. Some thirty were converted. The last day Brother E. W. White, our district superintendent, was present to set this work in order. Brother White spoke to over three hundred people in the afternoon and evening services. Eight received the Baptism in the Holy Spirit this last day. We organized a Sunday School at this place February the 28th with seventy-five out to start ... C. E. Thurmond was elected Pastor of this church. They are having meetings at three-thirty every Sunday. Sunday School is at two-thirty.

("Bassett, Nebraska," *Nebraska Pentecostal Fellowship,* Vol. 1:1, March 1932.)

*Bassett—Assembly of God, 1931

The Assembly of God church in Bassett had its beginning in a series of revivals conducted by C. E. Thurmond in late 1931. There were thirty-two charter members of the Bassett Assembly of God. The locations of Sunday school and church were varied until a lot was purchased in the spring of 1934. The first church building was erected later that year with everyone helping to get it enclosed before the cold weather came.

In May of 1947 the lot where the present church stands was purchased because of the growth of the congregation. The new church was built with larger facilities for the Sunday school and the regular services. Then in September of 1950 the present parsonage was added to the east end of the church. Various renovations have taken place since that time.

Many young people from this congregation have been called into full-time ministry....

The list of pastors who have ministered in Bassett since 1931 includes C. E. Thurmond, M. F. Brandt, Hannah Johnson (first resident pastor), Kenneth Baker, H. W. Lebsack, Fred Stading, Herman Rohde, Lynn Nichols, George Rohde, Wayne Hall, Joseph Kisser, Jerry Hackett, Charles Davis, Gerald Veicht, Paul Wilton, George Bingham, and Gary Graesser.

Praying for a Pastor in Bassett

In an interview with Lois (Goodwin) Randall, 1999 she tells the following story: Lois was starting high school about 1937; she was a young Christian; her church didn't have a pastor! Many times they would meet in homes for midweek prayer meetings. Before this while M. F. Brandt was pastoring Ainsworth, he'd hold Sunday afternoon services.

During this particular time without a pastor, much prayer was sent up to God to send them a pastor. One night, while in her early teens, Lois went with her dad, Lloyd Goodwin, to a prayer meeting in the Aubert home. For some time the people prayed, and among the prayers were petitions for a pastor.

There came a knock at the door, and there stood Velma and Herman Lebsack. This young couple was driving through town on US Highway 20, and stopped at a filling station for gas. While there, they asked if there were any Assembly of God people living in Bassett, and were directed to the Aubert home. Of course as they knocked on the door, they were unaware of the prayer meeting. But God knew all about the needs of His people.

The Lebsacks became Lois' pastors from 1938 to 1940. This immediate answer to prayer during a home prayer meeting made a lasting affect on Lois' life. During the past sixty years, she has seen God's Faithfulness many times.

Another story of prayer that Lois remembered was told to her when she was a young girl by C. E. Thurmond. During a revival in the Bassett Opera House, Brother Thurmond witnesses her grandparents, parents and six of their children all kneeling at the altar. What a legacy of prayer!

Bayard, Nebraska, 1924

We have just closed a revival meeting here which has been running for three weeks with much success. The building, which seats about 225 people, would not hold the crowds, and there was much interest shown by all that attended the meetings. It is one of the greatest revivals that we have been in for some time. Some nights there were as high as 32 at the altar seeking the Lord. During the three weeks over 50 were saved and 30 received the Baptism according to Acts 2:4. Several were healed instantly. Among them were two women that were healed of goiters; others were healed of different diseases, including tumors. Among them that received the Baptism in the Holy Spirit was a Free Methodist Minister, who has come out strong for the Pentecostal doctrine. Surely God is working in our midst. On the last Sunday of the meetings we had a water baptismal service at which 51 were immersed and took their stand for the dear Lord. This is a new field and people of this community are stirred, and are saying, "What meaneth this?" We set the assembly in order last Tuesday night, 41 signing the roster to stand strictly for the Pentecostal doctrine; for which we give God all the glory. Merle W. Roll and Evangelist Irl J. Walker....

("Bayard," *Pentecostal Evangel*, August 16, 1924, p. 12.)

*Bayard—Assembly of God, 1924

... On July 22, 1924, the church was officially set in order with Rev. Irl J. Walker being elected as pastor.

In the fall of 1937 a tent revival was held at the Gering Park. Many came to know Christ as their Savior and became members of the church at that time.

While Rev. J. M. Cummings was pastor ... the present sanctuary was built in 1952 and the older part was remodeled and was used for Sunday school and educational purposes....

In 1971, the church body elected to add a fellowship hall to the present facility...and the present 25' x 65' hall was added.

In 1979, Don Burry donated the steeple from the old German Lutheran Church to the Assembly of God church. The steeple was restored and mounted on top of the entrance tower in 1980 with the original bell from the old United Brethren Church, which was purchased in 1924....

The list of pastors includes Irl J. Walker, Million Smith, Clearance Darrow, Bert Talcott, Wallace Ross, A. M. Albers, E. M. Stanely, Raymond Sherman, J. M. Peck, J. M. Cummings, Dale K. Eden, A. H. Farrington, John W. Smith, Donald Reid, Wayne Nestor, Alan Schaberg, and Todd Tabor.

*Beatrice—First Assembly of God, 1937

Harold James, my Dad, pastored Beatrice 1943, 1944. We lived in the basement of the church building. I remember it was war years; supplies were scarce; oleomargarine was used instead of butter and was white when we bought it with a small colored capsule that when squeezed turned the package yellow like butter; the congregation was very small; all the men including my Dad and brother worked wherever there was a need.

There was one gentleman that stands out in my memory bank. His love for Jesus was evident to me even though I was very young. I knew he lived at the Beatrice Home (the correct name I don't recall). I don't know how he found transportation to the services, but was often able to attend. I can still see his face light up with a smile when there was an opportunity to suggest his favorite song. His voice would call out loud, but not clear as he would request *Such Love!*

Through out the years of my life this unknown man's love for this song, *Such Love,* has been a wonderful reminder of the love of our God for each of us. I believe this memory burnt a hole in my heart for the good in my life, causing me to never doubt the Love of God for me.

~ Elisabeth James Lemp

The list of pastors since 1950 includes William Womersley, Guy D. Hamer, Lyal McCormack, Kenneth Krivohlavek, E. W. Rosenkrans, James Benedict, Brian Ubben, Forrest Frazier, and David Bigley.

Youth Alive Bible Study Club Meets in Beatrice High School

Recently students who attend First Assembly of God in Beatrice started a Youth Alive Bible Study Club. The following article appeared in the school newspaper (Warnsing, M., Staff Reporter. Bible Study Begins Weekly Meetings).

Some students may feel that a Bible study would be boring and a waste of their time, but others feel that it is worthwhile and could change their life. A Bible study group started on January 5 and continues every Wednesday at 3:45 in room 148.

Tim Gunn, mid-term graduate, is the founder of the Bible study. Gunn said he wanted to start the Bible study because, "There are a lot of people who have a lot of depression, think life is a party, and hide their depression in a beer can. I used to be like that, but I was saved; and I just want others to understand God and be saved too."

Norma Mercer, the Bible study adult sponsor, said, "I believe it (the Bible study) is important for the students and the school."

Some students may feel that a Bible study is just a bunch of kids learning about God and reading the Bible. Not entirely true. They will do some of this, but they will also have guest speakers for different interests and will have open discussions on a subject that concerns teens.

... Right now they have ten or twelve participants, but are expecting more since they only started at the beginning of January. They have invited other students to find out about their group.

They hold their meetings at the high school in room 148, announce it in the bulletin, and put signs all over the school

Gunn feels that students should come because, "a lot of people are just lost and don't know their purpose in life. They are too involved in cars, beer, money, and women; and they don't know Christ is the only true happiness, and the Bible study strives to point that out."

Mercer gives up hours of her free time to help with the Bible study because it is easy to go to and the students are already there.

The Bible study doesn't go against the policy of not mixing religion and state. According to Mercer, "You go by choice and it forced upon anybody. You don't have to come if you don't want to. It's not like making students say a prayer at the beginning of a class—that's illegal, this isn't."

... The only guidelines set up by Principal Richard Kunde and Superintendent Stephen Joel was that they had to have an adult sponsor at all the meetings, and Norma Mercer was happy to do it.

Gunn feels that the real focus of the Bible study is for students to be saved or find their meaning in life. They're not there just to teach, they're there to help.

(M. Warnsing, "Youth Alive Bible Study Club Meets in Beatrice High School," *Nebraska Fellowship*, May/June 1994, pp. 4-6.)

Beaver City, Nebraska, 1924

We had a wonderful visitation of God's power at our camp, August 7 to 17. Brother Thomas K. Leonard was our evangelist. We thank God for his plain, deep, effective Bible teaching during the ten days. There were 6 saved; 7 baptized with the Holy Spirit as in Acts 2:4; 14 were baptized in water. The last night, the crowd was estimated at 2500 people. Many cases of healing were manifest the last night. Three were instantly healed; 2 were saints who were near 70 years of age. It was a wonderful demonstration of God's mighty power to heal. We covet the prayers of God's children. ~ A. R. Shaffer, acting pastor, Cambridge, Nebraska.

("Beaver City," *Pentecostal Evangel*, September 20, 1924, p. 14.)

*Bellevue—Bellevue Christian Center, 1972

... Charles Turner, founder and president of the Bethesda Foundation, consented to lead the church group from its beginning until it was ready for a full-time pastor. His able leadership and the financial assistance given by his Bethesda foundation made it possible for the church to flourish.

When the church was only six years old the congregation recognized the need for larger facilities. They purchased a 14-acre plot on Harvel Drive, and began planning for not only a new church building but also a complete Christian Center.... and the dream became reality with ground breaking and construction beginning in the spring of 1976.

Originally people got Credit Union loans themselves and then gave the money to the church. The Credit Union manager was impressed by sacrifices people were making and the miracles he saw take place and he began to attend the church services.

Senior pastors from 1972 include Charles Turner, Sam Mayo and Gary Hoyt.

God Uses BankAmericard

The Nebraska District's newest church, Bellevue Assembly, has the "fastest growing Sunday school" in Nebraska, and is listed as one of the 50 fastest growing Sunday schools in the nation, according to the November Christian Life magazine.

Only 3 years old, the church has engaged in 2 building programs and recently began a Sunday school extension program at the local Betz Elementary School.

Bellevue, a city of more than 25,000 that sits on the edge of Omaha, claims the American Defense Systems of the Strategic Air Command as its main tenant. Its inhabitants are well acquainted with the new church.

Here is a thrilling story Pastor Sam Mayo (formerly of Atlanta, GA) related to me concerning what happened when three families connected with the Strategic Air Command desired to see an Assemblies of God church established in Bellevue.

The dilemma of acquiring a building seemed insurmountable. Then one of the three military men, Captain Keith Hendrick (whose father is an Assemblies of God minister), pulled out his BankAmericard and asked the Realtor, "Can we use a BankAmericard for the $100 down payment on the closed Lutheran Church building"?

The Realtor laughed and said, "Sure, But I really shouldn't let you men do

The last Sunday of October was a memory-filled day for Sgt. Bob Thomas, Sgt. Duane Iglehart and Captain Hendrick. Exactly three years earlier their three families, along with two other families, had their first service in "the church that Faith built," as they call it.

"The two things that impressed me most about coming to be the pastor of Bellevue Assembly in April," said Pastor Mayo, "were the enthusiasm of the people to see the church grow and build, and the response of 20 people to the altar call on my first Sunday.

"Enough could not be said about the man who led the small band of worshipers during their pioneer days," Brother Mayo continued.

"Charles Turner, founder and president of the Bethesda Foundation, consented to lead the church group from its beginning until it was ready for a full-time pastor. His able leadership and the financial assistance given by his Bethesda Foundation made it possible for the church to flourish"

Assistant Pastor Tom Compton is quickly becoming known around Cornhusker country as "Mr. Bus" since the new church buses in between 175 and 200 people every Sunday with its fleet of four vehicles....

While growth from a first-month average of 42 to a present average of more than 350 may seem unusual, the recent growth in the youth group is even more phenomenal.

With an attendance of only 5 young people at the youth meeting the week before Pastor and Mrs. Mayo came to Bellevue, it was evident this area of church ministry needed attention. Mrs. [Jeanne] Mayo, affectionately known to the youth as "Sister J." slanted her imagination and natural abilities to youth ministry, and another miracle was born.

Within 6 weeks more than 100 young people were attending the "Spireno (Spiritual Revolution Now) meetings.

In Sister Mayo's words, "It became a usual occurrence to have at least a dozen young people come into a new experience with Christ around the altars each week. Our big responsibility now comes in teaching such a large group of 'newborn babes in Christ' and helping them to become established in the things of God."

"Sister J" also directs the five month-old "Noah's Ark" Preschool and Child Care Center.... Another part of the "Bellevue Miracle" was the fact that both the school and the center operated in the black the first month.

The young church now has a Monday-Friday broadcast on 2 local radio stations at prime time--when folk go to work in the morning and when they come home in the afternoon.

Offset printing equipment and office machines, recently purchased, have made possible the printing of more that 200,000 pieces of literature since late spring of 1974. "The Every Door in '74" campaign enabled workers to leave a salvation message at virtually every home in the city.

Pastor Mayo concluded, "Our next goal is to reach every home in Omaha with a personal message of love, concern and salvation.

"We anticipate an attendance of approximately 1,000 during our coming spring Sunday school campaign...."

(J. D. Wilkins: "God Uses BankAmericard," *Pentecostal Evangel*, March 30, 1975, pp. 18-19.)

Ministry to the Deaf at Bellevue Assembly

Attendance in Bellevue [Nebraska] Assembly's 1 1/2-year-old deaf church already has reached a one-time high of 115.

This new ministry which Cori Cook directs has attracted an encouraging number of deaf persons and a few with other handicaps.

Two classes--one for the deaf and handicapped children and one for adults--meet on Sunday mornings. The church also conducts a Sunday School and Worship service in the afternoons for the deaf who cannot attend morning services.

The deaf activities include the "Little Hands for Jesus" sign choir and drama group and the "Uplifted Hands" teen and adult sign choir.

All services at the church are interpreted for the deaf. Jeanne Mayo, the pastor's wife, has charge of the total youth program, which includes a deaf cell.

Eight deaf teens and adults have enrolled in the Thursday night Bible study group and a soul-winning class, as well as in an effective communication class for deaf ministry staff on Tuesdays.

The church provides transportation, with deaf attending from as far away as 35 miles. They also run a bus to the Iowa School for the Deaf on Sunday mornings, afternoons and evenings and provide a car on Wednesdays.

The church is listed as a supportive service for the deaf in the Metro-Omaha area and receives calls for counseling and interpreting. Through this service several deaf have found the Lord.

About 50 deaf persons, as well as a number of hearing persons, have responded to the convicting power of the Holy Spirit, and some have been baptized in the Spirit....

("Bellevue Assembly Adds Ministry to the Deaf," *Pentecostal Evangel*, April 23, 1978, p. 11.)

History of Bellevue, Nebraska Master's Commission

Toby R. Schneckloth (MC Director): *History of Bellevue, Nebraska Master's Commission*, 1998.

Master's Commission is a discipleship program that began in 1984 in Phoenix, Arizona, by a man named Lloyd Ziegler. It is designed to challenge a high school graduate with all that is necessary to prepare him or her for ministry, whether full-time or part-time....

The program began with the 1st term in January of 1995 ... It began with only 5 students, 4 males and only one female.... The program intensified greatly during the year of 1996. These six students traveled extensively across the Midwest holding retreats and services in many different cities: Gering, Beatrice, Minatare, Mullin, Hastings, Norfolk, and Grand Island in Nebraska; Oskaloosa, Madrid, and Grinnel, Iowa; Duluth, MN, Phoenix, AR, Chicago, IL, Champagne, IL St. Louis, MO, Rapid City, SD, and Kansas City, MO.

... September 1998 was the start of the 5th term. This team is the biggest yet, and it shows much growth from the previous three years. There are currently 22 students, 16 first year students, 6 second year students, 12 females and 10 males....

The Master's Commission strives to prepare the whole individual for a lifelong commitment to Jesus Christ and much activity serving the Lord.... We focus on four different areas of the MC's life: The head, the heart, the hands, and the homeopeners.... Each student comes into Bellevue and will live with a homeopener, which is a family who is willing to house them throughout the year....

("Bellevue Assembly Adds Ministry to the Deaf," *Pentecostal Evangel*, April 23, 1978, p. 11.)

Ainsworth Assembly of God

Dedication day of AG at Alliance, NE, July 19, 1981

A/G church at Atkinson , NE

Assembly of God at Bayard, NE

Unit 3: Communities Experience the Move of God

Chapter 8: Big Springs through Dalton

" ... Jesus stood and said in a loud voice, „If anyone is thirsty, let him come to me and drink. Whoever believes in me, as the Scripture has said, streams of living water will flow from within him.'"
(John 7:37-38 NIV)

Big Springs	Burwell	Coleridge
Blair	Butte	Columbus
Bridgeport	Carnes	Cozad
Broken Bow	Chadron	Crawford
Burton	Chappell	Dalton

*Big Springs—Assembly of God, 1926

The Big Springs Assembly of God church made its beginning in March 1926, when Rev. H. J. Ketner came to hold evangelistic services in the Legion Hall and became the first pastor. Hannah Wendt donated property, and the men of the congregation built the edifice in 1927. The church's original name was "Full Gospel Tabernacle." The church was officially recognized as an Assembly of God church on June 14, 1927.... According to the church's original handwritten records the congregation began with twenty-one charter members....

In 1930 Rev. Raymond Phillips was elected pastor, and during his pastorate a basement was added to accommodate Sunday school rooms and living quarters for the pastor. Under Pastor Phillips' direction the church body voted in its own constitution and bylaws on October 14, 1930. Later, property adjoining the church was purchased for a parsonage.... By 1933 the membership had increased to forty-four.

On November 6, 1973, a new church building was dedicated in a special service directed by Rev. Ivan Christoffersen, the pastor at the time. The new facility can seat 200 in the sanctuary, and has eight classrooms and a nursery, two offices, a completely furnished kitchen and a fellowship hall. By the summer of 1983 a new parsonage was completed....

Big Springs Assembly of God is an active missionary church, and for several years led the Nebraska District in missions giving. Many people who grew up in the church have become ministers, evangelists and missionaries.

The list of pastors, from the church's origin to the present date (1998), includes U. O. Ziegler, U. M. LeMar, Paul Copeland, A. R. Nichols, Ed Herrman, Lloyd Weed, E. J. Dewey, F. D. McClellan, Paul Wagner, Phillip Palser, Ivan West, Ivan Christoffersen, D. P. Wilson, H. F. Stiles, Ivan Christoffersen, Bobby Claycomb, Tim Munyon, Rob Mumm, Fred Benton, John Eisfelder, Clarence Rohde, and Chris Wadle.

*Blair—Lighthouse Fellowship, 1934

The Assembly of God in Blair was started largely through the efforts of the late LeRoy Baxter. Brother Baxter was born again in an Assembly of God church in Idaho. After returning to his hometown he felt a burden to start an Assembly. In 1934 Rev. Weaver was called as pastor and services were held in a vacant store building. Early in 1935 revival services were held with Sister Marjorie Ball from Ord, Nebraska as the Evangelist. Miss Ball later became Mrs.

Murray Brown and with her husband served as a missionary in Africa for many years. The young congregation continued with Bible studies and home prayer meetings after the Weavers left Blair in 1935 until Rev. Pollard became pastor in 1941. They then moved into the building known as Germania Hall (also called the Tin Hall because of its metal exterior) which had been used for a dance hall.

Rev. and Mrs. Ernest Aldridge came as pastors in October of 1945 and soon afterwards the congregation purchased the "Hall." The auditorium was remodeled, a nice apartment was added in the basement as well as Sunday school rooms and the outside of the building was stuccoed. Sunday school attendance jumped from 18 to nearly 100 during the four years the Aldridges served. Other improvements were made during succeeding years, and in 1971 the house next door was purchased for a parsonage.

The list of pastors includes Rev. Weaver, Rev. Pollard, Ernest Aldridge, R. V. Umphenour, LeRoy Hamburger, Nolan D. Blakkolb, M. S. Andersen, Perry Baublitz, William Ramsey, William Jay, David Corardo, Arthur Diaz, Perry Baublitz, and Joe Smith.

*Bridgeport—New Life Assembly, 1925

Brothers Irl J. Walker and Guy Cooper write, "We have just closed a three-week revival at Bridgeport, Nebr., in which there were 40 saved and a number received the Baptism of the Holy Ghost. Several were healed and the old town was stirred. At times there were as high as 42 seekers at the altar seeking the Lord and the tent, which seated 450 people, was packed to overflowing and many people turned away because there was no room for them. Bridgeport is just a new field and at the close of the revival meetings the people wanted an Assembly of God Church there but there was no building that we could rent for a place of worship, so different ones just simply walked up and subscribed so much for a building and we had $500.00 raised in just a little while so we have bought a lot and will build as soon as we can get at it. We ask an interest in all of your prayers that the Lord will save many more souls in Bridgeport."

(Irl J. Walker and Guy Cooper, "From Bridgeport, Nebraska," *Pentecostal Evangel*, October 17, 1925, p. 12.)

The list of pastors who have ministered in Bridgeport since 1950 include R.S. Denny, Kenneth Crouse, J.C. Garrett, R.V. Umphenour, B.F. Correll, Hugh Campbell, K. Melvin Johnson, and Greg Farmer.

Broken Bow, Nebraska

Here is information on Evangelist Blanche Brittain at Broken Bow, Nebraska.

I was introduced to Pentecost back in 1928 in Adams, North Dakota. I was only nine years old. Blanche Brittain (from Broken Bow, Nebraska) had come into Adams and rented the hall. She dressed in white, which looked like a nurse‘s dress. In that she was a powerful preacher, it‘s fair to compare her to Aimee Semple McPherson. And because she had this white dress, it reminded me of the pictures I‘ve seen of Aimee Semple McPherson. Of course, Aimee‘s was more classy, more fancy, because all Blanche‘s was -- was a nurse‘s dress. I never saw her dress in anything different. Blanche came up to the Dakotas in the summertime and went back to Nebraska in the wintertime.

We kids just looked up to her. We had never seen anybody preach like she did. She didn‘t stand behind the pulpit, she moved around. She preached with such tremendous force, she had life in her. It was very heartfelt, very loud, but she didn‘t shriek or anything. She conducted the singing herself, too. She was so different. Someone like her who has some life, some pep, was very captivating to a child. It was in the summer of 1928 that Blanche came for a few weeks.

(Darrin J. Rodgers, "An Interview with Doris Walker," Grand Forks, ND, July 23, 1995.

*Broken Bow—Assembly of God, 1939

The first services of the Assembly of God in Broken Bow were held in June 1939 under the leadership of Rev. and Mrs. Floyd Garrett in a portable tabernacle located on the old South Ward School grounds.... Hazel Bristol Hall and Opal Garrett took care of the tabernacle as pastors for a brief period following the resignation of the Garretts.

Rev. Paul Bredensen came on October 8, 1939, and established a Sunday school, which averaged about twenty in attendance. He served as pastor for two years. During 1942, the church was without a resident pastor, so Rev. Harold James, pastor of the Assembly of God at Westerville, conducted the services.... Rev. Carlyle Beebe became pastor, February 21, 1943. Several young people of the community were saved, and the work began to grow.... The Sunday school likewise grew and within a year the building was overcrowded, with a Sunday school attendance running up to 65.... Rev. Paul Wagner became the pastor in September 1945.

In 1945, the house at 614 South Third Avenue was purchased for a parsonage, including a vacant lot to the north for a total price of $3,500. Construction of the present building at 606 South Third Avenue was begun April 1946, under the leadership of Rev. Paul Wagner. The building was completed at an estimated cost of $7,000. Dedication of the new building was held on May 7, 1947.

One notable conversion was that of a Chinese University student in the employ of the Chinese Government, who had been sent to Nebraska to study soil conservation. His conversion was the result of personal work of a Sunday school teacher who worked in the county extension office. This Chinese man was invited to Sunday school, and the following Friday night at a prayer meeting accepted Christ as his personal Savior. A few days later he received word from his wife and family in China, saying that they had been saved in an Assembly of God Mission in China, and had been baptized in water. For a month he never missed a service. He was leaving to take further study preparing him for his return to China. In China he would be taking a leading part in the conversion program of the army. On the evening of his departure, he told the congregation that his greatest joy was that in his work he would be able to present Christ to the young Chinese soldiers whom he was to help get established in civilian life.

Rev. Clyde King became pastor in July 1949. Under his leadership, the church continued to grow reaching a high attendance of 130 in Sunday school....In May 1955, Rev. Wayne Hall was chosen as pastor of the church to succeed Rev. King. Rev. Lynn Nichols came in 1964, ministering until 1968, as was followed by Rev. Duane Roll, who ministered until 1972. Rev. A. E. Kleppinger came in December 1972.... Rev. William Jay came to pastor in July of 1984, and served until May of 1988. Since then the pastors include Rev. Bob W. Rudichar, Phil Parker, and Rick Johnson.

Carlyle Beebe and Broken Bow

"I was assistant pastor with E. M. Clark at South Sioux City, Nebraska. A relative of mine who was pastor at Madison, South Dakota passed away and I attended the funeral. While I was there, his wife thought that I resembled him very much. Thinking that it might help the people of the church to settle back to pre-funeral days, she asked me to come and conduct about three services. The three nights continued for one month of services.

While I was in Madison, South Dakota, we drove down to Sioux Falls and visited the District Superintendent, Rev. Arthur Berg. He told of a South Dakota town that didn't have a local pastor of any kind and since the South Dakota District had a church building there, he wanted me to go to Wall and look into the possibility of establishing a church there again.

I journeyed to Rapid City and met with the presbyter. While there I met Bro. Harry Dryer, a convert from Winner, South Dakota, and he invited me to conduct a children's revival for him at Hills City, so I spent one week there. While in Hills City, I called my parents, the Chester Beebee's, who were pastoring at Nebraska City, Nebraska. Rev. A. M. Alber, Nebraska District Superintended, was conducting a week of services there. He came on the phone and asked what I was doing in South Dakota? I told him I was looking into starting a church in Wall.

Bro. Alber replied, "You don't have to go to South Dakota to get into the ministry! Come back to Nebraska, and I'll find a place for you to get started." He said he would be in Bassett, Nebraska that weekend in services and that I should meet him there. We would go together and find something.

I took a train to Bassett and stayed that night with the Paul Wagners who lived there. Monday morning I met Bro. Alber and we took off for the central part of the state. He had plans to take me to Whitman, Nebraska where, he stated, that someone there wanted a church started. We proceeded to go south through Westerville and stopped to visit the Jameses. While we were with them, Bro. [Harold] James said that they were considering giving up the Sunday afternoon services at Broken Bow and perhaps that would be something for me to consider. I stayed with the Jameses, and Bro. Alber proceeded on his way somewhere else.

On Saturday afternoon of that week, Lena Mae [daughter of Harold and Marie James] had a piano recital at Broken Bow which I attended. I think she must have been around 12 years of age then. While the James were in Broken Bow that afternoon, I guess they told the people of the church they would have a guest speaker on Sunday afternoon, and they should come prepared to vote whether he should be a pastor for their church.

When that Sunday afternoon came, I spoke and afterwards went outside while the people voted to invite me to stay as pastor or not. I received their approval.

The church had a very good foundation to build a strong church on. There were the Conors, Flora Hogaboom, the Wooters, two school teachers (Emersons), and Betty Price, as well as a number of others. I had to rent an apartment and had no car for transportation, but the people did their best and things began to move forward as the people worked very hard for the Lord's cause.

In Broken Bow, we had no midweek services. The school teachers taught school at Oconto, Nebraska and would arrive back in Broken Bow on Friday night so we scheduled the services for Friday evening. I had the whole week pretty well open so I scheduled a trip or two to the northern part of the state where I had lived. I knew that a pastor should have a helpmate and I was handicapped without one as I had to take Grandma Emerson with me whenever I called on an ill younger lady.

I proceeded to court Betty Spearman whom I later married and took to Broken Bow as my helpmate."

(Carlyle Beebe, "Road That Led to Broken Bow, Nebraska," 1997.)

Carlyle Beebe was Nebraska District D-CAP from 1946 to 1949.

Harvest in Broken Bow

There had been no resident pastor at Broken Bow, Nebraska, for a year or more, when a young evangelist named Carlyle Beebe became pastor. That was in February, 1943. A nearby pastor, Harold James, had kept the field open by holding Sunday afternoon services, and the little congregation was worshiping in a portable tabernacle belonging to the district. The Sunday school attendance was under 20.

Then several young people of the community were saved, and the work began to grow. In a year's time a house was purchased to be remodeled and become the first permanent church home. The Sunday school likewise grew and within a year the building was overcrowded, with a Sunday school attendance running up to 65.

At this time Brother Beebe was ordained and elected to the office of District C. A. President (later to become also the District Sunday School Representative). When he resigned, the pastorate was taken over by Paul Wagner, who has been pastor for over a year.

The spiritual life of the church has had a continuous growth. One family after another has been saved in the regular services of the church and Sunday school.

One notable conversion was that of a Chinese university student in the employ of the Chinese Government, who had been sent to Nebraska to study soil conservation. His conversion was the result of personal work of a Sunday school teacher who worked in the county extension office. This Chinese man was invited to Sunday school, and the following Friday night at a prayer meeting accepted Christ as his personal Saviour. A few days later he received word from his wife and family in China, saying that they had been saved in an Assembly of God Mission in China and had been baptized in water. For a month he never missed a service, and on the eve of his departure to take up further study, preparatory to returning to China to take a leading part in the reconversion program of the army, he told the congregation that his greatest joy was that in his work he would be able to present Christ to the young Chinese soldiers whom he was to help get established in civilian life.

Although there were no rich members in the congregation at Broken Bow, the Lord's will seemed to be that a parsonage should be purchased, a pressing need because of housing conditions. Accordingly, the District Superintendent, M. F. Brandt, was consulted and invited to be present for Sunday services at which time the matter would be discussed.

At this service it seemed to be the will of God to receive pledges for this project. The enlarging of the present church, also, came up for consideration, and it was decided that this project should be included in the pledge.

A young working girl offered $500 of her savings. Then others began to pledge--very slowly, at first. After a time, a spontaneous spirit of worship and giving fell upon members of the congregation, and they began to pledge from $100 to $200 each--many showing a commendable spirit of sacrifice in so doing.

Pastor Wagner, who was accustomed to working each summer during harvest, had saved some funds which he expected to need for the support of his family. In his desire to see the work of God go forward, he challenged his people by stating that he would give $100 of his earnings for every $600 contributed by the people of the church. This sacrifice greatly inspired the giving of the people.

At present, the basement of a new $10,000 church is almost completed. Pastor and Mrs. Wagner and their congregation have done a great deal of the construction work themselves--excavating for the basement, pouring cement footings and laying the cement blocks. Mrs. Wagner and a couple other women mixed the mortar for the cement blocks. With such a spirit and with faith in God, is it any wonder the work of God is going forward in Broken Bow?

During the 1944-45 year the Sunday school was awarded the Blue Shield in connection with the Lighthouse Plan, the attendance showing a fine increase. Recently the grades for the 1945-46 year were compiled and the Broken Bow Sunday school took first place for the whole U. S. A., having a grade of 99 points at the time of this writing.

The purpose of this article is to inspire many of our Bible school students to lift up their eyes and look upon the many fields in our country where laborers are needed to garner in the grain that is already white unto harvest. "Pray ye therefore the Lord of the harvest, that He would send forth laborers into His harvest." Luke 10:2

(Loine C. Honderick, "A Thrilling Home Missions Project," *Pentecostal Evangel,* November 30, 1946, p 14.)

Paul Wagner Remembers Broken Bow

In September of 1945 while pastoring in Oxford where Frances and I had been for twenty-six months, we received an invitation to come to Broken Bow which had been in existence for only a few years. Carlyle Beebe, I believe was their only full time pastor and he had been voted in as C. A. President of the District.

The church building was a school house that had been moved into town to be used as a house. This little one room building was full to capacity. (Standing room for sixty people.) The four Sunday School classes were all in the one room so you could listen to your choice of four different teachers.

After being there only a short time it was decided that we needed larger quarters so we had the District Superintendent, Bro. M. F. Brandt, come spend a Sunday with us. Needless to say he urged us to start a building fund. As I remember it, people started to spontaneously raise their hands and say they would give different amounts as the service proceeded. And all were aware that some giving was sacrificial. A lady who had been one of the first to give, burst into tears and raised the amount she had first said she'd give. Of course this triggered others to do the same.

While in Oxford, a neighboring pastor and I had planted around thirty acres of pop corn and my share of the venture was $600.00 Since our family had been living on $12.00 a week offering, and now at Broken Bow, we were receiving $40.00 we were able to give the $600.00 toward the building fund.

Enough money was raised that Sunday so that we were able to start looking for property which we found just one half block from our present location. It included a parsonage with a lot beside it all of $3500.00. Big enough to build our 36x60 church with a full basement to include a number of Sunday School rooms, furnace room, restrooms, kitchen and fellowship hall.

During the time of building, we operated strictly on a cash basis. When we ran out of material to continue, we would present the need on Sunday morning and hands would go up saying they'd give a certain amount. Usually about $200.00 would be raised in this way.

This was during the war years (WWII) when lumber supplies were not very plentiful. So we bought an old barn for $400.00 and tore it down. This took care of much of our dimension lumber. A lumber yard in Omaha had an ad in the paper stating they had sheet rock which had a finish on one side so I remember going to Omaha for some supplies. The only hired labor that went in this building project was the installation of a coal furnace converted to an oil furnace and the metal duct work. The plumbing was done by the Lexington Camp caretaker. The electrical work was done by a neighboring pastor, Claude Sailors, who also was in a building project. E. E. Rohde and B. F. Correll helped me get the floor joist and sub-floor in place. The basement was laid up with cement blocks, which I laid up myself. The walls and roof of the building were assembled on the sub-floor during the day with the help of Brother Campbell, who had recently retired. Then in the evening when the men of the church got off work, they would come and help us put up the walls as well as the roof truss.

When the building was completed, we had a church in a beautiful setting with a four foot hedge around the church and parsonage. After a snow, the Custer County Chief came and took a picture and ran it in their paper. A number of ministers and District Officials were present for the dedication. The total indebtedness when I left the church to go to my next pastorate was around $3,000.00. The mortgage burning came a couple years later while Clyde King was pastor. All four of those who had been residing pastors at Broken Bow were present.

Since I did much of the work on this building myself, I had limited time to study and prepare my sermons. I firmly believe God gave me a special dispensation because of what I was doing. Many times I remember waking in the middle of the night and God would drop a complete outline into my mind for a sermon. Just what I needed for the following day. I am not saying this is an example to follow, but rather, God does unusual things when it is necessary. However, this is an example of what God can do when a pastor and congregation work together, having only one thing in mind and that--"we have a message for this community that they need to hear."

During my four years stay in Broken Bow, we had an evangelist each spring and in the fall with meetings lasting at least three weeks. In every meeting there were souls saved and believers filled with the Holy Spirit. Some of the evangelist I remember were: William Girke, a converted lawyer, whose messages inspired faith; Betty Baxter Hiatt, who had a wonderful testimony of a personal healing; A. C. Phillips from Oregon; Martin Baxter from Ohio; Forrest McClellin a pastor from Nebraska.

(Paul Wagner, "Memories of Broken Bow, 1945," 1999.)

Burton Park meetings, 1931

In August of 1931, Rev. C. E. Thurmond of Ainsworth, Rev. Chet Anderson and Rev. Gene Anderson and their families of Newport, and Brother and Sister James of Lucas, South Dakota came to the Burton Park to hold a Full Gospel meeting. This was the beginning of the Pentecostal work in this area. Some fifty were saved, over thirty became baptized Saints, and a new church was organized with fifty-three charter members. A class of thirty-five Christ Ambassadors was organized also. Because of the interest and potential of the community those ministers returned in October, rented the "White Church" and began meetings that lasted for six weeks.... Many souls were saved and in November a new church was set in order, the Burton Assembly of God. Rev. and Mrs. Harold James were the new pastors. ~ C. E. Thurmond

Memories of K. Duane Cook

I will tell you of the spiritual happenings in my life and the people of Burton during the great revival in the fall of 1931.

Lee and Jessie Snider were farmers and dairy people. They always milked their Holstein cows at 4:30 in the morning and 4:30 in the evening. They loved to square dance. One Sunday evening in November 1931, Jessie was milking when a voice said, "Jessie." She said, "Yes, Lee, what do you want?" No answer because Lee had taken milk to the house to empty and return to milk. She began to milk again and a voice said, "Jessie". This time she rather impatiently said, "Yes, Lee, what do you want?" No reply. Again the voice called, "Jessie", and this time she replied, "Yes, Lord, what do you want?" The Lord said, "Go to Burton to church." She and Lee went to Burton and were saved along with approximately 25 other people ... From the start, Jessie dedicated her life to the church. She would spend hours praying with those seeking the Holy Spirit. After Lee passed away, she spent much time in prayer and fasting.

Brother Evans, a black Christian showed up early in the starting of the churches in this area. [Burton] He had retired from some position in government services and was receiving a small monthly pension. He was from Chicago. He played a guitar and drums and, on some occasions, played both together. He fit in very well as all the churches had some type of orchestra. He sang specials. Being the first black person in the area, he was a new experience for most families and especially children. He would travel from one evangelistic service to another and at one time of another, was probably in every church in the State of Nebraska. He was always happy and ready with a testimony. I know he stayed with our family, probably on his first trip to Burton.... I am sure he encountered discrimination outside the church and, in some instance, in the church. This was during the 1930's and 1940's.... He was a special person in the early history of the Burton Assembly of God Church.

(From the Memory Book of K. Duane Cook from Burton's 75th Anniversary Booklet.)

Valee Peterson's Memory of Brother Evans from K Duane Cook's memories

We were living in Burton and Iris Dee and I would be very excited when Brother Evans stayed with Grandpa and Grandma Cook. He would play with us, give us rides on his knees, and then give us each a nickel. With this being the Depression years, Brother Evans was the richest person we knew. It was hard to get a penny from others. I was married at the Burton church in August 1950. We moved to Waxahachie, Texas for the next five years. Knowing only Brother Evans before, we were able to work and be with Black Americans without the chains of prejudice. With Brother Evans' memory in my heart, I became an active Civil Rights person.

(From the Memory Book of K. Duane Cook from Burton's 75th Anniversary Booklet.)

*Burton—Assembly of God, 1931

After a few years, the congregation purchased and moved to the present Assembly of God property. Rev. Charles Turner supervised the building of Sunday school rooms and enlarging the sanctuary while he served as pastor. A few years later the fellowship hall was added....

... God laid His call to the ministry on a number of young people, who dedicated themselves to a lifetime of service. Two former pastors have actively served as foreign missionaries, Rev. and Mrs. Norman Correll in Africa and Rev. and Mrs. Steve Groseclose in Suriname, South America. Perhaps one of the most outstanding arms of the church is its missionary vision, which has been felt around the world....

The list of pastors includes Harold James, Paul Copeland, Luke Brown, Chester A. Beebe, Edward M. Herrman, Cloyd Sailors, Forrest D. McClellan, James Bailey, Norman Correll, Charles Turner, LeRoy C. Eichmann, Wayne Jameson, Steve Groseclose, Howard Rice, Garry Swagger, William Jay, Mike Christian, John Rice, Jonathan Busch, John Gale, and Eugene Wilson.

*Burwell—Assembly of God, 1930

Rev. and Mrs. E. N. Stanley of Massachusetts assisted by Mrs. Christy and Mrs. Jones conducted the first meetings in 1930 in the building that is now the Burwell Hatchery. The Lord blessed and a new church was born. Pledges were accepted and construction of a Full Gospel Tabernacle was soon begun. In 1931 the Stanleys left and his parents the H. N. Stanleys were in care of the "little flock." In the summer of the same year Rev. and Mrs. Henry Comstock came to pastor the church. Rev. and Mrs. Glen Reed who served until June of 1934 followed them. Mrs. Reed will be remembered for her work with the children.

A parsonage was built across the street from the church on lots donated by Guy Laverty, a local attorney, while B. F. Correll was pastor. During Magnus Anderson's ministry the church was enlarged and extensive remodeling and redecorating done....

The list of pastors includes E. N. Stanley, Henry Comstock, Glen Reed, Joe Bushnell, B. C. Heinze, Harold Carlblom, E. C. Niles, B. F. Correll, L. L. Fogelman, F. L. Sobotka, Loren Triplett, Jack Risner, C. A. Beebe, Wayne Allen, Paul Marler, Duane Palser, Ellis Townsend, Leland Geer, M. S. Andersen, George Bingham, Dennis Romine, David Caley, David Nord, Clarence Rohde, and Mike Blatchley.

*Butte—Full Gospel Church, 1985

The list of pastors includes Vance Anderson, Douglas Overly, and Fred Moore.

Carns, Nebraska

... Brother and Sister Hugo H. Blumenthal, who were formerly in charge of the work at Torrington, Wyoming are at present stationed at Carns, Nebraska... At present we are working for the Lord in this place, which is 26 miles from a railroad in the canyons of the Niobrara River. There are young fold in this community who have never attended a Sunday School or heard a Gospel Message. After several weeks on our faces before God in prayer, He opened up the way for us to organize a Sunday School, and since then a home had been opened for young people's meetings. ~ H. H. Blumenthal

*Chadron—Chadron Community Church, 1949

Founded in 1949, First Assembly of God of Chadron was located at the intersection of Second and Lake. Rev. Robert Paul was the first pastor. The increase in average attendance from 55 persons to more than 200 over the years created the need for larger facilities. Construction was begun on a new building at 8th and Maple in March of 1973 and completed in 1975. The name of the church became Chadron Community Church in 1974. The church also actively engaged in Campus Ministries at Chadron State College with about 75 Chi Alpha members.

The list of pastors includes Robert A. Paul, Edward M. Hermann, C. G. Beebe, Jerry Spain, James Holden, Carl James Medearis, Bob Roos, Don White, Terry Petty, and Rod Smith.

*Chappell—Assembly of God, 1914

... In the spring of 1914 Rev. John McConnell held a meeting in the courthouse. During these meetings several families joined him. Then in August of the same year Rev. Joe Stevens came to Chappell from Texas and held a tent meeting on the main street of Chappell. He preached the Baptism in the Holy Spirit, with the evidence of speaking in other tongues. This teaching brought about much persecution. The tent ropes were cut, rotten eggs were hurled into the services, and seekers at the altar were dragged bodily from the tent. But in spite of all this, the nucleus of the church was born.

In the fall of 1915, a little mission down by the railroad was constructed. The first families included the Rankins, Cuttefords, Blanks, Ritcheys, Sanders, Welzes, and Matsons. Church and Sunday school were held on Sunday afternoons.... The church people were fasting and praying for a permanent pastor. In January 1921, a young evangelist, Irl J. Walker, came from Riverton, Wyoming to hold services at the mission. He preached with such unmatched zeal and enthusiasm that over forty young people accepted Christ during these meetings.... At the close of the services, Rev. Walker consented to pastor the church. He and his wife, and two small sons moved into the three rooms in the back of the church. It wasn't long until more room was needed for the church, so the partition was removed that separated the house from the church, and the pastor moved into a rented house....

In 1924, Zelma and Beulah Argue came from Winnipeg, Manitoba, to hold revival meetings. Because of the needed space, the meeting was held in the largest room in town: the courthouse. The crowds were large and interest in the services was high. One night at the close of the service, a group of Ku Klux Klan members, all dressed in their regalia came marching up to the platform. The service was halted—fear ran among the people. The girls were terrified. One of the Klan members walked up to Zelma, and reaching beneath his uniform, pulled out a large white envelope. Was it a summons or a warning? She opened the envelope and thanked God for a liberal offering. Then the Klan walked out quietly.

During the depression of the thirties, many of the faithful families moved to other cities. If it had not been for Rev. Clopine and the families that remained, the church might have closed.

In 1944, during the pastorate of Rev. Lester Dickinson, a new brick church was built on the corner of 4th and Court.... The church was dedicated, debt-free, in February 1945.... A major addition to the church was made during the pastorate of Rev. Harley

Stahl. At this time a kitchen was added in the basement and new pews were installed in the sanctuary. As attendance began to increase more space was needed, especially Sunday school rooms and fellowship hall.... The groundbreaking ceremony was held in September 1982. Phase one of the addition included the completion of a 50' by 52' basement. It houses a new fellowship hall and kitchen. Phase one also included the remodeling of the former basement into new Sunday school rooms. Phase two of the building project saw the completion of the new sanctuary and the remodeling of the former sanctuary into offices, nursery, and overflow area. This project was accomplished under the capable leadership of Rev. Al Rishowski. During the ministry of Dale Williams the church purchased the comfortable brick parsonage....

We have had thirty-nine pastors since the beginning of this church. The list of pastors includes John McConnell, Joe Stevens, Jess Snead, George Beckman, George Clopine, Irl Walker, Peter Davies, Harvey Babcock, Floyd Woodworth, Merle Roll, Otto J. Klink, Albert Alber, Virgil Shores, Bert Talcott, Loyal Miller, Ralph Ewing, Archie Nichols, Charles Jones, Lester Dickinson, Paul Bredesen, Herman Thieman, Walter Wagner, Douglas Ramsey, Earl Dewey, Chester Beebe, Elmer Swick, Eldon McNaughton, Floyd Garrett, Dean Markland, F. D. Cullens, R. Ballard, Joseph Kisser, Harley Stahl, Jim Reid, Terry Brown, Al Riskowski, Dale Williams, and Gregg Thee.

Chappell, Nebraska in 1916

Greetings in Jesus' dear name! Am glad to say that God is wonderfully blessing here, considering the meetings we have had, as there have only been meetings in a few homes. But God was with us and nine have received the baptism and two have been saved. We are expecting a tent any time and will begin a tent meeting as soon as it gets here. We covet the prayers of all God's that He will pour out His Spirit in a great measure here and in the surrounding country and that God will send forth laborers into the vineyard for this is surely a needy field.... We have not been here very long, having come from the state of Texas, and the high altitude affects our voices. So we ask you to pray that God will strengthen us and help us to preach His unsearchable truths. ~ J. F. and Emma Stephens

("Chappell, Neb.," *Weekly Evangel*, September 2, 1916, p. 11.)

Healing at Chappell, Nebraska

On June 8th, 1923, I fell down an old 12 ft. cistern and broke one of my right ribs as the result. I suffered severe pain for four days and could hardly get my breath. They took me to town to see the doctor, but I decided I would go to the Clark revival at the Pentecostal mission instead and be prayed for healing...

While Maxie A. X. Clark was preaching and while emphasizing the fact that we should use the little faith we have before asking for more, I received my healing. I felt fine. Glory to God.

~ Mrs. H. G. Smith, Oshkosh, Nebraska, August 1, 1923.

*Coleridge—New Life Assembly of God, 1978

The list of pastors includes Dan Thompson, Wilbur Tiahrt, George Rennau, and John Corder.

Columbus, Nebraska and Platte County

Northwest of Monroe the Evangelical Pastor held services in the original Congregational Church building in the O K Community. The Sunday school was organized by the Union Sunday School organization. There'd been a short revival after much prayer had ascended the throne of God. The Evangelist preached entire Sanctification as a second work of grace. Some people did receive an experience. In the fall of 1931, a young evangelist was invited to conduct revival services in a Country Community Church. Members of the Evangelical Congregation had attended home revival services in Genoa. Being impressed by the Word of God preached, they (the members of Evangelical Church) ask their pastor to invite the Evangelist to preach revival services for them.

The full gospel preached during that revival attracted the community and many attending received Salvation, Baptism of the Holy Spirit, Water Baptism by immersion and heard about the Second Coming of Christ. For six weeks, services were conducted every night and people attended, coming in any way they could get to church, horse and wagon, cars, and walking some miles. There were many home prayer meetings, people were so hungry for the Word of God. The Holy Spirit's outpouring upon those hungry for a deeper experience of God resulted in as many as thirty or more persons receiving the Holy Spirit Baptism with the evidence of speaking in tongues.

Controversy among the Evangelical Pastor and the community led to a decision concerning organizing the new Pentecostal believers. The Nebraska Assembly of God Superintendent conducted a legal organizational business meeting. This body of Pentecostal believers established the First Assembly of God church in Platte County.

Outstation services in surrounding towns were conducted, especially by the young people. In the summer of 1932, a tent meeting was held in Genoa. Not long after beginning the meeting, the tent was burned (believed to be arson). This curtailed further effort in Genoa at that time. However many street meetings were still held with good attendance in other surrounding towns.

During the original revival several young men and a farmer received their personal call for further Pentecostal ministry.

(Dorothy Brandt, "Revival in Platte County, Nebraska in 1931 and 1932," 1998.)

*Columbus—Word of Life Assembly of God, 1931

Revival came to the O K Community in Platte County in the fall of 1931. The full gospel was preached during that revival and many people received salvation, the baptism of the Holy Spirit, water baptism, and heard about the Second Coming of Christ.... The Holy Spirit's outpouring upon those hungry for a deeper experience of God resulted in over thirty people receiving the baptism in the Holy Spirit with the evidence of speaking in tongues.

The Nebraska Assemblies of God superintendent organized the First Assembly of God Church in Platte County with this body of believers. After the war years, in 1947 B. F. Correll came to Columbus as pastor. The congregation met in various store buildings until the white church on U. S. 30 was built.

In April of 1978 the little white church was sold and the congregation started work on the current building at 3701 23rd Street.... Gordon Harmon was pastor at this time. The new building was finished in November 1978.... An addition was added in 1982 and another in 1991. An outside facility was built to host community events....

The list of pastors which have served the church includes Keith Reed, C. Mikkelsen, Loyal A. Miller, E. H. Kent, Loyal A. Miller, Virgil Brooker, Cloyd Sailors, Julius Olson, James Bailey, B. F. Correll, C. T. Been, Harold James, A. H. Farrington, L. S. Nichols, Dale Eden, Paul Hebbert, Jim L. Reid, Gordon Harmon, and Terry Deffenbaugh.

Live Nativity at Columbus Word of Life

In the late 1990's, Columbus Word of Life Church presented its live, outdoor nativity scene complete with Mary and Joseph, the three wise men, shepherds, animals and angels for the Christmas season. Several years the snow covered ground with the subfreezing temperatures was the setting for the story of the birth of Jesus Christ, our Lord. In 1997, the nativity scene was on display from 7 PM to 9 PM with shows running every 20 minutes. As the narration of the ageless story was given, viewers could stand close to the manager and watch or view it from their cars, listening to 97.5 FM.

*Cozad— Living Hope Assembly of God, 1964

… In 1962 the Nebraska Home Missions Committee recommended to the district council that Cozad be the pilot project for "Breakthrough—8000" in the state. The District Women's Ministries provided enough dimes to purchase large lots in a new housing area.

District leaders engaged an architect who soon presented blueprints. Workers began laying the foundation. The beams arrived and brick layers and carpenters were busy. Everywhere Nebraska Assemblies of God people were praying. This was to be "their" church—a district project—yet all knew it would take more than just a new building. The sincere prayers were "Souls, Lord, and fill them with the Holy Spirit." The 36x72-foot structure was completely financed by the district.

Aware of volumes of prayer and keen statewide interest, Superintendent L. W. Dickinson officially opened the work on September 29, 1964, with 31 in Sunday school. The following Sunday LeRoy Eichman was installed as pastor. This day there were 44 in Sunday school with 55 attending morning worship.... God was working. Eleven adults and young people were saved that first year. Telephone calls to the pastor, plus visitors in almost every service, indicate a hunger for the Pentecostal experience. In March of 1965 a children's revival was conducted with Evangelists Mildred Larson and Linda Stivers. Community interest was outstanding. Even the postmaster helped enroll the children. Enrollment totaled 375 and average attendance was 154 with 229 children present for the closing night's program.

The list of pastors who have ministered in Cozad includes LeRoy Eichman, Harvey Herman, Ron Rice, Gary Erickson, David Farmer, and Kevin Jay.

*Crawford—Christ's Community Church

As a result of the outreach ministry of the Chadron Community Church through its Bible study ministries the Crawford Assembly of God was begun. The list of pastors since 1950 includes: Guy Hamer, Eldon Mincks, Jimmy Root, Jr., Ralph Russo, Earl Smith, Michael Kennedy, and Eldon Mincks.

*Dalton—Assembly of God, 1936

Prayer and Bible studies were held in the homes of those of the Pentecostal faith for several years before a church began. Rev. and Mrs. H. W. Lebsack began revival services May 3, 1936 in the old Woosley building west of Highway 385. Seventy were in attendance the first night and within three months the Sunday school averaged fifty. Evelyn Bethurum assisted the Lebsacks.

The group purchased the old Foster Hotel for their services. The upstairs served as living quarters for the pastor and family. In 1940 the congregation demolished this building. A large portion of the lumber was used in building a garage, a house and then the church. Rev. C. E. Thurmond was the pastor during this time. Our country was just recovering from the depression and the building program was a witness to the spirit and faith of the people.

Rev. and Mrs. L. E. Wilkins came in 1944 and under their leadership the church interior was finished, sidewalks run and trees planted to beautify the church property. In 1963 new pews were added, further sidewalk done and a permanent church sign was erected.

The list of pastors includes H. W. Lebsack, Earl Cummings, John Hodges, C. E. Thurmond, L. E. Wilkins, Clifford Case, P. V. Jones, James H. Holden, Gordon Harmon, D. B. Arnold, Paul Boyles, Elmer Burry, Gary Loutzenhiser, Jimmy Root, Jr., Richard Fisher, Dan St. Clair, Edd McCain, and John Mustoe.

Full Gospel Church at Butte

A/G Church at Chappell, NE

After this church building at Dalton was extended and remodeled, Supt. James Wilkins preached the dedication Message May 26, 1985. Jimmy Root, Jr. was the pastor.

Chapter 9: Dorchester through Grand Island

"If ye then, being evil, know how to give good gifts unto your children: how much more shall your heavenly Father give the Holy Spirit to them that ask him?" **(Luke 11:13 KJV)**

Dorchester	Franklin	Gibbon
Ewing	Fremont	Gothenburg
Fairbury	Geneva	Grand Island
Falls City	Gering	

Dorchester, Nebraska Revival

Guy H. Rake, Pastor, Milford, Nebraska, writes: Several months ago the Lord wonderfully baptized a brother living at Peetz, Colorado, with the Holy Spirit and told him to go back to the town and community where he was raised and witness for Him. As a result Brother Jess Huff and family landed in Dorchester, Nebraska, a short time later. Thru Brother Huff's efforts as a witness for the Lord a number of their relatives and friends were saved and baptized with the Holy Spirit ...

The Lord opened up the way for Evangelist Louis O. Rynning of St. Paul, Minnesota, to come and help in a campaign at Milford and Dorchester, and thru the kindness of the trustees of the unused Christian Church at Dorchester, the church was turned over to us for meeting--rent free, and the campaign began Sunday, Jan. 31.

Milford's Christ's Ambassadors have been doing fine work assisting in the regular services, holding services in the hospital, at the S. & S. Home and boosting the revival campaign at Dorchester. The C.A.'s constitute a fine group of young people and we would not be surprised if the Lord should call some of them as pastors, Christian Workers, and Missionaries. The Milford church is backing up the revival campaign at Dorchester where already some 45 have sought God for salvation, while 22 have received the Holy Spirit as in Acts 2:4. Evangelist Louis O. Rynning is in charge of those meetings and God has surely been using him. ~ G. Rake.

(*Nebraska Pentecostal Fellowship*, Vol. 1:1, March 1932.)

*Ewing—Ewing Full Gospel Church, 1945

Brother Chester Anderson started holding meetings in the town/village of Ewing, August 12, 1944. He believed the whole Bible so he taught that God would speak to people in many ways including dreams.... Therefore, when a certain young person dreamed that Brother Anderson was to hold evangelistic services in a town with an east/west main street, he began to look for such a town. The dream also revealed the appearance of the building to be used. Taking the young person who had the dream with him along with some others, they went searching. The drove through various towns but it wasn't until they drove into Ewing that interest began to really arise. The likeness of the building was there, also the main street ran east and west. Upon looking through the window of the nearly empty, unused, very dirty building it was affirmed this was the place. They acquired a lease and cleaned up the building. Services began August 12, 1944.

The Andersons, being a family blest with musical talent, drew a crowd. Most of the people, fearful to come in, sat in or on their cars parked up and down the curb and in the middle of the street. The open doors of the building let the music and the message reach many ears.

Later some land was purchased in the town. An old building on the property was torn down and what lumber that could be used made the new church less expensive for the small congregation. Brother Anderson drew the plans for the new building. The platform was raised to incorporate a place of water baptism. The pews were handmade, as were the oil burner stoves. Remember it was World War II and most things were not available. The new congregation with the help of the Butte Full Gospel Church built the church building which was dedicated in the late fall of 1945. The church through the years has made several physical changes with three additions to the building. The congregation is basically young families with teens and young children and is still a growing church.

In the more than 50 years only four pastors have served the church and been shepherds to the flock. These include Chester Anderson, Loris Anderson, Steve Shorette and Wayne Smith.

*Fairbury—Assembly of God

The list of pastors since 1950 includes: F. D. McClellan, Loren O. Triplett, Harold Mintle, James Wilkins, Leonard Herrmann, Howard Rice, David Hamilton, Eldon Walker, George Bingham, Kenneth Taylor, Daniel Moorhead, Daryl Lewis, Paul Reedy, and Gale Lund.

*Falls City—Good News Assembly of God, (Reopened) 1987

Good things are happening at Good News Assembly in Falls City. People are being won to Christ and discipled to follow Him as Lord. In 1987 when Leonard and Carli Reimer assumed the pastorate there were 35 in attendance. In 1992 according to an article written by George Edgerly for *The Pentecostal Evangel* the attendance was over 130. The congregation had peaked at 176 earlier in 1992.

The pastor gave this reason for seeing the growth of this church: "The Lord told me to reach out to the elderly, hurting, and needy." And the church did. The church operates a food pantry for the needy people. Working in cooperation with a food bank in Lincoln, they have distributed an average of $3000 worth of groceries a month. When the congregation moved to their present building in 1989, the former meeting place was turned into a clothing center. They coordinated the collection and distribution of good used garments. In the first two years of operation the clothing center had helped 3000 persons.... The pastors from 1950 include T. L. Beyer, W.O. Zeigler, Charles Kersey, Leonard Reimer, and Doug Overly.

Leonard Palmer Writes About Franklin, Nebraska

Leonard Palmer grew up near Franklin, Nebraska. He wrote the following in the early 1990s:

"Mama, why are Papa and Grandpa and the other men hitching all those horses onto that church?" That was the first of two of my early memories. I can plainly recall my utter astonishment. I was only a few months past my second birthday. The year was 1910.

Mama's reply was, "Well, son, they are going to haul the old Congregational Church across town where it will become our church. Now you stay out of the way so that the horses will not run over you!"

After that, probably days later, they dug a big hole under the building where coal, wood and kindling were kept. The building was about 100' by 50'. It was all one big room except for a small room above the vestibule. The ceiling of the main building was about 20' high. There was a platform in the north end for the pastor, choir and piano....

Not long after the people got into the church, and while they were without a pastor, God sent along a Baptist preacher who had come from the Chicago area. He had heard of a great revival, as of the New Testament times, and being hungry spiritually, he attended the revival. God was blessing. He could feel the presence of the Holy Spirit there and tarrying with them, he soon was baptized in the Holy Spirit as in Acts 2:4. Under the impulse of the new experience of the Holy Spirit‘s baptism, he went west preaching wherever he found an opportunity. Thus he landed in Franklin.

Hearing there was no pastor, he came to the newly organized church and was asked to preach. So, full of the Holy Ghost, George F. Fink poured out his heart with such an anointing that, like a prairie fire, the word swept through the congregation. Many received almost immediately and night after night and day after day in church or cottage prayer meetings, others were filled including my Grandfather and Grandmother Palmer as well as their son my father, Jesse Palmer....

Persecution started. Rotten eggs, tomatoes and stones were thrown at us inside and outside the church. Preachers preached, people shouted, "Amen! Glory! Hallelujah!" More were saved, healed, filled with the Holy Ghost. They testified and glorified God.

Our Sunday services were at 2:30 P.M. so that the people from other churches could come and again at 7:30 P.M. in the evening.... Without a pastor now that Brother Fink had left, they chose my father, Jesse Palmer, as their pastor and the revival continued apace. About a year later George Clopine succeeded Dad as the pastor....

Soon we heard of great camp meetings at Woodston and Alton, Kansas about 60 miles south. So away we went to hear the likes of Billy Millsaps, S. H. Patterson and Mrs. M. E. Woodworth-Etter.

So impressed were our fathers with these that a camp meeting was organized at Franklin. I do not remember the first years. But I know they brought people from all over Nebraska, Kansas and Colorado. The tent, a 40‘ x 80‘ size was located on the Republican River one mile south and one mile east of Franklin. Great evangelists such as John Goben of Iowa, H. E. Simms from Arkansas. Benson, Merwin and Draper would preach until sinners and saints alike cried out to God.... These camp meetings at Franklin continued annually until the mid-twenties....

Riverton was about ten miles east and one of the first out-reaches began there.... Revival meetings were begun. Not many came at first. That is, not until the wife of the town‘s saloon keeper got saved and filled with the Holy Ghost. The saloon keeper was mad but at her insistence he came one night. The power of God was so manifest and conviction so heavy that big old Walter B. Northrup fell into the altar crying out to God for mercy and was gloriously saved. He went to his saloon, poured out his liquor and closed shop. It was not long before he was filled with the Holy Spirit and went about giving his testimony of God‘s saving power....

About ten or twelve miles east of where we lived, a meeting was started in a country school house.... Amongst those saved in those meetings were a fine young farmer about 27 years old and his wife. They got a real experience and were on fire for God. When the camp meeting came that August, they and their little family of three came and stayed in a tent on the grounds. Every day and every night Irl J. Walker was earnestly seeking God for baptism in the Holy Ghost.... One afternoon his heart overflowed and he began to speak fluently in such a beautiful heavenly language.... Soon after this Irl J. Walker came to Brother Hoar, who was one of the Presbyters, and asked if there were a church where he could preach. He felt God calling him to go to tell others what God had done for him. Brother Hoar said, "I know of only one church now looking for a pastor. It is at Chappell, but I am not sure if you would want to go there because they have had a lot of trouble there."

Irl replied, "I will go if they will have me." He sold his farm stuff, and with his little family, launched out in faith for Chappell. The result was that God gave them a mighty revival. The church people got right with God. The church grew and the congregation multiplied. Irl J. Walker was launched on a God blest ministry that continued until God called him home a few years ago. If I am not mistaken, his last pastorate was in Portland, Oregon, in what has now become the First Assembly of God....

Leonard Palmer was superintendent of the Montana District of the Assemblies of God from 1943 to 1948, and assistant superintendent and then superintendent of the Northern California District from 1956 to 1959. In the early 1990s, Leonard Palmer wrote the early history of the Assembly of God Church in Franklin, Nebraska. The above are excerpts from the history he wrote.

Tent Travels by Rail to Franklin for Camp

In conversations with Gordon Harmon, he recalled family stories of his maternal grandparents, Warren and Stella Pennock. The Pennocks lived in Hopeville, Iowa and were early Pentecostal believers. When the brethren in Franklin, Nebraska needed a tent for their camp, Gordon Millard contacted Warren Pennock. Warren packed up the huge tent, took it to the train depot in Murray, Iowa, and shipped it via rail to Franklin. Gordon's aunt, Margaret, told how the family was excited about this coming event. After discussion, the entire family, along with the teenage sisters Margaret and Opal, loaded their camping supplies in the touring car and traveled to Franklin for the camp meeting.

Opal Pennock attended the Midwest Bible School in Auburn. She later traveled with the Roy Scott Evangelistic Team. While in Oklahoma, she met and married Roy Harmon.

Roy and Opal Pennock Harmon's three sons, Dale, Milo and Gordon served as Assemblies of God ministers in Nebraska.

The church at Franklin has closed. At this writing, no record of the closing was found or reported.

Mrs. M. B. Woodworth-Etter in Fremont, Nebraska

In her book, Marvels and Miracles God Wrought in The Ministry for Forty-five Years, *Mrs Woodworth-Etter describes her experience in Fremont including her arrest and the response of the news media.*

I decided to respond to a call I had from Fremont, Nebraska, at this time... They had a good sized tent pitched, but it soon proved to be too small. We decided to have a larger tent pitched at a different and better location...

We soon had a large tent pitched that held about three thousand people, and God worked in a wonderful way, healing the sick and afflicted...

Media Response:

OPENING SERVICES ARE HELD IN TENT IN FREMONT—Claim Aged Woman Can Perform Miracles in Making the Hopelessly Crippled Walk and the Deaf Hear (Reprint from Press).

> People were dumbfounded at the apparent miracles that the healer performed in straightening the limbs of hopeless cripples and making the deaf to hear. Last evening, a woman who has gotten around on crutches for thirty years, threw them away and walked without their aid.
>
> One man who had not heard a sound for two years shouted and clapped his hands for joy, crying, "I can hear." Unbelievers were at a loss for the explanation when the miracles were performed before their very eyes.
>
> Mrs. Woodworth-Etter is a prepossessing and refined lady of seventy-six years. She smiled and talked pleasantly before the meeting. She does not claim to have any supernatural power or magic words other than through the power of Jesus Christ.
>
> Some were brought to the evangelist on cots and in wheel chairs while others struggled to the platform on canes and crutches. Cripples who had lost all hope

of every regaining their health or the use of their limbs were smiling with a new hope and confidence that had long since faded from their wasted faces.

Every train is bringing to Fremont people with every ailment imaginable. It seems that the entire country is filled with afflicted people and none of them are missing any chance for recovery."

EDITOR -- MRS. WOODWORTH-ETTER PREACHES: I do not perform these miracles. It is Christ who is the "Healer". I am only an instrument through whom He works. "The prayer of faith shall save the sick and the Lord shall raise him up."

Extract from Press. GREAT CROWD OUT SUNDAY TO HEAR THE FAITH HEALER

A crowd said to number approximately 5,000 people attended the tent meetings of Mrs. Woodworth-Etter on Sunday at the new location at the corner of Second and Union streets.

There is certainly considerable interest shown by the attendance of thousands of people. There was an assemblage of both Sunday afternoon and evening, the like of which has never been seen at any religious exercises ever held in the city. There were probably as many people around the outside of the seating space and in automobiles parked as closely as possible on the two sides of the street.

("At Fremont and Omaha, Nebraska." In *Marvels and Miracles God Wrought in The Ministry for Forty-five Years,* by Mrs. M. B. Woodworth-Etter. Indianapolis: the author, 1922, pp. 411, 413-414.)

Hindrances Arise
(by Mrs. M. B. Wooworth-Etter)

God worked wonderfully in our last three meetings, so that the report of what God was doing spread far and near. I knew that it would be just a matter of time till the devil would get so stirred that he would do his best to have the good work of God stopped, if he possibly could. In this place at the close of the campaign, he tried it by having us arrested for practicing medicine without a license. We anointed the people with a little Olive Oil, as the command is in James 5:14. This they interpreted as using medicine. I have been told that the sheriff was given a command to take us during an afternoon meeting, but that he refused to do so. At the close of a very good meeting, a nice machine [automobile] came and took myself and workers--all of them ordained ministers--before a tribunal where the charge was read to us. Of course we plead "Not guilty," as we were not guilty. The saints provided bail for us, and we went on with our evening meeting and finished as we were advertised. Our trial was to come off the following January, but was postponed because of sickness of prosecuting Attorney; so I was informed. When the time finally came, the charge was dismissed. Of course they had no case against us: but had we desired we could have made a good case against them, so I believe and have been advised. But I always look to Jesus Christ as my lawyer, and what I feel impressed by him to do, that I make it my business to do.

People ask me many times why I do not stick up for my rights, more than I do. I have only one answer to these questions, and that is this: "Jesus Christ has not sent me out to fight the authorities, but to preach the everlasting gospel of the Kingdom." If I would do this He would be with me. I have been doing my part the best I know how, and some way or another I find that He always comes to my rescue. I just know that He will do this, so why should I put my dependence on the arm of flesh. My faith is stronger in the Jesus who said, "All power is given unto me in heaven and on earth." The authorities have power over us just as far as God permits them to have. This is why I do as I do, when the devil tries to stop us through those that are in authority.

("Hindrances Arise." In *Marvels and Miracles God Wrought in The Ministry for Forty-five Years,* by Mrs. M. B. Woodworth-Etter. Indianapolis: the author, 1922, pp. 416-417.)

Testimonies from Fremont, Nebraska

Here is a letter sent to the Pentecostal Herald *which tells about God's blessings in Fremont, Nebraska in 1922.*

Dear Sis Etter:

I wish to write you and let you know that I am well. The anointed handkerchief you sent me I received and place it on my feet and I am .... . When this brother was here I was taken sick with diphtheria, they all prayed for me at Omaha on Sunday evening in the meeting. I got some better, but Monday morning I was worse again. I was very sick all that day. I can't ever tell anyone how sick I was. But I kept praising the Lord for the healing. Then they prayed three times for me that day. I was in the meeting that night. Praise the Lord the next day I was able to do quite a little work. And in three days I was as well as I had ever been. Had my four little children, one a baby eight months old, right here with me and not a one got sick. Oh! How we praise the Lord for His goodness to us. Brother and Sister Long [M. G.] came over last Sunday and we had six young folks baptized in water.

It makes my heart rejoice to see the young folks come to Jesus. Brother and Sister Long will be with us now from Friday till Sunday. The Lord blessed them with the car that they prayed for so many years. They surely needed it. It was the happiest day of my life when the Lord answered that prayer. They can be with us more now. We need them here to teach us God's Word. We praise God for this dear brother and sister. May God bless you all, dear brothers and sisters.

Please pray for me that I may be humble and obedient to God. Your sister in Christ Jesus, Mrs. James Z. Hybl

(Mrs. James Z. Hybl, *Pentecostal Herald,* January 1, 1922.)

*Fremont—Calvary Temple, 1981

The list of pastors includes Brad Riddle, William Howell, and Nathan Ennis.

*Geneva—Assembly of God, 1982

The list of pastors includes Ron Rice, Stephen Fulks, and Chris Hoyer.

*Gering—Northfield Assembly of God, 1934

Northfield Church, as it is known today, found its beginnings when the Holy Spirit moved among the young people during a youth endeavor in Scottsbluff. One young man, returning to Scottsbluff from Portland, Oregon, had been baptized with the Holy Spirit. He then testified about the power of God to the youth. Many of this rising generation received the Holy Spirit with evidence of speaking in tongues. This took place in meetings at a church of another denomination. Immediately following the church services, the Spirit continued to move as they met together in individual homes to study the Bible.

Shortly after this great outpouring of the Holy Spirit, the officials of this certain denomination asked the "Spirit-filled" group to leave their church. The group withdrew, upon their request, and remained in search of God's leading, eager to see many of the German people receive Christ and be filled with the Spirit. Channeled in the direction of Rev. C.W. Loenser, Superintendent of the German Branch of the Assemblies of God, they received guidance....

It was the George E. Nazarenus family who opened their small home to be the meeting place of what became known as the "German Assembly of God." Regular Sunday morning and evening and Wednesday evening services were established with consistent attendance. The singing and preaching were done in the German language, while the Sunday school classes were taught in English. As the church began to become more established, a German-speaking pastor was sought. Rev. Fred Zeller answered God's call and thus became the charter pastor of the small, home-based congregation.

The first building program was birthed on July 13, 1935, with the formation of a building committee. The decision to build followed on July 22, 1935, and land was purchased at 12th Street and 11th Avenue in Scottsbluff. The total cost of the land and building was approximately $1,200. During the late summer and fall of 1937, the church board consented to building a parsonage. Rev. Alfred Jenson, who was a mason by trade, constructed the parsonage directly behind the church, with the continued help and support of the congregation. The addition of the parsonage was for the housing of not only the resident pastor, but for visiting evangelists and missionaries as well.... On June 10, 1945, a building project was promoted to expand the existing basement sanctuary with an upper-level, stucco addition. Once again the building project required prayer and the combined efforts of the congregation to complete the task. The willingness and fortitude of P. J. Hessler and Henry Schott, along with their valuable carpentry and building skills, led to the completion of the upper-level sanctuary.

Church services continued to be conducted in the German language and were of an evangelistic style. A spiritual hunger drew in crowds of 80 to 90 people, filling all the wooden-slatted folding chairs available, during the special meetings and revival outreach services. A German choir began in 1947 under the direction of Rev. Arthur Noetzel and warmly complemented the worship services. Their vibrant, happy singing enriched the congregation‘s emphasis on praise and worship in song. Those attending services during the ministry of Rev. Chris Stoudt in 1949 were led into expanding their body ministry—that is, praying for one another.... The church name was then changed to, "Full Gospel Tabernacle." Separate services were then scheduled in both the German and English languages.

The late 1950s mark a time of struggling growth for the church. Again God used the youth group and they made a significant contribution to the life of the church by cultivating attendance of other youth and ultimately bringing the church back into a vibrant, victorious lifeline. The zeal of this group resulted in meaningful time around the altar and six of the twenty-five youth eventually going into full-time ministry.

In 1967, a decision was made to purchase property for a new church building in Gering. Groundbreaking ceremonies were held in August of 1967 for the new sanctuary to be called, "Northfield Church".... As the church moved into the new sanctuary, the way was paved for additional ministry opportunities.... The Sunday school was growing and received acclaim in the state promotional campaign. Immediately following the joy experienced during the growth came a numerical decline in 1970. However, the congregation that remained continued on with the spirit of sacrifice and hearts of faith. God answered the people‘s prayers in a thrilling way with that time period ending in the Charismatic move upon the worshippers. It was a time of "giving up" traditional programs, contests, and competitions in order to bring about growth and maturity, and a time of "giving in" to relying totally on the Holy Spirit to orchestrate what needed to take place to complete His work.

Between 1974 and 1976, the church experienced a tremendous growth from 30 to 300 in attendance. In efforts to accommodate what Rev. Inman called a "spiritual renewal", an addition of a new sanctuary and office complex was proposed, accepted, completed and finally dedicated in July of 1976. The new sanctuary would allow the seating of 600 people for worship services. More additions to the building have been made and new ministries have been added....

The pastors of this congregation include G. Fred Zeller, Alfred Jensen, Jacob Rosine, Alvin Sprecher, Arthur Noetzel, Chris Stoudt, Edgar Moos, Edward M. Herrman, Larry V. Newman, Donald F. Stuckless, Paul Hebbert, John Stocker, Terry Inman, Dave Geary, George Cuff, William Bibb, David Houck, Tim Gross, and Leonard Reimer.

*Gibbon—Glad Tidings Assembly of God, 1953

In July 1953, the late Frank Sobotka, a native of Gibbon, Nebraska, and a minister in the Pentecostal Fellowship of the Assemblies of God, returned to his home town to hold a tent revival at Davis Park. This revival lasted for a month. The results of this revival were the erection of a church building and the organization of the Glad Tidings Assembly of God. In August 1953, property was purchased north of Highway 30. A church building was moved in from Eldorado, Nebraska, and repaired and remodeled by volunteer labor. The church was dedicated on November 3, 1953, with Rev. Sobotka preaching. Rev. Clyde Buck then became the first pastor, starting with fourteen charter members. In March 1955, the residence next to the church was purchased for a parsonage.

Glad Tidings Assembly of God celebrated its 10th Anniversary, November 3, 1963, with Rev. Buck as guest speaker. On July 11, 1965, a special service featuring the burning of the parsonage mortgage was held thus clearing all property debts. In 1975, the church purchased the parking lot south of the church property and a 54-passenger bus. In October 1975, the congregation added on a 40‘ x 50‘ sanctuary. Christmas Sunday 1975 was the first service in the new sanctuary.

The pastors include Clyde S. Buck, J. J. Kisser, Clifford Tuton, Rose Hallgrimson, Robert McCowen, Gordon Fraser, Harley Stahl, D. B. Arnold, Lawrence Gilmore, Bryan Correll, Harvey Herman, Richard Vernon, Mark Wetzler, and Larry Booze.

Hispanic Ministry at Gibbon

... From there we went to Gibbon, Nebraska. There was a small group of believers and soon after we arrived, the Lord began moving and gave us a mighty revival. So great was the visitation of the Lord night after night that the services would last until a late hour and often those under the anointing had to be picked up bodily and placed in vehicles. The blessing would continue even after they got home.

We met in a rented hall and immediately began a building program. In July, 1947, we held the dedication of the new church, debt-free. To God be the glory! ...

(Ysidro Ramirez, "Hispanic Ministry at Gibbon," *Reflections of Faith*, 1983.)

*Gothenburg—Victory Assembly of God, 1993

The only pastor to date (1998) is Jimmy Root, Jr.

Grand Island Receives the Gospel

Evangelist Edgar W. White and wife and myself began a meeting in the Cherry Street Dance Hall on Oct. 7, 1927. Over 40 have sought the Lord for salvation and many sick bodies have been healed. This is a new field and the Lord is working in a marvelous way. People starving for the Living Bread are becoming satisfied. ~ H. M. Steinle

("Grand Island Receives the Gospel," *The Pentecostal Evangel,* November 5, 1927, p. 12.)

*Grand Island—Abundant Life Christian Center, 1927

"Brother Larson, do you have any of God‘s money on hand?" Mr. Ivan Reed posed the question to Freudulph Larson in 1927. Mr. Larson chuckled as he answered his friend in the affirmative. Not only would he contribute to the need but he and his family could be counted on to come to the meetings. The three men talked excitedly of what God would do in Grand Island, then prayed together, committing the new faith venture to God.

Mr. Reed had traveled that day from Grand Island to Boelus to introduce Mr. Larson to Harley Ketner, a preacher of his acquaintance. Both Mr. Reed and Mr. Ketner believed it to be God‘s time for a full gospel meeting in Grand Island but they lacked the financial resources to rent a building. Mr. Reed explained to Mr. Larson that he could rent the Cherry Street Dance Hall and that Mr. Ketner would be willing to begin the desired meetings almost immediately. Mr. Ketner was a fiery gospel preacher and singer, a seasoned veteran in the relatively new full gospel movement. Mr. Ketner was affiliated with the Assemblies of God fellowship, which at that time was 13 years old. He had preached full gospel meetings in other Nebraska cities and now it was time for Grand Island.

The meeting was billed as "An Old Fashioned Revival Meeting." There would be good music and singing with services beginning at eight o'clock each evening. There would be "Special Divine Healing Services where the sick would be prayed for." And, everyone was welcome!"

From that gospel meeting in a dance hall a church was born. A three-month, every night of the week, meeting was begun with Evangelist Edgar White and following that meeting Mr. White was chosen to be the first pastor of the new church. It was decided to call the church "The Old Fashioned Church." During the first three years the congregation met in two storefront locations on Fourth Street. When Mr. White resigned to become the District Superintendent, Emmit R. Foster was chosen as the new pastor. Under his leadership in early 1930 the people of the new "Old Fashioned Church" agreed to incorporate and to purchase the former Trinity Methodist Church building at Sixth and Sycamore for $5,000 (with terms). This would be the home of the church for the next twenty-five years. God's blessing was upon the fledgling group, even though by then the Great Depression was on.

During this time Pastor Foster established the Assembly of God Church in Aurora in addition to pastoring the Grand Island church. Pastor Foster resigned in 1933 and Rev. White was asked to serve again as pastor, remaining until 1937. Silas Rexroat succeeded him and remained until 1941. B. H. Armes served until late 1945 and was succeeded by Harold Champlin. Under Pastor Champlin's leadership the people were motivated to relocate and build, securing the property at 15th and Eddy. Prior to the start of construction he resigned and on July 28, 1955, Erwin Rohde was chosen as pastor. Almost immediately plans were completed and approved and construction started on the new site. The people of the church, under Pastor Rohde's skillful leadership, built the lovely brick building with almost no outside help. Total construction costs were less than $40,000.00. Pastor Rohde was a progressive man of vision. In addition to constructing the building, he placed the first assistant pastor on staff. This quiet, but effective leader took many other steps of faith. In November 1966 he became the pastor of Central Assembly in Great Falls, Montana and Gene Arnold was chosen to succeed him.

The present twenty-seven acre campus on U. S. Highway 281 and Faidley Avenue was purchased in 1978. The first building on the new site was occupied on November 8, 1981. Since moving to the new location there have been two major building projects completed with all mortgage debt paid in full. Construction on a new office building began in August 1987 with completion by the end of that year. The building at 15th and Eddy was given as a gift to our new sister church, Calvary Assembly of God, in December 1986....

Pastors include Edgar White, Emmit Foster, Edgar White, Silas Rexroat, B. H. Armes, H. D. Champlin, E. E. Rohde, D. E. Arnold, and Steve Warriner.

*Grand Island—Calvary Assembly of God, 1985

Calvary Assembly of God is the official name chosen by the congregation of the new Assemblies of God church being started in Grand Island. The Rev. Robert L. Porter is pastor. Services are being held at Barr Junior High school, 602 W. Stolley Park Road.

This is the announcement given the church by the Grand Island Independent:

Services at Calvary Assembly of God began January 20, 1985. The Sunday morning attendance averaged 55. As the church grew they started to look for a place to buy or build. Then in September 1986 they were given a wonderful gift from the Abundant Life Christian Center. ALCC felt directed of the Lord to give their Children's facility at 15th and Eddy to Calvary Assembly. This came as a big surprise to the congregation and at that time they realized God was moving in a supernatural way. It was truly a blessing.

This building was actually home to many of the members as it had been the Assembly of God church built by Pastor E. E. Rohde in 1955. The church has experienced the many growing pains of a new congregation but God is faithful and with the sound Biblical teaching of Terry Brown the church has really stabilized. Missions are becoming a vital part of the church budget and prayer life. The church reaches out to families through a vital children's and youth ministry.

The list of pastors includes Robert Porter, Michael Neff and Terry Brown.

*Grand Island—Vida Nueva, 1995

The pastor of this congregation is Carlos Barcenas.

Chapter 10: Hastings through Lyons

"Enter into his gates with thanksgiving, and into his courts with praise: be thankful unto him, and bless his name." **(Psalm 100:4 KJV)**

*Hastings—North Shore Assembly of God, 1931

During the year of 1931 Evangelists Snow and Allensworth held a revival at the Chatauqua Park. From those services, a small band of believers began meeting in an old harness shop on First Street. Later that year, Evangelist E. N. Stanley came to hold services and stayed on to pastor the church. Under his leadership, the church was organized with a board of deacons and members. At that time property was purchased at South Hastings and C Street for $600 and the Full Gospel Tabernacle was built.

In 1945, the church building located on South Hastings and C Street was sold. A new building and parsonage were erected at 400 South Burlington. Building materials were scarce due to the war, so the men and boys of the church made their own bricks. The body of believers grew and soon more room was needed. A house at 400 South Lexington was purchased to provide a home for the Lebsacks, which allowed the previous parsonage to be converted into additional classrooms. As the congregation grew, it was apparent that more space was needed. In April 1967 the church began to build a new sanctuary and educational facility at 400 South Burlington. On July 9, 1967, the cornerstone for the church was laid, completing the building. Because of donated labor, construction expense was a low $75,000. In March of 1972, the church retired the debt against the building. On September 16, 1973, a new parsonage was completed and the old parsonage was moved to another location. The lot was turned into much needed parking space.

In 1976, after serving the church for 24 years, the Lebsacks retired to Colorado. Wayne Woody moved to Hastings from Odessa, Texas, to pastor the church. Under his leadership the bus ministry was expanded and Mrs. Woody laid the foundation for the Children's Church ministry. The church experienced revival with many souls coming to the Lord and growth in the Sunday school. During this time Terry Brown arrived to become the first youth pastor. In August of 1978, Dale Harmon accepted the position as Senior Pastor.... The house behind the church was purchased to use as an annex for classrooms. In 1985, Ted Britain took over the leadership of the congregation. Joe Masten moved to Hastings to be the youth pastor. Pastor Britain was instrumental in acquiring land in the North Shore subdivision along Highway 281. A building committee was initiated. After much time in planning, a tentative design was recommended. It was the birth of a vision for this body of believers. In 1988 the Britains moved to Idaho and Joe Masten accepted the position as Senior Pastor. Under Pastor Masten's leadership, the congregation began the stewardship program, giving of their resources to fund the building of a new worship center.

In July 1992, Ted Brust moved from Arizona to shepherd this flock. Due to the crowded sanctuary and classrooms, a committee was formed to proceed with the construction process.... In the fall of 1993, ground was broken to begin the first of a three phase building project located at 100 West 33rd Street. On February 13, 1994, the congregation chose the name "North Shore Assembly of God" for the new church....

Since the humble beginnings in 1931, God has poured out his blessings upon the church. Much planning and an abundance of prayers over the years have been shown and now we benefit from all those godly endeavors. We find ourselves in a wonderful facility that serves a multitude of needs. The building is being used as a tool to reach the community of Hastings with the gospel of God's love.

Pastors include Gordon Millard, W. O. Zigler, S. D. Garrett, Rev. Appleyard, Milton Smith, Guy Heath, John Waldron, B. C. Heinze, H. W. Lebsack, Wayne Woody, Dale Harmon, Ted Britain, Joe Masten, Ted Brust and Solomon Wang.

*Hebron—New Life Assembly of God, 1976

The nucleus for the New Life Assembly came into being when the Lord began touching hungry hearts of people in the Ruskin and Deshler areas in 1972. Through personal witness and the work of the Holy Spirit the number of individuals being born again and filled with the Spirit grew and the need for a meeting place prompted the purchase of a storefront building in Deshler in 1973. The building was named "The Lighthouse." Rev. Gene Boone who was led to come to the area about this time was a great help as he ministered to the group of young Christians. Services at the Lighthouse continued and included evangelistic meetings, ladies prayer and praise gatherings and youth activities.... September 8, 1976 Rev. James Wilkins met with the believers at the Lighthouse and introduced them to the Assemblies of God and their beliefs.

Rev. James Burnette came to candidate for pastor on September 26, 1976 and the vote of the people was "yes." Pastor Burnette and his musical family moved into the parsonage in Hebron on November 3. The first service of New Life Assembly was held November 7, 1976 with twenty-four attending. The body of believers met in the parsonage on Sunday mornings and in the rented Presbyterian Church for evening services for about three years. Later the morning services were held in the Lighthouse.

Property was purchased in Hebron in 1978 and dirt work began on the proposed earth-bermed church April 2, 1980. That same month an Easter sunrise service was held on the site. New Life Assembly at 1220 Union Street in Hebron was dedicated July 12, 1981.

The list of pastors includes James Burnette, Al Weiss, Tim Torrey, and Hugh Campbell.

Aimee Semple McPherson Campaign at Holdrege, 1919

Aimee Semple McPherson, Evangelist, Coming to Holdrege. The New York Press calls Mrs. McPherson the "Woman Billy Sunday." Old Time Power, Simple Gospel of Calvary and Pentecost.

The State Convention of the Assemblies of God and great revival campaign conducted by Aimee Semple McPherson, of Los Angeles, California, will be held at the Auditorium in Holdrege Oct. 12 to Oct. 26. Great preparations are being made for this meeting.

("The Aimee Semple McPherson Campaign at Holdrege, Phelps County," [Newspaper], Thursday, October 2 & 9, 1919.)

McPherson Campaign

In Nebraska Sister Aimee Semple McPherson has just closed a remarkable revival campaign at Holdrege, Nebr., lasting fifteen days. The meeting attracted a large number from several states. A goodly number were saved and a notable feature of the meeting was that nearly all the long-time seekers who came, received the baptism in the Holy Spirit. The mighty power of God was manifest from the beginning; the large stage that we used for the altar services was often literally covered by the slain of the Lord.

The local effect we believe to be all that we could have hoped for in the fifteen days meeting in a new place. Holdrege people had never seen a Pentecostal meeting before. There was no assembly nearer than forty miles. It was a strange thing for their great auditorium to be quietly engaged for a fifteen days' meeting at a rental of $50.00 a day by an unheard of people, calling themselves "The Assemblies of God." The advance advertising was given by the leading paper, whole columns of it unstintedly free of charge. The curiosity was great. The people came, thousands of them, from towns and surrounding country night after night. Sister McPherson's message of the cross drew the people and filled the great building night after night without the backing of any organization of local ministers and churches. It was a wonderful thing to capture the hearts of the people, pour in the marvelous truths of Pentecost with sweetness and overmastering logic. They were thrilled with Pentecostal signs, singing, and testimony. The last night the building, with its galleries, was full in spite of the fact that the weather was stormy and that a union Roosevelt Memorial meeting was being held in the large Methodist church. The great throng of 3,000 people were left reverent, tearful, inquiring and longing for the meeting to continue. Conviction was deep and pungent. A great number crowded around the altar and hung on till the lights went out. A leading business man told us the next morning that the people were just waking up when the meeting closed. We believe a week more should have been given to the campaign, but Sister McPerson felt that she could not remain longer at this time. As it is, we rejoice that the glorious truths of Pentecost have had so favorable a presentation to thousands of people. It simply shows what God's people can do when they will co-operate for the evangelization of new fields.

Our State Council was organized in July with J. C. Rediger, of Milford, Chairman, and G. W. Clopine of North Platte, Secretary and Treasurer. All the Assemblies of God in the state united in the movement to bring Sister McPherson into Nebraska for one great meeting. Bro. J. W. Welch, Chairman of the General Council, felt the great importance of the movement in Nebraska enough to come out and spend five days with us. Bro. Arch P. Collins, of the Colorado Council, and Brothers W. T. Millsaps, S. H. Patterson and C. A. Beckman, of the Kansas Council, were here and gave hearty support and encouragement.

We are looking forward to Sister McPhersons' coming again in June if the Lord tarries. In the meantime we are planning as God leads, to make Holdrege the center for an extensive evangelistic campaign to follow the good work begun. In this connection we are glad to mention that Bro. W. H. Pope and party, of Oklahoma, are to open a campaign here (D. V.) Nov. 9th, in the Congregational church. Let the saints pray earnestly that God will do a mighty work in this section of the country before Jesus come. ~ Hermon L. Harvey.

("McPherson Campaign," *Pentecostal Evangel*, November 15, 1919, p. 10.)

Many Traveled to Holdrege for the Aimee Semple McPherson Campaign

People traveled to Holdrege from across Nebraska, Kansas and many other states. Roads, weren't paved, few were graveled and stop signs weren't frequent until 1928. In 1928, stop signs with uniform design were erected wherever a road crossed any of the state highways all over Nebraska! Travel by train was more efficient and rails crisscrossed the state

Olafur and Skulina Hallgrimson were one couple from Long Pine, Nebraska the made the trip to Holdrege in 1919. They were driven to Burwell by their son, Balder (George) over trails through the Sand Hills. At Burwell they took a train to attend a few nights of Aimee Simple McPherson Revival.

That is where they both received their Baptism of the Holy Spirit!

*Holdrege—North Park Assembly of God, 1955

It was in 1955, under the leadership of Ted Beyers, that a small nucleus of people began to meet for worship in an old portable building. Under the authority of the Nebraska District Council of the Assemblies of God and in cooperation with the General Council, the group soon organized as an Assembly of God congregation. Rev. Beyers took the congregation through its first building program as the congregation erected a church building at Fifth Avenue and Tibbais in Holdrege.

The Rev. H. H. DeMent assumed the leadership of the church in 1961. During his tenure the congregation put up a new parsonage at 125 West 5th Avenue. Pastor DeMent led the congregation until 1966 when Steve Groseclose was elected. Earl Goodman pastored the church from 1969-1970. In 1971 Preston Hollis became the pastor, and following him was Ted Brust who came to the church in 1973 and remained until 1978. It was during Pastor's Brust's ministry that property was acquired at 14th and Burlington. It is interesting to note that both DeMent and Brust left Holdrege after being elected as the State Directors of Youth and Christian Education of the Nebraska District Council of the Assemblies of God. In 1979 Bob Satterlee became pastor of the Assembly. Feeling the pressure of limited space Satterlee led the congregation through another building project as a new church facility was constructed at 14th and Burlington. It consisted of a 300-seat auditorium, with a prayer room, choir room, Sunday school rooms, offices, fellowship hall, kitchen, nursery and rest rooms. When the congregation moved into the new building its name changed to North Park Assembly.

Pastor Satterlee finished his task of building then moved on in 1981. Rev. James Boardman who ministered until 1983 followed him. Rev. Tim Thomas was called to lead the congregation. In 1988 he followed the call of God to a ministry in Chicago.

Rev. Marvin Fulks came on the scene in 1988 and is credited with leading the congregation through a major building project. During its 35th anniversary year on August 26, 1990, the congregation dedicated a beautiful addition. It contains four offices, a conference room, library, nine classrooms, restrooms, showers, a kitchen and a gym, which serves as a multi-purpose room. Rev. Fulks resigned in August of 1992 and was followed by Rev. Jim Wilkins, who came from the San Francisco Bay Area where he oversaw the work of Central Assembly of Richmond and Ed Sorbrante Christian School. Rev. Wilkins was well known to many members of the Holdrege congregation as he had previously served two other congregations in Nebraska. He also held the position of State Director of Youth and Christian Education for the Nebraska District, and just prior to moving to the West Coast completed twelve years as the District Superintendent of the Assemblies of God in Nebraska. Pastor Wilkins resigned as pastor in 1997 and Rev. Bruce Dailey was called to fill the position of pastor.

Dedication of Kearney, Nebraska Assembly

It was in July, 1954, when a number of brethren gathered in Kearney, Nebraska (a city of 15,000), and pitched a tent, at 26th Street and Avenue "G". Revival services were started at once with F. L. Sobotka as evangelist. Brother Sobotka grew up in Kearney as a Catholic, and this fact attracted many to the meetings. Nearby pastors and their congregations helped in the services.

Interest was excellent and a number of people desired an Assemblies of God church in their city. We were asked to come and establish a church, and after much prayer we resigned the church at Lexington, Nebraska and took up our duties here.

We were granted the use of a hall (rent free) for the services, and it was our church for over three years. Seven people attended our first Sunday School session. Since then we have had a steady growth and are now averaging about sixty.

Construction of a new church at 28th Street and Avenue "H" was started in October, 1956. The building is 45 x 70 feet and has a full basement. It is a frame structure, veneered with "rose velour" split tile.

We have $15,000 invested in the property which has been appraised at $40,000. Only $1,500 was paid out for labor. We owe at present approximately $7,000. We are grateful to the W.M.C.'s of the district who gave a total of $3,000 toward our property and building program.

Dedication services were held May 6, 1958, with 250 people in attendance. Speakers of the day were Clyde King, district secretary-treasurer, Roscoe Leach, district C. A. president and L. W. Dickinson, district superintendent.

We are very grateful to the Lord for the wonderful group of people He has given us here. Also we appreciate the way in which the district stood by us in this new field venture.

(L. E.. Wilkins: "New Church in Nebraska," *The Pentecostal Evangel*, December 21, 1958, p. 9.)

*Kearney—New Life Assembly of God, 1954

... It was July 1954, when a number of pastors gathered in Kearney, and pitched a tent on a vacant lot at the corner of 26th Street and Avenue G. Services there were conducted by a native of Kearney, Rev. Frank Sobotka. Brother Sobotka grew up in Kearney as a Catholic, and this fact attracted many to the meetings. Nearby pastors and their congregations helped in the services. Interest was excellent and a number of people desired an Assembly of God church in their city. Subsequently, Sunday school classes and worship services were conducted in the old Youth Center above the old J. M. McDonald store in downtown Kearney. This hall was granted to the church rent-free and it housed the congregation for over three years. Rev. L. E. Wilkins became the first pastor. Seven people attended the first Sunday school session. Since then the church has seen a steady increase in this area.

The congregation built a new structure at 28th Street and Avenue H and moved into it in February 1958. The second pastor, Rev. D. R. Nelson, was elected in February 1972, and led the growing congregation in an addition to their facility. The present pastor, Rev. Bob Wine, became the third minister of the fellowship in October 1979. People responded to the congregation's contagious friendliness and on Palm Sunday 1983, they moved into a newly constructed facility located at 2715 West 39th Street, their present site. Growth from their dynamic ministry to the youth and children made it necessary for the construction of additional classrooms and a multi-purpose room. In 1991 they occupied their second building phase at the site. A third phase of construction is now being planned that will provide needed classroom and office space for their growing services to people in south central Nebraska.

The people place a high priority on contemporary and personal heartfelt worship, a variety of styles of home fellowship/Bible studies for adults they call "agape" groups, "Impact" (youth) as well as graded opportunities for children. Also important to them are their "Chi Alpha" (college) ministry and Sonshine World, a ministry to preschool children.

The list of pastors includes L. E. Wilkins, D. R. Nelson and Bob Wine.

*Kimball—Assembly of God, 1956 (reopened in 1976)

The list of pastors includes Robert L. Courtney, M. D. Markland, Jerry Hackett, J. D. Winscott, Eldon Mincks, James Mazurek, Max Graves, and Daniel Zitterkopf.

*Lexington—Calvary Assembly of God, 1936

The first pastors were Brother and Sister Herold Robeson. Times were hard, sometimes they didn't have groceries. Their little girl would go over to Ella Wilsey's apartment and Ella would give her pancakes. The church building was a portable tabernacle, supplied by the Nebraska District. It was erected on the Northwest corner of 12th and Harrison Street. The floor was gravel, the front had sawdust with old carpets over it so people could kneel at the altar benches. The only heat was from a pot-bellied stove that took tremendous amounts of wood and coal. It wasn't unusual to have rocks thrown on the roof and sides during services. Some people called it a sheep shed. What they didn't know was that the Lord was there, blessing His people and souls were being saved.

In 1937 the Robesons left the District and Brother and Sister Archie Duncan from Colorado came to pastor the church. Mildred Duncan became the minister, while Archie did the cooking, took care of their two children and led the song services.... It was time to have a permanent home for the church so a country church, 14 miles southwest of Lexington, was found. The church building was purchased for $500, which included the cost of moving the building. The building was moved to Lexington, painted and papered inside. It was dedicated debt free. It was the Lord that provided.

Brother and Sister Charles Blodgett followed the Duncans in ministry to the congregation. At this time another building by Elwood was purchased and torn down and the lumber was used to build a parsonage behind the church. (A number of the ladies helped pull nails.) While Cloyd Sailors was the pastor the church bought the lots across the street to the east of the church building. They moved the parsonage and put a full basement under it. In 1945-46 a new church was built from cement blocks and lumber from the old church. The men of the church and Brother Waldron, from Hastings, did the work. He later built the church in Hastings just like the one in Lexington. It took an enormous amount of cement for the church. Sometimes the work would have to stop until the money could be raised....

In 1969 Wayne and Hazel Hall came to be the pastors. At this time the people were getting excited about going into another building program. It was decided to sell the church and parsonage. It was sold on contract for $7500. The District allowed the church to have services at the District campgrounds. Services were held in Alber Hall for four years. Property was purchased on the corner of 13th and Adams. The cost seemed high, but with the congregation, the Nebraska District and many friends of the church, cash was paid for it. The cost of the land was $16,000. This was purchased in October of 1971 with less than $50 left in the building fund. The fund was replenished and a new building was dedicated to the Lord on May 24, 1974 at the cost of $115,000. On January 1, 1997 Joe and Tammy Masten became the pastors of the church....

The list of pastors includes Herold Robeson, Mildred Duncan, Charles Blodgett, Douglas Snyder, Cloyd Sailors, L. E. Wilkins, Milo Harmon, Dale Eden, Nolan Blakkolb, Clinton Thompson, Wayne Hall, George Jacobs, Clyde Brummett, Reggie Ballard, LeRoy Hopper, Henry Mohn and Joe Masten.

*Lincoln—First Assembly of God

The Pentecostal message came to Lincoln around 1930 when a group of people began to meet in a church at 21st and N Street. Rev. D. L. Cooper served as minister. Some members of that original congregation are still a part of First Assembly of God of Lincoln. The church moved to the larger building at 26th and Y and Rev. Thomas became the pastor in 1933. During the ministry of Rev. Thomas the church affiliated with the Assemblies of God. In the year of 1934 the church moved again to 15th and Q and Rev. and Mrs. Glen Millard became pastors and served for five years. Rev. and Mrs. M. F. Brandt accepted the pastorate in 1939 and under his leadership the property at 12th and

D Street was purchased. Rev. Brandt served the church for six years. He left the church to become the District Superintendent.

The L. W. Dickinsons came to Lincoln as pastors in 1945 and they too served six years and then he was elected as District Superintendent. Norman Correll acted as interim pastor for several months until Rev. and Mrs. Biffle, Jr. took up their duties as pastors in 1951. After the purchase of property at 29th and Randolph, First Assembly was instrumental in the beginning of two new Assemblies. One remained to worship at 12th and D and became known as Glad Tidings and the other is in Havelock, later known as Christian Life Fellowship. Ground was purchased at 56th and R in January of 1960 and a new structure was completed in 1961. A lovely new parsonage was added in 1962 and the west educational wing, fellowship hall, nursery and kitchen were added to the church building in 1968. There have been other additions and remolding since that time. The Biffles stayed for 17 years, then accepted a pastorate in Ohio.

The list of pastors include D. L. Cooper, Rev. Thomas, Glen Millard, M. F. Brandt, Lester W. Dickinson, S. K. Biffle, Jr., Daniel Rothwell, Jack Glass, Geoffrey Duncombe, Randy Dugger, and John Burpee.

*Lincoln—Christian Life Fellowship, 1951

This congregation was known as the Havelock Assembly of God until 1977 when the name was changed to Christian Life Fellowship. The list of pastors includes A. H. Edwards, J. Robert Birdwell, and Max Graves.

*Lincoln—Glad Tidings Assembly of God, 1954

In 1954 the Rev. John W. Smith, the first pastor of Glad Tidings Assembly of God came to Lincoln in search of a site for his church. It happened that the First Assembly of God Church was moving. They were looking for a buyer for the old building. Rev. S. K. Biffle, the pastor of First Assembly of God and Rev. Smith got together and negotiated for the sale of the building. Only one thing blocked the sale. Rev. Smith did not have enough money. The dejected pastor went back to his home in Kansas City, Missouri, where he was in evangelistic work, to find a way to raise the money. A short time later a friend came to him and offered to put up enough money to complete the sale. As a result Rev. Smith, his wife, Mary Ann, and son, moved to Lincoln. The church building had a varied history as a place of worship. Located at 12th and D, it was a Lutheran Church before the First Assembly of God congregation bought it. Before that it was a Jewish synagogue.

... The first Sunday Rev. Smith conducted services the only persons there were his wife, son, sister Bettie Smith and Martha M. Tagge. The next Sunday three persons other than his family attended the service. The next week that new person brought two of her friends and since that time attendance has steadily increased until soon there were more than 125 in attendance. After one year, in July 1955, Glad Tidings Assembly of God was dedicated.... The congregation grew until it reached the place where they needed a larger building and better facilities. On April 29, 1962, there was a groundbreaking service directly behind the old church.... Floyd Roll, one of the men from the Milford Assembly ... volunteered to bring his machinery and men to come and demolish the old church.... The new $35,000 structure including an auditorium, classrooms, education wing and a full basement was built next to the old building.

The list of pastors include John W. Smith, Gerald Spain, Nolan Blokkolb, Warren Gobel, Dan Thompson, and Chris Anderson.

*Lincoln—Christ's Place, 1976

Christ's Place was birthed in the prayers and dreams of several close friends as a creative alternative to the more traditional Pentecostal/Charismatic church. In the spring of 1975 this small core of people met to plan the beginnings of this new church. The first service was held on August 3, 1975, in the Cotner School of Religion located on the city campus. There were 26 people in attendance. The day started with a fellowship meal shared around two tables. Worship was then held and a teaching by Dave Argue followed. There were only six children at that time, the oldest being seven years and the youngest being an infant. There was no children's program.

As the church grew, the need for a larger facility became apparent. The goal being to always rent, Christ's Place then moved, in February 1976, to the Knights of Pythias building on the corner of 13th and Q. In the beginning, Sunday school consisted of one class taught by people on a six-week rotation. A nursery was held in the basement....

After five years (1980), the need for a new Sunday site once again became urgent. It was eventually decided to rent the Capitol View Seventh Day Adventist Church on 17th and Streets. We now had 219 in attendance, the majority of whom were young married couples. This meant that we also had a large growth in the number of children we were ministering to on Wednesdays and Sundays. By 1984, it was apparent that the congregation was "bursting at the seams." The search began, once again, for another rental facility.... Over 75 options were evaluated, however, there was nothing in Lincoln for rent that was suitable for the 400 people who now called Christ's Place their church home. Thus, the idea to erect a multipurpose building that was functional, roomy, durable, and yet attractive became the focus....

In 1991-92, the church expanded in two ways: 1) through the addition of 6400 square feet of space in two new wings to the original building, and 2) through sending 10% of those worshipping with us and 10% of our general funds with Pastor Randy and Christie Bartelt to begin a new church in northwest Lincoln, Highlands Community Church. For the last few years, we have now seen the Sunday attendance reach 1000, with missions giving projected to exceed $200,000 this year....

Pastor Dave Argue has been the only pastor of Christ's Place as of this writing, 1999.

*Lincoln—Highlands Community Church, 1995

Randy Bartelt has been the only pastor of this congregation so far.

Lincoln Revival Changes Lives

The following two articles by Bob Reeves appeared in the Lincoln Journal Star, *Lincoln, Nebraska on June 21, 1997. Used by permission.*

Love and mercy, fill my senses;
I am thirsty for Your presence;
Lord come and fill me up.

The words from a contemporary Christian praise song filled the air. Worshipers at Lincoln's First Assembly of God raised their hands in the air, swayed and stomped to the music. They felt the Holy Spirit moving in their souls.

"I can feel the river of God flowing through this place," evangelist Julaine Christensen exclaimed. Then she belted out another song with a pounding beat and chord patterns reminiscent of the Beatles or the Rolling Stones.

The message, however, was strongly Christian. "Let all fear and unbelief leave this place right now, in the name of Jesus," Christensen said. "Shake off everything you brought in except Jesus. Shake it off now."

Some people knelt on the floor and bowed their heads in their pews. Some had tears in their eyes. Others came to the front of the church and dropped to their knees or fell on the floor, "slain in the Spirit."

The dose of old-time religion with a contemporary music flair has infused new life into the Lincoln church, said it's pastor, Randall Dugger.

"People are hungry to see God touch their lives," he said. "We've seen so much happen. It's something that's stretching our minds and transforming us."

Dugger said many people have made a commitment to Christ and many others have renewed their faith since Christensen held her first three-day revival at the church in early May.

Christensen, an Omaha-based evangelist, returns to Lincoln to conduct weekly "renewal" services each Thursday evening. More than 200 people attended each session of the initial revival, and almost 100 attend the Thursday night services, which lasted up to three hours.

A number of faith healings reportedly have occurred during the services, Dugger said. Some people report physical healings; many more say they have been freed from addictions to drugs, alcohol--even overeating.

The church decided to invite Christensen to conduct the revival after 20 people from the Lincoln church spent a week at Brownsville Assembly of God in Pensacola, Fla., in early April. The Brownsville church has received national publicity for a mammoth, ongoing revival. More than 1 million people from throughout the United States--and many other countries--have flocked to the Florida church seeking salvation and healing. A sign outside the church claims that more than 100,000 people have been saved since the revival began two years ago.

Dugger believes that what's happening in his church could be the beginning of a similar phenomenon--albeit on a smaller scale--in Lincoln.

"It's a sovereign move of God; it's something we prayed for," Dugger said. "God wants to stretch our minds and let us know He's real."

Eleven-year-old Tiffany Lenhoff has no doubts that something very real happened to her during one of the revival meetings. She had hip surgery in 1995, and one leg was shorter than the other. Doctors told her she'd need another operation some day to stop the growth in her right leg so the left side could catch up.

But at the altar, while Christensen and her parents prayed over her, Tiffany said, she could feel her left leg getting longer.

"I felt a burning in my left leg," she said, "You could just sit there and watch it grow." Asked what caused her leg to change, Tiffany replied, "A real move of God was happening that night."

"I could see her foot moving in my hand," said her father, Wayne Lenhoff. "Then we put her up against the wall, and her leg was all the way straightened out. They were both the same length."

So far, no physician has examined Tiffany to verify the cure, but the girl has quit wearing shoes with a lift. On a recent Sunday, she walked across the front of the church to demonstrate that her disability was gone.

"She had been hobbling around before that," Dugger said. "Now her leg is just as straight as anyone else's."

Some people have criticized the revival for emphasizing a one-time experience of God, rather than long-term change. But Dugger said he believes that after people are transformed at one of the meetings, their lifestyle and devotion to God must change as well.

"It has to be something that lasts," he said. "It's great to jump and shout and be blessed in church—but how does it affect you Monday through Friday? That's what's important."

(Bob Reeves, "Lincoln Revival Changes Lives," *Pentecostal Evangel,* September 28, 1997, pp. 23-25.)

Kevin Gardner's Testimony from the Lincoln Revival

Kevin Gardner was a party animal. He loved to stay out all night drinking, drugging, and--as he once would have described it--"raising hell."

After graduating from Lincoln East High School in 1993, he got heavily into drugs. "I was addicted to crack and coke," he said. He enrolled in a radiology technician program at Southeast Community College, but dropped out.

"I decided to just take it easy and party it up."

His mother, Connie Dawson, kept at him to go to church, but Gardner preferred drinking and carousing. When home, he stayed in his room, smoking cigarettes and listening to rock music.

Then in early May, evangelist Julaine Christensen held a revival at the family's church, Lincoln First Assembly of God.

"I promised my mom I would go," Gardner recalled. "But I went to a bar the night before and stayed up real late." He woke up the next afternoon with a hangover.

His mother confronted him and begged him to go to the evening service. "I heard that tone in her voice, the disappointment," he said. "I decided to go just to get her off my back."

At the service, nothing earthshaking happened until Christensen invited anyone "who has any bondages in your life" to come up front. Gardner went forward, and Christensen told him to "lift your hands up and tell God you love Him."

"It was an act of surrender," Gardner said. "I threw my hands up and started crying."

After that service, Gardner tried to go back to his old lifestyle. He went to his favorite bar for a night of billiards and beer, but discovered "all the things I loved to do, I couldn't do. I felt guilty because God was working in my heart."

He wound up in the parking lot outside the bar, confessing his sins to God and asking forgiveness. "I kept saying to God, 'Give me peace,' and He did," Gardner said. "He gave me peace in my heart."

That night, he went home and read one of his mother's Christian devotional books. He said, "I love You God," and felt he could feel God reply, "I love you, Kevin."

Gardner said he had assumed for several years that he was on the way to hell, but "I suddenly realized that eternity is forever." He decided to take the plunge and accept God's promise of salvation for those who believe in Christ.

"I figured if He's not right, I didn't lose anything; but if He is I wanted eternal life."

After that, he threw away all of his cigarettes, drugs, and drug paraphernalia. He tossed his prized collection of 300 rock CDs, many of which contain obscene lyrics. "I just knew I couldn't listen to that stuff anymore," he said. He also threw out stacks of pornographic magazines.

Since then, he's been attending church regularly, reading his Bible, and making new plans. Last weekend, he stood before 50 people at Christensen's tent revival in North Omaha and testified to the changes in his life. This fall, he plans to enroll in a two-year training program at Brownsville School of Ministry in Pensacola, Fla., where he will study to become a revivalist preacher.

Since his own conversion, Gardner has witnessed to several friends and brought them to church.

"Three of my former drug dealers have accepted Christ," he said. "I'm so on fire for God, I want to tell everybody about Him."

(Bob Reeves, "Young Man's Change for Better Began at Revival Meeting in May," *Lincoln Journal Star,* June 21, 1997: Reprinted in the *Pentecostal Evangel,* September 28, 1997.)

*Lyons—New Life Assembly of God, 1943

In 1943, three families in Lyons began holding prayer meetings in their homes. District Superintendent A. M. Alber and other District brethren came to Lyons to help the small group look for property for a church building. The Swedish Covenant church at Fifth and Pearl Streets ... was purchased and Rev. and Mrs. Gibbs came to pastor the new congregation.... on December 15, 1944 dedication services were held for the Assembly of God in Lyons with Rev. M. F. Brandt, District Superintendent, officiating.

In early 1950 a parsonage was purchased and a Sunday school bus was bought and put into operation. The Sunday school bus ran in the Decatur and Tekamah areas. Attendance reached a high of 134 during this time. When Nathan Lutes was pastor the basement and sanctuary facilities were expanded and remodeled extensively. In 1976, with Ray Pile as pastor, a beautiful new facility was built in a new location. The dedication service for this new building was in January of 1980.

The list of pastors include Rev. Gibbs, Sister W. A. Hawkins, George Workman, Stanley P. Wicksell, R. D. Pick, Armond J. Mickelsen, Nathan Lutes, Fredrick Rosenkrans, Ronald Boswell, Raymond Pile, Rick Stevens, Rod Smith, and Gene Hinrichsen.

Church at Kearney constructed while L. E. Wilkins was pastor. He was founder of the Assembly.

The dedication services for this church building at Hebron, NE were held Sunday July 12, 1981. Superintendent James Wilkins brought the message. James Burnette was the pastor.

**North Park Assembly in Holdrege was dedicated July 13, 1980.
Guest speaker was former pastor H. H. "Spud" DeMent.**

Chapter 11: Maxwell through North Platte

"Lord, who may dwell in your sanctuary? Who may live on your holy hill? He whose walk is blameless and who does what is righteous, who speaks the truth from his heart." **(Psalm 15:1-2 NIV)**

Maxwell	Minatare	Niobrara
McCook	Mitchell	Norfolk
Melbeta	Mullen	North Platte
Milford	Nebraska City	

*Maxwell—Assembly of God, 1926

Rev. Irl Walker and Rev. Guy Cooper first brought the Pentecostal message to Maxwell. They held a tent meeting in July 1926 in which 30 some souls were saved. The first to be saved were Lena Anderson and Esther Yanken.... On August 15, 1926 Caroline Greeley organized the Sunday school with an attendance of 60. Henrietta Burnhart came to minister until we could find a pastor.

On November 8, 1926 the Nebraska District superintendent Rev. George Clopine set the church in order. There were 21 members on the original roster. At this time Rev. M. W. Roll was called as the first pastor, staying until May 29, 1927. On May 22, 1927 Rev. Ralph Ewing was voted in to serve until camp time. He left July 24, 1927. In August the Rolls returned as pastors. At this time the congregation worshipped in the old Everley Dance Hall.... In September 1928 Rev. Otto Gregg from California was visiting his sister in North Platte and came to Maxwell for service, as there was no Assembly of God church in North Platte. We had no pastor at that time so he decided to stay and fill in for awhile.

On December 2, 1928 we moved into the old Post Office building. It was also on December 2, 1928 that Pastor Gregg suggested we start taking a missionary offering the first Sunday of each month.... On December 30, 1928 Rev. Virgil Shores came as pastor for a few months. Under his leadership a building fund was established and the little church was purchased. F. G. Cline followed him....

In 1936 a parsonage was purchased.... June 20, 1937 was a record attendance day, 111 were present for Sunday school. There was a baptismal service in the afternoon with 24 being baptized. In 1952 under the leadership of Rev. Jimmy Mayfield the new church was erected and dedicated on January 2, 1956. During the early 1960s a Sunday school unit was added to the church. A new parsonage also was built during this time....

The list of pastors includes M. W. Roll, Ralph Ewing, Otto Gregg, Virgil Shores, F. G. Cline, J. C. Burkey, Rev. Campbell, A. R. Brown, Ed Herrman, John Hodges, Earl Cummings, Mervin Peck, Robert Paul, Rev. Edwards, Allen Peasley, Douglas Ramsey, Jimmy Mayfield, Noland Blokkolb, Ernest Hanson …, Julius Olson, Gene Arnold, J. E. Conell, A. R. Sutter, Clyde Buck, John Stocker, Jim Snyders, Irvin Jackson, Randy Robnett, Brian Correll, Ken Taylor, Dale Gosnell, James Benedict, Ed Warren, James Strating, and Tom McFarland.

*McCook—First Assembly of God, 1923

In 1922, a spiritual decadence in the churches of the city brought a group of spiritually hungry women together to pray for revival.... At first the little prayer band was afraid of what they were hearing about the phenomena of the speaking in tongues. But with hearing the reports of what was happening, they decided it could not all be bad, and decided to investigate.... When Lily Rouch and Sarah Bolles returned home they shared their testimonies with the prayer group about how they had received the Baptism of the Holy Spirit. By 1924 a number of the local ladies had been filled with the Spirit. Some of the ladies heard about a camp meeting being held in Beaver City and decided to attend....

They met Evangelist Charles Harris and asked him if he would take time to come to McCook for a series of meeting. In early October 1924 he came accompanied by Guy Dunbar of Guide Rock.... Immediately the fruit from two years of prayer and intercession became apparent, as from the first week, people began to be saved and filled with the Holy Spirit. Crowds grew, until hundreds of people were flocking to this little church which could not begin to contain them. As interest grew, there came the hunger for "tarrying services" in the afternoons where many more people received their Baptism of the Holy Spirit with speaking in tongues as the Spirit of God gave utterance.

Resistance broke out immediately among the pastors of the city, and the things that aroused the opposition was that people were "being slain in the Spirit" and "speaking in tongues." Local pastors began to warn against participation or even attending these "fanatical" happenings. But the more they warned their congregations, the more the crowds grew, until finally, even though it was winter the crowds became so large they overflowed onto the sidewalks and into the street. People brought stepladders to look through the windows, which were kept open so the people could hear the mysteries of the Word.

Persecution grew. After a few weeks it was decided to establish a congregation to meet regularly for the more than 150 people whom had been newly saved and filled with the Holy Spirit. A Sunday school was needed as well, as many of the people had no church ties. The worshippers agreed to invite Evangelist Charles Harris to become their pastor. He accepted and moved his family from Red Cloud into a small parsonage rented for him, and he assumed the duties of pastor.

The persecution did not quit. Early in 1925 when the congregation met at the Community building as usual for their services, they found a chain and padlock on the door. A newly saved engaged couple, Ed Raymond and Mary Rowland, were building their home only a few doors away. It was to that construction site the group went to conduct their prayer meeting by lamplight, and to discuss steps to take to secure a place of worship of their own. It was decided to look into the feasibility of purchasing property where they could build their church. Within the week, the present site at 807 East C Street had been purchased from the J. E. Kelley Realty Company, and plans were set in motion to erect a temporary board tabernacle and rough pine benches.... The first services in their building were held on February 27, 1925 and to this crude tabernacle people came from miles around to worship.

As the group worshipped in the little board tabernacle they proceeded with plans for a permanent building and on the lot next door a basement was excavated. Great urgency was added to the necessity to move into larger, warmer quarters when the eminent British Evangelist Smith Wigglesworth promised to come to McCook with his traveling team in November 1926.... At this time Superintendent Clopine was asked to set the church in order for affiliation with the General Council of the Assemblies of God of Springfield, Missouri. For thirteen years services were held in the basement of the unfinished structure of the church.... Then, under the ministry of Rev. Glenn Reed, building began again in October 1937, and was finished in 1938.... In 1950, to further meet the needs of this growing congregation, property was purchased and donated south of the church and converted into the church parking lot. In 1952 the lot just north of the church was purchased, making room for possible expansion....

The list of pastors includes Charles Harris, C. B. Thomas, Glen E. Millard, Glen A Reed, C. M. Smitley, C. T. Beem, Stanley Cooke, Walter Larson, R. H. DeLancey, C. A. Sailors, A. H. Farrington, Dale Eden, Jimmy Root, Sr., David Balliet, John Fransisco, David Nord, Woodrow Weidner, and Charles Hooton.

Nebraska District Camp Held at McCook

The Nebraska District Council Camp of the Assemblies of God was held at the Old City Park, McCook, Nebraska. August 7 to 16 with Brother T. K. Leonard of Findlay, Ohio, as Bible teacher and evangelist, assisted by G. W. Clopine, State Chairman. Perfect unity prevailed throughout the camp. Many received salvation and Baptism of the Holy Ghost. Some definite healings were manifested. All the saints were built up in the most holy faith. God's holy Word always has its effect and many scoffers were made to believe that this is that spoken by the prophet Joel.

(Pastor C. H. Harris, "McCook," *Pentecostal Evangel*, October 17, 1925, p. 12.)

Melbeta, Nebraska

A Pentecostal meeting was started here, April 17, 1924, with Brother Irl J. Walker as evangelist, assisted by Brothers Roll and Rankin. When this meeting began, there was only 1 who had received the Baptism according to Acts 2:4, but several were in sympathy with Pentecost, and when the meeting closed, 25 had been converted and 7 had received the Holy Spirit Baptism. We are praising God for such a grand meeting. Brother Walker and his helpers are truly on fire for God and are doing a wonderful work. ~ Mrs. J. G. Neighbors.

(Mrs. J. G. Neighbors, "Melbeta, Nebraska," *Pentecostal Evangel* June 7, 1924, p. 12.)

*Milford—Assembly of God, 1925

Shortly after the turn of the century a Pentecostal church sprang up about five miles southwest of Milford. From this nucleus the Milford Assembly of God came into being. In those beginning years the congregation held services in two different downtown halls and in 1925 purchased their first church building which had been the German Evangelical church. August 4, 1926 while W. O. Oliver was pastor, the church was officially set in order and affiliated with the Nebraska District of the Assemblies of God.

In October 1952 the old church structure was razed and a larger building begun. The new church was 80x40 feet with a full basement and seating for 280 in the sanctuary. The exterior of the building was faced with white stone and it has been estimated that 95% of the labor was donated. On July 22, 1953 dedication ceremonies for the new facility was held.... An addition to the building was completed while Terry Petty was pastor giving the church a beautiful fellowship hall, kitchen, nursery, and rest rooms on the main floor and educational space in the basement. Growth and revival has been a continuing experience for the Milford church. Many have gone out from the church into ministry around the world.

The list of pastors includes Joe Redliger, Edgar White, Henry Hoar, Stratton, J. Rerlizzi, Merle Roll, H. Griswold, Milton Smith, W. O. Oliver, K. Campbell, Mac Lamar, Guy Rake, M. F. Brandt, Roy S. Barnes, Harold Champlin, Harry Meyers, Eugene C. Bishop, George Acree, F. D. McClellan, Burrell R. White, Mel Jennings, Paul Sherman, James Wilkins, Arthur Kost, Frank Alexander, Terry Petty, Kent Anderson, John Walker, and Solomon Wang.

*Minatare—Assembly of God, 1944

The Minatare Assembly of God had its first service on May 14, 1944, with Rev. Elmer Burry as pastor. There were about a dozen in attendance. Several things had transpired to make this service possible, and God's hand can be seen in it all.

After spending his furlough with his family in Minature, Pardon "Bud" Loutzenhiser was hitchhiking to Sidney to catch the train back to Fort Dix, New Jersey where he was stationed. As he was walking east Rev. Charles Thurmond, pastor of the Assembly of God Church in Dalton gave him a ride. When they got to Dalton, Brother Thurmond said, "Soldier boy, is there anything I can do for you?" Bud told him that his mother was a good Christian lady and that she had been praying for a church in her hometown. The family had visited the church in Bayard a few times but not often. The men were in the army and they did not have a car. Rev. Thurmond promised Bud that he would see what he could do about that because he was the Presbyter for the Panhandle of Nebraska.

The Elmer Burry family had resigned the church in Newcastle, Wyoming in November of 1943. They came to Bridgeport where they had family, and decided to rest for awhile. Brother Thurmond contacted Brother Burry and asked him to come to Minatare to start a church. Brother Burry agreed, and they came to Minatare and found a little white church a block west of Main Street, which was owned by the Presbyterian Church. The church had not been used for sometime and they were able to work out a rental agreement.... They were able to have that memorable beginning service on Mother's Day, 1944.... Opal Martichewsky was an evangelist that God used in a revival that helped to begin 50 and more years of ministry. Many were brought into the church in the weeks of services with her.

Hazel Jay had been suffering for some time from gallstones and was to have surgery as soon as her husband was through with his trucking in the spring so he could care for their children. Her sister-in-law Lela Jay took her to the Assembly of God church in Scottsbluff, where the pastor and his wife prayed for her. She felt a warm feeling through her body and could breathe without pain. She was healed. Soon after that they heard that an Assembly of God was starting in Minatare. They began attending and Lela Jay became pianist for the congregation. Fred and Lillie Zimmerman, Hazel's mother and stepfather owned a pool hall. Fred was an alcoholic. They visited Hazel one afternoon soon after her healing, wondering what had happened that she was suddenly well. Hazel explained that God had healed her. Lillie immediately said she wanted healing too from the heart trouble she had and went to church to be prayed for. She was saved, healed and baptized in the Holy Spirit. Fred soon saw the change in her life, so he left the Christian Church and came to the Assembly with Lillie and was saved, and delivered from alcoholism. He sold his pool hall and worked at various jobs until his sudden death a few years later.... Alton Loutzenhiser married a girl from Wales, Marjorie Scheck. She joined him here and when their first child, a son, was born he had a tumor on his head, which was healed, when he was prayed for. Jim Loutzenhiser came home from overseas with malaria and was healed when he was prayed for.

In 1947 the congregation worked out plans to buy the church for $3500.... In the 1960s the need for a larger and better building became a necessity.... it was decided by the board to pay that amount and start a building fund. A church builder was contacted who designed and agreed to build the new church for $7.50 a square foot, which came to around $33,000.... James Neely was pastor at this time.

... The church developed a strong Sunday school soon after it began. During the first years as Brother Burry was pastor the Sunday school climbed to an average attendance in the mid 40s. The church has continued to maintain a strong Sunday school. In the 1960s there were a number of times when the Sunday school attendance was in the 80's. Wayne Allen's ministry saw the church at a strong state in its history. A strong Sunday school has kept the church moving forward....

The list of pastors includes Elmer Burry, Charles Turner, Elmer Burry, James Neely, Wayne Allen, Gene Schachterle, Norman Walker, Stanley Rutkowski, Elmer Hassler, and Dwight Sandoz.

*Mitchell—Assembly of God, 1944

In 1944 the W. O. Ziegler family started meetings in a hall on Center Avenue in Mitchell. On August 27 of the same year a revival meeting began and as a result a church was born. The group of believers held the first morning worship service on October 1, 1944. In November a Sunday school was organized. In 1945 a church building was erected at 1462 13th Avenue and dedication services for the Mitchell Assembly of God were held on July 19 of that year.... The first water baptismal service was held on June 23, 1946. A new parsonage was built while Robert Paul was pastor. The new church was built and dedicated while Troy Allen was pastor.

The list of pastors include Rev. Peasley, E. J. Dewey, Phil Palser, Robert Palser, W. E. Reynolds, Troy Allen, Ronald Hastie, Carl Swink, Harry Blakkolb, Gene Gilmore, Herb Christensen, James Moore, John Gale, Michael Christian, Ron Boswell, Kevin Jay, and Troy Allen.

*Mullen—Assembly of God, 1929

In 1926, a little band of people turned from the world of boozing, dancing, smoking, card playing, swearing, and the like and united under the name of crusaders. They stuck together through thick and thin, holding a young people's meeting on Saturday night's and Sunday school at the Cherry school house with a preaching service now and then by whom-so-ever would come through the Sand-hills as a preacher of the gospel. They had been praying for a long time for someone to come their way that would bring the old time Holy Ghost Gospel.... In 1926, a full gospel believer Mr. Newby from Oregon held the services in the second story of the old Tribune building where several people gave their hearts to the Lord. Then in 1929, the families then went together and bought the livery barn property. The barn was torn down, and a church was built. It was called it the Mullen Full Gospel Tabernacle. It was "Open Bible" for a few years and later changed to Mullen Assembly of God. After the people had organized their church they called L. W. James and wife to become their first pastors. In 1968, they purchased the old Methodist Church and moved into it. The congregation has increased so in 1980, they built on to the west and then in 1984, they had to have more room so built on to the back.

The list of pastors since 1950 includes Paul H. Marler, E. J. Dewey, Willis L. Dewey, Harry Walker, Duane C. Palser, Henry Mohn, J. D. Bruce, James O'Bryan, Jimmy D. Root, George Smith, Waldo Smith, Ray Anderson, Marvin Hancock, Ernest Rosenkrans, Richard Sing, George Greenwood, and Darrell Schmid.

*Nebraska City—Arbor Christian Fellowship, (reopened) 1993

The list of pastors since 1950 includes E. W. Thiemann, Virgil L. Conger, LeRoy Eichman, Willis Dewey, Kenneth Krivohlavek, George Gross, George Jacobs, Stanley Rutkowski, Harry Blakkolb, Kenneth Taylor, Steven Madrinich. The church was closed for a few years and then reopened as the Arbor Christian Fellowship in 1993 with Robert Schoenherr as pastor.

*Niobrara—Assembly of God, 1995

The pastors have been Mervin H. Kee and Shawn Gothard.

*Norfolk—Victory Road Assembly of God, 1934

Rev. Roy Comstock started the Norfolk Assembly of God in 1934. The first place of worship was a rented store building on downtown Norfolk Avenue, where special services were held nightly. Soon a larger place was needed, and an upstairs hall was rented. The church met there until 1937 when they moved into their first church building at Fourth Street and Omaha Avenue. Rev. Comstock and the church members built this building. It also provided living quarters in the back for the pastor. John Reitz donated most of the lumber and funds for the building.

Brother Comstock resigned in 1944, and the church changed leadership three times in the next three years. In 1946 Rev. Peter Pilot was instrumental in securing property at Third Street and Park Avenue, moving the house to one side, and constructing a basement which was finished for a place of worship.... Rev. Sylas Anderson helped the church sell the property at Third and Park to the Christian Missionary Alliance Church and purchase the property at Eleventh and Pasewalk in 1957. Rev. Nolan Christian became pastor in 1958 and began working on arrangements to construct the new church and pastor‘s residence.... The church building was then constructed using volunteer labor from the community, church and neighboring Assemblies. Many men would fly in from Western Nebraska in small planes and stay several days to help with construction.... One of the first services in the new facility was the 1959 Nebraska District Council, at which the church was dedicated.

Rev. Dale Lesher became pastor in 1968. In the fall of 1970 the church incorporated under the laws of the State of Nebraska as the First Assembly of God and was affiliated with the General Council of the Assemblies of God.... The church mortgage was paid in full on January 1, 1977. A new parsonage was purchased on Philip Avenue, allowing the annex to be used for Sunday school rooms.... In the fall of 1981, the congregation, due in large part to a gift from the estate of Irvin McGinnis, purchased 10.8 acres of the Northeast corner of Victory Road and Norfolk Avenue. The people began to pray for a miracle to somehow be able to build on that land. The total debt on the property was paid off in 1984, but there still seemed no way to build. Rev. Mark Richards became pastor in 1985.... The office was expanded, and overflow rooms developed. Pastor Mark Rose arrived in December of 1988....

The ground breaking for the new church took place in August of 1990.... Everyone there knew the Spirit of the Lord had already moved onto that property. Truly, we were standing on Holy Ground. As the congregation moved into their new facility they realized they had come a long way from the meeting in a rented storefront or basement facility and yet their purpose had never changed. "To see souls won for Christ and then discipled into mature Christians."

The list of pastors include Roy Comstock, Virgil Dickinson, Edna Shackelton, Peter Pilot, Lloyd Wead, Clyde King, Dale Hastie, Ervin Smith, Roscoe Leach, Sylas Anderson, Nolan Christian, Nolan Blakkolb, Mel Johnson, Dale Lesher, Mark Richards and Mark Rose.

North Platte, Nebraska, 1919

The Assemblies of God and Pentecostal Missions of Nebraska will hold a State Camp Meeting at North Platte, Nebraska., from July 17 to 30th, 1919 in the interest of a closer fellowship and better co-operation for State evangelization, etc. Evangelist F. Lohmann and others will be with us.

("The State Camp Meeting at North Platte, Nebraska," *Christian Evangel*, June 14, 1919, p. 15.)

First Assemblies of God Church in North Platte

The History of Lincoln County provides information about the location of the first Assemblies of God Church in North Platte.

What is styled the "Gospel Mission" at the city of North Platte, affiliated with the Assemblies of God, whose headquarters are at Springfield, Missouri, is located at Eleventh and Locust streets, and was organized October, 1919 by Pastor G. W. Clopine. The total membership is now (March 1920) almost thirty-five souls. (1919 the address for the Gospel Mission was 817 Locust.)

A Sunday school is conducted in conjunction with this mission work. Its superintendent is E. P. Blue and its enrollment is about forty.

The next mention of the Gospel Mission was at 903 W. 9th with George W. Clopine pastor and wife Emma P. The last found record was in the 1923 North Platte City Directory with George W. Clopine, and wife Emma P., the preacher at 1021 Locust, but no mention of the mission.

Emma Smith of North Platte

Elmer and Emma Smith were married in the summer of 1919 near North Platte. In a conversation with Emma Smith (a member of First Assembly of God in North Platte) when she was 92 years of age, she recalled a large "church tent" being set up and meetings conducted there. (This would have been the camp meeting G. W. Clopine organized, out of which came the Nebraska District.) She and her husband did not attend the meeting because they lived in the country at the time. The location Emma indicated would be the 1300 block of Jeffers (in 1919 known as Locust) between the swimming pool in Cody Park and 18th Street.

Pastor Steven W. Bell of First Assembly writes (1998) "Emma was one of the pioneer Pentecostals in North Platte, although she was associated with the Foursquare Church for most of her early life. She was not a charter member of First Assembly of God and did not begin attending until late 60's early 70's.

Of Emma's 9 children, three are in vocational ministry; all but two children are serving the Lord. Two are credentialed by the Assemblies and one by the Foursquare. The one credentialed with the Foursquare is Anna, wife of Jack Hayford. She has several grandchildren who are credentialed by the Assemblies and Foursquare. Emma was a precious saint and spent much of her time in visitation ministry. She was born in 1902, I believe ..."

(Steven W. Bell, "Emma Smith of North Platte." From First Assembly of God, North Platte, Nebraska.)

The North Platte Canteen

Just after the bombing of Pearl Harbor, the people of North Platte heard that Company D from the Nebraska National Guard was going to pass through their city by troop train going to the West Coast. About 500 people waited at the Union Pacific Railroad station with cookies, candy cakes and other gifts. After a long wait, a troop train rumbled into the station. As the crowd eagerly went to meet the boys, they were disappointed because the boys on board were Company D but from Kansas--not Nebraska. Nevertheless some one in the crowd of people said, "Welcome to our city sons, and here's a little something for you."

So the idea was born to meet all the trains carrying servicemen and women. Rae Wilson contacted businessmen, housewives, railroaders and everyone who would help. Christmas Day 1941 as a troop train rolled into North Platte, they were met by smiling young ladies with baskets of treats. Thus the birth of the North Platte Canteen. This continued to April l, 1946. In 1942, Mrs. Helen Christ, wife of a UP conductor was appointed general chairman.

Each day from 3,000 to 5,000 soldiers, sailors and marines passed through North Platte riding the trains. The trains stopped for an average of 10 minutes only long enough to be serviced. By the end of the war, there were as many as 8,000 military people from 23 trains served a day. Food was freely given by businesses, churches, clubs, and individuals. The most popular were sandwiches, fired chicken, hard boiled eggs, pickles, fresh fruit, cookies, doughnuts, pie (anything that could be eaten by fingers), coffee, milk and iced tea. On an average day, roughly 4,000 sandwiches were made and served. Minced ham-salad was a favorite! These snacks and treats were free of charge for the men and women in uniform regardless of rank. One of the best remembered practice was the giving of an entire birthday cake. An average of 20 birthday cakes were given each day and always on the honor system. Area children gave up their cakes to be given to the military and pen pals with old and young developed from names placed with these gifts. Ed Launer recalled his mother giving a birthday cake going to a sailor. Bill, the sailor, and Anna Launer corresponded for many years.

North Platte the place on the prairie where time changed from Central to Mountain time became a bright spot in the travels and memories of the servicemen and women that passed through Nebraska for 51 months during World War II. The Union Pacific was a busy transcontinental route for public travel as well as the troop trains. Union Pacific gave the use of a kitchen and employees contributed labor and donations helping make the center successful.

Approximately 125 other Nebraska and Colorado communities contributed either labor or donations to help the North Platte Canteen coming from as far away as 200 miles to help with the 10+ hour day making sandwiches, sweeping floors, washing dishes, serving food, etc. Beulah Imhoff recalls her mother, Esta Wolveston, who lived in Dickens, Nebraska helped one day each week because neighboring communities took their turn. Esta never missed a day of her community‘s turn! It has been estimated that over 55,000 people worked at the Canteen 1941 to 1946. The center opened at 5 AM each day until the last troop train passed through North Platte. During these years, it never closed for one day and operated in all kinds of weather!

Local churches gave sing a-longs at Easter and Christmas. There was a magazine table filled with Bibles and reading materials of all faiths, magazines, song sheets and playing cards to help pass the long hours for the service men and women. Writing materials were also provided as well as baskets of fresh fruit for them to take from. Names were sometimes written on magazines giving another opportunity for pen pals.

Ed Launer recalls that each day KODY would prerecord a program to be broadcast in the evening. He couldn‘t interview the service personnel, but could tell of the days events and interview the workers. He‘d also report what was given for that day. Beulah remembers his reports as being extremely interesting and inspiring as many as possible to pitch in. Ed remembered one day people from a town north of North Platte brought baskets of fried pheasant, bakeries donated bread; dairies gave milk, and all that could donated labor. He recalled many an early evening after work, he and his wife would put their baby girl, Mickey, in her buggy and walk to the Canteen to give a few hours of help.

(James J. Reisdorff, "North Platte Canteen." from "Conversations with Beulah Imhoff and Ed Launer," (Radio announcer with KODY, North Platte, during World War II).

*North Platte—First Assembly of God, 1943

A full gospel movement was again started in North Platte on December 7, 1936. Services were held in several homes at first, then in March of 1938, a box car was purchased to hold services in. Brother and Sister Clarence Koch of Hershey held services faithfully for some time there. Later the Lloyd Pounds of Ogallala held services from April until September of 1939. The George Pappases followed them from Big Springs and came to hold services every Sunday from October of 1939 until September of 1941. When they were no longer able to come for services, the Colliers from the Foursquare Church held services for the next year. In July of 1942 the Clarence Kochs again took over the work and remained until Rev. E. M. Herrmann came to be the first pastor in 1943.

The District of Nebraska had been hesitant about starting a full gospel work in North Platte, since there was already such a church there, but the time had come when both Brother Pappas and Brother Koch felt a great need to start an Assembly of God church in this city. Rev. A. M. Alber, the District Superintendent, came to North Platte to look over the possibility of starting a church and brought Rev. Herrman with him. Brother Pappas had already purchased lots for a church at 701 S. Pine Street and some time later the Clarence Kochs bought a church in the country to be moved on the lots, so the work was on its way. The first service was held in the little white church at 701 South Pine on September 7, 1943 and 19 people were present. The first year the Sunday school average was 38 and the second year it was 59. The church only had a seating capacity of 70, so they were already beginning to feel crowded. The third year the attendance continued to climb and on the third anniversary the attendance was 96 in Sunday school. By 1946, it was obvious that it would be necessary for the church to build a larger building, so they began looking for lots. Lots were purchased at the corner of "C" and Dewey streets for $2250.00 and soon the work began.... The work was finally completed and on September 2, 1948 the new church was dedicated. The E. M. Herrmanns continued to pastor the church until 1951.

... Lots were purchased in 1967, in a very choice location at Philip and Oak Streets, when Clyde King was the pastor. The lots were paid for in a short time and ready for the time when the new church could be built. After Rev. L. E. Wilkins arrived he was very anxious to get started on the new building and work began on the parsonage in March of 1972.... The parsonage was dedicated in July of 1972. The ground breaking for the church was held on August 20, 1972 and work began three days later. The first service was held in the new church on May 20, 1973, just nine months after the work began....

The list of pastors include E. M. Hermann, L. L. Roggow, F. D. McClellan, Clyde King, J. L. Alder, L. E. Wilkins, Danny Swearengin, James Huffman, Tim Munyon, and Steven Bell.

*North Platte—Calvary Assembly of God, 1982

On Friday, May 21, 1982, a number of people met at the Carpet Market to discuss reasons for, and the possibilities of starting a new Assembly of God church in North Platte. The following Monday, May 24, District Superintendent Jim Wilkins, came to North Platte. He met with this group of people for an informational meeting. The purpose of the meeting regarded requirements and guidelines for establishing a new Assembly of God church. It was agreed upon that they go ahead and organize a new congregation....

Sunday, May 30, 1982 came very fast. The people gathered together at Madison Jr. High School for this church's first Sunday service. Through the assistance of the district office, Rev. Milo Harmon from Omaha, Nebraska, came to speak and was appointed as the interim pastor.... After much discussion, phone calls, prayers, and a trip to North Dakota, Rev. R. E. Corlew was asked to come for an interview and candidate on June 27, 1982. The Corlews were asked to come to be the first pastor of this new congregation and they accepted. August 1st was the first Sunday for pastor and people. On Sunday the 15th the name Calvary Assembly God was chosen as the official name of the church. After much searching and prayer, the congregation voted to purchase the "Old Telegraph" building at the cost of $60,000. The first Sunday service held in the "Old Telegraph" on November 21, 1982. Today, Calvary Assembly of God meets at 315 East 5th Street....

The pastors of this congregation include Ray E. Corlew, Mark Klingengerg, and David Jones.

Maxwell Assembly of God, Maxwell, NE, 1984

The old Norfolk Assembly of God. The church later sold this building and built a new one.

Calvary Assembly, North Platte, NE

Assembly of God at Fairbury, NE

Chapter 12: Ogallala through York

"The Lord will guide you always; he will satisfy your needs in a sun-scorched land and will strengthen your frame. You will be like a well-watered garden, like a spring whose waters never fail."
(Isaiah 58:11 NIV)

Ogallala	Riverton	Valentine
Omaha	Scottsbluff	Wahoo
O'Neill	Sidney	Walthill
Ord	South Sioux City	Whitney
Pender	Springview	Winnebago
Plattsmouth	Taylor	York
Red Cloud	Thedford	

Ogallala—Radiant Life Assembly of God, 1934

Ogallala's Radiant Life Assembly of God's ... first meeting place was an upper room in Johnson Hall, a converted barn and later a dance hall. Adeline Mayden and Mary Leverton initiated the founding. They had been members of the Assembly of God in Bridgeport and after moving to Ogallala, decided they wanted a church of their own faith in Ogallala. On March 20, 1935, the church was officially organized. H. W. Lebsack was elected chairman of the Board of Trustees, and W. O. Ziegler, Mrs. Mayden's pastor of Bridgeport became the pastor.

Caught in the middle of the Great Depression, the little church struggled through the early years. On April 9, 1935, the offering totaled 16 cents. A stove purchased for the parsonage cost $9 and it took two months to pay for it. In 1936, the assembly decided to build a permanent church. On ground donated by Lilly Mahaffey, they erected a small frame building with a two-room parsonage. It was east of the Ogallala High School Auditorium.

Several items of interest are found in the church records of the 1930s. On April 20, 1938, the congregation voted to require that each prospective member prove himself for three months before becoming a voting member. In the field of women's rights, the Assembly of God was far ahead of its time. On February 14, 1939, the Board of Directors asked the superintendent of the Nebraska district if a woman could be voted a deaconess.

By January 3, 1951, the congregation needed a new church building. A building program was initiated March 27, 1951, and by August a church building was completed at 419 East Fifth Street. In 1959, the Assembly began another building project, this time to construct a new parsonage. The Rev. Clyde Buck was instrumental in both of these projects.... In 1978, the congregation started to build a new church at 700 West 13th Street. The first service in the new, larger facility was held in October 1981.... At that time the church had 110 members.

The list of pastors include W. O. Ziegler, Rev. Campbell, Alvin Kite, John Hodges, E. M. Hermann, Bernard Correll, Rev. Edwards, Ben R. Harris, Clyde Buck, George Workman, Harold Powell, Clyde Buck, Willis Dewey, Gerald Hansen, Elmer Craver, David Cordaro, Frank Sarvabui, David Kersting, and David Gill.

Revival at Omaha in 1914

Omaha, Nebraska was another early center of revival. Here are a couple of early reports from the Christian Evangel.

Brother Gaskill and I have opened a mission here in Omaha and it is the only mission standing for the full Gospel. The field is large and there are many adversaries. Please pray that God will mightily pour out His Spirit and give us a revival. The mission is located at 123 No. 12th Street. We have called it the "Assembly of God" with meetings every night and Sunday beginning at two p.m. ~ Fred E. Poole

(*Christian Evangel*, October 31, 1914, p. 4.)

Greetings in Jesus name. A few lines to let you know how the work is getting along. We were tested and pressed it seemed beyond measure until last week and spiritually there was somewhat of a break. God brought in two souls that had never been saved and baptized them before they got off their knees and they spoke in tongues as in Acts 2:4. God has been manifesting His healing power also and a number of remarkable healings have taken place. There are a number of seekers and new ones coming in all the time. Pray for us. ~ Fred E. Poole

(*Christian Evangel*, March 6, 1915, p. 3.)

Healing at Omaha

I can certainly praise God for the wonderful healing of my boy in February, 1923. We took him to Omaha, Nebraska, to the hospital and first we took him to the eye specialist, as he was blind. After examination of the eyes he sent us to the brain specialist; and he told us there was not much hopes of his recovery for he was seriously ill. He told us he had one of three things, either tuberculosis of the brain, tumor, or cancer of the brain.

They put him to bed and said they would do all they could for him, but the night before we took him to the hospital, I wrote to Brother and Sister Clark and told them to pray for him, and they wrote right back and sent an anointed cloth, but their prayers were answered before the letter and cloth came to us; for the third morning we were there the pain left his head, and he did not vomit another time.

When the cloth came he wanted to put it on his head and face for one side of his face was paralyzed. The doctor had not done a thing for him only examine him, so we give God all the glory for his healing. He is well and strong, has been home eight months and has never had a pain, and can see as well as he ever could...

They took eight X-ray pictures, and the doctors said they must give up for the first ones showed plainly that the growth had even lifted and separated the skull, and the last picture after prayer showed that it appeared to be normal again. They, however, thought it just temporary relief. He had been troubled with his head for two years before, till at times he would have such pains he would just walk the floor and ring his hands, and he gives God and Brother and Sister Clark the praise for healing his head. His name is Loraine Dennis.

(Earl W. Clark, "Healed of Tumor on Brain Through Anointed Cloth." *The Need of the Hour: Healing for the Body.* Springfield, MO: Gospel Publishing House, 1924, pp. 60-61.)

Earl Clark was married to the granddaughter of Maria Woodworth-Etter. The Clarks traveled extensively with Maria Woodworth-Etter in her ministry.

*Omaha—Glad Tidings, 1936

Glad Tidings started in January 1936 when Evangelist and Mrs. L. E. King from East St. Louis, Illinois, conducted services at the First Assembly of God in Lincoln, Nebraska. Pastor Glen Millard, Secretary of the Nebraska District of the Assemblies of God, and other ministers shared with them the need of establishing an Assembly of God Church in Omaha. The Lord led in every step of preparation for opening day. Services began August 9, 1936, with 23 present for Sunday school. Initially, the church was named “The Full Gospel Tabernacle.” However, after a few months, the name was changed to Glad Tidings Assembly of God to avoid confusion with a similarly named church. The church was officially organized as an Assembly of God Church with elected officers in March 1937. Growth continued through the years requiring more Sunday school rooms. During this time, Sunday school attendance peaked at 332. A few years later, additional rooms were needed, so the property across the street, 1824 Cass was purchased as an annex. Income, from renting half the building provided the entire monthly payment, while the other portion of the building met the expanding needs. With the added facilities, Sunday school attendance reached 430 by 1962. Interstate construction included the area of the annex, making it necessary to relocate. The property at 75th and Hickory was selected. The first service conducted in the newly constructed church was November 9, 1969. Official dedication was held April 7, 1970.

In November 1970, Rev. John G. Walker was elected Pastor of Glad Tidings.... Under the leadership of Pastor Walker, Glad Tidings began a new pattern of growth that was to continue for years to come. In early 1973, a balcony was added to the sanctuary, providing for a total of 750 people. With continued growth, the need to add a second morning service was evident. Because of this growth, the pastor and board met May 5, 1975 to discuss ways for expansion. The following day, May 6, Omaha experienced one of its most damaging tornadoes, which cut a path through the property of the church, severely damaging the building. The loss exceeded $300,000.00, but the spirit of the people was not damaged.

At a special-called meeting, Wednesday night, June 4th, the congregation voted to approve the recommendation of the church board to rebuild and expand the facilities. This included a 1300-seat sanctuary, an atrium, a new entrance on the south side with a canopy drive, special nursery and toddler facilities, projection and sound room, and three acres of parking. Groundbreaking services were held Sunday afternoon, July13, 1975....

On July 11, 1984, Rev. Val Munson was elected Senior Pastor of Glad Tidings. Under the leadership of Rev. Munson, Glad Tidings increased its support for missions to an all-time high of $165,000. Preparations were made for a great “harvest” throughout Omaha in the “Lord‘s time.” The Lord has blessed Glad Tidings with pastors who had a vision for the church and the city.

The list of pastors includes L. E. King, John Walker, Val Munson, Rick Cole, and Al Toledo.

*Omaha—South Side Assembly of God, 1955

In 1955 the first services for the Omaha congregation were held at the Odd Fellows Lodge at 25th and K Streets with twelve people present. The congregation moved into the building at 23rd and H Streets in 1958 with Rev. Fred Smith as pastor. Three years later on October 25, 1961 South Side Assembly became affiliated with the Assemblies of God with twenty-six charter members.

Rev. and Mrs. Wesley Reynolds came in 1962 to serve the church and during their ministry growth and revival was experienced.... Property for a new church was purchased March 31, 1967. On August 3, 1969 Rev. Robert Strand of Minnesota came to the church as pastor. Rev. Dale Harmon followed Rev. Strand and on November 12, 1972 ground was broken for a new church building. The building is located on 6 ½ acres at 4815 Harrison. The building includes a sanctuary which seats 450 with space for 75 choir members on the platform. There are 15 classrooms, offices, a kitchen, and a large fellowship hall, making the total floor space 12,600 square feet. In recent years a Family Life addition including a gym has been added.

The list of pastors includes Fred Smith, W. E. Reynolds, Robert Strand, Philip Hastie, Dale Harmon, David Houghton, Dennis Woodruff, and Charles Davis.

*Omaha—Cornerstone Assembly of God, 1985

Cornerstone Assembly of God originally was the vision of Jack Vetter, who had felt a "nudge" from the Holy Spirit to pursue the development of a new church in Southwest Omaha. Jack investigated and found that of the 450,000 people in Omaha, there was no more than 1,000 attending an Assembly of God Church. As there was a void in this area, groundwork was laid to establish a new church to minister to the large growing population of the Millard area.... Once the plan was in progress, Pastor Donald White was appointed to the arduous task of bringing it all together. Cornerstone met as an assembly for the first time in the Norris Elementary School on March 3, 1985 with an initial gathering of 111 people. After holding services at Norris for only one month, Cornerstone had the opportunity to lease the Millard South High School Auditorium.... With regulations only allowing churches to use public schools for approximately two years, God in His Greatness again opened a new door. In September of 1986, Cornerstone entered into a lease agreement for our current facility. After many laborious hours and approximately $75,000, a once barren warehouse became Cornerstone Church. The first service was finally held at the "new" facility in December of 1986.... However, the lack of space has always been undeniably a drawback.

Attendance has grown steadily over the years from the original 111. Cornerstone averaged 166 in attendance in 1986 and soon could boast an average in excess of 230. The Lord has been good to us.... In 1998 Cornerstone Assembly of God experienced some troubled waters within the congregation. They are in the process of rebuilding the body after a significant loss in membership. God is faithful and the congregation and pastor are experiencing His grace in difficult times.

Pastors include Don White and Dirk Roeder.

*Omaha—Christian Center, 1986

Omaha Christian Center was started in September 1986 in a motel (Omaha Inn) at 108th and L Street in Omaha. In March of 1987 a space was leased at 5420 North 99th Street in Omaha. The congregation worshiped in this facility until September 1996 at that time the existing facility was purchased from Bethany Baptist Church. Although the history is somewhat limited many have accepted Christ and God is blessing in many ways.

Ronald Edward Helmick is the pastor of this congregation as of this date (1998).

*Omaha—Evangel Assembly of God, 1987

The list of pastors includes Tom Jacobs, Robert Conner, and Kevin Nygren.

*Omaha—Freedom Assembly of God, 1991

Troy Vanderment has been the only pastor of the Freedom Church as of this date (1999).

*Omaha—Grace Community Church, 1997

The only pastor to date (1999) is Bart Wilkins.

*Omaha—Rios De Alabanza, 1995

Francisco Martinez is pastor of this church as of this date (1999).

*O'Neill—Assembly of God. 1943

In 1943 Rev. and Mrs. Harry Walker accepted the challenge to pioneer a full gospel work in the predominantly Catholic town of O'Neill. A store building was rented, cleaned up and opened for services.... While Harry Walker was the pastor lots were purchased for a church building. J. M. Cummings was pastor when the new church ... was dedicated in May 1946. Pastor Joe Clapper partitioned the church basement to serve as a parsonage during his stay in O'Neill. In 1949 Wayne and Hazel Hall came to O'Neill. A time of diligent visitation and children's services was experienced. A gracious outpouring of the Holy Spirit and revival among the youth took place. A new parsonage was also built during this time. In 1966 while Duane Palser was pastor there was a groundbreaking for a new sanctuary. Dedication of the new facility took place on March 30, 1969. The former church was used for a fellowship hall until under the direction of James Loutzenhiser, the parsonage was sold, the former church moved out, and a new fellowship wing was completed. A new parsonage was purchased at 901 West Cedar. Pastor Harry Brotzman was the first pastor to reside there. Dave Graves with the help of laymen completed the classrooms in the basement of the fellowship wing. Lee Warriner finished the basement of the parsonage on West Cedar, adding three bedrooms, office space, utility, full bath and a large family room.

The list of pastors include: Harry Walker, J. M. Cummings, Joe Clapper, Jonah Hamburger, Wayne Hall, Egan Kirschman, Robert Paul, Ivan Christoffersen, D.E. (Gene Arnold, Duane Palser, James Loutsenhiser, Harry Brotzman, David Graves, Mike Neff, Lee Warriner, and Paul Ready.

*O'Neill—Word of Life Assembly of God

Pastors include James Loutzenhiser and Jim Loutzenhiser.

*Ord—Assembly of God (reopened), 1975

The *Pentecostal Evangel* reported in 1978 that a new church ... has been started in this central Nebraska farming town of 3,000 which has been without an Assemblies of God church for several years. The Ord Assembly of God was one of the older, flourishing churches in Nebraska at one time. After the Depression years, most of the people left the area. The church struggled for several years but finally closed in the 1960s. M. S. Anderson, who had a burden to see an Assembly of God church in Ord again, began holding services in the community May 20, 1975. Almost immediately he purchased property and made plans to construct a church building.

For two months the new congregation of 22 rented the Odd Fellows Hall. Then the local high school made space available rent-free for 20 months. The new church building was dedicated May 17, 1977.... The beautiful new building will seat 250, or 325 with overflow. The facilities include seven classrooms and a large fellowship hall and kitchen.... Brother and Sister Anderson and the congregation did most of the construction, although a number of others donated labor and materials. In addition, local merchants donated an organ, two stoves, a refrigerator, and a 650-piece stainless steel flatware set.... In the first 2 ½ years, attendance has reached 50, and 10 persons have been saved.

Pastors include M. A. Anderson, Howard Rice, and Lonnie Carpenter.

*Pender—Cornerstone Assembly of God, 1925

The Pender Assembly of God had its beginning in 1925. Rev. G. A. Comstock held cottage prayer meetings and a number of people were converted. These folks continued to attend their respective churches but as the prayer meetings continued, the interest and attendance increased. In August of 1934 Pearl Wallway and Viva Keeling conducted a seven-week revival. More people were saved and filled with the Holy Spirit. A place of worship for the group was needed and Mr. and Mrs. William Cornwell donated lots and ground was broken for a church building in March 1935.... the building was completed and dedication services were held on July 14, 1935. In August of the same year the Assembly of God in Pender was officially chartered with eleven members.

Lots were purchased and a parsonage was built in 1946.... In 1980 construction began on a new facility. Charles Davis was the pastor during the construction. The facilities are in the shape of a cross. Included are a sanctuary with baptistery, six classrooms, two offices, fellowship hall, and kitchen.... The congregation is excited about what God is doing in their church and community.

Pastors serving this congregation include G. A. Comstock, Pearl Wallway, B. C. Heinze, Pearl Wallway, D. C. Hastie, V. C. Dickinson, Maynard Morehouse, L. S. Nichols, George Clarke, Ernest Rosenkrans, Gary Sherman, Don Warford, D. B. Arnold, Fred Rosenkrans, Ron Rice, Harvey Hanson, Charles Davis, Jeffrey Slosson, Sammy McKay, and Doug Overly.

*Plattsmouth—New Life Assembly of God, 1990

The *Pentecostal Evangel* reported the opening of New Life Assembly of God in the following article:

Plattsmouth, Nebraska ... been known for having the highest alcohol rate of any city its size (63,000) in the United States—14 bars for every one church.

... An estimated 60 to 70 percent of the people of this city do not attend church. Plattsmouth Police Chief Ron Duckworth believes that 90 percent of the city‘s high school students have tried drugs.

It was to this setting that Kim and Teresa Robarge were called, after spending 4 years in Kenya, East Africa.

Pastor Gary Hoyt of Belleuve Christian Center was sensitive to the burden that the Kim and Teresa felt and to God and asked his congregation to help plant a church in the neighboring community of Plattsmouth. The response was overwhelming.

Several families from the congregation agreed to go with the Robarges and churches in the Metro Omaha area joined with resources and prayer. The harvest field in Plattsmouth is great.

(Kim Robarge, “The Harvest As Close As Our Doorstep,” *Pentecostal Evangel*, October 7, 1990, pp. 24-25.)

Pastors of New Life Assembly of God include Kim Robarge, Doug Nurss, and Jonathan Busch.

*Red Cloud—Assembly of God, 1929

The Pentecostal message came to Red Cloud in 1919 when Brother Hoar and Brother Northup held meetings upstairs over the Central Café.... Charles Harris came in 1925 and held a tent meeting. During this revival Roy Barnes answered the call of God into the ministry and his wife was the pianist.

In 1929 Ira and Lois Shuck with their three boys came to Red Cloud to start a church.... Not only was 1929 the beginning of the great depression, but it also included the dust bowl days. To top all this off the Pentecostal message was rejected, and most people agreed that Red Cloud didn‘t need another church to support. Even with all this opposition they knew God had called them there.

... Hiram Moger remembers this about his childhood.

“The Lord led my family to Pentecost through Brother Shuck‘s son Raul. There was a big snow and the Shuck boys were giving rides on wooden sleds they made.... Raul and I had a lot of fun that afternoon.

While we were walking home Raul‘s younger brother Don came running up the street. He wanted to walk with us. As we were walking Raul asked his brother what they were going to have for supper. His younger brother replied “Two slices of bread and a bowl of wild plums.” ... I found out later that bread and plums were all they had to eat all week. I told my mother about the Shuck‘s food situation and my mother quickly responded to the need. We loaded our car up with potatoes, eggs and a few other things that we had raised in our garden and took it to the Shuck's home. That food gift was received and greatly appreciated. A few days later Sister Shuck visited with my mother. In this conversation a deal was made. The Shuck family would go with the Moger family on Sunday morning to church and the Moger family would attend the Shuck's service on Sunday nights, which was their home."

They attended the services and especially enjoyed the exciting music.... Sister Shuck started an afternoon prayer meeting and it wasn't long before many of the women were saved and filled with the Holy Ghost. The little house soon became to small to contain all the people that started to come. They needed a church building, but it seemed impossible.

The Assemblies of God sent an Evangelist named Charles "Earl" Schriner who came from the Riverton area. He began to hold tent meetings at 32 N. Seward Street. The tent meetings were full because this was the first time people had heard of the Assemblies of God movement. During an icy cold evening the tent they were meeting in blew over forcing Brother Schriner to find a new location to hold their meetings. Through God's great provision they finally got a building called the "old south end mission" which was located at 205 S. Seward Street. They met every Sunday afternoon, and their services included Sunday school for the children.

Brother Schriner became the pastor of this new church. Most of the town people didn't like the new church, ... It seemed that anyone who was seeking the Holy Spirit received it, however, because of lack of direction everyone who received the Holy Spirit also felt called into the ministry. This problem split the church several times. Shortly after these problem Sister Schriner died, and Brother Schriner moved away. The people that were left in the church began to quit. Finally the little corner church could not financially be maintained so they found themselves meeting once again in the home of Brother Shuck.

In 1937 Charles and Irene Blodgett came to serve as pastors. Times were hard, so hard that crow meat was a part of the Blodgett menu. God did bless in spite of difficult trials with 22 youth and an average of 50 in Sunday school. The Blodgetts resigned and moved to Riverton as pastors in May 1938. Again Brother Shuck assumed the role as pastor.

In June 1949 the C. W. Livers family came to pastor the Red Cloud Assembly of God. Improvements were made on the "Little Mission" including strengthening ceiling trusses and stucco on the outside. Work was begun a while later on a new building on lots purchased in 1950 on North Seward Street. Lumber was salvaged from the depot at Bloomington, Nebraska. The new church was completed as church folks and friends from the community worked together and Superintendent Lester W. Dickenson dedicated it on April 6, 1953....

The list of pastors includes Ira Shuck, Earl Schriner, Ira Shuck, Charles Blodgett, Ira Shuck, O. R. Shaffer, Lyle Herrick, Roy Herbig, C. W. Livers, Earl Fread, Harvey Herman, George Bingham, Mildred Larson and Linda Stivers, Harvey Herman, Kenneth Thee, Dan Moorhead, Harvey Herman, Ralph Russo, Scott Dunning and Ken Hansen.

*Riverton—Assembly of God, 1918

Saloonkeeper, Walter Northrup, was a key figure in starting the Assembly of God church in Riverton. He attended Pentecostal services in Bird City, Kansas and was marvelously saved. He sold his saloon and made his living by truck gardening and carrying the U. S. mail. Later, in 1918, Rev. Henry Hoar was persuaded to come to hold meetings and to begin a church. The Northrups held meetings in several neighboring towns in the area and followed Brother Hoar as the second pastor of the newly born church. This was the first Assembly of God church in Nebraska.

The third pastor was Rev. G. W. Clopine, who came from Franklin. The children were in school in Franklin, and the family never moved to Riverton. Rev. Clopine was elected the second District Superintendent and Brother Singeltary, a single young man followed him. The next pastor was a "cowboy preacher" from Texas. He arrived on the scene at a baptismal service out on the riverbank. He was traveling in a covered wagon—pulled by a beat up old truck! He and his wife had three little girls and they had measles, mumps, whooping cough and pneumonia—what a likely bunch to pastor a church! The Alvin Hawes were well liked and pastored Riverton twice....

In 1933 Robert Skelly went to Riverton as pastor and during his ministry the downtown mission burned and the congregation used rented store buildings or houses in which to worship. Alva Kite, a 17-year-old preacher followed Robert Skelly. Alva was quite a cartoonist, and he was liked by the kids and as well as the adults.... Others followed but it was in 1935 Ruth Gerber and Daisy Jones came.... They only stayed a few months but Ruth returned later. When Ruth returned in 1936 the new stucco church on Main Street was built. The church was blessed with a large group of young people who loved the Lord. She had one of the most outstanding ministries of all the history of the church....

Charles Blodgett came to pastor in 1938, then James Melton, and Walter Stahlecher. During these years (1940-41) Evangelist Moses Copeland conducted meetings and souls were saved and filled with the Holy Spirit and miraculous healings were witnessed. Numerical growth accompanied the spiritual growth. In 1942 Richards came from the Kansas District, they only stayed three months. In October of 1942 Christopher Livers was elected as pastor. He was one of the very best Sunday school builders ever in this district. In 1944 Moses and Ruth (Gerber) Copeland returned to server as pastors.... While LeRoy Eichman was the pastor the stucco church building was sold and a new building was built and the mortgage was burned.

Rev. Duane Roll began their ministry in 1960 and an active youth ministry and Sunday school work continued.... There were over 90 children enrolled. This was quite an event for a small town. During the ministry of the Elmer Cravers (1963) the church annex and basement were built and dedicated. The Sunday school grew and stayed in the 70's and 80's.... In 1972 Frank and Jeanie Alexander came to Riverton. Pastor Alexander was quite a carpenter and a new parsonage was built in approximately 4 months after their arrival from Colorado. Extensive remodeling was done on the church building. A large foyer was added, a nursery and 2 rest rooms were built into an overflow area, and new church furnishings were purchased....

The list of pastors include Henry Hoar, Walter Northrup, G. W. Clopine, Brother Singeltary, C. Alvin Haws, Grace Smith, A. R. Shaffer, Brother Felicy, Brother Rhoades, Walter Nelson, Robert Skelly, Alva Kite, Gordon Millard, Ruth Gerber and Daisy Jones, Marjorie Ball and Mercades Forhman, Dwight Chaffin, Ruth Gerber, Charles Blodgett, James Melton, Water Stahlecher, James Richards, Chris Livers, Moses Copeland, Roy Herbig, Ervin Smith, Earl Haight, Charles Spence, LeRoy Eichman, Duane Roll, Elmer Craver, George Smith, Irvan Jackson, Frank Alexander, Arthur Taylor, Steven Patterson, Larry Foster, Merle Headding, Frank Alexander, and Bill Holt.

*Scottsbluff—Assembly of God, 1924

Scottsbluff Assembly of God came into being as a result of a tent revival which began on September 5, 1924 near the old West Ward Elementary school with Irl Walker of Bayard as the evangelist. Florence Klitzing of Chappell provided the music. Following the revival the group of believers was pastored by the Merle Rolls and later by Florence Klitzing. The congregation moved into the West Ward Elementary school, which had been condemned for public school purposes. A lot was purchased later at 6th Avenue and 15th Street and a frame church building erected. It was dedicated in 1926 while Edgar White was pastor.

In 1945 during the ministry of E. M Clark a new face tile building was erected. Later while Clyde King was pastor a lot and a house was purchased for the purpose of providing additional Sunday school facilities. The name of the church officially became First Assembly of God in 1955. In 1960 Milo Harmon became the pastor and during this time the old parsonage became the educational facility and the house north of the church was redecorated for the parsonage.... Under the ministry of Troy Allen a three-acre plot was purchased on East 27th Street and a beautiful new building was built.

The list of pastors includes Merle Roll, Florence Klitzing, Logan Sturat, Rev. Griswold, A. M. Alber, Ray Sherman, W. Mac Lamar, Rev. Farrar, Herman Meyer, E. M. Clark, M. F. Brandt, Clyde King, Milo Harmon, Ernest Illum, Troy Allen, James Call, Lewis Hootman, Rev. Reece, Dick Dube, Alex Montgomery, Neal Hail, Mike Schaaf, and Rob Conner.

Hispanic Ministry at Scottsbluff and Gibbon

... It was in the summer of 1933 that the Lord, in His mercy, led us to the Assembly of God in Ft. Morgan, Colorado, where C. L. Walker was the pastor. Like most Spanish-speaking people, we were deeply religious, but we did not know the Lord.

On our second visit, a Wednesday night youth service, a young man read Matthew 11:28, and God spoke to my wife through that verse. She accepted Christ as her personal Saviour that night and this was the beginning of the transformation of our lives. Soon after that the Lord saved our young daughter and me, as well as my parents. Wanting to share with others what we had received from the Lord we began witnessing to every Spanish-speaking person in and around Ft. Morgan. We held services in our home and as the Word was preached, souls were saved, healed and filled with the Holy Spirit.

... Ever since the Lord saved me, I felt a call to preach. However, it wasn‘t until 1943 that I answered the call of the Lord for full-time service. So we left our jobs, church, and family and went to Scottsbluff, Nebraska, to pioneer a work for God. The Lord confirmed His Word; souls were saved and filled with the Holy Spirit and many were healed. In due time, we had an established church. Many times He performed miracles to supply our material needs and the remembrance of His faithfulness continues to fill us with joy! In Scottsbluff we were blessed with the precious fellowship of two other churches and their pastors. They were the English Assembly, pastored by E. M. Clark, and the German Assembly pastored by Alvin Sprecher.

(Ysidro Ramirez, “Hispanic Ministry at Scottsbluff and Gibbon,” *Reflections of Faith*, 1983.)

The German Church in Scottsbluff

... It must have been about in 1941 when we accepted the invitation to pastor the German Church in Scottsbluff. We had been pastoring in North Dakota at that time. The church had its beginning a number of years before this, when a number of young people of the German Baptist got hungry for more of God and the Lord poured out His Spirit upon them in the young peoples meeting. However, the Board of deacons did not look upon this manifestation with favor and told them that they did not want that Holy Spirit in their church.... So I believe the young people had their own meetings till finally some of their parents contacted the Superintendent C. W. Loenser of the German Branch of the Assemblies of God. I believe one of the first pastors was Rev. G. F. Zeller, under whose ministry the basement church was built. The following pastor was Rev. Jensen and after that Rev. H. Rosin, who was there only a short time, then after that they gave us the call. We were at this church about five years.... During that time the superstructure was built on the basement. Following us Rev. Arthur Netzel pastored for a number of years, followed by a few others then finally the church went over to the Nebraska District, some time after that they relocated, moving to Gering where the Lord graciously gave a time of awakening and the congregation had quite a growth for a time.

(Alvin Sprecher, "The German Church in Scottsbluff," 1998.)

Robert L. Nazarenus Recalls His Roots, 1999

I was born and reared in Scottsbluff, Nebraska. I am third generation in Pentecost and the Assemblies of God.

My father‘s parents and family attended a German Baptist church in the early 1930‘s. One Sunday evening following the evening service, several young people began seeking God and were baptized in the Holy Spirit. My father, Harry Nazarenus, his brother, Henry, and Pete Hessler were among those young people.

The elders and pastor of the church met on Monday and promptly dismissed my Grandparents and the other families of the youth that had received their Pentecost. My Grandfather, opened his home (a two room tar paper shack) located at 924 East 12 Street for services. Eventually, contact was made with the German Assemblies of God, and a church was born. After several years, the church became affiliated with the English speaking Assemblies of God and is presently known as Northfield Assembly of God in Gering, Nebraska.

I had my personal Pentecost on Easter Sunday Evening, 1959 in Scottsbluff at the Neighborhood Church. That Fall, I left Nebraska and enrolled at Northwest College of the Assemblies of God, in Kirkland, Washington. In June of 1962, I married Mary Peterson, from Bridgeport, Nebraska. Following graduation we moved to Great Falls, Montana, to pastor Bethel Assembly of God. During the summer of 1968, we moved to Aurora, Nebraska to pastor the Assembly of God. In the spring of 1976, we accepted the call to pastor in Lincoln. After eleven years there, we were elected in 1987 to be District Superintendent.

Robert L. Nazarenus served as district superintendent of the Nebraska District from 1987 to 2005.

*Sidney—Christian Life Center, 1948

The Assembly of God in Sidney began on Sunday afternoon, October 17, 1948. Rev. and Mrs. Clinton Thompson conducted the first Sunday school and worship service in the Odd Fellows Hall. From this start and with the favorable response they continued services at this location until a lot was purchased and the present brick building was erected at 1545 King Street. Ground breaking was held in the spring of 1950 and the construction began. Services were held in the basement as work continued on the upper structure. Living quarters for the pastor were also included. Later a parsonage was purchased. The Thompsons continued to serve this congregation until May of 1966 when they entered the evangelistic ministry.

The list of pastors includes Clinton Thompson, Harvey Herman, James Moulder, Mildred Larson and Linda Stiver, Mark Moore, Lloyd Gordon, Paul Hill, Gary Ribble, Toby Tyler, and Jeff Clark.

South Sioux City in 1924

We feel like sending in our testimony as to the mighty working of the power of God in our midst. We were definitely led of God to this little mission, from the Sioux City Assembly of God, two years ago last March. For almost 20 months, we have held on, as God had promised us the latter rain. We have had many fierce battles with the powers of darkness and spiritual wickedness in heavenly places and have sought the Lord many times for release from the work, always putting His will first. And He always said, "Stand in your places; I will keep My Word and give you souls." Just before Christmas, one was saved and received the

Baptism. With encouraged hearts we renewed our petitions, and, on Christmas night at our Christmas program, He poured out His Spirit in a mighty way. It was the real break we had been looking for. Since that night, He has been saving and baptizing in the Holy Spirit men, women, boys and girls, also healing divers diseases, and some evil spirits have been cast out. In all, about 12 have received the Baptism with the perfect Bible evidence of speaking in tongues.

~ Brother and Sister W. H. Brown.

("South Sioux City," *Pentecostal Evangel,* June 28, 1924, p. 12.)

Springview, Nebraska in 1932

Last June I went to Springview for a revival. A new congregation organized there after a stirring revival. About twenty have received the Holy Spirit there. Brother Lester H. Sheets is now pastor of this church.

(Nebraska Pentecostal Fellowship, Vol. 1:1, March, 1932.)

*Taylor—Assembly of God, 1940

It all started in 1940 when a young evangelist, Hazel (Bristol) Hall came to the Blake community and held revival services. The Raymond Harris family and some of the Goas family were saved during this revival. Burwell was also experiencing revival in early 1941 and several of the Lewis families were saved.

Vere Harris conducted a revival in the Goas school. Several were saved and filled with the Holy Spirit. Brother Harris continued on as pastor and the Congregational church was rented for services. The Drake family, Dan Sthrals, Henry Hydes and others who had attended services at Knobby Ridge joined the congregation for worship. The Congregational church was rented until September at which time Pastor Harris obtained a tabernacle from the district. Two lots were purchased and the tabernacle was set up. Vere Harris left in November 1941. Raymond and Marie Harris then filled the pulpit from November 1941 until February 1942.

W. W. Appleyard held a revival in February 1942 and remained as pastor until the next fall. The church was organized at this time. J. A. Vosika accepted the pastorate in November of 1942. During a revival with Paul Hill the Tom Rittenhouses, Fritz Brockmans and Thelma Smith were saved. Also at this time members of the Chet Dunbar family joined the congregation. During the ministry of J. A. Vosika a house was moved in for a parsonage. In June 1946 Erin Rhode came to pastor this growing congregation.... Groundbreaking for a new building was held in September and at a fellowship meeting June 1, 1947 the church was dedicated, debt-free. Superintendent M. F. Brandt gave the dedication message.

The list of pastors includes Vere Harris, Raymond Harris, W. W. Appleyard, J. A. Voseka, Erin Rhode, George Rhode, James Loutzenhiser, David Prescott, George Smith, Frank Alexander, Harley Stahl, Richard Schoonover, Don Dennison, and Dan Varns.

Thedford, Nebraska in 1925

Brother Thurmond writes, "My brother, W. E. Thurmond of Buckner, Illinois, and I just closed a meeting at Thedford, Nebraska, where I worked for a period of 4 years, there being about 25 turning from Satan unto the Lord. The people say they never witnessed such a revival meeting before. We were there for 2 weeks only and left the people rejoicing in the Lord. The Congregational church opened the doors of their church and turned it over to us."

(C. E. Thurmond, "Thedford," *Pentecostal Evangel,* October 17, 1925, p. 13.)

Thedford—Bethel Assembly of God, 1928

In June 1928 Rev. and Mrs. Claude Thurmond went to Thedford to conduct a tent meeting revival. About 40 people were saved in this old-time revival meeting. The church was then organized and set up as an independent unit with no affiliations with any group or denomination. For the first few weeks meetings were held in the town auditorium. The Thurmonds moved to Thedford in the fall of 1928 to become the pastors. Weekday services were held in what was then the Zavadil house for over a year. During this year the Holy Spirit and the Pentecostal message were received in the Sandhills area, first in a little schoolhouse north of Mullen known as the Cherry school. Some of the folks from the Thedford church attended these meetings and became very interested. Shortly after this a Pentecostal outpouring was experienced in Thedford. The first church building was erected in the winter of 1928-29 on land donated by Sylvester Blauvelt. Rev. and Mrs. Frank Wickham came as pastors for approximately one year. Rev. and Mrs. Skelly followed them. During this time living quarters were built on the back of the church. Alice Nichols served as pastor for a short time followed by Rev. and Mrs. Jay Bushnell.

From 1934 through 1938 Rev. and Mrs. Harry Walker served the congregation. While they were pastors the church became affiliated with the General Council of the Assemblies of God with headquarters in Springfield, Missouri. Rev. and Mrs. C. A. Sailors served from 1938-43 followed by Rev. and Mrs. Harry Balkkolb, 1943-48. At this time a house was purchased and remodeled for a parsonage and the old living quarters was converted into Sunday school rooms. From 1948-55 Rev. and Mrs. E. E. Rohde were pastors. This was the time of the ‘49 blizzard which will long be remembered by many. All through the years the congregation experienced growth and during this period the Sunday school attendance reached 144. Excavation for a new church building began in the spring of 1950. The first service in the new building was held in the fall of 1950. The old church property was sold.

The summer of 1955 brought Rev. and Mrs. R. S. Denny as pastors. Rev. and Mrs. Paul Sherman who began their ministry in 1957 followed them. During their stay the old parsonage was sold and a new parsonage west of the church was built. It was completed in March 1961. From September 1962-1968 Rev. and Mrs. E. L. McNaughton served as pastors. Rev. and Mrs. K. Melvin Johnson served the congregation from August 1968 through August 1978.... Pastor and Mrs. Kenny Dickenson and family moved to Thedford in October of 1978.... In 1981 a beautiful new sanctuary was built and the former building was remodeled to provide a modern kitchen, fellowship hall, offices, nursery and restrooms.

In December 1987 Ron Blauvelt was invited to come home and pastor the Bethel Assembly of God. During this time the church saw the need of taking Christ to the people. They erected a tent in a community 30 miles from Thedford for 4 nights of meetings. This was the first event of the nature in Brownlee, population “20 or so”, as the sign reads. At the Saturday steak cookout Randy Weaver, chaplain to professional cowboys, presented the gospel to more than 130—many had never been in a church. When Bethel Assembly purchased a large tent and held its first tent revival, people came from 36 towns and 7 states. It was an exciting time in the history of the church.

Pastor Joe and Tammy Masten followed the Blauvelts. Clarence and Ruth Rohde followed the Mastens. The Rohdes retired in 1999 and moved to California.

1938 Revival in the Sand Hills

In 1938 Brother Clark held a tent meeting in the sand hills where he met his wife-to-be. Estella Burry was playing the piano for the revival services. The Lord gave a tremendous revival in the Thedford area at a place called Seven Corners near Dunham. It wasn‘t long before Brother Clark knew Stella was the lady he wanted to marry. After a couple weeks, Stella returned to her home in Bridgeport. But it was several weeks before Brother Clark was able to close the revival because of the great response to the gospel the Lord gave them. He then followed her for their wedding.

While preaching this revival in the sand hills, Brother Clark didn't feel it was O.K. to pray for healing for the unsaved. One night a woman with a deformed hand came to him and asked for prayer for the healing of the claw-like, curled up fingers on her hand. Brother Clark told the woman, "You need to be saved." The woman answered she couldn't be saved because her husband wasn't saved, but she wanted to be prayed for anyway. So Brother Clark prayed for her. But he said, "I didn't pray the prayer of faith." The next evening she returned to the services with a normal hand and with her was her husband and several other family members. Her husband was a very big man only thin. Because of an ulcer, he was on a milk only diet. That night Brother Clark prayed for the husband. God healed him and he was able to eat anything.

(E. M. Clark, *"1938 Revival in the Sand Hills,"* October, 1995.)

Reaching Rural America

With the urgent need to take the gospel to the millions in urban America, we must not overlook those scattered over the vast rural areas.

My ministry is to those in and around Thedford, Nebraska, a county seat of 245. The county has some 850 residents. In the heart of the Sandhills area, Thedford is noted for its large ranches and quality cattle.

The culture here dictates learning to be self-sufficient early on and handling life with little outside help. Small boys learn that when they get thrown from their horses, they get up, brush off the dirt and get back on.

Most ranchers believe in God; but because of their self-sufficiency, they are often unwilling to accept divine intervention in their lives....

In December 1987, the congregation of Bethel Assembly of God in Thedford invited me to pastor their church.

... Rural ministry involves more than preaching. A minister must live with the people. To reach the unsaved I must first establish a trust relationship. Respect develops and opportunities to witness result. Rural people, when saved, are hard working, dependable, and dedicated to sharing the good news.

Because people are so scattered in this area, the church often must go to them. Presently Bethel Assembly buses Royal Rangers and Missionettes who live up to 50 miles away.

We erected a tent in a community 30 miles away for 4 nights of meetings. This was the first event of this nature in Brownlee, population "20 or so," as the sign reads. At the Saturday steak cookout Randy Weaver, Assemblies of God chaplain to professional cowboys, presented the gospel to more than 130 -- many of whom had never been in a church.

A year ago Bethel Assembly helped reestablish a church which had closed in a community some 40 miles from Thedford.

When Bethel Assembly purchased a large tent and held its first tent revival, people came from 36 towns and 7 states. This year we are planning six similar outreaches.

We must hear the call of the people scattered throughout the hills and lead them to Christ.

The question has been asked, "When is Bethel Assembly going to settle down to be just a normal church?"

Our answer is, "Not until our region has been reached for Jesus Christ."

(Ronald Blauvelt, "Reaching Rural America," *Pentecostal Evangel*, October 13, 1991, pp. 19, 30.)

*Valentine—Assembly of God, 1938

According to Ralph Hayford, the Assembly of God in Valentine, Nebraska began in the Norden area. Prior to 1925 a small group of people consisting of a few families started meeting in the Shadley Creek schoolhouse about 14 miles from Norden. The O. G. Hayfords and the Wilbur Andrews families along with others were involved with these meetings. Close neighbors also started attending. Milton Glendening, an uncle of Roy and Edward Cutler and a Methodist lay preacher had greatly influenced the people in the area in a spiritual revival. After Milton Glendening moved on the people were hungry for more of God.

Records in the Cherry County Court House show that on March 22, 1928 Frank and Pearl Kuskie Copeland purchased from John W. and Maud E Harvey Lot 20 in block 2 in Valentine. The property apparently was purchased with the intent of establishing an Assembly of God, for just four days later on March 26, 1928 this same property was sold to the Assembly of God in Valentine for a small sum of money. Construction on a small, wood frame church building began soon on the corner of 5th and Ray Streets. With the Great Depression, which began in 1929, the small congregation was unable to pay off their indebtedness on the building. The next record at the courthouse show that on March 10, 1931 the "Assembly of God Church of Valentine, Nebraska, a corporation," entered into a mortgage with Bertha C. Sparks. The Trustees signed this document.

The next record of interest is dated March 23, 1931 and is a record of the minutes of a business meeting of the church. The congregation voted one hundred percent to change organizations and become the Bible Standard, Inc. (also known as Open Bible Standard Church). The church remained part if the Bible Standard Inc. for about five years. During this time they did not have a regular minister. Due to the deepening depression, the congregation was unable to pay off their mortgage and there is a record showing that on December 18, 1935 they were forced to relinquish their rights to the property and it is believed the building was closed for about one year. However, the congregation was enthusiastic and continued to meet in various homes during this time.

A few of the previous members became desirous to return to the Assembly of God organization. They pooled their personal resources and bought back the church property. A record at the courthouse shows that on April 20, 1936 the property was again conveyed to the "Assembly of God Church, a Corporation." The remaining debt was fully paid off September 30, 1938. In January of 1938 the church secured their first full-time pastor. The Nebraska District Superintendent of the Assemblies of God, A. L. Albers, sent him to Valentine. It can be said that Rev. James Mervin Peck and his wife Velma, "pioneered" the church in Valentine. There were 10 people present for the first service with the new pastor.... Records show that the church applied for affiliation with the General Council of the Assemblies of God on May 5, 1940. In 1941 the Sunday school averaged 66.

In 1941 Rev. and Mrs. E. J. Dewey came as pastors of the church.... The church experienced growth and revival. In May of 1943 the H. W. Lebsacks were called to be pastors. God gave revival and growth with the Sunday school reaching a high of 200 in attendance. The church held revivals in surrounding schoolhouses and established an outstation in the town of Crookston ten miles west of Valentine.... A number of ranch families were saved and filled with the Spirit. In 1946 a house was bought and moved into Valentine and remodeled for a parsonage. The new church was built in 1949 and the congregation rejoiced with the new facilities. In 1951 H. J. Blakkolb began his ministry in Valentine.... A number of people have gone out from the church into the ministry as ministers and missionaries. God has blessed this church that had such a hard time getting started.

The list of pastors includes J. M. Peck, E. J. Dewey, H. W. Lebsack, H. J. Blakkolb, Gene Schachterle, Jimmy Root Sr., Ron Murray, Richard Fisher, Henry Mohn, Stephen Gill, and Jimmy Root Sr.

*Wahoo—Cathedral of Praise, 1985

Rich Vernon has been the only pastor as of this date, (1999).

*Walthill—Assembly of God, 1922

The Assembly of God church was started in Walthill as a result of a tent meeting held on Main Street by Rev. G. A. Comstock of Sioux City, Iowa, in the summer of 1922. After this meeting there were several families who accepted the Pentecostal doctrine and started having prayer meetings and services in the different homes. A Sunday school was organized on April 29, 1923, with six or eight families in attendance. In October 1924, Rev. Comstock held a revival meeting. On November 21, 1924, Rev. Charles F. Cox was called to act as the first resident pastor. In the fall of 1925 the Sylvan Creek property east of the railroad tracks was secured and converted into a church building. On April 20, 1925, Rev. Roy E Scott called a business meeting; Superintendent of the West Central District of the Assemblies of God to get the church set in order. At this time the people unanimously declared that they wished to be associated with the General Council of the Assemblies of God. At this meeting Charles F. Cox was elected as pastor and Mrs. Edley G. Keeling, assistant pastor.

In 1934 the old building was moved from east of the tracks to the present location and in the spring of 1938 it was torn down and work was begun on a new and larger building. The dedication services for the new church was July 4, 1940, with Rev. M. F. Brandt, Assistant Superintendent of the Nebraska District, giving the dedicatory message. The Walthill Assembly is one of the older churches of the Assemblies of God in Nebraska and has been one of the leading churches in the state in foreign missions giving.

Pastors of this assembly include Charles Cox, J. G. Unruh, Charles Cox, E. R. Swick, Ivan E. West, J. Robert Birdwell, E. L. McNaughton, Henry F. Stiles, John Bellar, Robert Pederson, and Harold Ross.

Revival at Whitney

December 31 we closed our meeting with Evangelist C. D. Quackenbush. In the very first service, December 4, the Lord began pouring out His Spirit. Before the meeting began a couple of our men made the remark that they would be unable to attend every service because of so much work they had to do. After this first service, the thought of not being able to come never entered their minds again. When God begins to work the people will come. Eight high school students knelt at the altar for salvation. Others were reclaimed, and some were filled the Holy Spirit. There was one outstanding Baptism. This lady came into the church from another denomination sometime ago, but was never entirely convinced that the Baptism in the Holy Ghost was for her. Oh, what a wonderful experience she had! We shall never forget this meeting with Brother Quackenbush. ~ J. E. Troyer, Pastor.

(J. E. Troyer, "Revival at Whitney," *Pentecostal Evangel*, January 31, 1942, p. 13.)

Mrs. M. B. Woodworth-Etter at the Winnebago Indian Reservation

In her book, Marvels and Miracles God God Wrought in The Ministry for Forty-five Years, *Mrs. Woodworth-Etter describes her experience while conducting a camp meeting at the Winnebago Indian Reservation in northeast Nebraska. As Mrs Woodworth-Etter concludes her meeting at Winnebago, she decides to respond to a call to hold meetings in Fremont, Nebraska. In this narrative she shares both the Winnebago and Fremont experiences including her arrest at Fremont and the response of the news media.*

The meeting among the Indians was in many ways a marvelous one. I received great sympathy and love for these people as I saw them come from their reservation in such large numbers to our meeting at Sioux City, Iowa. [September 1920]

It was not possible for me to pray for all the people who came to the meeting at Sioux City; not even all the Indians, so some were always disappointed because I could never get to them on account of the throng. They then sent me the urgent invitation to come to their reservation and hold a few meetings, even if I could stay no longer than a day or two. I consented to go if they made the necessary preparations, which they readily agreed to do....

On Tuesday morning, September 14th, we started for Winnebago, Nebraska, the Indian reservation. For this place we received an invitation, signed by ninety-three people to come and hold a meeting as follows:

"We, the undersigned Indians of the Winnebago Tribe, are firm believers in your ability as a divine healer, and as we believe you can do much good for other members of our tribe, and other citizens of this community we earnestly request that you spend a few days in Winnebago. It is impossible for some of our people to get to Sioux City for various reasons and these are the ones most badly in need of your assistance. We will assure you that we will be very glad to have you among us. Winnebago is about 25 miles from Sioux City."

The Indian people came and carried us there in the finest automobiles we ever rode in; and when we arrived there at noon the tent was nearly full of people. We commenced meeting in the afternoon, although the meeting was not advertised to start before night. The Indians were so hungry for the gospel that we could not deny them, and it did our hearts good to see them get down at the altar and seek for more of God, with tears running down their faces....

It was a beautiful scene to look at the preparation that these people had made for the campaign in their community. They pitched two large tents on a beautiful common close by their little village, and had it nicely arranged, and well lit up. A number of the workers were amused over the substantial timber (bridge timber) that was used in the large platform; but when they saw some of those large, stout men and women, come and line up on it, they were glad that it was well built.

The Indians came for miles around to attend this meeting; scores camped on the grounds, or close by, and when the meetings were closed at nights, the humming of the motors and the people running to and fro, reminded me of a Fall Fair.

God worked in a marvelous way in the healing of those hungry Indians, for they came upon the platform in simple faith, believing that they were going to receive what they asked for, and they surely received a touch from God in nearly every instance. In some of the meetings people were healed in the audience, without coming to the platform to be prayed for. One says: "I was healed of cancer in the breast and rheumatism, while in the audience at Winnebago." Another said, "I had a stiff knee for ten years, and it pained very much. I was healed, and the pain and stiffness is all gone. I did not get to the platform to be prayed for." This meeting lasted until the 21st of September and people came from far and near. There were over 200 autos on the ground at one time. Reports later state that practically the whole tribe turned out to seek God.

A lawyer, president of all the Indian Societies of the United States said: that he and a prominent Indian had hated each other but they had made up and now love each others. Many Indians gave marvelous testimonies of healing....

While I was at Winnebago, Nebr., calls came in from all directions for me to come and help them. Even many of the unsaved took quite an interest in the meetings. One man came from a town about one hundred miles away, with his machine [automobile] full of spiritually hungry people; some of whom were greatly afflicted. He stayed for some days and then went home. When he got home and saw what God had done for his people; the change wrought in them spiritually, and the afflictions of their bodies removed; he made up his mind to take up another load of sick people, which he did, with the same results. He did this three times in a very short while, and always came back with a "Macedonian Cry": "Come over and help us, we want you in our town."

(Mrs. M. B. Woodworth-Etter, *Marvels and Miracles God Wrought in The Ministry for Forty-five Years*. Indianapolis: the author, 1922, pp. 407-411.)

Meetings in Winnebago in 1924

Evangelist R. Fields [Rik Field], from Oregon, has just closed a meeting here. All were blessed by receiving the Word of God. The meetings started in a private home. Soon the crowd compelled us to rent a larger building located on Main Street, which was also crowded. The congregation was about one-half Indians. The sermons were interpreted for the Indians, and they gladly received the Word. Some were saved and baptized in the Holy Spirit, and some wonderful healings took place. One Indian came to the meetings on crutches, and could hardly walk. Brother Fields prayed for him and he was instantly healed. Two others came with canes, and were healed and left their canes in the building. Another person was healed for paralysis. We praise the Lord for the meetings and ask the Lord's blessing upon Brother Fields wherever he goes.
~ Joe Lameres, Jr.

(Joe Lameres, Jr., "Winnebago," *Pentecostal Evangel*, August 23, 1924, p. 12.)

*Mission Work in Winnebago

Louise C. Gray pastored in Allen. Also she was the pastor of the Hiway Mission in Winnebago in the 1930s as well as working in Macy.

In 1988, Louise C. Gray received recognition for fifty continuous years of service to the Assemblies of God.

*York—New Heights Assembly of God, 1933

Revival fires were spreading across Nebraska and in 1933 they spread to the small community of York, Nebraska. Mrytle Gorman and some young people from Aurora were instrumental in its beginnings. They came to York and held meetings in the vacant Dean Theater, located between 7th and 8th Street, on Lincoln Avenue. Later they rented a church building with a parsonage in the basement. This church was located on the corner of 8th and Grant. In 1933 the congregation called E. N. Stanley to come as pastor of the congregation. G. D. Baker, Jack Ireland and Earl Cummings served as pastors at this location. During Rev. Baker's time he had a radio program on the York radio station KGBZ. In 1936 a decision to tear down this building caused the move to a location between 18th and 19th Street on Platte Avenue … On September 30, 1936 the church was established under the name of Full Gospel Church. Rev. Earl Cummings of Hastings was the pastor. At the time of chartering there were 14 members listed. Today descendants of these early charter members can be found among the congregation.

The year 1944 found the church on the move again. This time it was to the location of 8th and Platte.... On April 22, 1959 another step was taken by the congregation to further establish themselves in the community. The church became an incorporated church under the name of York Assembly of God Church. In 1963 a building program was launched.... In 1995 Kerry and Linda Andrews moved to York to be the pastors of this congregation. They brought the congregation to a new plateau of change.... The new building is located on the South Grand property the church purchased in 1982. The new facility was dedicated in the fall of 1997.

The list of pastors includes E. N. Stanley, G. D. Baker, Jack Ireland, Earl Cummings, John Gorman, Virgil Hall, John W. Church, Clyde King, Dale Hastie, John W. Church, Delbert Turner, Jack Risner, B. H. Armes, James Mayfield, Troy Allen, James K. Richard, Leonard Herrmann, Hugh Campbell, Toby Tyler, Jeff Congdon, and Kerry Andrews.

Pender A/G church dedicated 11/21/80. Charles Davis became pastor shortly before dedication. Harvey Hansen was pastor during most of the building program.

Sidney A/G church

New ramp built on church at Valentine, NE

This Assemblies of God church was built to minister to the needs of the inner-city in downtown Omaha. It was called "His Church." Rev. James Twamley was the pastor. Supt. James Wilkins conducted a dedication service on Sept. 1, 1985.

Chapter 13: Closed Churches

"So shall my word be that goeth forth out of my mouth: it shall not return unto me void, but it shall accomplish that which I please, and it shall prosper in the thing whereto I sent it." **(Isaiah 55:11 KJV)**

This next section of the book includes some brief history of closed churches and a listing of pastors as gleaned from record cards maintained by the General Secretary's office at the Assemblies of God Headquarters. These churches are listed alphabetically. Although the churches in this section all have closed, there still was much planting watering and harvesting of souls as God gave the increase. God's word does not return void.

Allen—Assembly of God

This church was affiliated on June 25, 1940. In later years it was listed as a district affiliated church. For most of the time the church had 20 members or less. The membership in 1946 was 24. The church closed on June 12, 1964. At that time the church was located at 438 E. 31st Street. Known pastors are:

Earl J. Dewey (1940-1946)
W. C. Womersley (1956-1964)

Alliance—Alliance Full Gospel Tabernacle

This church affiliated in 1941. This church appears to have dissolved or merged by the 1960s.

C. E. Thurmond (1941)
Clyde King (1942)

Alliance—Bethel Assembly of God

This was a new church that opened on July 6, 1982. It was located at 11th and Toluca Streets. It merged with Calvary Assembly of God in Alliance on September 20, 1984. Known pastors are:

Howard A. Rice (1982-1984)

Alma—Assembly of God

This was a district affiliated church that existed prior to 1956. It was located at 5th and Carlyle Streets. The last pastor was Steven Groseclose, who was also the pastor at Holdrege. The church closed on February 29, 1968 because "the people have moved away." Known pastors are:

James E. Mayfield (1956-1957)
James Brown (1957-1959)
Everett M. Lee (1959-?)
Byron T. Luckey (?-1965)
Dee Lynn (1965)
George Smith (1965-1966)
Steven Groseclose (1967-1968)

Alma—New Life Assembly

This was a new church that opened on August 13, 1979. It was located at 302 W. Main. The congregation disbanded on October 26, 1982. Known pastors are:

Mark A. Wetzler (1979-1981)
Jonathan Wetenkamp (1981-1982)

Amherst—Assembly of God

This church was affiliated on August 16, 1934. The church was closed on May 14, 1957. Known pastors are:

Lecil Divine (1934)
V. W. Weaver (1956-1957)

Anselmo—Center Pentecostal Assembly of God Church

This church was affiliated on June 25, 1940 as Center Pentecost. It was located at Route 1, Anselmo, Nebraska. The attendance fluctuated between 15-40 parishioners. The church was closed on February 22, 1955. Known pastors are:

Harry Walker (194)
F. B. Wickham (1944-1947)

Arcadia—Assembly of God

This church existed for a few years. The church closed in February 1959.

Arnold—Assembly of God

This church was located 15 miles east of Arnold. This was a district affiliated church that was opened prior to 1952. There are no records of this church from the 1950s through the 1960s. The church was closed on November 22, 1976 due to "insufficient interest." Known pastors are:

Clinton Thompson (1969-1973)
Cornelius William DenHoed (1974-1976)

Auburn—Auburn Pentecostal Assembly

This congregation was organized in on May 31, 1917 as Auburn Pentecostal Assembly and affiliated on June 2, 1917. Evangelists Rev. and Mrs. W. B. Oaks were assisting with the church at that time. This congregation would have been the home church of the faculty and students of the Midwest Bible School that operated in Auburn from 1920-1921. The church closed sometime after 1921.

Bartley—Assembly of God Church

This church was affiliated on July 13, 1937. It had 17 members at that time. The church was closed probably in the 1940s. Known pastors are:

Carolyn Roach (1937)

Beatrice—Glad Tidings Assembly of God

This church was affiliated on September 28, 1942 as Glad Tidings Assembly. It was located at 218 N. 8th Street. (at the corner of 8th and Elm). In 1952 the church had 25 in attendance, and in 1953 it had 15 in average attendance. The church was closed in 1954. Known pastors are:

Herman W. Lebsack (1942)
Guy D. Hamar (1952-1954)

Beaver City—Assembly of God

This church was affiliated on June 15, 1925. The church disbanded on May 26, 1994. Known pastors are:

Allen R. Shaffer (1925)
Russell V. Umphenour (1956-1961)
Robert Courtneys (1961-1962)
W. O. Ziegler (1962-1964)
Donald Winter (1964-1966)
Larry G. Hessler (1966-1969)
Harvey C. Smith (1969-1972)
Robert O. & Eunice Brown (1972-1976)
Brad Riddle (1976-1979)

Lloyd Gordon, Jr. (1980-1981)
Forrest W. Frazier (1981-1983)
Edward Warren (1983-1984)
Forrest W. Frazier (1984-1985)
Lowell Imhof (1986-1989)
Les Loebs (1989-1993)

Bellevue—First Assembly of God

This church opened on October 1, 1966 and became affiliated on June 30, 1967. For temporary quarters it was meeting at the junior high school. By 1967 it was located at 2002 Franklin Street. It closed on October 10, 1968. Pastors include:

Clifford C. Sutton (1966-1967)
Kenneth Wray (1967-1968)

Benkelman—Assembly of God

This was a home missions church that opened on September 29, 1959. It closed on June 18, 1965 with a note that "We had several workers in this town, but we were unable to establish a church." Pastors include:

John A. Mazurek (1959-1964)
S. LeRoy Sailors (1964-1965)

Benkelman—Harvest Time Assembly of God

This was a new church that opened on April 12, 1991. It was located at 722 B Street. The church closed on October 20, 1997 due to "lack of interest." Pastors include:

John Corder (1991-1993)
George Rennau (1993-1995)

Bloomington—Woody Assembly of God

This church affiliated on April 27, 1926. At that time the church was meeting at the Woody School House in Bloomington, and the church was being pastored by Evangelist Sadie Shaffer. It is not known when this church closed. Pastors include:

Sadie M. Shaffer (1926)

Bridgeport—Assembly of God

According to records of the Eastern Colorado District of the Latin American District, there was a Hispanic congregation located in Bridgeport, Nebraska in 1943 and in 1947. This appears to be a different congregation than the church currently located in Bridgeport. It probably never joined the Nebraska District.

Broadwater—Assembly of God

This church affiliated on November 18, 1935. This church closed prior to 1956. Pastors include:

H. W. Lebsack (1935)

Buda—Assembly of God

According to records of the Eastern Colorado District of the Latin American District, there was a Hispanic congregation located in Buda, Nebraska in 1943. It was not listed in 1947.

Burwell—The Blake Community Church

This church was affiliated on April 17, 1942. In 1944 it had an attendance of 25. It was district affiliated and closed sometime in the 1940s. Pastors include:

Miss Hazel Bristol (1942)

Butte—Anoka Butte Assembly of God

This church affiliated on September 24, 1935 as Full Gospel Tabernacle, located at Anoka, Nebraska. In 1944 the church had an average attendance of 100. It later became known as Anoka Butte Assembly of God. It closed on December 30, 1954. Known pastors are:

Chester G. Anderson (1935-1944)

Central City—Assembly of God

This was a district affiliated church that existed prior to 1956. It was located at 22nd Street and 18th Avenue. It closed on January 23, 1967 because the "people moved away." Known pastors include:

Gaylord A. Correll (1956-1960)
Merlin D. Markland (1960-1962)
K. Melvin Johnson (1962-1965)
Gary Sherman (1965)

Chappell—Assembly of God

This was a district affiliated church that existed prior to 1943. It disbanded on March 23, 1944. Known pastors are:

George W. Clopine (1943-1944)

Coburg—Coburg Assembly

This church affiliated on July 13, 1937. The district report the church disbanded on March 23, 1944. Pastors include:

E. J. Dewey (1937)

Crawford—Assembly of God

This was a district affiliated church that existed prior to 1954. It was located at 3rd and Annin Streets. It was closed on December 30, 1954.

Crete—Assembly of God

This was a cooperative church that existed prior to 1961. It was located at 19th and Main. The church closed on January 29, 1965. Known pastors are:

Bill Bradway (1961-1963)
Harvey Herman (1963
Gary Sherman (1964)

Dalton—Assembly of God Mission

This church was recognized as a congregation in 198. It never had more than about 30 in attendance. William Cummings and John Hodges were the pastors between 1938 and 1944. This congregation disbanded on March 23, 1944. Known pastors were:

William E. Cummings (1938-?)
John W. Hodges (?-1944)

Decatur—Assembly of God

This was a home missions church that was active in 1956. It was closed on February 16, 1965. It was reported that a few of the remaining members began attending the Lyons Assembly. Known pastors were:

Loretta E. Plummer (1956-1959)
Herbert DeMent (1959-1960)
Robert Ayers (1961-1963)
Nathan Lutes (1963-1964)

Emerson—Assembly of God Church

This congregation was affiliated on March 30, 1937. It was located on the south side of Emerson. The attendance during the 1940s was around 20 members. The church closed on May 14, 1957. Known pastors were:

B. C. Heinze (1937)
Miss Pearl Wallway
Melvin Drews
Frank Moffat (1953-1954)

Franklin—Assembly of God

This church was affiliated on May 21, 1917 and was still in existence in 1931. It closed sometime in the late 1930s or early 1940s. Pastors include:

G. W. Clopine (1917-1931)

Fremont—Bethel Assembly of God

This was a district affiliated church that existed prior to 1956. It became General Council affiliated on October 16, 1967. The church was located at 1205 N. Hancock Street. The church closed on May 23, 1988 because the attendance dropped and the income was not sufficient to keep the church open. Known pastors were:

Allen Wine (1956-1963)
Leo Gaston (1964-1966)
Paul A. Luckey (1966-1969)
Robert G. Hutsell (1969-1980)
Gerald Begley, Jr. (1980-1984)

Gering—Pentecostal Assembly of God

This church affiliated on Jun 2, 1927. It was closed in 1932.

Geneva—Assembly of God

This was a district affiliated church located at 310 S. 8th Street. It existed prior to 1956. The church was closed on May 14, 1957. Known pastors were:

Howard L. Smith (1956-1957)

Gibbon—Bethel Temple

This church was set in order on December 8, 1940 and affiliated on July 15, 1941 as Betel Church (also known as Bethel Church). This was a Spanish-speaking congregation that was part of the Eastern Colorado Conference of the Latin American District Council. The church closed for awhile but reopened in 1947 under the name Bethel Temple. It is not known when this church closed. Pastors include:

T. R. Gonzalez (1940-1941)

Gordon—Bethel Chapel

This church was a district council affiliated church located at 302 E. 3rd Street. It existed prior to 1947. The attendance during the 1940s and 1950s fluctuated between 10 and 35. The church was closed on February 25, 1957. Known pastors include:

Marvin O. Green (1947-1954)
Harold Powell (1954-1955)
James Loutzenhiser (1955-1957)

Guide Rock—Full Gospel Mission

This church was a home missions church that was first recognized on August 20, 1956. It was closed on May 14, 1957. The only known pastor is:

E. V. Dunbar (1956-1957)

Hartington—Assembly of God

This was a district affiliated church that existed prior to 1956. It was located on Lemon Street. The church closed on June 12, 1964. Known pastors include:

Earl S. Fread (1956-1958)
Anne Bohan (1958-1961)

Hay Springs—Assembly of God

This church was recognized as a congregation in August 1955, and it closed on November 28, 1955. The only known pastor is:

Charles Turner (1955)

Hendley—Assembly of God

This church affiliated on December 11, 1922. It closed sometime before 1956. Pastors include:

Daniel L. Cooper (1922)

Hershey—Assembly of God

This church affiliated on March 29, 1930. The church closed on August 10, 1964. The district made this note: "Most of the people moved away and those remaining voted to close the church at Hershey and attend a neighboring church." Pastors include:

Rose Hallgrimson (1941)
Wesley E. Reynolds (1956-1958)
M. E. Ellis (1958-1959)
Robert D. Sinner (1959-1963)
Edgar Baker (1963-1964)

Homer—Assembly of God

This church was active in 1924 and affiliated on April 28, 1925 with Charles F. Cox as pastor and Fred Kipper as assistant pastor. Cox was pastor of the church continuously through 1935 at least, except for two years he spent pastoring at LeMars, Iowa. This church closed prior to 1956. Pastors include:

Charles F. Cox (1924-1925)
Charles F. Cox (1935)

Johnstown—Moon Lake Assembly of God

This church affiliated on February 4, 1935. In 1942 it had an attendance of 50 members. The church closed sometime in the 1940s. The only known pastor is:

J. J. Clark (1935)
Harry Walker (1942)

Kearney—Assembly of God

This church affiliated on January 22, 1932. This church closed prior to 1956. Pastors include:

H. D. Stanley (1932)

Lincoln—Assembly of God Mission

This church was set in order on April 30, 1930 and affiliated on May 9, 1930. It moved to 6135 Morrill Avenue in 1931. It was a country church that remained small. It existed at least until 1935. Pastors include:

Joe C. Burkey (1930)
Opal Wiley (1931)

Lincoln—Faith Tabernacle Assembly of God

This was a new work that started in 1954. At that time it had an attendance of 13 members. It was located at 834 ½ North 27th Street. The church closed on May 4, 1955. The only known pastor is:

Duane E. Woods (1954-1955)

Lincoln—Garden View Church Assemblies of God

This was a new church that opened in February 1976. This church affiliated on June 13, 1977. It was first located in a temporary worship center at 4444 S. 52nd Street, and then 48th and "A" Street. In 1980 the congregation moved to 2500 S. 84th Street. The church closed on January 31, 1998 due to lack of interest, financial support, and the pastor leaving. Known pastors include:

Robert L. Nazarenus (1976-1987)
Wayne Newcomb (1987-1988)
Steven Fenton (1988-1995)

Thomas M. Swihart (1996-1998(

Lincoln—Gates of Praise

This church was affiliated on February 20, 1935. At that time it was called Lincoln Gospel Tabernacle and later called First Assembly of God. It was located at 29th and Randolph Streets. The church moved to 340 N. 56th Street in the early 1960s. (the intersection of 56th and "R" Street). In 1999, the church moved to 740 N. 70th Street. At the same time, the church changed its name to Gates of Praise. The church closed on November 3, 2004. Known pastors include:

C. B. Thomas (1935)
S. K. Biffle, Jr. (1956-1969)
Daniel O. Rothwell (1969-1973)
Jack L. Glass (1973-1981)
Geoffrey Duncombe (1982-1994)
Randall Dugger (1994-1998)
John G. L. Burpee (1998-2004)

Lincoln—Lighthouse Pentecostal Mission

This church affiliated on July 31, 1926 with Sister Pearl Gilliland elected as interim pastor through August 1926. The church later withdrew on August 29, 1926. Pastors include:

Pearl Gilliland (1926)

Long Pine—Lighthouse Assembly of God

This church was district affiliated on June 1, 1922 as the Assembly of God at Long Pine, Nebraska. In 1942 the church had 30 members. It changed its name to Lighthouse Assembly of God on January 4, 1977. The last location of the church was at 266 W. 3rd. The church disbanded on June 1, 1995 due to lack of interest and economic conditions. Known pastors include:

F. E. Anderson (1922)
Sophia Skoff (1942)
Luella Cutsinger (1956-1966)
Dennis G. Pigman (1966-1968)
James Snyder (1968-1970)
Elmer Swick (1970-1971)
Merritt Nickerson (1971-1972)
Willard Hutsell (1972-1975)
Edwin G, Scribner (1975-1976)
Steve Williams (1976-1978)
Edward Warren (1978-1981)
Ron Lint (1982-1986)
Dale Williams (1986-1989)
Maynard McCarthy (1989-1991)
John Gale (1991-1993)
Gary Graesser (1993-1995)

Macy—Assembly of God

This church was district affiliated on April 5, 1927. It closed for a short time during the 1950s and reopened in October 1959. It served as a mission to Native Americans. The church officially closed on May 4, 1964. Known pastors include:

Susan Miller (1927)
Mrs. Louise C. Gray (1950)
Walter J. Hamilton (1959-1964)

Mills—Assembly of God

This church affiliated on September 3, 1932. It closed sometime prior to 1956. Pastors include:

F. E. Anderson (1932)

Minden—Assembly of God

This church affiliated on July 28, 1936. It closed sometime prior to 1956. Pastors include:

A. E. Brown (1936)

Naper—Assembly of God

This church was district affiliated on August 27, 1937. During the 1950s it had an average attendance of 30-40 members. The church closed on May 14, 1957. Known pastors include:

Elmer R. Swick (1937)
James D. Brown (1950-1951)
Olfert Rettedal (1953)

Nebraska City—Harvest Time Assembly of God

This church was affiliated on July 28, 1936 as the Assembly of God at Nebraska City, Nebraska. It was located at 1112 Fifth Corso. It changed its name to Harvest Time Assembly of God on July 18, 1984 and moved to 1020 N. 10th Street. The church closed on August 31, 1985 when the congregation dwindled, and it didn't seem feasible to keep it open. Known pastors include:

George Baker (1936)
Virgil L. Conger (1956-1960)
Leroy Eichman (1960-1962)
Willis Dewey (1962-1965)
Kenneth Krivohlavek (1965-1967)
D. George Cross (1967-1971)
George R. Jacobs (1971-1975)
Stanley J. Rutkowski (1975-1977)
Harry J. Blakkolb (1977-1981)
Kenneth D. Taylor (1981-1984)
Steven Madrinich (1985)

Neligh—Assembly of God

This was a district affiliated church that existed prior to 1956. It was located at 10th and Sycamore. The church closed on January 23, 1967. Known pastors include:

Ernest Rosencrans (1956-1958)
Mildred Larson & Linda Stivers (1958-1962)
James Strieby (1962-1964)
Dennis C. Pigman (1964-1966)

Newcastle—Assembly of God Full Gospel

This was a district affiliated church that was affiliated on May 19, 1927 as the Assemblies of God Mission. The high attendance in the early 1950s was 30 people. The church closed on March 3, 1955. Known pastors include:

Frank Thomas (1927)
J. Willis Rilea (1935)
J. Wilber Copenhaver (1944-1950)
Allen Wine (1950-1952)

Oak—First Community Church

This was a new work (district affiliated) that opened in 1951. The original name was Oak Assembly of God. Then it was changed to the Church of Oak. Then to First Community Church. At its peak in 1954, the church had 80 members. The church was closed on April 3, 1958. Known pastors include:

E. V. Dunbar (1951-?)
Estel L. Krause (?-1958)

Ogallala—Spanish Assembly of God

This was a home missions church that ministered to Hispanics. It was opened in about 1960. It was originally part of the Midwest Latin American District and was located at 909 W. 9th Street. In 1971 the church became part of the Nebraska District. The church was closed on March 18, 1976 because there were not enough Spanish speaking people for a church. Known pastors include:

Mrs. Francisca Figueroa (1960-1964)
Abraham Valenzuela (1964-1965)
Mrs. Fransisca Figueroa (1965-1976)

Omaha—Ashland Park Assembly of God

This church was located at 5260 South 48th Street in Omaha. It was closed on June 10, 1963.

Omaha—Christian Center

This was a new church that opened on October 2, 1978. It was located in the high school auditorium. The church was closed on August 13, 1979 because there was not enough interest to carry on. Known pastors include:

Charles R. Turner (1978-1979)

Omaha—Cornerstone Assembly of God

This was a new church that opened on March 20, 1985 and affiliated on June 30, 1986. The original name was Millard Assembly of God. It was located at 12424 Weir Street at Norris Elementary School. The church changed its name to Cornerstone Assembly of God later in 1985. Then it moved to Millard South High School at 149th and Q Street. Lastly, it moved to 133rd and I Streets (13305 I Street). The church disbanded on February 12, 2001. Known pastors include:

Donald L. White (1985-1998)

Omaha—Good Report Assembly

This was a new church that opened on April 21, 1986. This was a black inner city church. At that time it was called Believer‘s Good Report Outreach Center, located at 4426 Florence Boulevard. By the fall of 1986 it was known as Good Report Outreach. In 1987 the church moved to 5830 Maple Street and changed its name to Good Report Assembly. The church withdrew from the Assemblies of God on May 1, 1990. Known pastors include:

Frank Elia (1986-1990)

Omaha—His Church

This was a new church that opened on June 19, 1985. This was an inner city church located at 512 S. 13th Street. It was closed on June 30, 1987 because of a dwindling congregation and the expiration of the lease on the downtown facility. Known pastors include:

James Twamley (1985-1987)

Omaha—Calvary Assembly of God

This church was originally called Bethel Assembly of God and was affiliated on March 27, 1958. It was located at 67th and Corby (2814 N. 67th). During the 1960s the church moved to 10303 Boyd Street. The church changed its name to Calvary Assembly of God in 1969. On September 24, 1982, the church merged with a sister congregation called Living Faith Assembly of God. Known pastors include:

Kenneth H. Wray (1958-1965)
Arlo A. Johnson (1965-1970)
Rex Herndon (1970-1976)
Gene L. Ansell (1977-1979)
George R. Jacobs (1980-1982)

Omaha—Living Faith Assembly of God

This was a new church that opened on June 29, 1981. It was first located at 655 N. 108th Avenue where the church was renting a place at the Holiday Inn. In 1982 the church merged with a sister congregation called Calvary Assembly of God. The combined church was called Living Faith Assembly of God and was located at 10303 Boyd Street with D. Wes Daughenbaugh as pastor. A few years later, the pastor resigned and the congregation made a decision to withdraw from the fellowship. The church withdrew on October 8, 1985. Known pastors include:

D. Wes Daughenbaugh (1981-1985)

Ord—Assembly of God

This church affiliated on May 13, 1931 as Pentecostal Full Gospel Church. By 1955 it was called Assembly of God and by 1963 it was known as Full Gospel Assembly of God. Ord Assembly of God closed on June 1, 1968. Pastors include:

Gordon S. Fraser (1966-1967)

Oxford—Assembly of God

This church affiliated on June 25, 1940. It was located at the corner of Colorado and Odell (700 Odell Street). The church was closed on March 13, 1989 after the pastor left and attendance and finances dropped. Known pastors include:

Miss Ruth Gerber (1940)
A. J. Mickelson (1956-1957)
Howard Smith (1958-1961)
E. E. Baker (1961-1963)
Byron Lucky (1963-1964)
Miss Rose Hallgrimson (1964-1977)
Mark Moore (1977-1984)
Steve Olson (1984-1985)
Dan Hutsell 1986-1987)

Palmer—Assembly of God Church

This church was district affiliated on April 18, 1931. The attendance reached 20 in 1943. The church closed probably in the early 1950s. Known pastors include:

H. E. Comstock (1931)
J. A. Mydland (1943)
Ruth McKenney (1947)

Plainview—Revival Tabernacle

This church was a district affiliated church that existed prior to 1955. The church was first called Plainview Assembly of God. By 1956 it was known as Revival Tabernacle. The church withdrew from the fellowship on April 23, 1959. Known pastors include:

Virgil L. Conger (1956-1957)
C. R. Spence (1957-1959)

Red Cloud—Assembly of God

This church originally affiliated on June 24, 1921. It closed sometime after 1936. Pastors include:

Miss Marjorie Ball (1921)
Ira D. Shuck (1933)

Reynolds—Assembly of God

This church affiliated on October 15, 1936. It was located on Main Street. The attendance in the 1940s was around 40 people. The church closed on June 12, 1964. Known pastors include:

J. L. Huff (1920)
Edward C. Maser (1941-1946)
Mrs. Loren Duis (1956-1964)

Riverton—Assembly of God

This church affiliated on December 15, 1920. The church was closed on November 21, 2005. Known pastors include:

C. R. Spence (1956)
LeRoy Eichman (1956-1960)
Duane W. Roll (1960-1963)
Elmer Craver (1963-1966)
C. E. Smith (1966-1969)
Irvin V. Jackson (1969-1972)
Frank Alexander (1972-1976)
Arthur Taylor (1976-1979)
Steven O. Patterson (1979-1981)
Larry Foster (1982-1990)
Merle Heading (1991-1992)
Frank Alexander (1992-1998)
William C. Holt (1998-1999)
Brian Carroll (2000-2002)
Audry Beaty (2003-2005)

Rosalie—Assembly of God Church

This church affiliated on April 5, 1927. It disbanded sometime after 1930. Pastors include:

Mrs. Frank A. Samson (1927)
G. M. Haight (1927-1928)
A. L. Schoonover (1929)
G. M. Haight (1929-1930)

Scottsbluff—German Assembly of God

This church was set in order on June 9, 1935 and affiliated on September 23, 1936 as German Assembly of God (Gemeinde Gottes) and was part of the German Branch of the Assemblies of God. It later became part of the Nebraska District. It is unknown when it closed. Pastors include:

G. Fred Zeller (1935-1936)

Scottsbluff—Iglesia Beth-el

This church affiliated November 1, 1943 as Iglesia Beth-el and was part of the Latin American District of the Assemblies of God. It later became part of the Nebraska District, probably in the early 1950s. Pastors include:

Isidro Ramirez (1943)

Sidney—Assembly of God Church

This church affiliated on June 21, 1932 and disbanded on March 23, 1944. Pastors include:

Bert Talcott (1932)

Simpson—Simpson Assembly of God Church

This church affiliated on June 25, 1934. It closed sometime before 1956. Pastors include:

Chester Anderson (1934)

Springview—Assembly of God

This church affiliated on December 8, 1931 and disbanded on March 23, 1944. Pastors include:

C. E. Thurmond (1931)

Stapleton—New Life Assembly of God

This was a district affiliated church that was started before 1956. It was located at 605 "C" Street. The original name was Assembly of God. The church closed on November 16, 1982 due to dwindling numbers and insufficient funds. The church reopened on October 22, 1984 and changed its name to New Life Assembly of God. Known pastors include:

James Loutzenhiser (1956-1960)
C. W. Livers (1960-1967)
James D. O'Bryan (1967-1970)
Robert C. Ingle (1970-1971)
George E. Smith (1971-1972)
Daryl Lewis (1972-1979)
Gary A. Swagger (1979-1980)
Clinton Thompson (1981-1982)
Richard Bartz (1984-?)

Superior—Assembly of God

This church was first recognized on October 6, 1958 and was located at 906 E. Fifth. That pastor at that time was C. W. Livers. The church was closed on April 23, 1959. Known pastors include:

C. W. Livers (1958-1959)

Superior—Assembly of God

For the second time, a new church was opened at Superior, Nebraska on February 24, 1978. It was meeting at the Coaches Inn at 420 Fourth Street. In 1983 the church moved to Tenth and Dakota Street (959 Dakota). In 1985 the church moved to 145 S. Kansas. This church closed on March 13, 1989 because attendance dropped and the income was not sufficient to keep the church going. Known pastors include:

John M. Rolli (1978-1979)
Robert Albin (1979-1984)
Arthur Taylor (1984-1986)
Maynard McCarthy (1986-1989)

Thurston—Assembly of God Church

This church was affiliated on December 14, 1925. It was located on Main Street. The pastor in 1938 was Pearl Wallway, and the attendance at that time was around 25 people. The church was closed on February 25, 1956. The only known pastor is:

Pearl Wallway (1938)

Wahoo—Cathedral of Praise

This was a new church that opened on January 10, 1985. At that time the name was Cathedral of Praise Assembly. By 1987 the name was shortened to Cathedral of Praise. The church was located at 1335 N. Locust Street. In 1998 the church moved to 950 N. Chestnut Street. The church disbanded on December 31, 2005. Known pastors are:

Richard Vernon (1985-?)

Wallace—Assembly of God

This church affiliated on June 21, 1932. It closed on October 25, 1978 due to lack of interest and lack of finances. Known pastors include:

George T. Cummings (1932)
Nolan E. Christian (1956-1957)
David T. Holden (1957-1959)
Clarence Brotzman (1959-1960)
Duane C. Palser (1960-1964)
E. E. Baker (1965-1966)
Clyde Buck (1966-1967)
Leland Geer (1967-1969)
Maynard Brantlier (1970)
Harold Allen (1970-1977)
Gary A. Swagger (1977-1978)

Westerville—Assembly of God

This church affiliated on November 1, 1934 as Full Gospel Church. By 1940 it was called Full Gospel Assembly. The district reported it disbanded on March 23, 1944; however it reopened again soon afterwards. By 1955 it was called Assembly of God. It closed on August 25, 1981 because of an insufficient number of people to carry on. Known pastors include:

A. C. McIntyre (1934)
Harold James (1940-1943)
Carlyle Beebe (1943)
Frank Sobotka (1948-1949)
Howard Dixon (1950)
Harley Stahl (1950s)
Guy D. Hamar (1956-1960)
Harley E. Stahl (1960-1965)
Robert G. Hutsell (1965-1969)
James D. O'Bryan (1969-1974)
Mildred Larson & Linda Stiver (1974-1976)
Carlton J. Wyckoff (1976-1979)
Robert O. Brown (1979-1981)

Whitman—Assembly of God Church

This congregation was listed as a new work in 1950. The highest attendance was 20 members. The church was closed on January 23, 1956. Pastors included:

Rose Hallgrimson (1950-?)
Roy Herbig (?-1956)

Whitney—Assembly of God

This church was affiliated on April 8, 1935. It closed on June 12, 1964 with the district giving this report: "The Whitney, Nebraska is a very small village in North west, Nebraska that has almost ceased to exist. The potential is very limited so far as the church is concerned. The congregation elected to join with the congregation in Chadron, Nebraska which is only twelve miles for most of them to drive. This congregation is not lost, but are in our church in Chadron." Known pastors include:

Loyal A. Miller (1935)
Clyde S. Buck (1956-1957)
Earl J. Dewey (1957-1958)
Leonard G. Herrmann (1958-1964)

Winnebago—Assembly of God

This was a district affiliated church that existed prior to 1956. It was closed on January 23, 1967 because the "people moved away." Known pastors are:

Ralph Archer (1956-1966)

Wood Lake—Assembly of God

This was a district affiliated church that existed prior to 1956. The church was closed on June 12, 1964 with the district giving this report: "Woodlake is a small village in the ranch country of northern Nebraska. At the close of the school year 1963 they lost their high school. This made it necessary for the families with children to move elsewhere. We have not lost any of this congregation, but they have affiliated with our other churches in that area." Known pastors are:

Howard A. Dixon (1956-1963)

Chapter 14: Laying the Foundation (1919-1929)

"Peter replied, „Repent and be baptized, every one of you, in the name of Jesus Christ for the forgiveness of your sins. And you will receive the gift of the Holy Spirit. The promise is for you and your children and for all who are far off — for all whom the Lord our God will call.'" **(Acts 2:38-39 NIV)**

The next section of the book outlines historical information relating to the Nebraska District's development and ministries. Beginning with 1919 — the year the Nebraska District was organized — each chapter covers a different decade of growth within the district.

Nebraska District Council of the Assemblies of God Organized

In accordance with the call issued in June in the Christian Evangel and other papers, the brethren in Nebraska came together at North Platte, Nebraska, and organized the Nebraska District Council of the Assemblies of God, declaring itself in fellowship with the General Council with headquarters at Springfield, Missouri, and adopting as a basis of work the Preamble and Constitution adopted at Hot Springs, Arkansas, April 2-12, 1914, and the Fundamentals adopted at St. Louis, Missouri, in 1916. J. C. Rediger of Milford, Nebraska, was elected Chairman, and G. W. Clopine of North Platte, Nebraska, was elected Secretary. Other officers are H. L. Harvey, Henry Hoar, T. Timmons. For further information address the officers as above. We ask the prayers of all the saints that we may prosper in the Lord and walk in the Spirit while standing for New Testament order. The Secretary.

(G. W. Clopine [of North Platte, Nebraska], *Christian Evangel*, September 6, 1919, p. 14.)

Accessibility to North Platte

North Platte was ideally located for this historic gathering of Pentecostals from all over the state of Nebraska. In these early years of the twentieth century, east/west transportation was advancing with the main line of the Union Pacific Railroad and the Lincoln Highway going over the gently rolling prairie. Both transcontinental means of transportation went through North Platte in 1919 enhancing its accessibility.

With Nebraska having a length from north to south of 205 miles and east to west is 452 miles, the Nebraska Legislature proposed the first State Highway System comprising approximately 4,500 miles in 1919. The name of Nebraska comes from the Oto Indian word nebrathka, which means "flat water," referring to the Platte River which flows all across Nebraska. The south and north branches of this river join near North Platte making it the longest river in the state as it flows eastward to the Missouri River south of Omaha. The total area of Nebraska is 77,355 sq. miles making it the 15th largest state (1990).

From a 1919 Union Pacific train schedule, there were as many as twenty-eight passenger trains going east and west stopping in North Platte in addition to freight and mail trains. During the early decades of the century, North Platte became a major center for the railroad.

Trains, in 1919, were more reliable than automobiles since the roads were just trails from town to town with few people owning this modern machine. The first roadway to cross the United States was the Lincoln Highway, and it went directly through North

Platte. This plain dirt, sand, or mud road was established in 1913. Fence post were markers for the Lincoln Highway. The post were painted with red, white and blue stripes to keep travelers from wandering off the highway. At the beginning, it was little more than a line on a map connecting existing roads and trails. In 1925, the Lincoln Highway became U. S. Route 30. In 1928 Boy Scouts across the nation placed 3,000 markers along the highway distinguished by the letter "L". In 1932, the road was paved.

Hermon Harvey Reports

Our State Council was organized in July with J. C. Rediger, of Milford, Chairman, and C. W. Clopine of North Platte, Secretary and Treasurer. All the Assemblies of God in the state united in the movement to bring Sister McPherson into Nebraska for one great meeting (in Holdrege, Nebr.). Bro. J. W. Welch, Chairman of the General Council felt the great importance of the movement in Nebraska enough to come out and spend five days with us. Bro. Arch P. Collins, of the Colorado Council and Brothers W. T. Millsaps, S. H. Patterson and C. A. Beckman of the Kansas Council were here and gave hearty support and encouragement.

(Hermon L. Harvey, *Pentecostal Evangel*, November 15, 1919, p. 10.)

E. N. Bell on the Mid-West Convention

What we trust will be a great and blessed convention will be held at Auburn, Neb., June 10-20th. All the saints of Nebraska, Kansas, Missouri and Iowa are especially invited to attend this Mid-West Pentecostal Convention

This convention will be in the interest of the Master's work in all these stations, especially in the interest of the Mid-West Bible School of the Assemblies of God, at Auburn, Neb. The Lord has graciously undertaken and sent in $4,000 of $5,000 needed to buy a splendid building at Auburn, Neb. It is said this building cost about $22,000, and perhaps it would cost $40,000 to put it up at the present time. In order to encourage Pentecostal people to have a Bible school at Auburn, Neb., this building was offered to us for $5,000; $2,000 of this was given by two brethren interested in the school in or near Auburn. Putting our faith in the Lord we have taken over the building and now hold the deed to the same, and we are trusting the Lord to send in another $1,000 immediately to finish paying for the same, and then to send in some more for repairs and with which to start the school

The building will be used for the camping headquarters of all who attend the convention. We believe that the visitors can be accommodated in this building. We expect to have a large tent in which to hold the meeting.

Bro. S. A. Jamieson is to be present and give a teaching service each day out of the Word of God, and there may also be another day service for the saints. The night service will be of an evangelistic nature, and a rousing time is expected at this convention. Let the brethren keep this convention in mind and plan to come up to the help of the Lord on June 10th. For further information address Elder Geo. W. Hawley, or Elder J. C. Rediger, Auburn, Neb. Funds for the convention should be sent to the above brethren, and anything for the school may be sent either to them or to the Secretary of the Board of Trustees of the school, as below.

~ E. N. Bell, Secretary, Springfield, Mo.

(E. N. Bell, "Mid-West Convention: Midwest Bible School, Auburn, Nebraska," *Pentecostal Evangel*, May 1, 1920, p 10.)

Helping The New Bible School

Lately I have been considering what would be the best means for raising funds for the school, as there are pressing needs on every hand and not much in sight.

Thought perhaps that we could press the need more forcibly upon the people by suggesting that they plant an acre or so, such as potatoes, vegetables, etc., especially for the school.

As all four states are engaged in agricultural work it could easily be done and sent in this fall. Every little helps in these times when the cost of living is continually soaring higher and higher.

The government in times of war spent millions in the training of our boys and advised everyone to raise foodstuffs and sacrifice as much as possible. Why cannot we, as Christian people, concentrate our forces and help in the training of our boys and girls so they become well equipped soldiers of the cross. ~ J. C. Rediger, Auburn, Neb.

(J. C. Rediger, "Helping The New Bible School," *Pentecostal Evangel*, May 1, 1920, p. 10.)

The Midwest Bible School Remembered

Located at Auburn, Nebraska, this was the first General Council operated Bible school in the U.S. It lasted for one year.

Anticipation ran high in 1920 when groundwork was laid for the establishment of the first General Council operated Bible school at Auburn, Nebraska. That was 70 years ago. The Assemblies of God fellowship was 6 years old at that time and well on its way toward impacting the world for Christ.

Many of the founding fathers were anxious to see this school started since education was one of the five purposes for organizing the Assemblies of God in 1914. When "the call" had been issued for meeting at Hot Springs, it was announced: "We may also have a proposition to lay before the body for a general Bible Training School with a literary department for our people."

A school was not established in 1914, but two already existing schools were promoted there--T. K. Leonard's Gospel School and R. B. Chisolm's Neshoba Holiness School in Mississippi. Other independent or church sponsored schools were in operation between 1914 and 1920, but there was no General Council school.

By the providence of God, the first General Council school became a reality in 1920. A few years earlier, a Methodist minister in the little Midwest town of Auburn, Nebraska, had received the baptism of the Holy Spirit with the evidence of speaking in tongues. He decided to become affiliated with the Assemblies of God in 1919. This man, George W. Hawley, had been ordained by the Methodist Church in 1887 and had been a pastor for over 30 years. Now, at age 67, he could have easily retired from the ministry, but instead he decided to launch out on one of the biggest ventures of his life!

Having a seminary education himself, Hawley felt a need to promote Bible education in the Assemblies of God. Almost immediately after he received credentials with the A/G in September 1919, he was able to secure the Avenue Hotel in downtown Auburn. This seemed to be a suitable building for a Bible school, so he contacted the officials in Springfield.

After a season of prayer, the officials agreed to Hawley's offer to convert the building into a Bible school. Plans were made to purchase it from Hawley for $5,000, the amount he had originally paid for it. The Avenue was a 3-story brick building, 70 x 80 feet in dimensions, with a basement, and was constructed in 1903 at a cost of $20,000. It contained 57 rooms with steam heat and electricity and was likely worth at least $10,000 in 1919 when Hawley purchased it and offered it to the Assemblies of God.

By November 1919, a board of directors had been established and an announcement was made in the Evangel concerning the opening of what was called the Midwest Bible School to begin January 1, 1920. Twice during the winter of 1919-20 plans were made to open the school, but the official opening did not come until much later.

The temporary board of directors in 1919 was composed of representatives from Nebraska, Missouri, Iowa, and Kansas. By January this board consisted of: J. C. Rediger, Milford, Nebraska, chairman; George W. Hawley, Auburn, Nebraska, treasurer; E. N. Bell, Springfield, Missouri, secretary; John Goben, Lucas, Iowa; J. Kelly Campbell, Mt. Ayr, Iowa; Howard D. Stanley, Topeka,

Kansas; J. W. Welch, Springfield, Missouri; John Holman of Nebraska; and J. E. Shaw of Kansas.

Because of a cracked furnace in the school building and a strike which prevented buying coal, the school first had to postpone its opening until March. The trustees and board of directors agreed to hold a convention at the school from February 13-22 to earnestly seek God in behalf of the school and for personal needs. The last week of February was set aside as an adjustment time for new students arriving at school. S. A. Jamieson, Oklahoma District Chairman, and pastor of the famed "Fifth and Peoria" Assembly of God at Tulsa, Oklahoma, had been secured as principal, and plans were in order for the spring opening of the school.

But then another unforeseen circumstance came along.

In early February a flu epidemic spread through southeast Nebraska and closed in on the town of Auburn. The mayor of the city declared all churches and schools closed because of the epidemic and requested the convention be delayed.

Final plans for the upcoming semester were to be discussed at the convention, so it was impossible to proceed with the March opening date. Once again, the school opening had to be postponed.

It seems that the earlier scheduled openings for the school were not in God's time plan. With the extra months of preparation and time to raise funds for the school property, repairs, etc., the school was able to launch out on better footing for the coming year of study.

After urgent appeals to readers of the Evangel and district officials in the Midwestern States, the $5,000 needed to purchase the building was raised. The Assemblies of God purchased the Avenue Hotel from George W. Hawley on April 12, 1920.

The promised Midwest Convention which was to precede the opening of the school was held June 10-20, 1920. S. A. Jamieson gave Bible lectures during morning sessions of the convention, other services were held in the afternoon, and evangelistic meetings were conducted in the evenings. The meetings were held in the school building, and overnight accommodations were provided on a freewill offering basis inside the school. The board and interested supporters of the school made plans for the school to open on October 4, and more than $4,000 in cash and pledges were raised to help pay for repairs and provide a fund for support of students and teachers.

Like other early Bible schools, Midwest was operated on a "faith" basis, with faculty remunerations and other expenses paid from freewill offerings. Still other monies were requested to help pay necessary expenses, including a $1,600 paving tax.

An interesting suggestion appeared in the July 10, 1920, issue of the Pentecostal Evangel. As a way for students to raise their own support to attend Bible school, they were encouraged to work in the wheat harvest during the months of July and August to earn between $5 and $7 per day to apply toward their school expenses. Whether anyone took advantage of the opportunity is not known, but likely some of the students did. Others were evangelizing during that summer and raised support from gospel campaigns. Still others likely traveled to Auburn with faith that God would provide for their needs.

One student, Nina (Englund) Renick, recalls that she had written to Bethel Bible Institute in Newark, New Jersey. The letter the school sent her told of all the things the students could not do. The school sounded overly strict and oppressive. Nina's father said, "I'm not going to send my daughter to a prison." When Midwest opened, her parents sent her there and paid her way so that she did not have to find outside work.

When the 1920 General Council met September 21-27, plans were finalized for the opening of the Auburn school. It was considered "a direct answer to prayer to meet a crying need." The school was intended to be a training center for young people called into the ministry, to promote the fundamentals of the gospel as taught by the apostles and endorsed by the Assemblies of God. It was recommended that students study the Word 3 1/2 years, following the example set by Christ in instructing the disciples.

Within the next week the students and teachers began arriving at the new school. The ground floor of the school was made up of a prayer room, classrooms, bathroom facilities, dining room, and kitchen. The Jamiesons had an apartment on the first floor. The second floor was used for the girls dorm, and the third floor was the boys dorm. The walk-out basement included a pump house with washing and recreation facilities.

Each day started about 7:00 a.m. with chapel services conducted by the instructors and staff. Then the students separated to attend their respective classes.

Faculty and staff included S. A. Jamieson, principal, as Bible and advanced doctrine instructor; Mrs. Jamieson; O. E. McCleary, Bible and homiletics instructor; Louise Albach, English and penmanship teacher; Eva Groomes, piano and orchestra teacher; Mr. and Mrs. Dront as dormitory supervisors; and Johanna Zou, cook. Calisthenics was also taught at the school.

The teachers were very strict. The students were instructed to call the staff members by "Mr." and "Mrs." or by their respective title. The principal was given the respected title of "Dr." Jamieson. He did have a seminary degree, but technically he did not hold a doctor's degree. The students themselves were charged to only refer to each other by last names to be prefaced by "Brother" or "Sister." They could not use first names. When going to church and other activities, the boys would walk ahead, and the girls would follow behind. There was no dating.

Eva Groomes, the music instructor, was not very Pentecostal, in the opinion of former students, but she was a committed Christian. Although very strict and thorough in her training, she was a good teacher. The matron was also very exacting. Jamieson, on the other hand, was a gentle and pleasant man who almost always had a smile on his face. According to Nina Renick "You'd have to go a long ways to find a greater leader than S. A. Jamieson." He was highly respected by all the students.

Mrs. Jamieson did not teach, but she helped her husband. She was considered strict and made sure the girls abided by the dress code. She would often pray for the students and wait up at night for any of the girls who were working. One night, while waiting up for Adele Carmichael, she scalded her arm on the tea kettle and was badly burned. She just walked the floor and praised the Lord. By morning she was completely healed. This left a deep impression on Adele.

On Sundays the students attended the local Assembly of God which, undoubtedly due to Jamieson's influence, was meeting in the First Presbyterian Church of Auburn, located across the street from the school. Jamieson had been a Presbyterian minister and district official for many years before he received the Holy Spirit baptism and joined the Assemblies of God. The school's orchestra played for the Sunday services, and the students were a great encouragement to the local congregation at Auburn.

Even though almost a year of planning and promotion had been made for the school, funds were still needed to get though the first year. A plea in a November Evangel asked for $1,600 to pay for repairs, necessary purchases, coal, and state ordered fire escapes for the building. Readers were also requested to help supply the following: 75 folding chairs, bedding, bedspreads, dishes, table cutlery, rugs, a bathtub, and a piano. Lastly readers were again exhorted to send support for the teachers whose only support was from freewill offerings. Some of the students also needed support to be able to attend school.

As the school year progressed, the young people gained practical experience through student-conducted meetings held twice each week. Tarrying meetings were held on Sunday afternoons, and several of the students received the baptism in the Holy Spirit at these services.

Adele Carmichael, one of the students at Auburn, remembers: "There was one solid week when all classes were dismissed. During this time the students prayed night and day, and many of them received their calling to service." The students also held street meetings in downtown Auburn, making quite an impression on the townspeople.

All of the students were required to work at the school on Saturdays. Mrs. Jamieson usually asked Nina Renick to help clean and straighten up their apartment. The students also took turns helping out in the kitchen. Some of the students were able to find outside work in the evenings and on weekends. Adele Carmichael worked evenings in the telephone office. Malinda (Yost) Shotts did housework for a Pentecostal minister, Leroy Kopp, and later worked for a high school teacher in Auburn.

The spring term opened on January 4, 1921, with about 12 new students and a few new staff members. Mrs. and Mrs. Dront returned home to New York after the first semester and a new matron was secured for the spring session. The music instructor, Eva Groomes, did not come until January. By the spring semester about 40 students were enrolled.

The students gave glowing reports of the many benefits they were receiving from the Bible training and spiritual atmosphere at Midwest Bible School. Some of their comments were published in the Evangel. There is no doubt the school helped to prepare and nurture these young people to be capable ministers of the gospel.

Sad to say, though, in March, Evangel readers were told that a critical need existed. The announcement stated: "None of the teachers have received enough to cover their personal needs while the school has been in operation. Ten dollars a month is the very most that any of them have been given so far ... None of them can continue long at the present rate." These instructors really knew what it means to count the cost of discipleship.

At the close of the school year, D. W. Kerr, from Southern California Bible School, came to teach a 2-week course on dispensational truths. This special course was made available to anyone who had been unable to attend during the regular school year. Then from May 26 to June 5, 1921, a special "Mid-West Bible School Camp-Meeting" was held with evangelist Jack Saunders, D. W. Kerr and others in charge. A newspaper account reported that Saunders, his wife and 2 children had traveled 2,068 miles by car to arrive at the camp meeting. It took them 2 weeks of travel through wind, snow, rain, and hail, following the Old Sante Fe Trail at times and going through plowed fields. The students carried folding chairs from the school over to the big gospel tent for this revival campaign. The school's board of directors also met during this time to discuss the future of the school.

Despite financial needs which weighed heavy on the school during its first year, and problems relative to running a new enterprise such as this, the board of directors and the faculty made plans for a much better school year for 1921-22. Jamieson must have carried a heavy load as Bible instructor and principal in the first year, as the board proposed that E. N. Bell take on the duty of principal for the coming year. This would allow Jamieson to concentrate his energies toward his Bible teaching. O. E. McCleary intended to continue on the faculty, with a new matron, new English teacher, and a new music teacher to be added.

The school was advertised in the Evangel with such comments as "This is not a school to manufacture preachers. We believe in an old-fashioned, God-given call from heaven to the ministry. No amount of education can take the place of the Spirit of God and a call from the Lord ... We are only God's helpers in aiding these students to obey God's command to 'study to show thyself approved unto God, a workman that needeth not to be ashamed, rightly dividing the word of truth."

Applications were received that summer and plans were made for the second school year to commence after the General Council, with October 3 designated for registration and orientation and October 4 as the day classes would begin. New students were expected to pay in advance $5.00 per week for board, lights, and steam heat for the coming year. As late as October 1, 1921, advertisements still appeared in the Evangel to promote the second year of the school's operation, but at the last minute the term was canceled.

Over the course of the summer, badly needed funds did not come in. Another factor was that Auburn was too small to provide adequate employment for the Bible school students. Last of all, the school was unable to secure enough teachers and staff to operate for another year. Considering the meager offering the teachers received (less than 10 dollars a month), it is no wonder the school was unable to obtain faculty for a second year.

E. N. Bell, who was chairman for the Assemblies of God, was reelected at the 1921 Council, so he was unable to take on duties as principal of the school. By the end of the summer, O. E. McCleary decided to return to his hometown of Findlay, Ohio. He had previously taught at T. K. Leonard's Gospel School there which had been closed for several years. Now, with the fall term of 1921, Leonard had decided to reopen the Gospel School, so he had enlisted his old friend O. E. McCleary to help in this venture. McCleary became principal of that school and taught there for several more years, before becoming principal of Peniel Bible Institute which opened at Dayton, Ohio, in 1928.

The official decision to close the Auburn school was made on the last day of the General Council meeting in St. Louis: "On account of being unable to secure suitable teachers at the present time for the 'Mid-West Bible School,' at Auburn, Neb., it was decided that the school would not be opened for the fall term."

This announcement undoubtedly came as a surprise to new applicants and to students who had made plans to attend a second year. Some of the students continued their studies at other recognized school and others entered evangelistic work.

The Midwest Bible School was destined to never open its doors again. On April 28, 1922, the Assemblies of God sold the building back to George W. Hawley for $3,325, an amount lower than the original price paid 2 years previous. Presumably the General Council officers felt indebted to Hawley for his aid in securing this property for a Bible training school, and likely they were glad to have a willing buyer when the school closed its doors. Two months later Hawley was able to resell the structure for $7,000.

The building was operated again as the Avenue Hotel from 1922 until the early 1940s when it was converted into apartments. At that time the kitchen, dining room, lobby, and other rooms on the lower floor were remodeled to form five separate apartments, one of which boasts two enormous thermopane picture windows in its living room. The dome on the building always leaked and was removed after a hail storm did further damage around 1940. The structure is still standing in downtown Auburn and today is known as the Auburn Apartments. The First Presbyterian Church, where the students met for Sunday worship, is also still in use.

The Midwest Bible School only operated for one year, but as far as Adele (Boatright) Carmichael is concerned, it was ordained of the Lord. Not only did she receive Bible training, but she met her husband, the musically gifted Richard Carmichael. He and two of his brothers were students at the school. About 40 students attended Midwest, and according to Adele, "Most of the students of the Auburn School became active ministers and missionaries."

Although the closing of the school was a shock, had Adele continued at the school she perhaps would have missed out on a great blessing God had in store for her that next year.

She joined her father and Evangelist Maria B. Woodworth-Etter in a camp meeting in Des Moines and was healed of a goiter during this campaign. "Mrs. Woodworth-Etter came to the piano while I played, kissed me on the head, and laid her hand on my neck. She told the goiter to go. It went, never to return!" That experience gave her strength in praying for others with similar needs as she ministered with her husband in later years.

After the Midwest Bible School was closed, the Assemblies of God officials immediately began looking for a more suitable location for a General Council school. They visited a number of towns in Missouri and strongly considered two sites in Webb City, about 75 miles west of Springfield. However both buildings were badly in need of repairs. Having learned from the financial problems faced at the Auburn, Nebraska, school, the officials ruled out the Webb City location. It was also decided that the school should be in a large city where the students would have greater opportunity for missionary and evangelistic work.

Then in August 1922 the Commercial Club of Springfield donated a 15-acre tract of land on the north side of town to be used for a Bible school. Thus the new General Council school was located in the headquarters city.

That fall Central Bible Institute was started in the basement of Central Assembly, and the students lived in the homes of church people. By 1924 the campus was ready for occupancy and classes were held in what became known as Bowie Hall.

Midwest Bible School at Auburn, Nebraska, not only left an impact on the students during its one-year existence, but it left its mantle on Central Bible College, the second school to be fully owned and operated by the General Council, which has now trained thousands for Christian work.

Thus the educational needs of the Assemblies of God which were voiced at Hot Springs over 70 years ago are being fulfilled through the impact of the Midwest Bible School, Central Bible College, its successor, and through many other recognized schools in our fellowship.

(Glenn Gohr, "The Midwest Bible School Remembered on its 70th Anniversary," *Assemblies of God Heritage*, Summer and Fall 1990.) *(Used by permission).*

From the *Pentecostal Herald*

The following articles appeared in the Pentecostal Herald *which was published by George C. Brinkman in Chicago, Illinois. Brinkman was part of the Assemblies of God in the early years and many A/G churches are listed in his paper. Later Brinkman and his followers helped to found the Pentecostal Church of God. That denomination is still in existence with headquarters at Joplin, Missouri.*

Dear Bro. Brinkman:

At the winding up of the old year, I thought I would write a few lines. We are very busy in the battle for our Lord here in Omaha. Have been here over five months. God is wonderfully blessing in the work. We have a little mission located at 4002 N. 24th Street where we have services each Tuesday, Thursday and Saturday evening at 7:30 and Sunday afternoon at 3 o'clock and 7:30p.m. We also have a special meeting each Thursday afternoon for the sick and afflicted and God is wonderfully blessing in this service. Some marvelous cased of healing are being wrought by the mighty power of God. Wednesday afternoon is our service at the county hospital. A number of workers go there and spend all afternoon and God is doing a great work there saving and healing folks. On Friday evening we go to Fremont, Nebr., for a service. There we have a nice little band of people.

We welcome any Pentecostal people who may be passing through Omaha to stop off and see us, especially ministers. You will find your self made welcome in our home and mission. Please pray for us. Yours in the Master's service. ~ Mr. and Mrs. M. B. Long, 4002 N 24th St., Omaha, Nebr.

("Omaha, Neb.," *Pentecostal Herald*, February 1921, p 1.)

Greetings in Jesus precious name. Just a few lines to tell you all how wonderfully the Lord has been blessing the saints here at Fremont. Praise His name! Bro. R. Field was with us one week. We had eight receive the Holy Ghost. We sure praise God that sent Bro. Field* here. Our meetings were just wonderful. While not feeling well, I went to prepare some hot tea and a sandwich. I thought that would bring relief. My body had gotten so cold, instead of relief it just made things worse. I got so cold and my stomach bloated and I did not look like myself in the looking glass. Then I realized I was poisoned. I claimed the promise, *"And if ye drink any deadly thing it shall not hurt you."*

I held on tell my husband came and prayed for me, rebuking the cause and asking Jesus to heal. It was wonderful how the poison was cast out of my body ...

When it was over I was weak, but this morning I feel refreshed and my strength is back. I praise God we can prove Him and there is not one promise in the Bible which we can claim but that He will verify it. Praise His name!

Sincerely, your sister in Christ. ~Mrs. J. J. Foster.

("Fremont, Neb.," *Pentecostal Herald*, January 1922, p 3.)

Rik Field in the above article was an Assemblies of God evangelist who later joined the Pentecostal Church of God.

From Omaha, Nebraska

Well, praise the Lord for Victory. Am glad to report that my trial was called Monday, April 24th, and my accusers failed to be able to arrange their stories till they would hold together. And when the case was turned over to the jury it only took them a few minutes to unanimously decide Not Guilty and once more for the first time in four months I could say that I was free and not under bond.

When the jury returned and verdict was read there was a great roar of Praise the Lord, and Hallelujahs went up from that old crowded court room. Brother R [Rik] Fields of Portland, Ore., was here and heard the trial, if you want to make inquiry about the case you may write him. His address at present will be Kimball, South Dakota.

("From Omaha, Nebraska," *Pentecostal Herald,* May 15, 1922, p. 4.)

Long Not Guilty

The following is a clipping from the Omaha papers sent to the Pentecostal Herald; LONG NOT GUILTY.

"The Rev. M. G. Long, Pentecostal preacher, on trial in District Judge Day's court Monday, on appeal from police court, where he was sentenced to thirty days, charged with making improper advances toward a 13-year-old-girl, was found not guilty."

The reporters didn't write as much this time as they did before. The papers in Omaha are controlled by class of folks that don't like to say anything good about a Pentecostal Preacher. Please pray for me that the Lord will keep me sweet and humble in everything. Yours in the Master's glad service. ~ M. Long.

(Note: The writer knows very little about this case, but was told by one who was in Bro. Long's house, that he believed Bro. Long to be straight. As the matter was given publicity through other papers we believe it due to Bro. Long to say that the court found him "not guilty." Editor)

Revival at Ord, Nebraska in 1923

An Old Time Revival To Be Held In Ord, Nebr. Beginning May 10 and will be held for an indefinite time at 15tj and O Streets. One and one-half blocks southwest of the court house.

Evangelist Mrs. Ida Tribbett of Sturgis, Mich., is classed as one of the greatest workers on the field today. God is wonderfully using her in praying for the sick. Signs and wonders follow her ministry. All manner of diseases have been healed. Souls are saved and believers baptized with the Holy Spirit. You cannot afford to miss hearing her. Count on being present in the beginning of the meeting. Bring the sick and all that are in need of the water of life.

Remember the time and the place. Those from a distance who bring bedding and toilet articles, and who wish to do their own cooking will be furnished a 4-room house, supplied with stove, table, cots, etc. at reasonable prices, cots $1.50 per week. Rooms at private homes will be furnished to those who stay for more than a day at very reasonable prices. Those desiring same write to Mrs. John Chatfield, Ord, Nebr.

("Revival at Ord, Nebraska," *Pentecostal Herald,* May 1, 1923, p. 3.)

Victory in Fremont, Nebraska, 1923

Dear Bro. Brinkman and Saints:

Praise God for Victory. Just a few words to let all the dear ones know that the little assembly at Fremont is still on fire for Jesus. In the great battle for lost souls. It is nearly 3 years ago since the Lord first sent Sister Etter here with her full Gospel message. The devil was stirred then to crush the Saints of God. Thank God a few of the seeds fell on good ground and are growing every day in the Lord. After Sister Etter left, the Lord sent Rev. M. B. Long here once a week to bring food to the souls that were hungry for more of God. It was just like when Jesus fed the multitude, we had lots of folks who came. But when the power of God fell and the Holy Ghost came, men and women realized what it would mean to go all the way. Many turned back. The things of the world meant more to them than Jesus. One man who was so hungry for God told our Pastor one night after service. "Any man who fails to go all the way with the Lord after the lesson you gave tonight is nothing but a coward." In a short time God put him to the test and like the young man who came to Jesus and said, "Master what must I do to be saved." Jesus said, "Sell all you have and give to the poor." He became sad and turned aside. The cost was more than he was willing to pay. May God help His people to keep their eyes so fixed upon Jesus that we will not see any of the worlds good to draw us away from Jesus, that the cry of our hearts may be, give me more of Jesus.

Glory to His name. In the last 8 years, my husband was a drinking man. I knew at the time that I married him that he drank, but like many others he just knew he could give it up. The Spirit is willing but the flesh is weak. He tried so hard to keep from it. But in just a little while it got the best of him, it seemed like for four years I lived in the very brink of Hell. There I was just a girl with two little children. Night after night, weeks and weeks I walked the floor at a loss what to do. Friendless, in sorrow and disgrace. I had the best mother. She tried her best to do all she could for me but she like others said, "If he don't change, leave him." But my heart was set, live or die, I was going to stand by him. For no one knew better than I did how miserable his life was. I have never been taught anything about God. Never heard a prayer in our home. But some how one day I came across a small tract. How a mother prayed for a son who was a drunkard and how God saved him. Praise God it turned my heart. From that day, I turned my back upon all human beings and called upon God. I taught my little girls to pray. Out of the very depths of sorrow God heard our cries and set him free. Praise His Holy name. After God had done so much for us we failed to live worthy because of lack of knowing His ways. So God again let trouble come upon us. The little babe who has prayed the great blessing down upon her father was taken sick with lung trouble. The doctors took her tonsils out but nothing would help. She got weaker and weaker every day.

Then the Lord sent Sister Etter here. Through her prayers our little girl was healed. Glory to Jesus. Today she is well and strong, the sunshine in our in our home …

Then they cried unto the Lord in their trouble and he saved them out their distresses. He brought them out of darkness and the shadow of death and broke their bands in sunder. Praise God when he broke the old bands of drink and sickness it put the Praise of God in my soul. I feel that is the best I can do. I can't begin to Praise God for what he has done for me. I love the battle. We are going to win I know because Jesus is our Captain. The Captain who never lost a battle. Thank God. We are looking forward to a great meeting the 10th of August. We ask the prayers of all the saints everywhere. That God may have His way in this meeting that souls may be saved. May God bless all His children is my prayer. Pray for me that I may be willing to be as the very clay in God's hands. That my life may be spent for His Glory. Your Sister in Jesus. ~ Mrs. Jas. Z. Hyble

(Mrs. Jas. Z. Hyble: "Victory in Fremont, Nebraska," *Pentecostal Herald*, August 1, 1923, p. 4-5.)

Bayard, Nebrska, 1925

Brother Irl J. Walker writes, "We have just closed a two-week revival here with Evangelist Gay Reeves in charge and a number were saved, healed, and baptized with the Holy Ghost. Sister Reeves preaches a straight, clean Gospel and her messages were enjoyed by all those that heard them.

(Irl J. Walker, "From Bayard, Nebraska," *Pentecostal Evangel,* October 17, 1925, p. 12.)

Debate on Name Changes

At the 1927 General Council, there was lengthy debate on whether they should change the name of the church from the Assemblies of God to the Pentecostal Evangelical Church. That motion eventually was tabled, and at the next General Council that topic did not come up again, and so we are still called the Assemblies of God.

Also at the 1927 General Council the title of the chief officer was changed from general chairman to general superintendent. So there was a lot of talk about name changes, etc.

Anyway, George Hawley of Nebraska (if you remember, he was the chief motivator behind getting the Midwest Bible School started at Auburn, Nebraska), remarked that "the name was not the most important part of the office." Then he related a little incident that occurred in Nebraska several years previous to 1927. I don't see exactly how his story related to the issue of changing the name of the chief executive, but it is a cute little story. I thought it might make your day."

(Excerpted from a note from Glenn Gohr, to Elisabeth Lemp regarding a proposed name change for the Assemblies of God which was discussed at the 1927 General Council.)

The October 15, 1927 issue of the Pentecostal Evangel *reports the following discussion regarding the name of the chief executive officer.*

The Twelfth General Council Meeting, Brother George Hawley remarked that after all the name was not the most important part of the office. He related an incident that occurred in Nebraska some years ago when they were running the line between Nebraska and Kansas. "An old lady lived in a little hut near where they were drawing the line. She was very anxious about which side of her house the line would run on. When the surveyors came along she found the line ran on the Kansas side of her house and left her in Nebraska. She was exceedingly glad for she said she had always heard the air was very much purer in Nebraska than in Kansas."

It was finally agreed that the name of the chief executive should be General Superintendent.

("The Twelfth General Council Meeting," *Pentecostal Evangel*, October 15, 1927, p. 2.)

1929 District Council

At the 1929 Camp-Council Edgar White was elected to serve as Superintendent. Under his supervision the District adopted a constitution and by-laws at the 1930 Council which was held in Milford.

Chapter 15: The Great Depression Years (1930-1939)

***"How excellent is thy lovingkindness, O God! therefore the children of men put their trust under the shadow of thy wings ... thou shalt make them drink of the river of thy pleasures."* (Psalm 36:7-8b KJV)**

1930 District Council

The 12th annual session of the Nebraska District Council was at the Assembly of God Church in Milford, Nebraska.

District Superintendent's Report for Sept.—Oct.—Nov.—Dec.—Jan.

Income for five months	$638.07
Expense	249.66
House Rent	125.00
Stationery and Stamps	6.44
Printing Minuets	24.00
Envelopes (advertising)	2.50
500 Letter Heads	5.50
Advertising	5.80
Total expense	$418.90
	$253.17

Miles traveled were 8,322; Assemblies visited—23; Assemblies set in order—2; Revivals held—4. ~ Bro. White.

Reports from Hershey and Carns, Nebraska in 1930

The Saints at Hershey have sent in an offering for the Advocate. Sister Goldie Matson, who is pastor of the Assembly there, writes; "We are praising the Lord for Victory in Hershey. We have only a small assembly her, but we have some real saints of God. We surely do enjoy the Advocate. We covet your prayers that God will send us a mighty revival."

Brother and Sister Hugo H. Blumenthal, who were formerly in charge of the work at Torrington, Wyoming are at present stationed at Carns, Neb. Brother Blumenthal sends greetings to the Advocate family. He writes in part of the need of that field: "We are enjoying God's blessings. We miss the brothers and sisters of the Rocky Mountain District. But we realize the Lord has other sheep which are not of this fold. At present we are working for the Lord in this place, which is 26 miles from a railroad and in the canyons of the Niobrara River. There are young fold in this community who have never attended a Sunday school or heard a Gospel message. After several weeks on our faces before God in prayer, He opened up the way for us to organize a Sunday School, and since then a home had been opened for young people's meetings. We do not have a large church to worship in, nor a big choir, just a humble little school house. But we have a great God and we are believing Him for great and mighty things.

Will you pray with us that God will cause "wells of living water to spring up in this dry and thirsty place, that souls may drink of the water that cometh from God?" John 4:13, 14.

("Reports from Hershey and Carns, Nebraska," *Pentecostal Advocate* [Official organ of the Rocky Mountain District of the Assemblies of God], June 1930.)

Nebraska, A Divided State

When Sister Etter was in Sioux City in 1920 the Indians at Winnebago, Nebraska, persuaded her to come and hold a meeting for them. Sister Etter asked Brother Comstock of Sioux City (Iowa) to help in this meeting, and a new work was begun there. Following this meeting Brother Comstock conceived the idea of going to other places in that section and starting other places too.

(Eugene N. Hastie, "Nebraska, A Divided State," *History of the West Central District Council of the Assemblies of God*, p.106.)

The Lord blessed Brother (Daddy) Comstock in these endeavors in a remarkable way, and in a few years time good churches were begun at Homer, Dailey, Pender, Macy, Walthill, Thurston, Emerson, Allen, New Castle and Rosalie.

At this time the Assemblies of God wasn't active in this part of Nebraska, and it was felt this new territory should be included with the Iowa District. At the General Council meeting in Springfield, Missouri, in September, 1927, the former name of Iowa and North Missouri District was changed to that of the West Central District, and the Nebraska territory was taken in. The new western boundary line began at a point south of Yankton, South Dakota, and ran in a southeasterly direction to a point just north of Omaha, Nebraska. In a 1929 letterhead of this Assemblies of God District, all three states Iowa, North Missouri and Northeastern Nebraska District Council were used, and in 1930 the West Central District Council of the Assemblies of God was used.

Within a few years, it seemed reasonable for the Nebraska churches to return to the Nebraska District. However, this took a few years to achieve. Over a period of three years from November 1931 to December 1934, Roy E. Scott, Mercer, Missouri, Superintendent of the West Central District Council wrote several letters to Eld. J. R. Evans, (General Secretary) in Springfield, Missouri, and also to Edgar White, Grand Island, Nebraska, Superintendent of the Nebraska District concerning the return of the churches in the northeastern corner of Nebraska to that Council.

Roy E. Scott, states the following in a November 30, 1931, letter to J. R. Evans:

Our agreement in the past with Brother Gaston and Brother McDowell also with Brother Smith, the former Superintendent of Nebraska, was to let the churches themselves settle the matter. I still feel that this is the proper course in-as-much as we recognize the sovereign right of the local church, above all other authority over them.

The churches in Nebraska do not know about this request that the General Presbytery has requested of us nor about Brother Whites appeal to the General Presbytery, but I expect to inform them about it and ask them to be present at our convention. If they have anything to say and lest I should be misunderstood, I shall simply state that Brother White appealed the matter to the General Presbytery, and that the General Presbytery asked us to settle the matter and recommended that we turn this corner of Neb. to the Nebraska District then of course request their presence at our convention."...

In a December 4, 1931 letter, J. R. Evans responds to Elder Roy E. Scott as follows:

... Regarding the boundary line situation we realize that it is rather a delicate matter to deal with, and would suggest that you invite Brother White to meet with you in January (at their council meeting) and any others who may be interested that this matter may be thoroughly gone into and see if some amicable agreement cannot be reached....

In the West Central District Council annual business meeting in Newton, Iowa, January 2 to 10, 1932 the churches of Nebraska voted to stay with the West Central District.

From a January 19, 1932 letter to Eld. J. R. Evans from Roy E. Scott, Brother Scott writes:

...Brother Evans I have said it many times and I repeat it that this matter will never be settled until the two Superintendents visit every church and explain the matter.... I have expressed myself repeatedly as willing to make this trip and have invited Brother White to meet me over there, but he has not seen fit to do so as yet....

Then from a February 21, 1935, letter, Roy E. Scott, writes to Eld. J. R. Evans:

Your letter received and I was just thinking that I had failed to notify you that the N. E. Corner of Neb. was turned over to Neb. on Dec. 14, 1934. Bro White did not ask for an appointment, nor ask any other thing after the (1931 General Council) San Francisco convention, and as you know failed to meet me at my suggestions, and never at any time asked for any kind of a meeting so the thing just had to drift until Brother Albers was elected, and then I took the matter up with him, A most peaceable agreement was reached, and they are cooperating with us in our camp next July with Dr. Price ...

Thus when the members of the committee to adjust boundary lines of some of the Assemblies of God districts for the 1935 General Council received correspondence (February 13, 1935) from J. R. Evans, General Secretary, he stated: ... "For a number of years the assemblies in eastern Nebraska were considered as belonging to the West Central District, but now they are included in the Nebraska District.... The Nebraska District includes the state of Nebraska only."

A report on the Geographical Divisions of the District Councils of the Assemblies of God in 1996, states:

... the following districts conform to state boundary lines including Nebraska except Naponee, Nebraska is in the Kansas District. This Kansas community, Pleasant Green Church, has a Naponee, Nebraska address. Pleasant Green Church is twelve miles North of Agra, Kansas, and about ten miles from Naponee, Nebraska. The church was set in order in 1928, but by 1935 used the Nebraska address.

Today (1999) the church is using the Agra, Kansas address.

Christ's Ambassadors

The Second Annual meeting of the Christ's Ambassadors of the Nebraska Assembly of God was held in Chappell, Nebraska, August 29, 1931.

1931 District Council Report

The annual meeting of the Nebraska District Council of the Assemblies of God convened at the Full Gospel Tabernacle at McCook, Nebraska, February 10th through the 12th.

Superintendent's Report of 1931 showed the following figures:

Income for support of office
$1,507.02
Offerings from Camp Meeting
63.23
Missionary offering
65.00
Song Books
30.00
Offering for Minutes
12.50
<u>Total</u>
$1,677.75

Miles traveled were 27,172; Assemblies visited were 60; Assemblies set in order—2; Revivals held—2. ~ Bro. White.

Heavy Gains In Nebraska District

The 14th annual Nebraska District convention, which convened in Grand Island, Feb.9-11 closed with a testimony from all that it was good to be here. The smile of approval from the Lord seemed to rest upon all business transacted. District Superintendent E. W. White reported that we had made a gain of between 500 and 600 members the past year, 9 new churches set in order, and two others were ready to unite with us.

("Heavy Gains in Nebraska District," *Pentecostal Evangel*, March 26, 1932, P. 13.)

The Nebraska Pentecostal Fellowship

Volume 1:1 of the *Nebraska Pentecostal Fellowship* was published March, 1932 at $1.00 per year or 10c per copy. A. M. Alber,

2216 Avenue B, Scottsbluff, was the Managing Editor.

Brother Alber writes: It is with praise and thanksgiving in our hearts to the Lord that we announce the initial number of the Nebraska Pentecostal Fellowship. For some time we have felt the need of giving to our fellowship a district magazine...

Remember that this is your paper. No one is receiving a salary for getting up this paper. Every article is contributed freely, and all the work of compiling and getting the paper ready for the printer is done without charge....

In 1978, Albert M. Alber received recognition for fifty years continuous service to the Assemblies of God. A. M. Alber was Nebraska district superintendent from 1934 to 1945.)

From Over the State: A Growing Field

C. E. Thurmond of Ainsworth writes: We went to Burton last November for a revival assisted by Brother and Sister James of Lucas, South Dakota. Some fifty were saved and a new church was organized with fifty-three charter members. A class of thirty-five Christ Ambassadors was organized also. Brother and Sister James were elected as Pastors of this work and it is thriving splendidly under their leadership. They have over thirty baptized Saints in this place.

Last June I went to Springview for a revival. A new congregation organized there after a stirring revival. About twenty have received the Holy Spirit there. Brother Lester H. Sheets is now pastor of this church.

February the 28th we closed an eight weeks revival at Bassett assisted by Brother Lester H. Sheets. Some thirty were converted. The last day Brother E. W. White, our district superintendent, was present to set this work in order. Brother White spoke to over three hundred people in the afternoon and evening services. Eight received the Baptism in the Holy Spirit this last day. We organized a Sunday School at this place February the 28th with seventy-five out to start .... C. E. Thurmond was elected Pastor of this church. They are having meetings at three-thirty every Sunday. Sunday School is at two-thirty.

Leland R. Faith closed a revival at Ainsworth last month. In the four weeks fifty-three were saved and three received the Holy Spirit. We have a Christ Ambassador class here of thirty three charter members. Pentecost is sweeping this part of the country....

("From Over the State: A Growing Field," *Nebraska Pentecostal Fellowship,* Vol. 1:1, March 1932.)

Pastor E. R. Foster of Grand Island, Nebraska, writes:

We wish to take this opportunity of sounding a note of praise through the columns of the Nebraska Pentecostal Fellowship to the King of Kings and Lord of Lords for His mighty visitation to Grand Island in the last few weeks....

This district council meeting which convened in our church from February 9th to 11th proved to a great blessing. Brother C. B. Thomas of McCook, Nebraska was with us a few nights following the convention as Brother Shields was delayed. God made his ministry a blessing to us. Bro. S. G. Shields of Amarillo, Texas continued the meeting for two weeks. The presence of the Lord was so near. At times the spirit of weeping would settle down over the people. Other times He seemed to come as a rushing mighty wind. The altar was filled each night with hungry seekers....

Our Young People's work is moving forward. I noticed Sunday evening we had between forty and fifty in the Christ Ambassador class.

A "Hatching" of Preachers from This Area of the Country!

In 1997, Carlyle G. Beebe made a list of people from these Nebraska—South Dakota border towns that went into ministry with the Assemblies of God as a result of the revivals in the 1920's and early 1930's. He listed the towns of Valentine, Burton, Coberg, Ainsworth, Butte, Bassett, Burwell, and Thedford, Nebraska; Clearfield, Lucas, Winter and Wewela, South Dakota. (Probably, Gregory and Herrick, South Dakota as well as other Nebraska towns could be added with more names.) There are over 65 names on his list—first and second generation going into full time service for the Lord.

I may have missed some—but to my knowledge all those listed had some papers from the Assemblies. Of this grand total, five (5) were District Superintendents and a number were Assistant Superintendents. At least eight (8) have been Foreign Missionaries. The greatest amount have been pastors of churches. Many founded churches. Some are at present pastoring churches with over 1000 people.

So this area of the country has been good for the Lord's work. A regular 'hatchery of preachers.'

Carlyle G. Beebe's parents, Chester and Elsie, from Lucas, South Dakota were 1920s pioneer Pentecostal preachers in South Dakota and Nebraska. Chester was a converted bootlegger who loved a good fight. Jesus changed his life. Many came to know Jesus as their Lord and Savior and accepted the Pentecostal message because of the Beebes' straight forward manner along with their powerful testimony of transformed lives. The Beebes later pastored in Nebraska for many years.

1934 District Council at Hastings, Nebraska

A wonderful time of fellowship and blessing from God was enjoyed at the District Council meeting April 10-12. P. C. Nelson, President of Southwestern Bible School was the main speaker. Entertainment was provided for all by the local assembly and their Friends. Gordon H. Millard, Pastor arranged this most creditably.

The Council accepted an offer of a large pavilion in a park in the edge of Hastings for the camp meeting July 19-29. The pavilion and park make a most excellent place for the camp and we are looking forward to a large attendance and blessed time. Glenn Millard, Secretary

The 1934 Nebraska District Council Minutes state that the resolution that the Superintendent give his entire time to District work was adopted.

("1934 District Council at Hastings, Nebraska," *Pentecostal Evangel*, May 12, 1934, p. 13.)

1935 District Council April 9-12 in Grand Island, Nebraska

Superintendent's report by Brother Alber.... Eight churches were set in order this year: Amherst, Mullen, Westerville, Forty Four, Whitney, Ogallala, Falls City, and Lincoln. Two of these came to us from the Bible Standard and the Lincoln Church should have been set in order before, but the records never reached Springfield. Then there are about thirteen churches that have come to us from the Iowa district. These are located in the northeast section of the state. There are a number of other churches at the present time that are waiting to be set in order. Unity prevails in general over the district and we praise the Lord for what He is doing.

We purchased three tents and paid for them this past year. One 30 x 60 and two 30 x 50. These cost us a total of $295. Pioneer work is now going on in Chadron, Broadwater, Guide Rock, Campbell, and in other places such as schoolhouses, etc.

Three camp meetings were conducted this past year – the state camp at Hastings, a local camp at Bayard and also at Naper, Nebraska.

Total offerings for Superintendent
$2036.60
Traveling expense, etc.
$1085.00
Received for Superintendent's house rent
81.75
Paid out
141.00

Deficit
59.25
Offering for camp meeting at Hastings
1061.20
Paid out
1061.20
Offerings for camp meeting at Bayard
471.48
Paid out
462.37

In 1935 it was Resolved "That the District Superintendent shall not hold a pastorate." Also Resolved "That this Council makes provision for the payment of the District Superintendent's house rent by each assembly contributing one dollar or more a month."

Also Resolved "That, we have one DISTRICT CAMP MEETING hereafter, said camp to be centrally located in the state with a permanent camp site as the object in view."

1936 District Council Held in McCook on April 7-9

In 1936, the Nebraska District Council was held April 7 through the 9th, in McCook, Nebraska. Superintendent's report from Brother Alber for the year ending April 1. This year like last year, has been a very busy year, having been over the entire state a number of times …We were also called to officiate at many of our church elections. We traveled approximately 30,000 miles in the interest of the state work. This is about the same number of miles traveled last year.

Five churches have been set in order this year: Anoka, Broadwater, Thedford, Nebraska City and Minden. Pioneer work has been going on in a number of towns, and plans for this summer.

We purchased one tent for gospel work, size 30 x 48. Also ten 10 x 12 living tents for our camp meetings.

The work of our Sunday Schools is still progressing with a great deal of interest.... Some of our Schools have doubled and tripled their attendance this last year ... The vision is growing and God's people are realizing the all-important advantage of having a good, live, effective, well organized Sunday School.

Three camp meetings were again conducted last summer. All were greatly blessed of the Lord. Hastings was our large state camp which was well attended … Brother McMullan was the main speaker. Dr. Chas. L. Thornton was the principal speaker at the Bridgeport camp … The camp at Meadville, although the cold weather hindered much in the meeting, ended with a great shout in the camp and with many coming to the altar the last day. Brother E. W. White, of our own district, was the principal speaker at this camp.

As much as we know, there is good unity in the District among the brethren and a great desire among us to see the work of Nebraska forge forward....

Our missionary effort still is in need of improvement. We feel that we are below normal in this respect. We have had more missionary effort the past year, however, that for some time. Missionaries have visited the state and brought us the needs of the field and this has awakened many of us to our responsibility, and we trust that the Nebraska District will forge forward in this all-important work for the Master.

We accepted no outside engagements for meetings this year because of the abundant labors of our own District. It seemed we could not find time to do all there was to be done. Certainly the harvest is ripe …We can report the highest financial income in the history of the District. This all speaks of loyalty, faithfulness and godly sincerity on the part of our ministers and churches. The doctrine of tithing is more strictly practiced than formerly, and the results are indeed gratifying and commendable. May the God of heaven bless every faithful servant—is the prayer of my heart.

Total offerings for Supt.	$2,750.33
Traveling expense, etc.	$1,167.96
Received for Supt's house rent	119.00
Paid out	144.00
Balance from last year's camp	9.21

Deficit for the year	25.00
Deficit for last year	59.25
Total deficit	84.25

An offering was taken at the last Council meeting, of $27.19, but due to the fact that last year's books were closed, we added this amount to the first month's income for rent.

Camp Meetings

Offerings for Bridgeport camp	$185.00
Paid out	$185.00
Balance from last year's camp	9.21
Offerings for Hastings camp	1,297.86
Paid out	1,296.30
Balance	1.56
Owe state	50.00
Deficit on camp	48.44

This deficit is due to the fact that we purchased ten living tents 10 x 12 at a cost of: $135.00

1937 District Council Held in Grand Island on April 6-8

A. M. Alber writes in the Superintendent's Report: "Another year of our District work has passed into history. It has been a busy year for all of us. And although we have had many great problems in our churches and District work, the Lord has graciously brought us through on the victory side. We praise God for the manifestation of His power and blessing upon the entire work.

I have traveled about thirty-two thousand miles in the interests of our District. This is a few more miles than last year, but our new field program this year demanded extra work and miles. Besides these miles, we traveled about four thousand miles on our trip to the Northwest and West. I will to thank the District for allowing me the time to make this very interesting trip and receive a much needed rest.

This year six churches were set in order. They are as follows: Valentine, Dalton, York, Reynolds, Pender and Emerson. The church at Red Cloud was reorganized....

Although this has been one of the greatest drought years in the history of Nebraska, we are able to show one of the most progressive years of our District work. Besides building two portable tabernacles (worth about $500 to $600 each but only cost about $300 with no labor cost) for new field work, we also purchased the large camp-meeting tent, (a wonderful buy) and ten 12 x 14 living tents and a number of cots. Our Secretary-Treasurers report will show how liberal our people gave for the advancement of the District.

Sunday School interest is still on the increase, and attendance is gradually increasing in many of our churches.

Our District camp meeting was well attended, and the blessing of the Lord was greatly felt by all of us. The North Camp was at Burton.

I have enjoyed the fine fellowship of the brethren. Good unity has prevailed throughout the year. Again we say with the Psalmist, "How good and how pleasant it is for brethren to dwell together in unity." I thank you for your prayers and co-operation throughout the year. We have been able to accomplish some things because we have worked together in the unity of the Spirit."

Total income was $2961.01 and total expenses were $1269.49. Tithe from ministers $2611.19.

Resolved That we instruct the District Presbytery to set an allowance sufficient for the District Superintendent, and that a reasonable amount also be allowed for his traveling expense. After general discussion it was seconded and unanimously carried....

Resolved, That this Nebraska District Council of the Assemblies of God do hereby form themselves into a body corporate under the laws of the State of Nebraska, and do hereby approve and adopt the attached articles of Incorporation.... Unanimously carried.

"Whereas, The District is in need of a camp site, be it resolved that this Council empower the District Presbyters to purchase a suitable camp site, but that they shall be limited to place the camp within about sixty miles of the center of the state. By unanimous consent is was agreed.

" ... Be it Resolved, That each church send in at least $1.00 per month for campmeeting purposed to be used as follows: Two thirds for the purchasing of new equipment and one third for operating expenses of the camp. Ministers and their families shall receive meals and tents at half price. This offering may be raised by monthly pledges or by a booster trip arranged by camp officials." The resolution was adopted ...

An announcement from Bro. Alber: " We have no bills. We owe no man. Praise the Lord. We don't have much money in the treasury, but we don't owe any bills."

"In regard to the amount set for the District superintendent I want to say that because I proposed it, some might think I had something up my sleeve. When the finances reach a point they take care of an office, there is no need to pour more in than is needed. So the District Presbyters have set $175.00 per month as the salary for the District Superintendent and 3 cents per mile for traveling expenses ... If the income does not reach that sum, the District superintendent is still paid up in full and the Nebraska District is not in debt to the District superintendent, but if it shall exceed an average of $175.00 per month and 3 cents per mile for traveling expenses, it will go back into the District Treasurer for Home Mission work, for evangelizing new fields. It takes faith for District work as well as faith for healing."

"We have only one missionary for the District of Nebraska. We have two other couples who have made application for missionary appointment that are going to look to us for financial help for their equipment and support on the foreign field ...

Here is a l*etter from A. M. Alber to Elder J. Roswell Flower*, Springfield, Missouri, May 14, 1937:

Greetings! Your letter of inquiry in regard to churches at Kimball, Nebraska City, North Platte and West Point received. All of these churches have been discontinued but Nebraska City. Nebraska City at the present time is in no condition to give a report for our organization fell and rather lapsed into inactivity for a while, but is now being revived and I will be able to go there and hold a business meeting soon and bring this church back again to proper function...

1938 District Council Held in Lincoln on April 5-7

A. M. Alber's Superintendent's Report states: "It has indeed been a pleasure to serve the District another year. Not that it is such an easy matter to be responsible for the position I hold, but because the Lord has so graciously helped us through another year. Problems and difficulties have presented themselves and at times threatened to overwhelm us, but as we looked to the Lord and trusted in Him, we were brought on the victory side.

"Since placing an allowance upon the income of the Superintendent we have gone further and given the offerings from the fellowship meetings to Home Missions. Since then we have proposed the tithe of the Sunday Schools go to Home Missions. Some of the schools have responded and have been sending in their tithe. I trust that this will be discussed in this Council. We have found that the creating of departments alone does not make them function. They must be properly financed in order to be effective and reach their objective. Prayer and praise are valuable and we need more of it, but we also need God's money to carry on God's work. I feel we are at the place now where we can really do something worth while in new fields."

Other Reports from the 1938 District Council

... Sunday Schools are growing. Some have recently made a new high mark. I trust that we shall see many of our Sunday Schools now below one hundred reach the one hundred mark this year.

This has been a year of church building. McCook, Norfolk, Burton, Butte, and Riverton have new church buildings erected the past year. Falls City is building. Brother Cummings has built a portable tabernacle for Chadron. The District built another portable and sent it to Gordon. Maxwell remodeled and painted their building. Milford church put in a full basement with rest rooms, pastor's study, and Sunday School rooms. Burwell has done some work, enlarging the basement and some repairs above. A portable tabernacle was moved to Nebraska City, where Brother Davidson was holding meetings in a tent last summer. This has brought the work together there. Many of our churches need larger quarters. I trust God will give faith to our brethren to continue to provide better churches--to build where necessary.

The camp meetings last summer were well attended. God met with us in all three camps, and I feel they were a success for God. These are the greatest burdens of a district superintendent's work. The responsibility is very heavy. I trust that our churches will respond with their one dollar a month, that this burden can be shifted to more shoulders. The more we divide responsibility the safer our work will be and greater will be interest shown."

Gross income for the year was $2,764.28. 26,230 miles @ 3 cents was $786.84. North Camp was at Bassett and the State Camp at York….

"Whereas, Our District has been without a District paper for some time, be it ... Resolved, That a District paper shall be published, similar to trial issues as introduced by Brother Heinze."

It was moved by Brother King and seconded by Brother Brandt that the resolution be accepted. A discussion followed, with some explanation from Brother Heinze regarding the cost and work of the paper. Brother Millard added the amendment that the Presbytery be empowered to appoint an editor and that the price of the paper shall be three cents. Carried.

The Resolutions Committee than presented the following resolution: "Whereas, There is great need at present for funds for new field work, be it

Resolved, That this Council recommend that each assembly tithe their Sunday School offering for this purpose." Carried.

On Thursday morning, Brother Alber displayed the kit for the Daily Vacation Bible School and suggested that it be used by the different churches.

P. C. Nelson and the 1938 Nebraska District Council

... P. C. Nelson who was the president of the School in Enid Oklahoma, a very highly educated man who was saved out of the Baptists, I believe. When he was living in Detroit, was healed on his deathbed. Healed instantly and became a mighty believer. He spoke three or four languages and could read seven, I believe. He had great healing services....

His wife was very different from him. She had a very simple approach to everything. She helped him pray for the sick and had great faith for healing.

However she had some ways that were so straight forward it was very different. When he was preaching Camp or District Council or whatever it was, if he told a joke she would kneel on the platform with one hand lifted and say "Daddy is getting silly. Lord help him." This was in front of the whole congregation. Her husband only smiled and paid very little attention.

P. C. Nelson was a rather poor car driver. He was so preoccupied with other things. His wife had worn the lining of the inside of the roof or the car on her side raising her hand against the roof and pleading the blood. This is meant in no way to make fun of her. She was a very Godly woman and loved by the people.

P. C. Nelson was preaching the District Council at York, Nebraska in 1938, the year I was ordained. At the close of the service those who were ordained lined up and the preachers and then others came by to congratulate us. When P. C. Nelson came to me, he hugged me and cried and said, "My own dear Oscar, I have prayed so much for you. I am so happy for you. God bless you and use you in a mighty way."

He was so blessed that I didn't have the heart to tell him that I was not "Oscar." So, I got Oscar's blessing, I hope."

(E. M. Clark, "P. C. Nelson and the 1938 Nebraska District Council," 1995.)

E. M Clark grew up in Burton, Nebraska. Brother Clark was head of the Radio Department for the Assemblies of God in the 1950s. He was instrumental in establishing a national voice for the denomination. Under his leadership, "Revivaltime" developed into an ABC syndicated network program. In 1960, Brother Clark was elected superintendent of the Illinois District and served until 1970. In 1971, E. M. Clark became the fourth president of North Central Bible College.

1939 District Council Held in Grand Island on April 4-6

A. M. Alber's superintendent's report: "With thanksgiving and praise to God for His wonderful works to the children of men. I bring you my report at the District Council Meeting. The past year has been a busy one, filled with blessings and victories and lot of good hard work.

Some of our smaller churches have taken on a great deal of strength, attendance has increased, and the finance of the churches have greatly improved in many of them. Walthill, Allen, Wood Lake, Cliff, and Lexington have built new churches. A church was purchased in Beatrice. Three of these churches were in new fields.

We feel the Nebraska District is much stronger in membership and financially than a year ago. For this we praise God and give Him glory and adoration.

The District officiary purchased a District home and headquarters at 831 North Kansas Avenue in Hastings ... It is a seven-room house all modern with automatic gas heat ... It is a splendid location, and I am sure all of us are happy about this purchase.

The following is my financial report:

Total income for the year	$3,245.33
Allowed District Supt.	$2,100.00
28,883 miles at 3c a mile	866.49
Deficit last year	122.62
Sent to state Treasure	182.63
	$3,271.74
(A.M. Alber)	$3,271.74
Deficit last month	26.41
York Camp Meeting...	
Total Income	$1,051.15
Disbursements	832.19
Cash Balance	218.96
Bassett Camp Meeting	
Total Income	$719.45
Disbursements	639.52
Cash Balance	79.93

(A. M. Alber, "Superintendent's Report," 1939 District Council Held in Grand Island on April 4 to 6.)

Early History of the Nebraska C.A.'s

My first involvement in any type of District Work, was in 1937. During the C. A. Convention in Hastings I was asked to be the Secretary-Treasurer of the C. A. Department. At that time the C. A.'s were helping to start a new work in Broken Bow. We were pastoring in Ord. In July 1939, we went to the Northwest, Washington State, we returned to Nebraska in October of 1939.

November 1939 during the C. A. Convention in Ord, I was elected full time C. A. President and Sunday School Director. There was no set income or place to live. Our 1939 Chevy was our home, Sister Dickinson, Gary and I. (Sister Dickinson says they lived with her brother, Silas Rexroat, who pastored the Grand Island church. Their home was in Rexroat's spare bedroom. Many nights they came home late and other company occupied the spare room. Those nights were spent sleeping in the car.) ...

We conducted a few revival meetings, Ainsworth, Milford and one of the meetings was conducted on the Indian Reservation in Macy, Nebraska. We livied in an Indian lady's house. Carried water from the town well and bought milk for Gary in the little store. This was quite an experience as we did not know where the milk was delivered from as it had no label on it. It was a good experience for us as we saw some people blessed by the Lord.

Charles Blair followed me in this office, and he being a single man it worked out much better for him. J. M. Peck also served. Carlyle Beebe followed, then Forest McClellan, Delbert Turner. Brother McClellan and his family lived at the camp grounds. There was a two or three room apartment in the five room unit just west of the dining hall.

Delbert Turner was the pastor of the York Assembly when he took over the leadership of the department.... Soon after this a lot was purchased with the thought in mind to build a C. A. Home. The District paid the $1,000 for the lot. A house on South Sycamore came up for sale. The lot was sold and this money was used to make the down payment on the house. It was a two bedroom house. An old barracks building was purchased and a double garage was built on this property. One half of it was a garage and the other half an office. That house was sold in 1966.

Roscoe Leach followed in line for the Directorship of the Department. Norman Correll served in this office (before Roscoe) until he went as a missionary to Tanzania. Spud DeMent came into the office until he accepted a position with the Youth Department in Springfield. James Wilkins served until he became pastor of the church in Milford. John Stocker was elected to the Office of Director of Youth and Christian Education in 1972. Ted Brust served 1977 to 1982. David Graves 1982 to 1988. John Francisco 1988 to 1995. Rick Lorimer 1995 to 1999 and …

(Lester W. Dickinson, "History of the Nebraska C.A.'s.")

The Nebraska District of the Assemblies of God

THE NEBRASKA PENTECOSTAL FELLOWSHIP

A Magazine with a Full-Gospel Holy Ghost Message

VOL. ONE MARCH, 1932 NO. ONE

Resurrection Victory

"But thanks be to God, which giveth us the victory through our Lord Jesus Christ."—1 Cor. 15:57.

The word "victory" is often associated with the defeat of an enemy in battle. All victory is of the Lord. "The horse is prepared against the day of battle": but victories of heathen monarchs are due to Divine ordering. "Now have I brought to pass;" Jehovah said to Sennacherib, "that thou shouldest be to lay waste fenced cities into ruinous heaps," 2 Kings 19:25. Jehovah "doeth according to His will in the army of heaven, and among the inhabitants of the earth." Dan. 4:35. Ungodly monarchs and their armies unwittingly fulfill the purpose of God. They think they are merely carrying out their own evil designs, but the Lord uses them to chastise His own people and to fulfill His own purpose. They are but the axe in the hand of the Divine Hewer. Read Isa. 10:5-15.

Victory over the world is also of Jehovah, for the victory by which His people overcome is by faith in Him. We read also of "victory over the

(Continued on page two)

"Have ye received the Holy Ghost since ye believed?" Acts 19:2

$1.00 PER YEAR 10c PER COPY

Cover of the first *Nebraska Pentecostal Fellowship*, March 1932

Back row (l-r): C. E. Thurmond, Chester Anderson, Arnold Armstrong, Evelyn Anderson, Norine Armstrong. Front row: Rose Hallgrimson, Garlen Anderson, Viola Hallgrimson, Lara Anderson, Vance Anderson, Lillian Hallgrimson (Blakkolb); 1931.

Unit 4: Nebraska District Development and Ministries

Chapter 16: World War II Years (1940-1949)

***"Fear thou not; for I am with thee: be not dismayed; for I am thy God: I will strengthen thee; yea, I will help thee; yea, I will uphold thee with the right hand of my righteousness."* (Isaiah 41:10 KJV)**

1940 District Council Held in Grand Island on April 9-11

The District Superintendent gave an oral report of the work of the district adding appreciation and love for the loyalty and respect of the district shown him and gave a word of encouragement for the future building of the district. This was followed by a complete mimeographed report of all moneys handled by his office, also showing a full financial statement of the district....

Resolution 3. "Whereas, we have an opportunity to buy a five acre tract, one and one half miles west of Lexington, Nebraska on high-way No. 30, for the sum of one hundred and fifty dollars, be it, Resolved, That we empower the District Officiary to buy this plot of ground for a permanent camp ground, and be it further resolved that trees be planted and necessary improvements be made to be used as a permanent camp within the period of five years." ...

Adopted the next day. Pledges to the amount of $310.00 were received to buy and begin to improve the grounds.

Resolution 4. "Whereas, many of our Southern Councils have organized a Women's Missionary Council, be it Resolved, that we take steps to formulate a Women's Missionary Council of the Nebraska District. Motion carried.

Brother Alber read portions of the missionary report from Springfield stating amount of money given for Missions in the year of 1939. There was an increase of over thirteen hundred dollars.

Brother Alber made some remarks about the "Nebraska Pentecostal Fellowship" and encouraged all to stand by the paper and help to keep it going out to our constituency and also support the paper ...

Wednesday evening the Sunday School service opened at seven o'clock.... Sister S. S. Rexroat gave an example of teaching a Sunday school by using the visual board.

I remember as a small child the fascination with the "flannel-graph-figures." These figures were only outlines needing coloring, then cutting out, and a small square of flannel pasted to the back of each figure so it would adhere to the flannel board. But oh, how alive the flannel graph made the story. ~ Elisabeth Lemp

Beginnings of the W.M.C.'s in Nebraska

Nebraska has the distinction of being one of the pioneer districts in the work of the Women's Missionary Council ... It was in 1940 the Nebraska district was organized and the same year the New Mexico and Northern California districts.

The first local group of the WMC's to be organized in Nebraska was in 1939 at Omaha in the Glad Tidings Assembly. The work of these ladies inspired other ladies who had heard about what could be accomplished through women working together. Mrs. L. E. King talked with District Superintendent A. M. Alber about the possibility of having a district organization. He did not have to be convinced for he had already been encouraged along this line by Mrs. Etta Calhoun months before. It seemed he was waiting for some women to catch the vision.

("Beginnings of the W.M.C.'s in Nebraska," *50th Anniversary Booklet, Nebraska District*, p. 11.)

1941 District Council Held in Grand Island on April 8-10

Resolution 3. Resolved, That we pay our Superintendent $50.00 per week plus 3 cents mileage. MSC.

Resolution 4. Be it Resolved, that we incorporate in our District Minutes the article on "Military Service," Article 16 in our General Council Minutes.

"ARTICLE XVI. MILITARY SERVICE"

"While recognizing human government as of divine ordination and affirming our unswerving loyalty to the Government of the United States, nevertheless we are constrained to define our position with reference to the taking of human life.

"Whereas, We as followers of the Lord Jesus Christ, the Prince of Peace, believe in implicit obedience to the Divine commands and precepts which instruct us to 'Follow peace with all men' (Heb. 12:14), 'Thou shalt not kill' (Ex. 20:13), 'Resist not evil' (Matt. 5:39), 'Love your enemies' (Matt. 5:44), etc., and

"Whereas, These and other scriptures have always been accepted and interpreted by our churches as prohibiting Christians from shedding blood or taking human life; and

"Whereas, We, as a body of Christians, while purposing to fulfill all the obligations of loyal citizenship, are never-the-less constrained to declare we can not conscientiously participate in war and armed resistance which involves the actual destruction of human life, since this is contrary to our view of the clear teachings of the inspired Word of God, which is the sole basis of our faith; therefore, be it

"Resolved, That the General Council hereby declares it unswerving loyalty to our government and to its Chief Executive, and that we hereby restate our fixed purpose to assist in every way morally possible, consistent with our faith. (Reaffirmed 1927)"

1925 Statement from *General Council Minutes* concerning Pacifism

ARTICLE XX CONCERNING MILITARY SERVICE AND LOYALTY TO THE GOVERNMENT

While recognizing Human Government as of divine ordination and affirming our unswerving loyalty to the Government of the United States, nevertheless we are constrained to define our position with reference to the taking of human life.

Whereas, In the Constitutional Resolution adopted at the Hot Springs General Council, April 1-10, 1914, we plainly declare the Holy Inspired Scriptures to be the all-sufficient rule of faith and practice, and

Whereas, The Scriptures deal plainly with the obligations and relations of humanity, setting forth the principles of "Peace on earth, good will toward men" (Luke 2:14); and

Whereas, we as followers of the Lord Jesus Christ, the Prince of Peace, believe in implicit obedience to the divine commands and precepts which instruct us to "Follow peace with all men" (Heb.. 12:14), "Thou shalt not kill" (Ex. 20:13), "Resist not evil" (Matt. 5:39), "Love your enemies" (Matt. 5:44), etc., and

Whereas, These and other scriptures have always been accepted and interpreted by our churches as prohibiting Christians from shedding blood or taking human life;

Therefore, We, as a body of Christians, while purposing to fulfill all the obligations of loyal citizenship, are nevertheless constrained to declare we cannot conscientiously participate in war and armed resistance which involves the actual destruction of human life, since this is contrary to our view of the clear teachings of the inspired Word of God, which is the sole basis of our faith.

(*General Council Minutes*, 1925, pp. 24-25.)

1967 Statement on Military Service

The revised report of the special study committee on Military Service was presented by Howard S. Bush:

WHEREAS, the ideal world condition is that of peace, we as Christian citizens should use our influence in promoting peaceful solutions to world problems; and,

WHEREAS, We live in a world in which there may arise international emergencies which will lead our nation to resort to armed conflict in the defense of its ideals, freedom and national existence; and

WHEREAS, our first loyalty is to God, we recognize never the less that human government is ordained of God, and that there are obligations of citizenship which are binding upon us as Christians; and

WHEREAS, we acknowledge the principle of individual freedom of conscience as it relates to military service; therefore, be it

RESOLVED, That Article XXII of the General Council Bylaws be deleted and replaced with the following article:

Article XXII. Military Service

As a movement we affirm our loyalty to the government of the United States in war or peace.

We shall continue to insist, as we have historically, on the right of each member to choose for himself whether to declare his position as a combatant, a noncombatant, or a conscientious objector. MSC

(*General Council Minutes*, 1967, p. 34.)

It is noted that we have military chaplains and others in the armed forces.

Report of the Nebraska C.A.'s in 1941

Nebraska has approximately forty-five organized C. A. groups. Our district is divided into six sections, each section electing its own sectional representative....

C. A. rallies are held monthly in connection with the sectional fellowship meetings. The young people have charge of the afternoon services, which have been especially blessed of the Lord. Besides these we try to have at least one special all-day rally in each section during the year, at a time when it is most convenient for all C. A.'s to attend....

The District President is expected to attend the rallies as often as possible and to visit every local group once a year.

(L. W. Dickinson, "The C.A. Work in Nebraska," *Christ's Ambassadors Herald*, May 1941, p. 12.)

Letter from Private Leonard Barnes

Private Leonard Barnes sent greetings to the Nebraska District, April 1941:

Dear Brother Alber:

Your letter just came this evening and I was so glad to hear from you. Mail call is the big event in the daily life of a soldier, so a letter is always especially welcome....

Quite naturally I am among a great number of unsaved men, but I find that God's grace is equally sufficient even under the most adverse conditions. It has been my privilege to attend services at San Miguel on Sundays, and being in a good Pentecostal service is a great help. There are several Pentecostal boys here in camp, so I am not entirely separated from those of my own kind.

By the time this letter reaches you another glorious Nebraska District council will be in progress. Needless for me to say, I would be very happy to be present among those whom I love so dearly, but it seems that at this time of emergency the call of our country comes first. I would like to extend heartfelt greetings to the people of the Nebraska District at this time, and I know that God's blessings are going to rest upon His people at this Council Meeting.

For the benefit of the Christian young men who are subject to the call for military service, I might say the army can be a place of spiritual strengthening as well as it can be a place of spiritual decline. A little backbone and spine and a lot of God's grace can make an over-comer, even in the army. By the Lord's help I am expecting this year to be a fruitful one in my own life....

In Christian Love, (Signed) Private Barnes — C. C 80th Inf. Tng.Bn — Camp Roberts — San Miguel, California

Superintendent's Report, 1941

YOUR SUPERINTENDENT [A. M. Alber] was very happy to be able to tour the district with our beloved Brother Fred Vogler, Assistant General Superintendent of the General Council of the Assemblies of God in a series of Missionary conventions....

From Milford we went to Lincoln then on to Walthill, Ainsworth, Burwell, Scottsbluff, Bridgeport, Chappell, and McCook. We were not able to make our appointment with the Bayard Church Sunday Morning on account of the storm on Saturday that caught us in the vicinity of Ravenna, where we stayed all night Saturday and then proceeded through almost impassible roads west toward Bayard, but reached Bayard in the afternoon too late for a meeting.

I am sure that our people are much better informed in regard to Missions and the workings of our General Council than ever before.

~ Brother Alber

1942 District Council Held in Grand Island on April 7-9

Brother Alber introduced Sister Margaret Bass, from Springfield, Missouri, as the speaker for the Council on Vacation Bible Schools and Sunday Schools. After the opening sermon by Brother Rexroat from Kansas, Sister Bass spoke to us on Vacation Bible Schools …

Sister Bass spoke to the Council again on Tuesday afternoon, Wednesday morning; Wednesday afternoon from 1:30 to 3:00; Thursday morning Sister Bass spoke from 10:00 to 11:00 then again in the afternoon from 1:30 to 3:00. After the business , Sister Bass handed out the certificates to those who passed the examination given by her on Vacation Bible Schools and Sunday Schools.

A report was made from the Sectional Boundaries Committee by Brother Wilkins, chairman, which reads as follows: "Having observed the sections of the District and finding that many of the sections are too large for the churches to conveniently attend sectional meetings, the committee recommends that one more section be added, arranging the seven sections as presented." The recommendation was accepted as a resolution. MSC

... Resolution 11 Whereas, ... be it resolved, That the District Superintendent be granted the privilege of employing a stenographer when needed to help in the detail work of his office, the expense of said stenographer to be defrayed by the District....

The first Women's Missionary Council officers were: Mrs. L. E. King, Omaha--District President, Mrs. C. A. Beebe, Nebraska City--District Secretary-Treasurer. Sectional Officers were: Mrs. R. S. Barnes, Milford, Mrs. Elmond Clark, South Sioux City, Mrs. Earl Cummings, Maxwell, Mrs. Lester Dickinson, Chappell, Miss Cleo Mae Hink, Ainsworth and Mrs. L Roy Comstock, Norfolk....

A. M. Alber writes to Elder J. Roswell Flower, May 29, 1942

"Your letter received in regard to the renewal of ministerial fellowship certificates, and we do not have any ministers at the present time who are under any serious difficulty and we are not holding up any fellowship certificates for any of the brethren."

A. M. Alber's letter to Elder J. Roswell Flower, September 25, 1942

We are having a lot of rain in Nebraska and it is cold for this time of the year. We have a large Potato, Beet and Corn crop to be harvested and unless the weather clears off, and we get some sunshine it will make the harvest very difficult with the shortage of labor as it is. We have so many war plants now in the state and the draft is taking so many of our young men that labor on the farms is a real problem.

My boy Kenneth is now in the Navy Air Corps taking his basic training. He is taking up a plane by himself now, doing solo flying. My son-in-law who is married almost four years is called for his medical examination and the draft board says he must go in another month.

We solicit your prayers for the work here in Nebraska. We are getting short of Gospel Workers also in the state. Many of our ministers are going to the west coast.
~ A. M. Alber

Letter from A. M. Alber to Elder J. Roswell Flower, January 29, 1943

Your letter to the General Presbytery received and I would be in favor of having a General Presbytery meeting this fall instead of the General Council on account of war restrictions. It does seem to me that with the efforts of the war increasing and it is very possible that we will be at the very height of the war by that time and it may not be at all feasible to arrange for a large gathering at that time.

I also feel that you brethren are in a position to know the situation much better than any of us and I would be willing to leave this matter to the judgment of you Executive Presbytery.

Both my Son-in-Law and Son are in the war now and of course we are feeling the serious times with the millions of other Americans. My prayer is that God will give us a speedy victory and our boys will soon return to us again. I am, Your Brother in Christ, ~ A. M. Alber

Portable Tabernacles Used in the Late 1930s and Early '40s (*from Paul Wagner*)

They were made of plywood usually with a 2 x 4 frame. These tabernacles were made in sections that could be taken apart and loaded on a truck to move. The walls were 8 feet high, or sometimes less. The exterior size was from 28 x 40 to 30 x 60. Often the roof was of canvas, however could be of more durable construction. The floors were dirt generally covered with straw or sawdust. For extra endurance the buildings were staked down to the ground.

When we were in Oxford (1944), we took cardboard boxes, cut them up and made a ceiling. This way we could heat the building and keep some warmth with a space heater. This heater was probably oil heat.

1943 District Council Held in Grand Island on April 6-8

... Resolution 2. Be it Resolved, That all Home Missions offerings at Fellowship Meetings be retained in the respective sections by the Presbyter for the development of new field work. MSC

... Resolution 5. Be it Resolved, That an allowance of 4 cents per mile be allowed the district presbyter on his home missionary work and when called by churches where the offering from the church does not amount to 4 cents a mile. MSC

... Resolution 6. In as much, as the Gospel Publishing House will be unable to print our minutes and because the cost of commercial printing would be prohibitive,

Be it Resolved, That the district be permitted to mimeograph the 1943 minutes as a supplement to the 1942 minutes. MSC

Letter from A. M. Alber to Elder J. Roswell Flower, April 12, 1943

A. M. Alber made plans to attend the founding meeting of the National Association of Evangelicals.

... The Brethren of the District want me to go to Chicago for this convention of the Evangelicals for United Action and in talking to Brother E. S. Williams, he said I should let you know that I plan to be there so that you would know of my going.

I have been getting literature from them wanting us to register with them, but inasmuch as we are in touch with them from your office, I feel it would be better if you sent in the information as to who will be there from our movement....

...We are making plans for a united effort to bring this Full Gospel to every town in our state. We trust that we may be able to find the will of God in getting started in many of our Nebraska Towns. I am, Yours in Him, A. M. Alber

In 1978, A. M. Alber received a certificate for fifty years of continuous service to the Assemblies of God.

1944 District Council Held in Grand Island on April 11-13

Resolution 6: Whereas, the one year terms of the District Secretary-Treasurer and the Assistant District Superintendent are too short for them to thoroughly acquaint themselves with their official work. Be It Resolved, that their term of office be extended to two years. M S C

At the Thursday morning business session the recommendations of the Home Missions Committee were acted on as follows:

1) The evangelization of many more towns as yet untouched with the Pentecostal message, with a permanent church in view. MSC

2) That some means be worked out whereby the finances of the Home Missions Department would be increased to the point where these works and workers would be better able to present the gospel to the people. MSC.

1945 District Council Held in Lincoln on January 30 to February 1

Brother Alber, District Superintendent, told of how this District had grown from 12 active ministers and 8 or 9 churches in 1927 to the size it is today, bringing to our minds the thought that it was not the work or the responsibility of one or two but all of, the Lord helping us. There were 39 Ordained Ministers listed in 1945 and 9 with Christian Workers Permit.

Resolution 4: Whereas: It is desired to help the youth of our movement.

Be it Resolved, That a Boy's Camp be held at the Lexington Camp Grounds for one week for boys 9 through 16 at which they would receive supervised teaching and recreation. MSC

Resolution 5: Whereas, There has been an offer made to purchase the District Manse and Whereas, It is felt a change in location would be beneficial to the work of the District Superintendent.

Be it Resolved, That the change be made as the District Presbytery see fit. MSC

Wednesday Evening a lovely tablecloth was presented to Mrs. Alber and a solid gold 17-jewel wrist watch to Brother Alber in appreciation of their many years of service in the District. *(M. F. Brandt was elected District Superintendent upon A. M. Alber's resignation.)*

A. M. Alber acted as chairman for the Christ's Ambassador's Meeting Thursday ...

Resolution 1: Whereas, Traveling under war-time conditions is very difficult, Be it Resolved, That the resolution requiring the C. A. President to tour the District with the Superintendent be cancelled. MSC

Resolution 2: Resolved, That one day each year in each section be designated C. A. Rally day.

Mervin Peck Remembers the Youth Ministry *(Sister Peck writes, 1998)*

Mervin was C. A. President while pastoring in Maxwell, then resigned when we moved to Bayard (1946). At that time we could not cover the state and do justice to the youth.

He remembers a trip to Springfield, Missouri, to a Youth Convention shortly after our State Camp. He was responsible for a group of young people who went along. This was during W.W. II and the trains were loaded with young soldiers and our youth tried to share "Jesus" with as many as they could.

Bro. Peck covered a lot of miles to Fellowship Meetings where each afternoon or evening was a C.A. Rally. Bro. J. M. Peck especially thinks of the C. A. Conventions at Thanksgiving. The one he was responsible for was in Ord. Great Things From the Youth.

J. Mervin Peck was elected D-CAP in 1945. In 1984, he received recognition for fifty years of continuous service to the Assemblies of God.

Sunday School Harvest in Nebraska

Nebraska is a land of golden opportunity. Her fertile fields and vast plains produce abundant crops of corn, and white-face cattle thrive on her green hills. This wealth of land can be compared with the wealth of opportunity there is in Nebraska to interest Sunday School workers and win souls to the Lord Jesus Christ.

There are approximately seventy-five Assembly of God Sunday Schools in the State having five hundred officers and teachers and perhaps four thousand members. The Holy Ghost anointed people of these Assemblies are enthusiastic for Sunday School gains. They plan to invade the unreached homes of Nebraska and claim for the Lord more sheaves of golden grain--sheaves which are precious souls of children, young people and adults.

... There are at least eighteen cities of more than 2500 population which have no Assembly of God Sunday School. Moreover, there are dozens of smaller towns where strong Assemblies could be established. Then, too, there are countless numbers of closed rural churches which could be put into use once more for the glory of the Lord and the salvation of souls.

... Evangelists with a Sunday School ministry are badly needed to serve in this state. Several pastors are already asking, "Please send us an Evangelist who can help us build Christ-honoring Sunday Schools." These pastors are not looking for contest builders. They desire Sunday School Evangelists who can help them group the pupils, who can give instructions to their teachers and promote personal evangelism.

There is a great need for workers who are equipped to engage in Child Evangelism. Many are asking assistance with Vacation Bible School ... The foreign fields are calling many but because of world conditions, they may not obtain missionary appointments at this time. To such workers we would say, "Why stand ye here idle" when the unreached of Nebraska call, "Come over and help us?"

("Gathering Golden Grain in Nebraska," *Our Sunday School Counsellor,* June, 1945, pp. 1, 9.)

Nebraska Sunday School Tour, 1945

In a recent tour of Nebraska, District Superintendent M. F. Brandt, Sunday School Representative Clyde King and Gospel Publishing House Representative, M. L. Grable made up the Sunday school touring party. They ministered in Sectional Sunday School Conferences at Aurora, Taylor, Maxwell, Bridgeport, Bassett, Walthill and Lincoln. Additional evening sessions were held in a half-dozen assemblies; these being of special emphasis to boost attendance at the larger conference. Still other Sunday sessions were held at Grand Island, Bridgeport, and Omaha...

Your "Counselor" editor feels very kindly toward all the Nebraska brethren. Talk of southern hospitality! Why, it extends at least as far north as Nebraska, and it not affected by cold northwest winds or snow drifts.

Your Editor.

("Nebraska Spring Conference Tour," *Our Sunday School Counsellor,* June, 1945, pp. 8, 9.)

1946 District Council Held in Grand Island April 2-4

On Tuesday morning, G. F. Lewis, Assistant General Superintendent, from Springfield, Missouri was the speaker. Before he delivered the message he told of some of the problems Headquarters in Springfield were experiencing. C. B. I. needed enlargement, as 175 ex-G.I.'s were to be trained there and the institute was too small to accommodate all the applicants. He told of the Missions Department and its lack of funds. Our hearts rejoiced as he indicated that the radio broadcast "Sermons in Song" was a greater success than had been anticipated … they were heard over 101 stations in the U. S.; some in Canada; one in Cuba and they were negotiating for a station in Alaska; they are negotiating for a station in Ecuador that would blanket all of South America.

M. F. Brandt's report to the 29th Council of the Nebraska District Assemblies of God, 1946:

Fourteen months have passed since we have taken up the duties as District Superintendent, it was rather hard at first to become adjusted to the work but the Lord helped us. We have made a few mistakes but have discovered what will do by finding out what will not do …

Five churches have been dedicated, Chappell, Mitchell, Hastings, Laurel and Blair. The church at North Platte was set in order.

A number of churches have acquired a parsonage and others have remodeled their living quarters and some are busy building new churches and making improvements for Sunday School facilities.

There has been considerable work done on the Camp Grounds the past year. Building two units, 12 x 60 with seven rooms each. A storage shed 26 x 40; pouring approximately 1350 sq. ft. of sidewalk; built a cabin 18 x 24 for my own personal use, also purchased three acres on the north to enlarge the Camp Grounds.

A boys camp was held which was a new adventure but proved a great blessing. 117 boys registered.

We traveled 29,705 miles.

As we are in the midst of turmoil, distress and unbelief let us PRAY, WORK, AND LIVE so when JESUS comes we can hear him say WELL DONE.

The camp meeting committee reported that shortage of materials had prevented the building of new cabins.

1947 District Council Held in Grand Island on April 1-3

... Before bringing the Wednesday afternoon message, Thomas Zimmerman, Assistant District Superintendent of the Southern Missouri District advised the Council that at the present time in the United States alone the Sermons in Song broadcast was reaching 10,000,000 people per Sunday. He advised that the Assemblies of God radio program blanketed about every section of the United States and covered eight foreign territories.

... On March 5, 1947 the program was released through a station in Chungking, China 10 times stronger than the strongest station in the United States. The Chungking station was 500,000 watts, a government-owned station. English is the second language in China. The Sermons in Song is released through 90 stations in the United States besides the foreign releases. They have a potential listening audience of 10,000,000 per week....

Sermons in Song is not primarily planned to bring spiritual exhilaration to our own constituents. It is designed to reach the unreached thousands. Every $.25 invested in Sermons in Song will reach a potential 1,000 listeners. $1.00 will reach 4,000 … An offering was taken for Sermons in Song, and a few cents more than $296 was received.

1948 District Council Held in Omaha on April 5 to 7

At this council the mileage rate for the C. A. President and the Executive Committee was raised from 4 cents to 5 cents per mile.

... Resolution II: Be it Resolved, that the Sunday School tithe, now used for Home Missions, be used instead to apply on the support of the Sunday School Secretary. MSC

... The recommendations of the Home Missions Committee: That all assemblies adopt the World Mission Program for the raising of funds as soon as possible. After such funds shall have been raised they shall be sent to the Missionary Secretary at Springfield, Missouri, who will return 20% to the District Treasurer for Home Mission work of the district; said funds to be disbursed at the discretion of the District Presbytery, and a report of all disbursements to be given at the annual meeting of the Council.

1949 District Council Held in Grand Island on April 5-7

George Flattery, returned missionary from Upper Volta, French West Africa told of the work being done by missionaries and the great need for workers. He revealed that statistics from the American Bible Institute showed twelve new languages receiving at least a portion of the Word of God in 1948.

Wednesday morning Noel Perkin told us something of the missionary policy of the General Council. Some pertinent facts gleaned from Mr. Perkin's talk: There are 200,000 members of the Assemblies of God denomination in foreign countries. There are between 560 and 700 missionaries. It costs $2,000,000 a year to maintain this group. There are 1600 native ministers. There is an investment of at least $3000 in every missionary we send out …

Among several recommendations in 1949 from the Camp Ground Committee there was a recommendation to develop a bathroom in the caretaker's quarters.

... The Radio Committee report was given by Clyde King. The following recommendations were made:

1. That B. F. Correll, pastor of the church at Columbus, be appointed radio secretary of the broadcasts over the Columbus station. That all offerings for the support of Sermons in Song and The Gospel Rocket be sent to B. F. Correll, and that he acknowledge all such offerings with a receipt. That a financial report of the broadcasts be place in the District paper each month.

2.That all churches contributing to the support of the programs be given publicity in connection with each broadcast, in the announcement of the name of the church and its location, name of the local pastor, and an invitation extended to the people of the community to attend the local church.

3. That all pastors of the district take it up with their church boards and churches to see if they can send in a monthly offering to the support of these program.

4. That B. F. Correll, the radio secretary of the Columbus station, send out a letter to all the churches and seek to secure their interest and support in regard to the programs.

5. That we seek to change the time of the program to later in the afternoon so that people living farther west who have mountain time would have a chance to listen to the program. MSC

... Resolution V: Resolved, That Section II, Article XI under Finance on page 13 of the 1948 minutes be amended to read: All ordained and licensed ministers and Christian workers are requested to support the District office, with the tithe from their ministry with voluntary contributions. MSC

... Resolution XIII: Resolved: That this Council recommend that every church take a love offering for Carlyle Beebe, and said offering to be considered full payment for his past deficit. MSC

Thursday evening … E. G. Aldridge, Sunday School Evangelist presented the need for Sunday School evangelism by means of a flannel board. Three essentials were given: We need prayer. We need preparation. We need presentation. PREPARE FOR THE GLORY OF GOD.

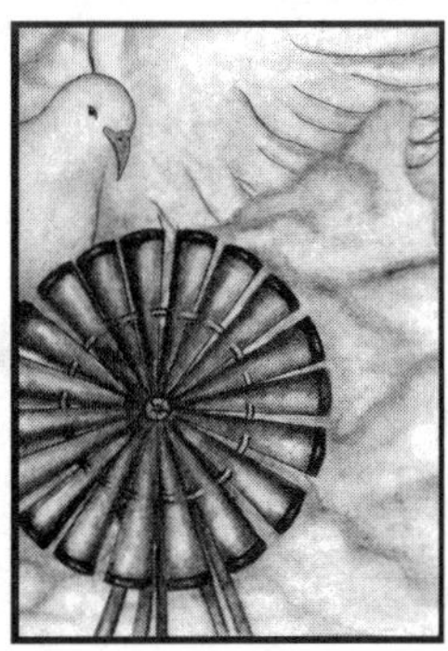

Lena Mae James, 5-year-old soloist

Albert M. Alber, 1943

Baptismal service and cars

Chapter 17: Progress in the Fifties (1950-1959)

"And a man shall be ... as rivers of water in a dry place, as the shadow of a great rock in a weary land."
(Isaiah 32:2 KJV)

1950 District Council Held in McCook on April 4-6

There were sixty-two churches in the district. There was much discussion concerning the location of the District Home at this council. Resolution II (As amended): Because of the debt on the District Home of $5000.00, "Be It Resolved, That we sell the District Home at a price agreeable to the District Presbyters, and purchase or build another home debt free. Amended Resolution carried. (The home was to be in Grand Island.)

Early Assembly of God Kansas/Nebraska pioneer, Mrs. Herbert Buffum of Stockton, California, gave an original reading entitled "Pentecost In Action" on Tuesday afternoon and Tuesday evening gave an original reading "Beautiful Bride." Mrs. E. G. Aldridge and Mrs. L. E. King taught a chorus to the group from the Buffum book of songs, "Let's Talk About Jesus." Wednesday morning Mrs. Buffum gave another original reading, "The Rupture."

... Resolution VII (As Amended): Resolved, that the district financial records be audited by an authorized auditing firm annually at the closing of the fiscal year, and that the report of the auditors be included in the District minutes. MSC

Resolution XIV: Be It Resolved, That the new program "Revival Time" be put under the supervision of the District, and each Presbyter act as Secretary. MSC

1951 District Council Held in Lincoln on April 2-5

W. A. Brown, General Treasurer, was the main speaker. In his opening message he mentioned that in the current issue of "Time" magazine it was stated that the Assemblies of God had grown 474% in 23 years.

... On Wednesday afternoon there was a motion to move the Nebraska District Council to the State Camp Ground at Lexington and also to hold the Council meeting prior to the state camp beginning in 1952. After being brought to the floor for consideration this resolution lost.

Also a motion was made to have the Christ's Ambassadors annual business meeting be held during state camp, beginning in 1951. SC

... Resolution VIII: Be It Resolved, That we endorse the Temperance League of Nebraska and affiliate with them. MSC

At the Thursday morning session the Camp Ground Committee report contained some of the following recommendations:

1. A recommendation was made at District Council last year that water be piped to the caretaker's house. Whereas this has not been done, we reaffirm this recommendation, and that this work be done this summer, or before cold weather sets in.

2. We recommend that a large gas tank be installed, adequate to meet the need for the entire season, and that a gas burner be installed in the water heater. MSC to accept these, as well as other recommendations.

This was the first year that an audited report was included in the minutes book.

1952 District Council Held at Lexington on April 15-17

Paul Marier spoke on "Evangelism in the Sunday School," using Ephesians 4:11 and 13 as basic scripture. He stated that 95% of the active ministers had been converted through the Sunday School, and 85% of the Sunday School teachers were saved in Sunday School; 95% of the church workers and 75% of the church organizers were saved through the Sunday School . He stated that 5,000,000 souls had been saved through the Sunday School in 64 years.

... BE IT RESOLVED, That the Nebraska District Council, under the direction of the District Presbytery, purchase a new automobile to be used in the work of the District, and under their direction and supervision, pay operating expenses, maintain and replace as is necessary this automobile used by the District Superintendent in the District work.

The Pioneer Spirit Still Lives!

In two or three weeks our Folding Church Trailer will have completed its function in opening another Assembly of God work in Alma, Nebraska, and then it will be free again. This time we are moving it to Hebron, Nebraska, a town of two thousand." So writes J. M. Ruthven, of Reynolds, Nebraska.

We will provide the use of the folding Church Trailer, an 8x14 well equipped house trailer, and a car (if needed) all free to an Assemblies of God couple if they will come in and open an Assembly work in this town.

Brother Ruthven, is affiliated with the Pentecostal Assemblies of Canada, but is working now in Nebraska. He has been pioneering for over twenty years, and together with his wife, has sacrificed freely and labored without thought of reward in order to establish churches in unreached communities. They have used the folding Church Trailer, designed by Brother Ruthven, as a means of opening works, and then left the works with Assemblies of God workers.

About a year ago they re-opened an old denominational church at Geneva, Nebraska. They painted and redecorated it, and began services. Now the church is growing under the leadership of Assemblies of God pastors, Brother and Sister Armond Mickelson.

Brother Ruthven states that he has blueprints for the Folding Church Trailer which are available at a nominal cost. Anyone interested in securing information concerning the blueprints, or in pioneering the work at Hebron, Nebraska, should contact Brother J. M. Ruthven, at Reynolds, Nebraska.

(J. M. Ruthven, "The Pioneer Spirit Still Lives!" *Pentecostal Evangel*, August 3, 1952, p. 13.)

1953 District Council Held at Lexington on April 7-9

... The subscription price of the Nebraska District Fellowship was raised to seventy-five cents per year.

The Camp Ground Committee report was given by C. T. Beem, chairman, who took the place of E. E. Rohde on this committee and the six laymen from the various sections in the District, as follows: 1) J. S. Rihanek from Pender recommended that another pump be added to the grounds, and that the house covering the pump be repaired or replaced as it was deteriorating rapidly. He also recommended that the present pump be put on the first floor to get it out of the dampness in its present location. 2) R. R. Roberts from Bayard recommended modernization of the rest rooms, insulation and air-conditioning of the tabernacle, and that attention be given to the floor in the kitchen and the floor in the laundry room. 3) Roger Rosenkrans from O'Neill recommended fixing up the piano on the grounds. It was estimated that the cost of such repair would cost approximately $300.00 or more. 4) George Campbell of Aurora recommended that the camp grounds and the tabernacle be used for one or two large evangelistic or healing campaigns each year. 5) D. B. Pierson of Thedford talked on Boys and Girls Camp and the long range building program: the possibility of building another tabernacle and using the present tabernacle for a dining hall.

After this report everyone stood to their feet and gave God thanks for the work that had been done at the camp.

Motion to accept the report of the laymen of the Camp Ground Committee. SC

Motion was made that at the discretion of the Executive brethren a tour be made through the state, with whatever promotion aids they choose, to promote the camp ground. SC

... Resolution XI, Whereas, There is a need of furthering the Home Missions Program, and that the interest for Home Missions needs to be broadened among the sectional ministers.

Be it Resolved, that there be a Sectional Home Missions Committee consisting of the Presbyter and the Sectional Pastors, and that distribution of Home Missions funds in the section be under their direction, subject to the approval of the Executive Presbytery. MSC

1954 District Council Held at Scotsbluff

An offering was lifted to help erase the deficit incurred at the last C. A. Convention.

The Psalmster's Quartet from North Central Bible Institute provided special music for the Council. Tuesday afternoon Howard Cummings, the Nebraska member of the Psalmster's Quartet, told a few things concerning N. C. B. I. He mentioned curriculum, faculty, sports, living conditions, employment possibilities, etc. An offering was taken for the Psalmster's Quartet. While the offering was lifted, the quartet sang "God Is Real," a southern melody.

... RESOLUTION 7, Whereas, there is a need for a fund to obtain property in new fields, be it resolved that we adopt the "500 Plan." Each member contributes $5.00 with a goal of 500 members or over. MSC

Wednesday evening Mrs. Wayne Hall presented a short Sunday School program with Bonnibel Roll, Loretta Lebsack, F. D. McClellan, Robert Paul, B. H. Armes and George Clark each taking part. It was announced that Bonnibel Roll and Loretta Lebsack were to be the new State Sunday School directors

... RESOLUTION IX, Whereas our Nebraska District is growing, and as time goes on there will be a need for an established central office for the furtherance of the work of the Nebraska District,

Be It Resolved, that we establish an office building fund, placing $500.00 per year into this fund from our tithe fund. Additional sums may be added to this fund as they are available and authorized by the District Presbytery.

Be It Further Resolved, that when sufficient funds are available, we do hereby authorize the District Presbytery to purchase necessary property and proceed with the building of a District office. MSC

... RESOLUTION XI, Be It Resolved, That the Nebraska District Council proceed to organize a Men's Fellowship, the details and appointment of a director to be in the hands of the District Presbytery. MSC

L. W. Dickinson announced that the Men's Fellowship director had been appointed. C. A. Sailors was appointed to fill that post.

1955 District Council Held at McCook

... RESOLUTION V, ... Be It Resolved, that we recommend that all ministers participate in the National Social Security Program. MSC

Tuesday evening the District Male Quartet comprised of Russell Umphenour, R. D. Turner, Roscoe Leach and Egon Kirschman sang two numbers "Hide Thou Me" and "I'm Redeemed." They were accompanied by Mrs. [Lena Mae] Leach at the piano.

... Wednesday morning Mrs. H. D. Champlin reported for the Women's Missionary Council. She reported that the Nebraska District rates 17 in support to the National office and tied for second place in per capita support. As to projects: In the past a foreign missions and a home project had been carried out each year. This year they were focusing all their attention to the needs at the camp ground. They have taken all the responsibility of furnishing 7 rooms at the camp. To make curtains for all the cabins at camp. There will be no display at camp this year but there would be a W. M. C. booth. Dimes for souls in Nebraska last year totaled $1,788.60. They were believing for $2,500.00 this year in dimes. MSC to accept the report....

The Youth Department report was given by R. D. Turner. He reported on the Youth Camp in 1954--5 saved, 8 received Baptism. He reported $2,082.17 given in Speed-the-Light offerings, that Nebraska was first in per capita giving for this program and fourth in total giving....

1956 District Council Held at Alliance

Monday evening Christ Ambassadors Rally opened with Norman Correll, C.A. President leading the C. A. Chorus.

... The mileage rate was changed from five cents per mile to seven cents per mile.

... RESOLUTION VIII Paragraph 5, under Resolution 8, Page 31, be amended to read as follows: Wherein a goal has been set by our National Headquarters to have one Assemblies of God Church to every 10,000 population within the next 4 years, it will be necessary for Nebraska to establish 40 new churches in that time to fulfill our quota. We recommend publicity and promotion be given the 500 plan by each local pastor. We further recommend that all ministers of the Nebraska District become members of the 500 plan. MSC

RESOLUTION IX, That the City Council of Lexington be urged to open 10th Street, which is now less than one fourth mile from the Campgrounds, to the Campground. That the purchase of the additional two or two and one half acres that lay straight north of the field now used for a ball park, be made. That the District should endeavor to raise funds in the next Camp Meeting to put in a sewage system. That a pay telephone be put on the Campground for those who want to make long distance calls. That the Campground be platted out in streets. MSC

RESOLUTION X, Since our Home Missions program has grown, and since we are endeavoring to establish a number of new churches by 1960, therefore be it

Resolved, that Article 6 of our Articles of Incorporation be amended to read $75,000.00 instead of $50,000.00 MSC to accept the resolution....

1957 District Council Held at Omaha

... On Thursday afternoon R. V. Umphenour read the Home Missions report. One new church has been started during the past year, that being Wayne, Nebraska. No more new churches have been started because it was felt that the present new works should be established before starting more new works.

On Thursday evening L. W. Dickinson announced that Norman Correll intends to go to Africa as a Missionary, and asked God's blessing upon the lives of Brother and Sister Correll and their family.

1958 District Council Held at Grand Island

... On Thursday morning L. W. Dickinson read the report of the Nebraska Fellowship. 184 new subscriptions were received during the year.

Recommendations: a bulk mailing permit be purchased. That subscription price be raised from 75 cents to $1.00 per year. MSC to accept the report. MSC to raise the subscription rate for the Nebraska Fellowship from 75 cents to $1.00....

... RESOLUTION IV. Since there is a growing need for additional office and study space for our District superintendent; and since the home of our District Superintendent does not have a convenient study and also needs some enlargement in other places.

THEREFORE BE IT RESOLVED, THAT; The District Executive be empowered to appoint a committee of three or more who will explore the needs of our District home and make recommendations to the District Presbyters who shall then act upon the findings of the committee. Moved for adoption by Nolan Christian. Seconded

Erwin Rohde spoke in favor of the resolution. He suggested that the garage be enlarged and a study added.

Clyde King stated that a few years ago the Council made provision to set aside $500.00 each year to some day establish a District office. He asked if this fund would be used.

Nolan Christian stated that is the committee recommends that a district office be built separately from the District home, it would be legal to use this fund. However, the proposed resolution leaves this entirely with the committee.

Wayne Hall stated that in his opinion the $500.00 put aside yearly for that project should be done until a building is built.

R. L. Leach, D-CAP, asked if the C. A. Office would be in that separate District Office, if built.

... Charles Turner recommended that the resolution be changed to be more specific as to whether a study for the District Superintendent or a District Office is to be built.

... The Chairman asked all those in favor of motion to adopt Resolution IV to stand; also all those against. Motion carried.

RESOLUTION V. Clyde King presented the following substitute resolution and moved its adoption: We will take the money which has been designated for an office several years ago and build an office and a study at our present District Home location in accordance with the advice of the Committee suggested in the Resolution and that will be considered a fulfillment of the legislation passed before concerning a district office, canceling the District Office Fund. SC The amount contained approximately $2,000.00....

First Men‘s Fellowship Day, 1958

"Men‘s Fellowship Day Observed at Nebraska Camp Meeting," *Pentecostal Evangel,* November 9, 1958, p 9.

Approximately 90 men were in attendance at the First Men‘s Fellowship Day at the Nebraska Camp Meeting on Wednesday, August 13. The meeting was under the direction of C. A. Sailors, the district MF director. A 20-voice male chorus, led by District C. A. President Roscoe Leach, sang "The Battle Hymn of the Republic."

Two laymen of the Assemblies of God gave testimonies as to how God had blessed their business activities and spiritual lives. They were Darold Conner, insurance salesman from Lexington, and Brother Nelson, head maintenance man at the Hastings Ammunition Depot.

District Superintendent L. W. Dickinson brought a stirring message entitled. "Daniel—the Forgotten Man."

A Men‘s Fellowship camp project was presented. The men agreed to furnish ten picnic tables and a number of park benches for the campgrounds.

1959 District Council Held at Norfolk

... L. E. Wilkins gave the Camp Committee report. The committee recommends that the present buildings at the camp ground be repaired and painted.

There is a need for more room in the dining hall, and the committee recommends that a lunch stand be built north of the present dining hall, and that the present lunch stand be used by the dining hall.

The sanitation buildings need screens at both windows and doors. More shower facilities are also needed. There is room for about three more showers in the present building. The committee recommends that this be done.

New bleachers are needed at the recreation grounds. This should be taken care of immediately.

There is a need for more class rooms and additional space in the tabernacle. It is recommended that the north wall of the present tabernacle be moved 18 feet and the platform be moved to the north side. The cost for this would be approximately $1607.00.

A few years ago a recommendation was made concerning a new tabernacle. The committee recommends that a committee be appointed to get prices for a building desirable for this purpose.

Motion to accept the work of the committee seconded and carried.

MSC that steps be taken to take care of the maintenance, dining hall space, screens, showers and bleachers recommended by the Camp Committee.

Charles Turner asked if a new tabernacle is included in the recommendations of the committee. L. E. Wilkins answered that if a new tabernacle were built, the old one could be used for dining facilities.

Thursday morning L. W. Dickinson asked for a report from the boundary committee.

... RESOLVED: That the Nebraska District Council of the Assemblies of God divide the state into nine sections ... MSC ...

Louis Roggow gave the Foreign Missions Report:

Since Foreign Missions is a vital part of our district program, the Foreign Missions committee recommends that we continue to encouraged increased giving and cooperation in every phase of the program.

Robert Paul gave the report for the Home Missions Committee:

We the members of the Home Missions Committee, after due consideration, feel that in line with the National Home Mission goal of four new churches for the Nebraska District, and considering the enormous growth in population of the Omaha area, which only has three Assemblies, be it recommended that:

1. The District take proper steps to open two new churches in the Omaha area this year. We also recommend that Bellevue be considered for a location for one of the new churches.

2. We further recommend that these churches be made district projects, being supervised and financed with the cooperation of the entire district.

3. We also recommend that the outlying sections be encouraged to survey their local areas for possibilities of opening new works in their respective sections, making them sectional projects.

4. We also recommend that all pastors encourage their congregations to stand with these new works in prayer, donated labor, as well as finance, food offerings, and to assist in any other way possible in order to make the works strong for God.

5. We further recommend a special Home Mission emphasis with a district wide approach such as the exchange of pulpits services, this to be annually. Also greater emphasis should be placed upon the "500" Plan through District publications, District and sectional meetings. We recommend that pastors cooperate with all such efforts. MSC.

On Thursday evening L. W. Dickinson asked the Tripletts to come to the front of the auditorium and there the ministers laid hands upon them and prayed for them.

Chapter 18: Growth in the Sixties (1960-1969)

***"If you knew the gift of God and who it is that asks you for a drink, you would have asked him and he would have given you living water."* (John 4:10 NIV)**

1960 District Council Held in Grand Island

A men's quartet consisting of James Wilkins, Jerry Spain, Robert Sinner, and Herbert DeMent sang "*I'll Be Led by the Master's Hand.*"

... Wednesday afternoon L. W. Dickinson read a letter in regard to liability insurance for the churches. The Presbyters voted to take out liability insurance on all district churches. The premium is based on the membership of the church.

L. E. Wilkins gave the Camp Committee's report. The committee recommended an investigation be made of the possibility of connecting the camp sewer system to the Lexington sewer system.

In view of the fact the price of real estate continues to rise, they recommended the purchase of the land east of the camp to square up our property.

Due to the need of more housing for various camps, they recommended the erection of a unit of cabins.

They recommended that instead of remodeling and piece building to meet State requirements, that a new tabernacle be built and the present tabernacle be made into a kitchen and dining hall.

They recommended that any further district building of homes or offices be done on the camp grounds. MSC ...

... Nolan Christian asked for an estimation of the cost of the new tabernacle. Mervin Clopine reported an estimation of $24,000, L. E. Wilkins estimated $21,000. Erwin Rohde estimated $24,600 and L. W. Dickinson $30,000 which would include the heating....

Pulse of the District in 1960

I trust everyone in our Nebraska District is becoming more Camp Meeting minded as the days go by. The dates of our State Camp are drawing very near. August 5-14 ...

Brother Jimmie D. Brown who was our Evangelist last year is returning as our Camp Evangelist for this year.... Brother U. S. Grant, the pastor of a fine church in Kansas City, Kansas, is the Bible teacher this year....

North Camp plans are materializing as the time draws near. The dates of the camp will be June 26th through July 4. Brother Klaude Kendrick is to be the special speaker again this year and Brother Dickinson will be speaker in the afternoon service of the July 3rd service. The C.A.'s usually have the afternoon service of the fourth of July ...

ROSCOE LEACH, President (D-CAP) writes: We greet you again this month from here in Grand Island ... The last two months your D-CAP has traveled 4,460 miles in direct District Youth work. I have also traveled 2,000 miles in youth activities outside our state. We are thankful to the Lord for His blessing as we have visited 12 churches.

In all of these services, it was wonderful to see the C.A.'s respond to the Spirit of the Lord as He moved upon their hearts. Surely it is wonderful to have the Lord in these days.

... The C.A. Department is planning a College and Career Camp, August 26-28, at Camp Kinaki in Lincoln ... I will look forward to seeing you at one of the camps this summer or in your local C.A. Rally ...

FROM MRS. R. V. UMPHENOUR, President, WMC's: A letter has come from Sister Niles (missionary to Venezuela) concerning the items which were sent to them at Council time. The following is a portion of it: "What a thrill it was to see each lovely article, conscious of the sacrifice necessary for the purchase of the many things, and the knowledge of the care in selection....

SISTER LILLIAN TRASHER is seriously ill: therefore she will not be speaking at Camp Meeting as was announced earlier. She wants to return to Egypt as soon as her strength allows. Pray God's blessing and guidance in her life. 1960

(L. W. Dickinson [superintendent], "Pulse of the District," *Nebraska Pentecostal Fellowship*, June 1960, pp. 2-13.)

1961 District Council Held in McCook on April 11-13

W. E. Reynolds, C. A. Vice-President did not feel, because of the present building program at Mitchell, that he could take the District Office of C. A. President vacated by Roscoe Leach in February.

... L. W. Dickinson stated that the additional acreage had been purchased for $1,000 an acre [*Camp Grounds*].

Revivaltime Broadcast from Lexington

I feel Revivaltime is one of the answers to the prayer which has been upon my heart for a number of years.

The ranch areas of Nebraska, covering hundreds of square miles, contain scores of families with no church home. Many of them live miles from any church. Often as I have driven through the ranch country my heart has been burdened, and I have wondered how we in Nebraska could ever reach these people. I believe Revivaltime is going to meet a real need in these rural areas.

For a number of years I have felt KRVN, a 25,000-watt station in Lexington, was the strategic station over which to release Revivaltime in our state. It is strategic in that it is beamed to cover the greater part of Nebraska, plus parts of Kansas, Colorado, Wyoming and South Dakota. In some areas of Nebraska, particularly in the ranch country, KRVN is virtually the only station which comes in clearly.

During March of this year, I felt God was directing us to inquire into the possibility of releasing Revivaltime over KRVN. I visited Bill Freeman, one of our own Assemblies of God men and an announcer for the radio station. He assured me he would look into the matter. Within a few days I had word from Brother Freeman that time was available and the station would carry Revivaltime.

In a survey of our district we found some areas where stations releasing Revivaltime overlapped in their coverage, while other areas were not receiving Revivaltime at all. By discontinuing two other stations and adding KRVN our district will receive a far greater coverage than before.

We prepared this data and presented it to our district council in session last April. The ministers attending the district council enthusiastically endorsed this change in releasing Revivaltime.

As Revivaltime went out for its first airing over KRVN on Sunday morning, June 4, there was praise in my heart for this God-given opportunitiy to bring the gospel to many who have not heard this full-gospel message.

(EDITORS NOTE: Nebraska is currently leading the nation in percentage of churches giving to Revivaltime. During the first six months of the year, [1961] 65 percent of the Assemblies of God churches in Nebraska gave regularly to this radio ministry. With a concerted effort by the pastors, they have been able to "blanket" their district with the Revivaltime broadcast. Your prayer and support can help not only to "blanket" Nebraska but also to take this ministry to "blank" areas where Revivaltime is not heard.)

(L. W. Dickinson, "Nebraska Assemblies Release Revivaltime on Lexington Station," *Pentecostal Evangel*, September 3, 1961, p 24.)

1962 District Council Held in Lincoln on April 10-12

... RESOLUTION I: Whereas, a number have felt a need of some type of hospitalization, medical coverage, and life insurance, several committees have been set up to explore group coverage for the pastors and families of the Nebraska District Council. Be it therefore resolved that we authorize and recommend, as a committee to the Presbytery Board, to set up the following benefits for the Pastors and families: MSC on a standing vote....

The Sunday School Department announced that Milford had given the most per capita in the United States to BGMC the past year....

1963 District Council Held in Grand Island on April 2-4

James Wilkins congratulated the Youth of the Omaha Glad Tidings Church for their victory in the "Learning Luke" contest held that day. They will represent Nebraska in the Regional playoff.

Warren McPherson, of the Servicemen's Division, Springfield, Missouri, presented a visual—"What Do You See." He presented the great need for funds that his department might broaden their ministry to the Servicemen. An offering and pledges for this purpose were received.

… L. W. Dickinson urged that all continue to promote the 1000 Plan that the annual payment of $3,000 on the Camp Ground loan might be met. The increase in the Ministers' Tithe fund was noted with thanks. It was found that the expense of keeping the District car for two years was nearly as much as trading for a new one each year.

... In the afternoon, Loretta Lebsack presented the Sunday School Report and announced that Nebraska ranked second in per capita giving for BGMC the past year.

The District Headquarters Committee Report was read by C. A. Sailors as follows:

... It is recommended that we purchase the property at 1503 West 2nd Street and that we put up for sale the existing house, to be moved off by the purchasing party, then develop a new building approximately 38 x 76 feet with offices built on ground floor level, for the District Superintendent, Secretary Treasurer, Youth Department, Sunday School Department, reception room and conference room. To also have additional area that could be developed into office space as the need arises.

The final details and furnishing of the building to be determined by a committee appointed by the District Superintendent and District Presbytery.

Since there would be no further need for the District office in the Superintendent's home, be it resolved that we sell the property (appraised value at about $25,000) using said funds to develop a district headquarters building. Be it further resolved that the District give the superintendent a house allowance to provide an adequate home for him, the amount to be set by the District Presbytery....

During discussion concerning an office secretary, E. E. Rohde stated that a competent office secretary in Grand Island is paid about $2800 a year.

Motion that the District establishes a District Headquarters Building. Carried by a standing vote with no opposition.

MSC that the Headquarters Building be located in Grand Island.

Paul Ackerman gave the following Men's Fellowship Report for the year March 2, 1962 to February 28, 1963: Warm Christian greetings …

In some areas, we have not seen the progress we had anticipated, however, we are not discouraged … We serve a big God and can accomplish great and mighty things through His name.

In a recent survey conducted by *Moody Monthly*, it was stated that ninety-five-percent of the people of evangelical churches have never won a soul to Christ … May the Lord increase our vision for lost men in our local community before His soon coming …

It was a pleasure for the Men‘s Fellowship Department to issue 125 certificates to individuals in Nebraska who read the “Bible Through in ‘62.” The Broken Bow Assembly, pastored by Wayne Hall had 20 individuals who completed their reading the Bible in 1962.

The program of Royal Rangers should thrill and be very close to the heart of every pastor and layman in our district … The men or our fellowship are becoming aware of the Light for the Lost and to see the great potential which it carries for the church. Light for the Lost provides literature for foreign city crusades and will be expanded in 1963.

... Jim Wilkins gave the following Christ‘s Ambassadors Report: ... Plans are under way to conduct the new Bible Quiz in our District. The book being emphasized this year is “Corinthians.” A survey will soon be made to determine whether or not our pastors want the finals to be conducted at the fall C.A. Convention....

Because of the fine response to the Talent Search which the C. A. Department conducted at State Camp last summer, we are planning to follow a similar course … We want you to note the fine achievement of our Nebraska youth in their giving to Speed-the-Light during the past year …

In the evening service of April 4, L. W. Dickinson announced that total World Missions giving for the District showed an increase of $10,000, the highest gain in any year in the history of the District .

1964 District Council Held in McCook on April 7-9

... R. B. Umphenour gave the following “Nebraska Fellowship” report and financial statement for the year March 1, 1963 to February 29, 1964: It has been my privilege to again serve the Nebraska District as editor of The Nebraska Fellowship.” This is the sixth year I have edited the district magazine. This responsibility is gratefully acknowledged ... As of February, 1964, we were mailing 260 individual copies of the Nebraska Fellowship.... The subscription price is $1.00 per year. MSC to accept the report.

... C. A. Sailors, Chairman of the District Office Building Committee, gave the following report: The committee meeting for the planning of a District Office was called to Grand Island in December, 1963. Those present were C. A. Sailors, L. W. Dickinson, E. E. Rohde, and L. E. Wilkins. Time was spent in looking at types of buildings that would serve best for the District Office. At that time the Hall County Assessor assured us if we constructed additional office space than we needed, only the rented would be taxed.

After careful study, it was the committee‘s opinion that we should build the building so that we could have an income of at least $250.00 per month from the leased area, to retire the debt and make the payments of the building. The rate of rental in Grand Island is $1.75 to $2.50 per square foot per month and this type would bring about $2.50 per foot. The lot is located at 1503 West Second Street in Grand Island, and would be adequate space to build a building 38 by 90. A frame building with brick face could be constructed for about $10.00 per square foot. MSC to accept the report as read.

C. Turner asked, “Does this finalize the plan to build?” L. W. Dickinson replied that there will be further study made before the actual building. C. A. Sailors stated that donated labor for the project would be necessary.... J. R. Birdwell inquired regarding the fire zone of the location, and was informed that it had been checked. MSC on a standing vote to authorize the Presbytery to go ahead with the building.

Kenneth Wray gave the following World Missions report: … For the first time in the history of the Assemblies of God, World Missions giving for the year 1963 was in excess of eight million dollars ($8,000,000). May God help us to continue this trend.

This report presents the progress and recommendations for Radio, Foreign Missions, and Home Missions in the State of Nebraska.

REVIVALTIME. The international radio broadcast of the Assemblies of God, has received wide acceptance throughout the world and has proven a great blessing to many individuals and churches in Nebraska.... The cost of REVIVALTIME in Nebraska is one hundred ninety dollars and twenty-five cents ($190.25) per week. We recommend again that each church regularly support REVIVALTIME with offerings and prayer for this world radio voice.

FOREIGN MISSIONS. The year 1963 has been the greatest in the Assemblies of God missions. Overseas activities continue to focus upon the creation of a Biblical indigenous church. In countries where Assemblies of God missionaries have spent several years, the emphasis has shifted to the maturing of the church, particularly through the seventy-four Bible schools. Forty-one new missionaries were appointed ... four hundred sixty-six new preaching points were opened, and over one hundred new cities and towns were entered. One new field, Ecuador, was opened and four new Bible schools were established....

HOME MISSIONS: ... Recognizing that the metropolitan areas present the greatest challenge of evangelism in the state, we wish to recommend that any addition BREAK-THROUGH projects be established in these areas ... The Greater Lincoln area ... The Greater Omaha area ... Sarpy county ...

L. E. Wilkins, chairman of the Camp Committee, gave the following report: Whereas there is a shortage of altars in the tabernacle, we recommend that eight new altars be built; also that rugs be supplied to meet the needs around the altars.

We recommend that uniform trailer spaces be set up in a shady area and that a fee of fifty cents per day up to five days, or $2.50 for the entire Camp, be charged.

We recommend that trees be planted to add to the beauty of the grounds, where the future trailer parking area will be built, and where deemed advisable. MS to accept the report. After much discussion, the motion carried.

RESOLUTION VI: Whereas there continues to be an annual lack of sufficient income to finance the District Camp Ground; be it therefore resolved that the following be added to Article V, Page 27: The District executives and all pastors will make a special effort at least once a year to promote the "1000 Club" plan for the financing of the District Camp Grounds in each Church throughout the District. There will be an honor roll listing the names of all active members in the District tabernacle and special recognition will be given to those who contribute $100 or more a year. MSC for adoption of the report.

RESOLUTION VII: ... Ten per cent of the ministers tithes shall be transferred to the camp fund and that sufficient funds be immediately transferred from the general tithe fund to liquidate the current camp fund deficit. Be it further resolved that ten per cent of the cash offerings for missionaries be retained for the camp fund. MS

L. W. Dickinson asked that the Resolution be considered in three parts. Part I--That ten per cent of the minister's tithes be transferred to the Camp Fund. MS ... L. E. Wilkins explained that the camp expenses are nearly $7,000 a year and this was the only way the Camp Committee could see to carry it on. H. Dixon expressed his belief that the "1000 Club" should take care of the Camp needs. On a standing vote the motion carried. Part II--That sufficient funds be immediately transferred from the general tithe fund to liquidate the current camp fund deficiency. MSC Part II --Be it further resolved that 10% of the cash offerings for missionaries be retained for the camp fund. MS for adoption. Motion lost.

L. W. Dickinson asked that each one make the Camp a matter of prayer and stated that one dollar per Sunday School member in the District would take care of the Camp expenses. E. E. Rohde thanked Brother Dickinson for his efforts in making the Camp a success. The entire body gave him a standing vote of thanks.

RECOMMENDATION; That the local churches include in their yearly budget an amount for the camp grounds, paid monthly if possible. MSC.

L. O. Triplet informed the Council that it was recently passed that the Foreign Missions Department will retain three per cent of all missionary offerings to be transferred to an Emergency Missionary Fund for the purpose of taking care of emergencies that might arise on the foreign mission field.

1965 District Council Held in South Sioux City on March 30 to April 1

... In the business session the morning of March 31, the World Missions Report, read by L. W. Dickinson, revealed Big Springs as tops in the District with a total giving of $7,327.61. A drop of $9,942.08 from the previous year's total was noted with regret ...

... Loretta Lebsack gave the Kids Kamp and Sunday School director's Reports. We have 11 Gold Crown Sunday Schools, 11 Silver, 17 Blue, and 31 Co-Operative. She reported that the Valentine Church had contributed $332.17 to BGMC with a per capita giving of $4.43. This entitles them to keep the Gold Barrel Award.

Loretta announced her resignation effective April 30th, as Nebraska Sunday School Director to accept the position of Coordinator of Child Evangelism in Springfield, Missouri. L. W. Dickinson expressed his thanks to Sister Lebsack for her good work in the Nebraska District and a love offering was received for her. MSC to accept the report.

L. W. Dickinson read a letter from Melvin Hodges, field secretary for Latin America, commending the outstanding work of two Nebraska missionaries in Central America. Harold Mintle and Loren Triplett, Jr. Brother Mintle is due for furlough but will be staying on the field another year in the interest of the work in Honduras. The Loren Triplett family will be returning to Nicaragua in June.

L. E. Wilkins gave the following Camp Committee Report: Whereas there is a need for more housing for various camps, we recommend that the Little Chapel be converted into rooms for sleeping area.

- We recommend that four houses that are presently connected to a septic tank be connected to the main sewer.
- We recommend that the parking area be improved by installing mercury lights and laying out a parking pattern.
- We recommend the developing of a house-trailer parking area.
- We recommend that a P. A. system be installed in the tabernacle by a technician and the control system be installed in the rear of the tabernacle.
- We recommend that all-weather accommodations be provided on the grounds.
- We recommend the cabins be rewired with heavier wire.
- We recommend that Men's Fellowship groups plant trees, this to be done this spring.

Motion and seconded to receive the report. It was stated that the $394 that had been received for dormitories was to be used to convert the Little Chapel. L. E. Wilkins suggested that such a dormitory could be heated and used during the winter meetings as well as summer.

L. W. Dickinson asked which of the recommendations were for immediate action. L. E. Wilkins answered, "All of them." E. Craver spoke against the all-weather building, stating that the cost would be out of proportion to the need for such a building. F. [Floyd] Roll encouraged the replacement of old cabins with modern ones. L. E. Wilkins expressed his desire that the Men's Fellowship undertake the planting of trees immediately. He announced that Floyd Roll was chairman of the committee to lay out plans for the trees, parking area, and trailer-park for approval by the Executive Board. The P. A. system was discussed and F. Sauer recommended that a Mr. Kruger in Grand Island be engaged to work out the difficulties in the present system.

L. W. Dickinson called for a vote on the motion. Motion carried.

The evening service of March 31 was the dedication service of the new sanctuary in South Sioux City where B. F. Correll was pastor. Brother and Sister Norman Correll, serving as missionaries in Africa, sent a cablegram of congratulations to his parents. The service was recorded to be sent to them.

Mrs. L. E. King gave the following Women's Missionary Council report; 64 active groups with a total membership of 845; Dimes-For-Souls offering for the past year of $5,066.34; and a grand total giving of $16,902. MSC to accept the report.

Paul Ackerman gave the following Men's Fellowship Report:

... On September 5, 1964 Nebraska's first Light-for-the-Lost Banquet was held in Grand Island. The attendance at this banquet was very gratifying. Over 125 were in attendance from twenty different churches. Our National Men's Fellowship Director, Rev. Howard Bush, was the guest speaker. Also attending were Everett James, National Secretary for Light-for-the-Lost and our missionary guest, Loren O. Triplett. Over $1500 was given in pledges for the Light-for-the-Lost Literature Crusade for Managua, Nicaragua....

The Royal Ranger program is increasing its outreach. There are now nine chartered outposts in Nebraska, with 150 boys. This program for boys ages 9-17 will be a blessing to any church, if it is willing to accept the responsibility.

L. W. Dickinson asked the Council to continue to pray concerning the building of the new office building in Grand Island. An attorney has inquired about the leasing of some space in the building.

1966 District Council Held in Grand Island on March 29-31

The missionaries home on furlough were: Marjorie and Murry Brown, Africa; Bonnibel Roll, Ghana; Byran Niles, son of Elmer Niles, South America. In the march 30th morning service, the Combined Cooperative Fellowship Giving Report was presented by L. W. Dickinson with a 1965 total giving for Nebraska of $115,131.54. This again of 414,402.89 over 1964. The Big Springs Church was in first place for highest total giving of $6,845.09.

... L. E. Wilkins reported the following for the Camp Committee: "Whereas the shower house is inadequate, we recommend shower rooms be built on the present rest room building.

We recommend a trailer area be developed by running sewer, water & electricity to the area between the two North units of cabins.

We recommend a furniture drive be made to replenish the needs in the cabins.

We recommend some new housing be developed.

We recommend the Royal Rangers sponsor a clean up of the grounds on a Saturday soon.

To inform and develop interest in the camp program, we recommend a film be developed showing the activities of the Camps to be shown in our churches throughout the state.

For financing of the Camp, we recommend instituting a companion club at $10 to supplement the present $5 plan. Also a Junior Club of $1 for children.

Respectfully submitted--Camp Committee."

L. W. Dickinson expressed his thanks to the Camp Committee for their good work.

The clean up recommendation was discussed. Motion by M. Johnson to encourage the Royal Rangers to sponsor the clean up. Seconded by E. Blauvelt. F. Roll felt that it should be encouraged as an all young folks picnic as well. L. W. Dickinson made it clear that this did not take the place of the regular Camp Clean Up Day later in the spring. Motion carried.

MSC to accept the Camp Committee Report in its entirety as amended.

In the March 31th morning sessions the Presbyters Financial reports were considered ... L. W. Dickinson reported that in Cozad the lots, church building, parsonage came to a cost of $35,170. This low cost was partly due to the fact that Cozad did not have so many building regulations. He said the same amount of property in Omaha would cost $100,000, the lots probably costing as much as the entire Cozad. A. Johnson suggested that we get a long range plan looking father ahead and working with Chambers of Commerce to find desirable church sites … L. W. Dickinson explained that when a Council decides they want to go into a city with a new church, we are obligated to see the work get on its feet. When an individual wishes to do so, we will help as much as we can, but are obligated to see the District project through.

RESOLUTION: Be it resolved that Article II, District Sectional Boundaries on Page 13 (of 1966 minutes) be deleted and the following be substituted: The district shall be divided into eight sections. These sections shall be known as Northwest Section, Lower Panhandle Section, Republican Valley Section, Niobrara Section, Sandhills Section, Siouxland Section, Metropolitan Section and Tri-City Section ... MSC to adopt the Resolution.

RESOLUTION: Whereas the Kids Camps of our district are a very important phase of our Sunday School Program and, Whereas our Kids Camps require a great deal of planning, foresight and organization, be it therefore resolved that our District Kids Camps be under the direction of our Director of Youth and Christian Education. He will appoint a coordinator and other necessary committees to minister in the camps. MS for its adoption.

... J. [Jerry] Spain pointed out that according to Article XIII of the Constitution and By-Laws, Boys and Girls Camps are listed under the activities to be mainly administered by the District Sunday School Director. C. [Clyde] King stated that if this resolution were adopted it would be, not mainly ... J. [James] Wilkins said that he understood that the resolution allowed him to delegate some of the responsibility ... Motion carried on a standing vote.

Mrs. L. E. King gave the following WMC Report: 61 active groups with a total membership of 845; Dimes for Souls offering for the past year of $5,272.61; a grand total giving for the past year of $21,421.87. It was interesting to note that in the past ten years the WMC has given a grand total of $137,703.45 and have collected Dimes-For-Souls in the amount of 440,441.59.

... In the March 31 evening service, L. W. Dickinson read a letter from headquarters appointing Mr. and Mrs. Jerry Spain as missionaries to Tanzania, Africa. Majorie and Murry Brown came forward with them and offered prayers of thanksgiving and blessings for their lives as missionaries.

1967 District Council Held in Grand Island on April 4-7

L. W. Dickinson gave a summary on the New Office fund which was started by a loan the first part of 1966. He also stated we are thankful the Lord has been so good to us by giving us such a nice place for our Headquarters and a wonderful W.M.C. room so that our missionaries can come to do their packing.

He also gave a report of selling the District Home for $24,500.00. He stated at the Ministers Institute held in Lincoln that it was the executive board‘s responsibility to secure a New District Home. Much planning and consideration was given to this project. It was decided to build on the Park and Ruby lots a 1500 Square foot home to be bricked half way up, with a double garage. At this report it is almost ready for finishing of the inside.

In the Wednesday evening service, L. W. Dickinson brought forth the dedication ceremony of the District Headquarters Office building. He stated that "God‘s anointing touch be on each personnel and that our lives be so dedicated that when people enter our office they may feel God‘s presence."

Mrs. L. E. King gave the following W.M.C. report: 60 active groups reporting, giving total membership of 809. Dimes for souls the past year was $5,539.98. A grand total of Giving for the past year of $20,972.45. It was interesting to note that in the past ten years the W.M.C. has given a grand total of $151,953.83, and have collected Dimes-for Souls in the amount of

$50,566.04. Mrs. L. E. King presented Bro. and Sis. Spain a check for $1200.00 to be applied on purchasing their outfits for Tanzania, West Africa, the land of their calling. Rev. and Mrs. Jerry Spain gave inspiring talks and thanked everyone for their part in giving saying "The Lord Bless you abundantly."

Mrs. Wayne Hall presented Bro. Dickinson with a check for $500.00 to help with the expense of the W.M.C. room at the New District Office Building. ... In the Friday morning, April 7, session L. W. Dickinson announced to adopt the entirety of Home Resolutions, was seconded and carried.

1968 District Council Held in Hastings on April 2-5

... Brother Charles Turner emphasized that the Men's fellowship department is comprised of three main outreaches; National Action Crusades, Light for the Lost and Royal Rangers.

Brother W. E. Reynolds, read the World Mission Report: REVIVALTIME, the international voice of the Assemblies of God, continues to bring Spiritual life and blessing to countless thousands "BEHIND CLOSED DOORS" throughout the world.

A report from the Radio Department shows that presently there are NINE REVIVALTIME releases throughout the state of Nebraska. In addition to this the report shows that a deficit of $1,896.23 has occurred in the radio budget of the Nebraska churches during the year 1967.

An increase in giving to REVIVALTIME by each church would provide for the release of this Full Gospel Message to a greater foreign, national and local audience. We recommend again that more of our churches consistently contribute to the support of REVIVALTIME ...

FOREIGN MISSIONS Department continues to expand its ministries in the propagation of the Gospel.... This work is being carried out by 920 missionaries in 72 foreign countries with training facilities for National Workers being furnished by 80 Bible schools....

There was a drop in foreign missions support from the Nebraska churches last year, but there were gains in other areas which increased the over-all World Missions giving ...

HOME MISSIONS--Realizing the necessity of reaching more of the people in Nebraska with the Full Gospel Message we present the following:

That sections which have no definite project at a given time be encouraged to:

1) Send an offering to a newly established Home Missions Work ...

2) That they help make it financially possible for a new work it its initial stages to engage an Evangelist or musical group for special services ...

We recommend that more emphasis be given to strengthening of the established churches and Home Missions Churches ...

We further recommend that definite, immediate action be taken toward purchasing land tracts in outlying areas of metropolitan cities for the purpose of a long range program of church extension. MSC to accept the report.

On Friday morning, April 5, Wayne Hall, Chairman, gave the Camp Ground Committee report.

REPORT ON NEW DORMITORY: Each room has an adjoining room with shower and stool. a lavatory has been installed in each room and a vanity with four drawers on each side ... Regarding painting the walls, we suggest that each section paint two rooms. They gave six recommendations. MSC to accept the Camp Ground Committee report.

1969 District Council Held in Gering on April 8-10

... On Thursday afternoon, April 10, a resolution was read by A. A. Johnson, after which he moved its adoption--whereas, there is a need to preserve the History of the Nebraska District Council of the Assemblies of God and its affiliated churches for the future generations, be it therefore resolved that there shall be a Historian appointed by the District Presbytery to keep the historical records of the Nebraska District. This record shall include District Meetings, Speakers, Pastors and Churches, Dedication of Churches and any other events of historical significance. SC

Further recommendations which will not be presented in the form of resolutions came out of our meetings. They could also improve the effectiveness of the Dept. of Y & CE.

1. It is suggested that a "policy pamphlet" be made available--especially for new pastors in the District.

2. Suggested that careful consideration be given to the assignment of personnel to positions of responsibility at camps.

3. Suggested that presbyters and sectional representatives could possibly assist the District Director in recruiting help for the camps.

4. Suggested that job descriptions be made available well ahead of each camp.

5. Suggested that a list of available Children's Evangelists and Worker's Training Course instructors be compiled ... and made available to pastors.

6. Suggested that the Department study the possibility of conducting Sunday School tours and Speed-the-Light tours on alternating years.

7. Since the Office Secretary has the bookkeeping responsibility for the District as well as the Dept. of Y & CE, and since along with many other tasks leaves virtually no time for her to supply the secretarial help our Director urgently needs to accomplish the things that we demand of him, the Study Committee recommends that part-time secretarial help be provided for our District Director as needed.

REVIVALTIME REPORT: Revivaltime, the International voice of the Assemblies of God, is currently released on nine Nebraska Radio stations. it is presently supported by fifty-eight of our churches. The 1968 income for this ministry totaled $12,893.48.... During the last 6 months there have been 15 new responses received by our District Office from the Revivaltime Office.

HOME MISSIONS REPORT TO THE 1969 DISTRICT COUNCIL:
... A study by this committee has found a strong shifting population from the rural areas to the cities in the past decade. (Many of these have moved out of the state.) The State of Nebraska's population grew from 1,395,000 in 1958 to 1,535,000 in 1968, a growth of 40,000. (round figures) While during the same decade the number of Nebraska Assemblies of God churches has declined from 77 in 1958 to 66 in 1968, the average Sunday School attendance slipped from 4,889 in 1958 to 4,252 in the past year. Although there may be several realizable conclusions for this decline, yet let us recognize that we have not kept pace with state population growth trends.

FOREIGN MISSIONS REPORT: It appears that the Nebraska District has quite a large and successful Foreign Missions outreach. We commend the unselfish attitude of our people as they have provided the needs of these missionaries through Foreign Missions, Speed the Light, Women's Missionary Council, and Men's Fellowship.

We have begun churches in Cozad, Auburn and Arnold in the past 10 years that are still open today. In beginning a new work, the emphasis must yet be upon the man God will call and lay upon his heart a burden for that community. Many a good work has been started and flourished when such dedicated men and women stepped out to work for God and trust Him. As much as money is needed to begin new works, the man of God is still the Key.

However, it is completely inconsistent for Nebraska Churches to support so strongly our Overseas Missions and do little or nothing for the lost souls of men here in Nebraska. Most capable personnel are sent overseas by us while it seems to this committee that also such capable men and women can be called and well supported for a work here at home for God. This is a call for balance in World Missions giving.

Reminiscing the 1960s and Moving Ahead to the '70s

It is always interesting to reminisce when we come to the conclusion of a year. We not only think of the passing of 1969, but the passing into history a very productive decade so far as scientific advances are concerned. This decade brought us a new era. The conquering of space by man is no longer a fantasy, but a reality. In this decade four men left their footprints on the surface of the moon. During the sixties man was permitted to explore a little more of God's wonderful creation. This achievement by man has brought to us a message loud and clear, "The coming of the Lord draweth nigh." Surely the Lord will come before the end of another decade.

We praise God for the accomplishments He has permitted us to achieve during the sixties. A great advancement has come to our camping program. The erection of the new air conditioned tabernacle and the remodeling of the old tabernacle into a spacious kitchen and dining hall. In 1968 a new eighteen room dorm was completed. Not only have we seen progress in the physical improvements of the camp, but during the sixties the attendance in the different camps have steadily increased. In 1969 an all time high in attendance was reached. We give to God all the glory for these accomplishments.

During the past decade the Lord permitted us to construct and occupy our new District Headquarters Office. This has facilitated the operation of the District and made the work so very much lighter. We praise God for these new facilities.

The Lord enabled us to dispose of the old District home and office at 1704 West Division Street here in Grand Island and from the amount received from the sale of this property we constructed a new residence for the District Superintendent at 1324 North Park in Grand Island. God enabled us to complete these building projects before the rise in building costs.

God has wonderfully blessed some of our congregations with new church buildings during these past ten years ...

The decade before us presents great responsibilities and each responsibility is a challenge. I personally desire to see a number of new churches established in Nebraska. United under God and empowered by the Holy Spirit we will see our desires materialize into realities....

(L. W. Dickinson, "Reminiscing the 1960s and Moving Ahead to the '70s," *Nebraska Fellowship,* January 1970.)

District office at1503 W. 2nd, Grand Island, NE

C.A. parsonage for the D-CAPs, located at 1028 S. Sycamore in Grand Island.

Jim Wilkins Family in D-CAP parsonage about 1964

Chapter 19: Continued Growth (1970-1979)

"Every day they continued to meet together in the temple courts. They broke bread in their homes and ate together with glad and sincere hearts, [47]praising God and enjoying the favor of all the people. And the Lord added to their number daily those who were being saved." (Acts 2:46-47 NIV)

1970 District Council Held in Omaha on April 7-9

... Brother Melvin Jennings presented the following revised resolution on College Campus which was in printed form and distributed:

COLLEGE CAMPUS MINISTER - BE IT THEREFORE RESOLVED THAT,

1. A minister be appointed to the ministry of the College Campus and that such minister shall also serve as the District Chi Alpha Director.

2. That a District College Youth Committee be formed to act according to the guidelines of the National C.A. Department ...

3. Funding: The support of this ministry shall be the responsibility of every church in the District...

4. The selection of the District College Youth Minister and his salary shall be made by the District Presbytery with recommendations by the District Youth Committee.

5. This ministry shall be considered a Home Missions Project and thus shall be promoted by the District Committee on Evangelism.

MSC that the resolution be adopted.

RESOLUTION--WHEREAS, there is quite a lot of concern to have the C.A. Convention at an earlier date in the fall, BE IT THEREFORE RESOLVED THAT, the C.A. Convention be held on the date of the Nebraska Teachers Convention, October 29 and 30. MSC that the resolution be adopted.

Mrs. L. E. King, President of W. M. C., presented her report. She stated a grand total of $24,292.24 was given the past year. Since 1953—17 years of giving for "Dimes for Souls," making a total of $66,558.64. Total over all giving in 30 years was $254,000.00. She stated that 1970 marks the 30th Anniversary for the Nebraska W. M. C.'s. MSC to accept the report.

REPORT OF COMMITTEE ON EVANGELISM: ... Home Missions accomplishments during the past year have been:

1. The $10,000.00 goal set by last year's District Council has been met and exceeded.

2. Money received by the Nebraska District through returns of World Ministry giving has increased $713.00 over the previous year.

3. A revolving loan fund has been established by the Presbytery, as recommended by last year's District Council.

4. Impact Omaha has been underwritten with Home Missions funds.

1970 Special Session of the District Council Concerning College Youth Held in Lexington on August 5

Dr. John Murphy ... I am thus acting as chairman with the recommendation that I serve as "Pro-Tem" Chi Alpha director until such time that our College Youth Minister can be appointed. This recommendation was approved by our Nebraska Executive Presbytery and allows us to move ahead with the naming of our committee.

If we were to continue making progress, it was necessary to name this committee. Our District directives state that a budget for the Chi Alpha director and the college youth program be established by the District College Youth Committee, and approved by the district presbyter. Our committee was thus named and is as follows:

Dr. John Murphy, Chairman

Rev. L. W. Dickinson, Superintendent

L. E. Wilkins, Secretary-Treasurer

H. H. DeMent, D-Cap

R. [Robert] Nazarenus, C. A. Representative

Earl Goodman, Jr. Pastor

To continue with progress, our committee then approached the problem of the budget. We studied the budget as proposed by the makers of our resolution. We have approved this although we feel it is perhaps marginal. We have submitted this budget to Executive Presbytery as such:

Salary	5200
Housing	1800
Travel	1200
Office Expense	250
	$8450

Dr. Murphy asked for the voting of the budget. SC ...

RESOLUTION—The Executive Presbytery be authorized to withdraw from the Home Mission Fund $1,000.00 to be placed in the College Youth Ministries Fund for the purposes of meeting current expenses. MSC

Dr. Murphy also explained this would be a Home Mission project and does not conflict with the C. A. Program.

Congratulations for Benevolences Giving

We congratulate the Nebraska District for first place in the total number of churches participating in Benevolences giving with 69.7% of your churches giving to some phase or phases of Benevolences throughout the year. The report also reflects that your district placed second in the nation (28.7%) in churches giving to Highlands Children‘s Home and third in the nation (42.4%) giving to the Hillcrest Children‘s Home.

In support of other Benevolences ministries, Nebraska placed tenth in the nation with 16.6% of the churches giving to Bethany Retirement Home, and eleventh in the nation in supporting AMA, with 30.3% of your churches contributing to AMA last year.

("Congratulations for Benevolences Giving," *Nebraska Fellowship*, October 1970, p. 3.)

David Argue Appointed Campus Minister

... David Argue of Victoria, British Columbia will be moving to Nebraska in the near future to take up his responsibility as campus minister of Nebraska under the appointment of the Nebraska District Council of the Assemblies of God. There are 60,000 students enrolled in our Universities and Colleges in Nebraska. This is an extensive home missions field. I urge you as a member of this fellowship family to earnestly pray that God will use our church to reach these people with the gospel. ~ L.W. Dickinson

(L. W. Dickinson, "David Argue Appointed Campus Minister," *Nebraska Fellowship*, November 1970, p. 2.)

"You Were Speaking in Tongues!"

Here is a testimony from the 1970s, when Dave Argue was directing campus ministry at the university in Lincoln, Nebraska.

Shortly after I became a Christian through a coffeehouse ministry in Fairbury, NE, a group of us attended a Bible study at the University in Lincoln, NE. It was called Agape Fellowship and was led by Dave Argue. Being a new Christian, I had heard no teaching yet about the Holy Spirit but I was hungry for more.

At the end of the meeting, we were all standing around in a large circle singing. I thought to myself, "Wow, that's a beautiful song, it sounds like angels singing, but I can't understand the words." (I was told later that they were singing in tongues.) Dave invited those that wanted the baptism in the Holy Spirit to come to the center of the circle. I remember thinking, "I don't know what it is, but if there's more I want it!" I don‘t recall what was said to me, or prayer over me in that circle and I didn‘t speak in tongues then but felt great about the decision to "go for it."

Since the coffeehouse kids were from many different denominations, the sponsors felt the need for teaching us regarding the Holy Spirit after Dave's ministry. So, I soon was made aware of the gifts of the Spirit, speaking in tongues, etc. and started wondering when I'd start speaking in tongues.

It was shortly after that teaching that an evangelist that worked with the kids at the coffeehouse had a flashback from the drugs he'd done prior to salvation. He was at the coffeehouse and started throwing furniture, knocking things down and tearing the place apart. A lot of the kids ran upstairs to the balcony in fear.

But the Holy Spirit gave Dawn (adult sponsor) and I boldness and we went to him, laid hands on him and started praying. I was at a loss for words, "What should I pray?" I hesitated a moment and then started praying. After we finished and he calmed down, Dawn said, "You were speaking in tongues!" And I answered, "Well, I didn't know what else to pray."

~ Joni Clarke, Christian Education Director, Word of Life Church, Columbus, NE

1971 District Council Held in Grand Island on March 30 – April 1

... Thursday morning, April 1, 1971, Rev. Wayne Hall, Chairman of the Camp Committee gave the camp report. The following recommendations were made by the Committee:

1. We recommend that the Little Chapel building be renovated for use as large dormitory type rooms for campers. It will be necessary to repair this building in order to bring it up to minimum State Approved Standards.

2. We recommend that the camp fees for cabins, campers, and trailers be raised to present day costs.

3. We recommend that the tabernacle be painted on the outside, with an economical, home-made covering to seal the blocks and improve the appearance.

4. We recommend that the two District cabins and the four privately owned cabins south of the New Dorm be removed. This is in accordance with a letter received November 20, 1970, from the Nebraska State Health Department. This area will than become a playground for the small children.

5. It was suggested that song books used at the General Council and offered at reduced price be purchased for use in the tabernacle. New song book racks would need to be made for the new books.

6. We recommend that Northwest Bell Telephone Company be contacted and asked to install a pay phone on the grounds for public use for local and long distance calls.

MSC to receive the report as read.

Brother John Stocker, Chairman of the Financial Committee of the Department of Youth and Christian Education gave the following report—

... It was the opinion of the committee that the needs of the department could be met within the existing framework if greater cooperation at all levels were achieved ...

The following are its recommendations: ...

D) That the camp tuition be increased to provide added revenue for the Department.

E) That the C.A. Representatives work more closely with the Pastors in their section, keeping them informed of District and National programs.

F) That the financial condition of the Department Executives, and in the event of an unforeseen emergency, this situation be considered by the District Presbytery and Department Executives. MSC

Men's Fellowship report for 1970-1971 submitted by Charles R. Turner:

... We now have 24 R.R. Outposts with two hundred boys participating. We have been quite pleased with the enthusiasm in most churches for this work. Brother Burdine and his helpers have been doing a good work in this outreach.

Light for the Lost response has been very gratifying this past year; our total offerings and pledges have totaled over $8,000.00 for literature besides the nearly three thousand dollars given by councilmen for the expense account.

... RESOLUTION--WHEREAS, the Saturday closing of Kids Kamp creates considerable inconvenience for those traveling long distances to and from our camp grounds: BE IT THEREFORE RESOLVED THAT, Kids Kamps close Friday noon of each week. SC.

Mrs. H. W. Lebsack, District WMC President, gave the WMC report of the year. Mrs. Lebsack reported that there were 60 active groups, total membership 746. She also stated that "Dimes for Souls," the past year was $5,371.13 ... Mrs. Lebsack, also presented the Murray Browns a $1,000.00 check to purchase what is needed for their personal needs, and 250 points from the "Heart Room," at the District Office.

1972 District Council Held in Lincoln on April 4-6

... The present youth movement sweeping our country, including that in the state of Nebraska, is creating a vast mission field among previously un-churched youth, as well as opening the hearts of our own Assembly of God young people, and since many of these young people are demonstrating the urgent need of teaching ... and the necessity of instructing in conducting a valid person-to-person confrontation with the Gospel message and teaching in organizing and conducting a meeting of praise and worship emphasis ... The old cliché "today's youth are tomorrow's leaders" is quickly being replaced due to the shortness of time before the return of our Lord, to that "today's youth are today's evangelists!"

Rev. Wayne Hall, Chairman of the Camp Committee read the following camp report: The following were discussed:

1. Finishing the new dorm which has fourteen rooms with a shower, stool, and lavatory in each room. A good crew of workers are needed for a couple of days to put on the plywood ceiling, hang the doors, install the furnace, and paint. A firm in Lexington will blow in 5 1/2 inches of insulation. A hundred bunk beds with thirty inch mattresses with plasticized coverings are needed.

2. Finishing the Little Chapel: The new windows are in. The walls and ceilings are insulated but the walls are not paneled. About two-thirds of the floor still has to be run with a new layer of concrete. The central bathrooms have to be finished.

The Committee reviewed the State Inspection report and saw several improvements that are to be made. MSC to accept the report.

1973 District Council Held in Hastings on April 3-5

... In the April 5, Thursday morning session, Mrs. H. W. Lebsack, WMC President read the following annual WMC report ...

We had 62 organized groups in Nebraska, with 846 members. These 62 groups held 427 services in rest homes and made 11,213 visitations. Through the efforts of the WMC, 30 souls were saved. They gave out 7,444 Bibles and gospel portions.

Last year we praise the Lord for helping us go over our goal in our giving to "DIMES FOR SOULS." We gave $7,443.35. Our goal for 1973 is $7,600.00. By the help of the Lord and our "HUSBANDS" we'll exceed that goal.

From our Dimes for Souls offering, we gave the District $3,163.42. We gave to the Foreign missions $1,581.72 and for new beds at the Camp Grounds $1,450.35.

Through the ministry of the HEART ROOM we outfitted three missionary families: Harold Mintles, Jerry Spains, Gene Schachterles and a home missions family.

Through the ministry of the coupons and stamps we purchased a number of very needed articles for three foreign missionaries and for the Camp Grounds.

We thank God for the wonderful cooperation from the ladies of Nebraska. With an open heart, they are always willing to work and sacrifice to further the Kingdom of God.

The 1973 Camp Committee recommended the following:

1. We recommend that all privately-owned cabins be repaired or otherwise improved to meet state requirements and to compare with the standard of other buildings on the camp grounds ...

2. We recommend siding the dining hall and Alber Hall. Also covering the walls that have been insulated in North Alber Hall before camp.

3. We recommend the Men's Fellowship tool project be completed and a riding mower with attachments be purchased as soon as possible for use in 1973.

4. We recommend that a man be appointed from each section to act as a camp representative to promote the 1000 Club and other projects.

5. We recommend that camp projects be promoted at Home Missions Rallies across the state ...

6. We recommend installation of two additional mercury lights: one west of the Swedberg Dorm, and one south of the Roll Dorm.

7. We recommend that the green cabin just south of the Swedberg Dorm be torn down.

8. We recommend that those cabins south of the 18-unit dorm be town down, with the exception of Dewey's cabin, to make room for a recreation area ... Any lumber salvaged from the cabins will be saved for future use.

9. We recommend the following improvements be incorporated into a ten-year Master Camp Plan:

a. A chain-link fence be installed along the south edge of the camp ground.

b. Additional lighting be installed.

c. A lighted sign, "Assemblies of God Conference Grounds," be erected by the highway.

d. Consider landscaping in south area.

e. A 28-30 room, family dorm be constructed north of the dining hall; and one more open-bay dorm be built.

f. A croquet, volleyball and badminton courts be included in the recreation area.

MSC to accept the report.

In the Thursday afternoon session Rev. Troy Allen, Chairman, read the resolution after which he moved its adoption: WHEREAS: Our camping program is constantly expanding, WHEREAS: There is ever a need to look toward future development, WHEREAS: Building projects often take a number of years of planning and consideration before actual work is begun, BE IT THEREFORE RESOLVED THAT: That a committee be appointed to: (1) Study the need of a multi-purpose type of building on the camp ground. Such a building to be used as a multi-purpose recreational building with gymnasium facilities. (2) Study the cost of building such a facility. (3) Study the means of financing such a project. SC

Troy Allen, Chairman, read the resolution after which he moved its adoption: WHEREAS: The Campus Ministries program is expanding throughout the state, and WHEREAS: In the Omaha area alone there are 23,000 students that are virtually untouched by the Gospel, and WHEREAS: Our present Campus Minister's responsibilities will not allow any further expansion of Ministry in that area: BE IT THEREFORE RESOLVED THAT: Approval be given the District Presbytery to institute such a program that would bring about the expansion of personnel on the field adequate to meet the present need, and that investigation and proposals be instigated immediately in this regard. This resolution was seconded and much discussion took place. The resolution carried.

Rev. A. M. Alber, former District superintendent, gave a most interesting talk saying he was voted in as superintendent in 1934 with an income of $2300.00. Bro. and Sis. Alber were given a standing ovation.

1974 District Council Held in North Platte on April 2-4

... On Thursday afternoon, April 4, a motion was made to adopt this Resolution. Seconded. WHEREAS, the Nebraska District Council unanimously approved the exploration of the expansion of Campus Ministries in the Omaha Area, and WHEREAS, some investigation relative to this matter during the course of this past year has resulted in the desire for an expression of firm direction on the part of this council, BE IT THEREFORE RESOLVED THAT, the Campus Ministries committee be empowered by this body to expand the Campus Ministries program in the Omaha area along the following guidelines:

1. That the following budget be suggested--$5000.00 salary

a. ($2500.00 to be raised from churches)

b. $2500.00 to be raised by private concerns and interested parties.)

c. Other expenses as mileage, and office expense be raised from the 10% Home Missions return on Speed the Light funds.

2. That a person be sought for this position.

After much discussion was made on this resolution both Pro and Con, it carried.

RESOLUTION-WHEREAS, the direction of Kid‘s Camp is under the Youth and Christian Education Director WHEREAS, this creates an excessive work load on the Director of Youth and Christian Education implementing of Kids Camp programs to have them under separate direction; WHEREAS, it has been mutually agreed between the Kids Camp Director, Presbyters and the Director of Youth and Christian Education that separate direct supervision would be practical, BE IT THEREFORE RESOLVED THAT, the Kid‘s Camp program be removed from the supervision of the Director of Youth and Christian Education and be placed under the direct supervision of the Kid‘s Camp Committee, with all their plans being subject to the approval of the District Superintendent, BE IT FURTHER RESOLVED THAT, all other constitution and bylaw changes made necessary by the approval of the above resolution be authorized. This resolution, was MSC.

Mrs. H. W. Lebsack gave the WMC report.

We appreciate the work of Loretta Blauvelt, our District Vice-President and Missionettes Director. We have 19 clubs in Nebraska with 200 members. 10 Missionettes were saved, 8 were baptized with the Holy Spirit. The Missionettes became STARS AND TWO WERE CROWNED HONOR STARS in our achievement program, “Stairway to the Stars.”

DIMES FOR SOULS: The WMC day at Camp, August 1973 was the great day that God has given to us. The WMC‘s brought in $8,463.87 in “DIMES FOR SOULS” OFFERINGS …

... We have 61 local WMC groups with 873 members. The WMC‘s held 378 services in rest homes, etc. They made 8,372 calls. According to the reports that were sent in, 88 souls were saved through the ministry of the WMC‘s. 2,141 Bibles and gospel portions were given. We gave two Leadership Training certificates.

... There was a resolution passed to have a committee of three, one sectional presbyter, one pastor and one district executive be appointed by the District Superintendent to edit the bylaws for clarity of expression and grammatical correctness. Following the completion of the work of this committee, the bylaws be submitted to another committee of three, named by the District Superintendent and this committee shall determine whether the editing has changed in any way, the meaning of any of the present bylaws. Following the approval of the second committee the bylaws shall be printed. MS and after much discussion both Pro and Con it was carried.

1975 District Council Held in Omaha on April 1-3

On Wednesday morning, April 2, Bro. Dickinson‘[s Superintendent‘s report he stated that he “appreciated the faithfulness of the churches in their giving.” Highlights of the World and Foreign Ministries were given showing $97,435.00 gain in World Ministries and $29,160.00 in Foreign. This shows the concern of the people and the sharing of their talents …

The Assets and Liabilities indicate that the district is in good financial condition and may God help you to move on to establish new churches. We only support one small one at the present time." Bro. Dickinson stated that we have now paid off a total of $45,000 in bonds on the district office, leaving a balance of $15,000. We lease 40% of the office.

Ella Masten, director of Kids' Kamp expressed her thanks to all those who helped in this area and the continued spiritual growth of the Kamps. She also stated that the tuition for Kids' Kamp will be increased this year due to the increase of food prices. Report accepted as printed.

Rev. James Wilkins was elected District superintendent. His acceptance speech was as follows: "I think that anyone who would find himself in the position of following a Superintendent such as Bro. Dickinson would feel a great load of responsibility descending upon his shoulders at a moment such as this. I know I haven't felt the full impact of it yet ... A good many of the delegates here today have known me a short time—many of you a long time ... I stand before you with a bit of awe, humbly accepting it, believing you will pray for us. I know that, if we work together, God will help us move forward for the glory of Jesus Christ ..."

... On Thursday morning, Mrs. H. W. Lebsack, president of the WMC, reported the following: We thank God for the opportunity of serving the Nebraska WMC's for another year ...

The total membership of the WMC in Nebraska is 779. The WMC's held 395 services in rest homes and made 6,793 visitations. They gave 283 Bibles and Gospels out.

"DIMES FOR SOULS" giving surpassed all past giving with a total of $9,904.59 ...

Rev. Dickinson stated that Rev. Thomas F. Zimmerman would install the newly elected District Superintendent after the Ordination service Thursday evening. He further stated, "This brings to a conclusion the end of my tenure in office. You have done more for us than we could ever expect or hope for. I've told many people to remember me for what has been accomplished, but please forget me when you new pastor takes over. God is going to use you new Superintendent with the leadership he has given him ... The Nebraska District has a great future—a tremendous future! The Lord is going to bless and help you all the way."

While we look with joy at the Foreign Missions program, we look with concern on our situation as it relates to Home Missions. We realize that there will be a decline in our Foreign Missions outreach unless the home base is kept strong. We will be unable to put more missionaries on overseas soil unless we plant more churches in our own district.

... In the early 1960's, the following goal was set forth to the Nebraska District Council in session: "ninety churches by 1970 (6 new ones in our two metropolitan areas)." At that time there were 76 A/G churches in our District. Since then because of shifting population and other reasons we have closed churches in the following places: Alle, Alma, Benkelman, Central City, Decatur, Fairview, Hartington, Hershey, Kimball, Macy Neligh, Ord, Reynolds, Whitney, Winnebago, Wood Lake. It should be noted that the majority of these people have not been lost to the Assemblies of God but are attending other A/G churches. While we have established a few new churches to take the place of those that have closed we can only boast of having the sum total of 67 churches in 1975--far less than the projected goal of 90 by 1970. With these things in mind we hope you can sense in some measure the burden that your committee has felt for a number of months. It is our desire to see:

1. The strengthening of existing churches ...

2. The planting and establishing of new churches on a regular basis.

... Your committee does not come to you with recommendations wherein we would ask this Council to give us machinery and a plan for reaching our state. These are already at our disposal. What we do ask for is your full cooperation as we seek to work along with the District Presbyters and the Lord of the Harvest to put laborers into the whitened fields ... The Great Commission is not optional. It is a command and it is the standard by which our stewardship will be judged. MSC to accept the World Mission report.

1976 District Council Held in North Platte on April 6-8

In the Wednesday morning session, District superintendent James D. Wilkins present his report. Brother James D. Wilkins, returned to the chair and announced that as a result of legislation passed last year, no other reports will be read at council.

... Reverend L. E. Wilkins resigned his office. He had served in the District Office in some capacity for 34 years. He expressed his appreciation for the opportunity of working with the Brethren in this Presbytery. He expressed his thanks for the people's confidence in him. Nebraska is a small state but has been first in many things. Nebraska was one of the first to have a Director of Kids and Youth Camp. Brother Wilkins expressed that he served under 5 District Superintendents.

Brother Wilkins stated, "It was expressed at the General Presbyters meeting in Denver that my son and I are the first to serve as father and son at a General Presbyter meeting." ...

The chairman Reverend James D. Wilkins added thanks for allowing a father-son team. The working relationship was enjoyable.

... AMENDMENT TO RESOLUTION #3. BE IT THEREFORE RESOLVED THAT: The 59th session go on record as approving a plan calling for the construction of a New Recreational facility on the District Camp grounds as follows:

1. The installation of a 30' X 60' state approved swimming pool and, the construction of a Multi-purposed basketball, tennis, and volleyball court and,

2. The construction of a building to house both of the two previously mentioned projects. Such building to be constructed with showering facilities and classrooms in 1976.

BE IT FURTHER RESOLVED THAT: The Camp facilities be prepared for year-round use and the same be used for all reasonable District activities.

BE IT FURTHER RESOLVED THAT: Proper financing for this project be arranged for through the District Office. That the project be under co-operative supervision of the District Presbytery, the Department of Youth & Christian Education and the Camp Committee. The main amended motion which calls for construction of a multi-purpose activity building, was put to vote and carried.

1977 District Council Held in Gering on April 5-7

From the FINANCE COMMITTEE REPORT (of 2-25-77): ... It was further recommended that fund balances be added to the work sheets in succeeding years, disability and hospitalization be considered for all full-time district employees and a report on the multi-purpose building be included in the budget at council time.

In the Thursday morning session, Reverend Wilkins introduced Reverend E. M. Clark, president of North Central Bible College, who shared information concerning the college. President Clark extended an invitation to the Nebraska District to join NCBC Region. This would give our district three seats on the NCBC Board of Regents.... The invitation was accepted by the district council ...

... From the Special Committee to Consider the Possibility of Changing C. A. Convention Date, Ted Brust, Chairman, Dave Geary, Ted Davis and Tim Rust. After checking all the factors, we recommend the following:

1. That the D-Cap look into the possibility of changing the dates from Thanksgiving Convention for 1977 ...

2. That in an effort to keep costs at a minimum, that the Speed-the-Light Banquet

be abolished and a STL Victory Rally be held in its place ... MSC ...

1978 District Council Held in Lincoln on April 4-7

... The Chair introduced Dan Betzer, Secretary of Radio and TV Division of the Assemblies of God in Springfield, Missouri. He spoke to the people and challenged our hearts with the new mission field presently before us—TELEVISION AND TURNING POINT TELECAST. He pointed out that this outreach is not Assemblies of God centered but "God Centered."

Reverend Stocker noted with great joy that Nebraska was first in the Nation with 7.9% growth in Speed the Light giving. He stated this growth was not just made by a few churches in the state, but the growth was spread out among many churches.

1979 District Council Held in North Platte on April 3-5

In the Wednesday morning session the presentation of awards was a follows:

1st Foreign Missions, Omaha Glad Tidings

1st World Ministries, Omaha Glad Tidings

2nd World Ministries, Gering Assembly

3rd World Ministries, Big Springs

The Director of the Department of Youth and Christian Education, Ted Brust, presented awards for STL giving. The top one was Bellevue. Top giving to the Youth Department was Grand Island. The BGMC award went to North Platte.

Mrs. H. W. Lebsack, W.M.C. director

Jim Wilkins family

Mel and Barb Johnson

Dave Argue

Irene Kisser

Chapter 20: Forward in Ministry (1980-1989)

***"The Lord's hand was with them, and a great number of people believed and turned to the Lord."* (Acts 11:21 NIV)**

1980 District Council Held in Scottsbluff on April 7-10

... BE IT THEREFORE RESOLVED THAT, The Nebraska District Council establish an extension school of the Bible using International Correspondence Institute (ICI) materials and that the executive committee be empowered to make the arrangements necessary to operate such a ministry under the supervision of the District Office. The resolution was adopted.

WHEREAS April 29th is the date for "Washington for Jesus," BE IT THEREFORE RESOLVED THAT, April 29th be proclaimed by the Nebraska District as a day of fasting and prayer. MSC

... The Nebraska District Council went on record as opposing abortion on demand.

1981 District Council Held in Omaha on April 7-9

... It was MSC the term of office for the District Superintendent would be for four years. Election in uneven years for the District Superintendent and all others on the even years.

A Special Study Committee Chairman, Reverend Jimmy Root, gave a verbal report to the council in session. One suggestion, which came out of the committee, was that the secretary-treasurer office be made full-time position. In the discussion which followed it was suggested that the council consider hiring a business administrator. It was pointed out that a qualified layperson could do most or all the things we would expect if additional full-time personnel were added.

1982 District Council Held in Hastings on April 13-15

... The chairman gave opportunity for questions concerning the budget report. A comment was made that due to improvement of the minister's tithe and two (2) percent church giving our funds should improve ...

The District Council gave approval for the hiring of a Stewardship Director and the strong possibility exists that this will come to be a portfolio for an Administrative Assistant.

1983 District Council Held in Gering on April 5-7

... In the Wednesday, April 6, session Jewel Tucker of Springfield, Missouri, gave a word of greeting to the District Council and expressed the importance of pastors and churches in fulfilling the Great Commission in sending out the Gospel over the radio ... Dr. Don Argue, president of North Central Bible College in Minneapolis, Minnesota, expressed the need for churches to help support the school.

Reverend Terry Brown was elected Assistant Director of Youth and Christian Education....

ICI Holds Developmental Meeting

"International Correspondence Institute recently held its annual Development Meeting in Brussels, Belgium. At this meeting the strategies for ICI reaching out to our world were developed. Representing the Nebraska District were Gene Schachterle, Spud DeMent, Eldora and Jack Vetter."

("ICI Holds Developmental Meeting," *Nebraska Fellowship,* 1983, Volume 4, Issues 1–6.)

Fastest Growing Churches

"According to the November (1982) issue of Moody Monthly magazine, in 24 states the fastest growing church is an Assembly of God! In Nebraska, Abundant Life Christian Center in Grand Island, Nebraska, Gene Arnold, Pastor, was named."

Church watchers may have suspected as much, but two new statistical studies make it clear: the fastest-growing denomination in America is the Assemblies of God (A/G)" *Dean Merill Christianity Today, January 7, 1983* in an article "The Fastest Growing American Denomination."

("Fastest Growing Churches," *Nebraska Fellowship,* 1983, Volume 4, Issues 1–6.)

1983 Camp "Rap-Up"

The 1983's camping season is now history! And what a history it is! Kid's Kamp attendance numbered 709 ... breaking all attendance records; and our Youth Camps brought more than 430 teenagers to Lexington to experience one of the most awesome outpourings of God's presence and power in recent years at our District's camping program, young people were saved, filled with the Holy Spirit (Jr. High Camp saw between 75-100 teens filled with the Holy Spirit), called into the ministry ... not to mention countless rededications to the Lord....

(David Graves (Director), "1983 Camp 'Rap-Up,'" *Nebraska Fellowship,* 1983, Volume 4, Issues 1, 6.)

1983 Missions Theme, Called to Pray

A/G Foreign missions giving was $56,779,964.00, 17% higher than in 1982. We have 1,261 Missionaries and National Ministers number 86,620. There are 99,574 number of churches overseas. 743 new churches were built in USA during 1982-1983. 320 Appointed Home Missionaries. 70 Active duty Military Chaplains and 91 Industrial and Institutional Chaplains.

Royal Rangers, Perry Baublitz, District Commander

The Nebraska District Royal Rangers annual summer Pow-Wow is history but it will live on as being one of those exciting years for Royal Rangers. God has been so good to send us one hundred and forty-six men and boys to make an exciting campout.

Once again the river float was one of the highlights of the Pow-Wow. Even Burlington Northern Railroad had fun tooting their train horns at the long string of floaters.

Women's Ministries, Mrs. Wayne Hall, President

1983 Ladies Fall Retreats were held at Lexington and Halsey. The Dimes for Souls offering was $13,475.00.

1984 District Council Held in Grand Island on April 10-12

... The subject of one of the resolutions was retirement income for minister. It was Resolved that the Nebraska District "enroll all its ministers into the membership of the Ministers Benefit Association, Springfield, Missouri."

Another resolution dealt with the dress code for youth camps. Immodest apparel was considered shorts, fish net shirts, tank tops, etc. No mixed swimming was to be permitted. This was referred to the new camp committee.

David Graves was reelected Youth and Christian Education Director.

District Staffing Changes

District Office hires Vickie Hesselgesser as new secretary.... As we welcome Vickie to our staff, we bid farewell to Leota Eigsti who has been a vital part of our District for the past 18 years. "

Leota Eigsti came on the scene when the superintendent's Office was on West Division Street and the D-Cap's Office was attached to a garage on South Locust. Her coming helped the District to begin to coordinate activities and eventually the District Office was set up in the basement of the Superintendent's home. That was when Reverend L. W. Dickinson was leading our District. Leota was here and was a vital part of the many of the improvements that have taken place over the years. She saw the new office erected on West Second Street and was a part of a growing staff.

The District Presbytery announces the appointment of Faith Tyson as the Director of the Nebraska Kids Kamp program. Faith holds a Specialized Ministries License with the Nebraska District Assemblies of God and is involved in child evangelism work.

("District Staffing Changes," *Nebraska Fellowship,* 1984, Volume 5, Issues 1-6.)

Royal Rangers

... We had a great time during this winter Pow-wow. Quite a few boys and leaders braved the unheated new swimming pool and not a few enjoyed the hot showers. The great news is that about 15 boys went forward to accept Jesus as their Savior.

Just over one hundred pinewood derby cars were entered and they all looked pretty good …

(Stephen Bowman [District Commander: Royal Rangers], *Nebraska Fellowship,* 1984), Volume 5, Issues 1-6.)

Department of Youth and Christian Education

... The attendance at both the Junior and Senior High camps were the highest it has been in a number of years, with 294 teens attending Junior High Camp, and 197 teens coming to Senior High camp, making a total attendance of 491 ...

Finally THANK YOU to two special families who have supported our camping program down through the years by donating meat to help keep costs down. The families of Kenny Lemp of Columbus, and Karl Hughes, of Wood River, both gave hogs this year. Thanks!

(David Graves [Director], "Department of Youth and Christian Education," *Nebraska Fellowship*, 1984, Volume 5, Issues 1-6.)

Women's Ministries

Mrs. Wayne (Hazel) Hall retired as President of Women's Ministries and Sandra Goodwin Clopine became the new President of Nebraska Women's Ministries.

The New S. T. L.Van — Steve Shorette, Director of Evangelism

Dear Nebraska Youth: We at Teen Challenge are extremely grateful for the energy you channeled toward our new van. It seems God is doing a new thing for us at every turn. God is providing for our Omaha reconstruction (fire destroyed much of the interior of the Teen Challenge home in Omaha) …

Just a few lines regarding the van. It will be used to transport Teen Challenge students to church services and other local functions....

Light for the Lost

The annual banquet tour is over and must be, by every measure, declared successful. The Nebraska District enjoys an enviable reputation as an ardent supporter of this effective mission's tool. Forty-three churches participated in the total giving of $54,809.18. This represents a substantial increase in both the number of churches involved and also the amount of cash and pledges received. This isn't "perfect," but I believe that if we chase perfection we can catch excellence.

(Myron Clopine [Director], "Light for the Lost," *Nebraska Fellowship,* 1984, Volume 5, Issues 1–6.)

1985 District Council Held in Kearney on April 9-10

In the Wednesday sessions, Chairman Wilkins informed the audience that the business sessions are being taped in order to assist those who take the minutes and prepare them for the printer:

Brother [Robert] Nazarenus, Secretary / Treasurer thanked the district presbytery and all past secretary/treasurers. He thanked Vickie for her patience and help in learning the job. The bookkeeper, Vickie Hesselgesser, then highlighted some of the new terms of the system. She then went through the Balance Sheets section by section and explained the format and the gain/loss for each department and fund....

Treasurer Nazarenus read the budget committee report. Discussions took place on the problem of the camp deficit and it was decided to have the District Presbytery handle this problem.

There was much discussion concerning the feasibility of establishing its own program of self-insurance or recommend to the General Council to consider the forming of such companies. BE IT RESOLVED THAT we urge the General Council as soon as possible to consider the forming of such companies or group policy insurance funded by a recognized company that would provide to our constituency nationally, or on a district basis, multi-peril/liability insurance for our churches, and health/accident and life insurance protection for our pastors, and employees in our district and church ministries.

Reverend Ray Pile made a motion to refer this resolution with all its amendments to the Executive Presbytery of the District. Seconded and carried.

It was voted "The Sectional Youth Representative and Christian Education Coordinator shall be a credentialed minister or qualified layperson of the section."

... From the presbyters came the changes from the 1984 District Council for the dress code for camps. BE IT THEREFORE RESOLVED, ... the policy will read as follows: ... modest sports apparel including recreational shorts and cut-offs as illustrated in our camp brochure will be allowed as wearing apparel at all camps for recreation times only, whether such recreation be indoors or outdoors. Campers are asked to continue the present policy of wearing dress or street clothing excluding shorts, tank tops etc., when in the dining hall or tabernacle. Campers and staff shall not wear swim suits while out on the grounds. Street clothes must be worn to and from the swimming pool. A policy of separate swim times shall be maintained for all camps sponsored by the district. This shall not apply to rental groups. (This means separate swim times for male and female.)

The Executive Committee has asked Youth Camp and Kids Kamp Directors to put something together in the form of an illustrated brochure....

1986 District Council Held in North Platte on April 8-10

... Pastor Sam Mayo presented Sister L. E. Wilkins with a certificate honoring L. E. Wilkins for his dedication to the campground. The dining hall at the campground will now be called L. E. Wilkins Dining Center.

In the Wednesday session, Chairman Wilkins introduced Todd Cram, who explained the changes in Minister's Benefit Life Insurance. He said they were offering an open period of enrollment for 30 days which would enable ministers to purchase insurance without a physical exam.

The College Ministries Outreach program must remain strong in the District. It was MSC "that the District Presbytery have the option to appoint a District College Ministry representative. He shall give general oversight to the program."

MSC "The District Presbytery" be amended to read: "The District Presbytery shall consist of the District Superintendent, the Assistant Superintendent, The District Secretary/Treasurer, The Presbyters of each section in the District and the Director of Youth and Christian Education."

Since there is a need for better and expanded housing facilities to accommodate children and youth attending our camps, and for Family Camp, and Paul Ackerman left a cash gift to the camp which now exceeds $36,000 with accumulated interest and the Presbyter Board and Layman's Council have endorsed a new building project for the camp:

BE IT RESOLVED THAT, we increase our borrowing limit to $300,000 and

BE IT FURTHER RESOLVED THAT, we authorize the borrowing of up to $275,000 for the construction of the new facility at the camp; and

BE IT FURTHER RESOLVED THAT, we authorize the Presbyter Board and the Executive Committee to sign all necessary legal documents and see the project through to completion. MSC

Thursday morning a Special Finance Committee to study the finances of the Youth Department gave the following recommendations:

1. That the present method of funding continue with the understanding that by action of the District Presbytery the District policy will be to forgive any reasonable shortfall.

2. That the salary, social security, and health insurance be assumed by the General Fund of the District.

A motion to receive the report was seconded. Chairman Wilkins said he believed that receiving the report would only place the recommendation before the Presbytery in the fall.... It was moved and seconded that the house adopt the whole report but just change the word forgive to subsidize. The report was adopted as amended.

Family Camp is designed to enhance the cohesiveness of families and families like to swim together as a family,

BE IT THEREFORE RESOLVED THAT, there be a time set apart at Family Camp for family swimming. MSC

1987 District Council Held in Omaha on April 7-9

... There was an inadvertent insertion in the resolution concerning the Campground Lodge and Retreat building program, which calls for the Presbyter Board and the Executive committee to sign necessary legal documents and loan papers in 1986. It was MSC that the Executive Committee is authorized to sign any and all necessary loan and legal documents which may be required in the construction of the Lodge and Retreat Center. (It was cumbersome and inconvenient for Presbyters to carry out this responsibility.) ...

Special District Council Held in Lexington on June 22, 1987

Superintendent Wilkins resigned to move to El Sobrante, California, and Robert Nazarenus became the Suerintendent-Elect.

... Chairman Wilkins expressed his appreciation for the privilege of working in the Nebraska District as, Superintendent for twelve years, Assistant Superintendent for one year, pastorates in two Nebraska churches and nearly five years as District Youth Director. Brother Sam Mayo asked that we gather together and pray for the departing Superintendent and the Superintendent-Elect, Robert Nazarenus ... Brother Mayo thanked Superintendent Wilkins for his wisdom and service to the District.

1988 District Council Held in Gering on April 12-14

The Tuesday evening service began at 7:00 p.m. with Missionettes Honor Star Ceremony conducted by Caroline Deffenbaugh, Missionettes Director for the state of Nebraska

Brother Rice commented on the Ackerman Lodge project, stating it was nearing completion ... He shared that the major concern is the cash flow as a result of this project. Brother Rice called attention to the Camp Fund commenting that there has been a shortage of cash flow in that area.

... He remarked that our Camp Ministry has been a beautiful opportunity to share ministry, and asked for their prayers and any special appeals to their church bodies so this ministry can continue uninterrupted.

District Director of Youth and Christian Education, David Graves, presented the awards for Boys and Girls Missionary Crusade Giving for last year. Brother Graves extended his appreciation to all the churches for their participation in BGMC. In 1986, $12,500.00 was given, which set a new record and won the award for the most improved district in the nation from our National Headquarters in Springfield, MO. In 1987, over $15,500 was received in BGMC giving.

... Chairman Nazarenus presented the Light-For-The-Lost Director, Brother Ed Canfield, with an award from the General Council‘s Men‘s Ministries Department recognizing the Nebraska District Council as being 2nd in the nation, in 1987, in giving.

Brother Sam Mayo shared the exciting adventure of "Decade of Harvest." He explained that a Task Force was appointed by our Executive Presbyters, and they have been meeting with the purpose of crystallizing strategy for our Fellowship, that will give to us a total church evangelism thrust through the "Decade of Harvest," which takes us up to the turn of the century. Brother Mayo asked the congregation to stand and join with him in prayer for the "Decade of Harvest," the new work in Wayne, and other home missions works through the state....

... BE IT RESOLVED THAT, the Nebraska District Council, in cooperation with the General Council of the Assemblies of God, declares the 1990s the Decade of Harvest, and that we affirm the national goals of the Decade of Harvest, which are:

1) To enlist 1 million prayer partners.

2) To reach and win 5 million persons to Christ.

3) To train and disciple 20,000 persons for ministry.

4) To establish 5,000 new churches.

It was moved, second, and the resolution was accepted.

Since the Nebraska District supports Teen Challenge of the Midlands, and there is a need to remodel and renovate many rooms at the Men‘s Center at Colfax, Iowa a resolution was presented which encouraged churches and/or Sections to participate in the "Adopt-a-Room" project. This resolution passed.

WHEREAS, the Ackerman Lodge debt service has placed stress on the cash flow of the District, and ... BE IT THEREFORE RESOLVED THAT, the District Home Certificates be cashed with the monies applied to reduce the debt on Ackerman Lodge. After much discussion the resolution carried.

Report of Special District Council, January 1989

A specially called district council was held January 12, 1989. The assistant district superintendent, Sam Mayo had resigned. David Argue was elected to serve in that position.

Chairman Nazarenus shared about legal items that had come across his desk. He emphasized the importance of being incorporated and making sure the fee was paid every two years to be current.

The next subject for discussion revolved around the screening of workers in churches and how important it was to know your volunteer workers as well as your paid staff. There had been many incidents of molestation and attacks by religious workers. Chairman Nazarenus said screening forms would be sent out from his office with instructions on how to protect your church from employing unknown staff.

Brother Nazarenus discussed the requirements in filing of Tax Exempt forms for each county assessor. He informed the pastors the assessors are now taking the posture that it is not their responsibility to inform the church they need to file the affidavit ...

Chairman Nazarenus shared that some insurance companies are making liability coverage available, including the one the District just signed with, that provides coverage up to $300,000. This covers our Executives, Presbyters, volunteer staff and paid staff. Each church should find out whether they are covered for this under their own policies.

1989 District Council Held in Lincoln on April 11-12

... In the Tuesday, April 11, sessions the Secretary/Treasurer, Howard Rice, made comments on the Financial Report. He noted Minister's Tithe for 1989 was up in comparison to last year. The campground budget showed a black figure, after many years of running in the red ... His concerns for the days ahead were the debt retirement of Ackerman Lodge, a new roof on the District Office and the Tabernacle.

In the Wednesday sessions Brother [Robert] Bornert from the Department of Benevolences in Springfield thanked the Nebraska District for what they were doing for Highlands, Hillcrest, Disaster Relief, and A. M. A. He reported that in 1988 Nebraska gave $20,785 to Benevolences. He said 29 churches didn't support Benevolences at all in Nebraska. Overall in the U. S., 33% of churches support Benevolences, and 17% of churches in the U. S. support A.M.A.

District Commander Perry Baublitz at 1982 Pow Wow

Harold and Marie James receiving 50-year awards from Superintendent Jim Wilkins (left) in 1982.

WM Day, 1983

Hazel Hall

Pastor Faith Tyson

1985 mortgage burning for tabernacle at Lexington Camp. (L-r): Jim Wilkins, Dave Graves and Indiana Supt. Charles Crank.

Chapter 21: The Decade of Harvest (1990-1999)

"For by grace are ye saved through faith; and that not of yourselves: it is the gift of God: Not of works, lest any man should boast. For we are his workmanship, created in Christ Jesus unto good works, which God hath before ordained that we should walk in them." **(Ephesians 2:8-10 KJV)**

1990 District Council in North Platte April 24-25

In the Tuesday sessions Chairman [Robert] Nazarenus introduced Sonny Salmon, District Director of Finance and Administration and thanked him for his expertise during the past year in the area of finance and budgeting.

... Brother [Howard] Rice, Secretary/Treasurer, shared observations in regard to the current budget before going onto the 1990 Budget. He shared that our camp fund in 1986 was minus $21,000 plus at the end of that year. In 1987 this fund was a minus $31,000 camp deficit. Brother Rice shared that we appreciate the support and help for the camp ministry. The 1989 fund is now at minus $5,000 and at the end of 1990 the fund will be in the black.

Brother Rice highlighted the 2% Advance Fund. He encouraged pastors to present this program to their Board. One half of this fund is used for Camp Operational expense, the other half is used for Ackerman Lodge debt retirement. Any help in this area would compliment the cash flow of our General Fund as Home Missions Ministry and Ackerman Lodge are the two primary drains on our budget....

First Place winner in the BGMC giving was Omaha Evangel Assembly of God with $2,023.50...

In the Wednesday sessions, Reverend Faith Tyson, Kids Kamp Director, presented a brief slide presentation about Kids Kamp.

There was a resolution concerning Campus Ministry. Brother John Fransisco shared there have been a lot of changes on the National level as far as College Ministries go. It used to be under ythe Division of Church Ministries and about two years ago they were moved to the area of Home Missions. This puts us in line with that move from Church Ministries to Home Missions. Resolution adopted....

Brother Nazarenus introduced the District office Secretaries, Sherry Hemmingsen and Wanda Hutchinson and extended his appreciation for their ministry to the District.

WHEREAS, the officers for Women‘s Ministries are selected through an appointment process in keeping with our Bylaws and WHEREAS, we desire that our bylaws be in harmony:

BE IT THEREFORE RESOLVED THAT, Article XIII, be amended to read as follows, “There shall be a Women‘s Ministries Department of the Nebraska District Council. All Executive Officers and Women‘s Ministries Representatives, along with any other positions, shall be appointed by the District Presbytery.... MSC

... BE IT THEREFORE RESOLVED THAT, in Article XIV, Men‘s Ministries, that paragraph 2 be changed to read, Each section shall have a Men‘s Ministries Representative who will be appointed by the Presbytery Board to assist the Director in promoting the work of Men‘s Ministries in the section. It is recommended that a layman be appointed where practical. MSC ...

Nebraska Missionettes Help New Churches Start Clubs

District Missionettes groups start projects to help new churches start clubs. Missionettes clubs in at least two districts have developed programs to assist with new church planting during the Decade of Harvest.

Linda Upton, Missionettes coordinator for the Women's Ministries Department, said the Southern New England District and the Nebraska District both have developed such projects....

("Nebraska Missionettes Help New Churches Start Clubs," *Pentecostal Evangel*, September 16, 1990, p. 28.)

1991 District Council in Grand Island April 15-17

The opening service of the Council was a Missions Banquet. H. H. "Spud" DeMent, Secretary of U. S. Relations for the Division of Foreign Missions, in Springfield, Missouri, was the banquet speaker. Special guest was James Byh, missionary to Benin, West Africa

... BGMC first place winner was Omaha Evangel Assembly of God with $2,612. Buddy Barrel watches were presented to Minatare Assembly of God for churches under 75 in Sunday School attendance with an increase of 260% in BGMC giving over the past year, and to Hastings First Assembly of God for churches over 75 in Sunday School attendance with an increase of 282%.

Dave Argue shared current Decade of Harvest projects in regards to Freedom Church in Omaha, pastored by Troy and Jennifer Vandament. David invited Pastor Dave Nord of McCook Assembly of God to share the progress of their church mothering a new work in Benkelman. Pastor Nord introduced Pastors John and Dorothy Corder from Benkelman.

... BE IT THEREFORE RESOLVED, that the name "Lower Panhandle" be changed to "Southern Panhandle." MSC ...

In the Tuesday evening service, Kerry Andrews, Minister of Music at Grand Island Abundant Life, directed a combined choir from Hastings First Assembly of God and Grand Island Abundant Life in the cantata, "Til The Whole World Knows Jesus."

Senior Adults Visit the Ozarks

Thirty-nine people from around the district took a chartered bus trip to the Ozarks the last weekend in October. They toured the Assemblies of God Headquarters and Gospel Publishing House in Springfield, visited the Bass Pro Shop, and then headed for Branson. They enjoyed the "Shepherd of the Hills," spent a day at Silver Dollar City, ate an elegant lunch at the Victorian Sampler Tea Room in Eureka Springs, and marveled at the Passion Play. Everyone had a great time, and we are looking forward to doing it again October 2-5. Start putting some money aside and join us for a weekend you'll never forget!

(Faith Tyson, "Senior Adults Enjoyed their First Annual Trip to the Ozarks!" *Nebraska Fellowship,* 1991.)

1992 District Council Held in Bellevue April 6-8

This Council was the 75th District Council of the Nebraska Assemblies of God.

... In the Tuesday sessions, Brother Argue shared a progress report on the new work that Christ's Place will be mothering in Lincoln. He also shared that the District as a whole was on target for their goal of planting 30 new churches by the year 2000.

Brother Nazarenus stated that loans which have been secured for Ackerman Lodge would be paid off by 1995. He announced that the new dorm which was recently purchased and is in the process of being remodeled, would be named the Clyde King Dorm.

CONSTITUTIONAL DECLARATION from the Revised, April 1992, Constitution of the Nebraska District Council

WE BELIEVE;

That God's purpose concerning man finds fulfillment in a priority reason-for-being: 1) to be an agency of God for evangelizing the world, 2) to be a corporate body in which many worship God, and 3) to be a channel of God's purpose to build a body of saints being perfected in the image of his Son....

Therefore we recognize ourselves to be a cooperative fellowship of Pentecostal, Spirit-baptized saints from local Pentecostal Assemblies of like precious faith in the Nebraska District Council of the General Council of the Assemblies of God, whose purpose is neither to usurp authority over the various local assemblies, nor to deprive them of their scriptural and local rights and privileges; but to recognize and promote scriptural methods and order for worship, unity, fellowship, work, and business for God so that results of our efforts may be considered and assemblies established and developed along the line of our distinctive testimony; and to disapprove unscriptural methods, doctrines, and conduct, endeavoring to keep the unity of the Spirit in the bond of peace, "till we all come in the unity of the faith, and of the knowledge of the Son of God, unto a perfect man, unto the measure of the stature of the fullness of Christ" (Ephesians 4:13).

1993 District Council Held Kearney April 19-21

... Mission Statement:

We exist to glorify God by loving Him and obeying His Word, being birthed, empowered, and taught by the Holy Spirit, thus becoming more and more like Jesus, taking on His character and ministry, that in these last days, Nebraska, the nation and the world might also glorify Him.

... At noon WM President, Pat Mohn, emceed the Women's Ministry Luncheon. Charles Hackett, National Director of Home Missions, shared his message on "What Time Is It?" ...

Our District gave over $20,000 to BGMC this past year for the first time.

... District Home Missions Director, Dave Argue, was called on to give a report on "Isn't It Time For Jesus?" Grand total of those present for Friendship Sunday (Easter Sunday) was 15,139, with two hundred twenty-one made first time commitments to Christ, seventy-eight making recommitments to Christ ...

In the Wednesday session, ARTICLE XI. DEPARTMENT OF YOUTH AND CHRISTIAN EDUCATION was presented.

There shall be a "Department of Youth and Christian Education" of the Nebraska District Council of the Assemblies of God

Purpose:

a. To win, build and send Nebraska Youth in the power of the Holy Spirit in harmony with both the National Youth Department and local Assemblies of God churches.

b. To promote Christian Education, to train teachers and leaders, to network resources and to cooperate with local pastors in fostering the development of various methods of Christian Education in local Assemblies of God churches....

Pastor Bob [Nazarenus] gave a report on "Isn't it time for Jesus." He received a call from Red Able stating that this was the most exciting ad campaign that he has ever been involved in, it was of top quality. James Wilkins of Holdrege stated some may hesitate to cooperate in this campaign because of not seeing results in their area ... Radio spots — they decided not to use radio but three weeks ago they had a call from radio station stating that they had heard ads on a radio in South Dakota and invited Holdrege to run ads over their station as Public Service spots with good reports.

The *Nebraska Fellowship*, September/October 1993, pp. 3-5, give us the following three items!

Royal Ranger Report Summer Pow-Wow Report

The 1993 Nebraska Royal Ranger Summer Pow Wow was held August 5-8 near Cairo, Nebraska. One hundred seventy-one boys, leaders, and fathers attended from all over Nebraska and were treated to not one but two special Pow-Wow speakers....

Missions Giving Report

NEBRASKA IS #1! Of course we already knew that, but now it's official—54.7% of our Nebraska churches held a Missions Convention in 1992. This is the highest participation rate in the United States. From Mark Rose.

Speed-The-Light

The Speed–The–Light vehicle provided by Nebraska Youth was given to Christine Frigoli, Missionary to the Children of Peru.

1994 District Council Held in Lincoln on April 11-13

... BE IT THEREFORE RESOLVED THAT: "Nomination for District Presbyters shall be made by each Section at a meeting prior to the annual District Council. The nominee shall be selected from the ordained ministers of the section. Nominations are to be made by ordained and licensed ministers of the section and an official delegate from each assembly of that section. The presiding officer shall appoint a roster chairman who will present the number of voting constituents before the balloting period." MSC ...

BE IT THEREFORE FURTHER RESOLVED, that each church of the Nebraska District be encouraged to contribute at least two ($2) dollars per Sunday morning worship service attendee (as reported on the 1994 ACMR) toward this 1995 evangelism media blitz. MSC

Bob Roos was invited to present the new Hispanic church meeting at South Side Assembly in Omaha, (Rivers of Praise Assembly).

1994 Royal Rangers Winter Pow-Wow
(Steve Bowman)

One hundred ninety-two boys and men attended the 1994 Nebraska Royal Rangers Winter Pow-Wow. The Pow Wow was held February 4-6 at the Assemblies of God Conference Center in Lexington. Those in attendance were from seventeen outposts throughout the state of Nebraska. Joe Masten of Lexington skillfully blended spiritual lessons with demonstrations, including his skill as a marksman with a bow and arrows ...

1995 District Council Held in Gering on April 24-26

... Bruce Riddle, Youth Pastor of North Park, Holdrege, gave statistics of pastors' and wives' involvement for 1994 camping season as general information. During the 1994 camping season in three Kids Kamps there were 672 campers, 221 workers, of these 14 wives and 27 ministers participated. Junior and Senior High Camp had 209 total workers, with 13 pastors' wives and 45 ministers participating.

Kids Kamp Director, Susan Wertheimer, gave a slide presentation of the Nebraska Kids Kamp and reported on its 50th Anniversary. Eighteen thousand (18,000) kids have attended Kids Kamp during the past 50 years....

... In the Wednesday evening Ordination Service, Dr. Wood announced that Pastor Bob [Nazarenus] will be honored along with Warren Bullock, District Superintendent of the Northwest District, as Co-Alumni of the Year at Northwest College, Kirkland, Washington.

1996 District Council Held in Norfolk on April 15-17

Loren Triplett was the speaker for the evening service. [April 15] He began by sharing a short history of his ministry in Nebraska and his call to the missions field of Nicaragua. He then recounted the miraculous way God provided his entire monthly support at a single camp meeting.

... Following the *April 15th evening* service, John and Kerri Fransisco were commissioned as missionaries to Peru, South America. Following the prayer of dedication, pastors from around the district were invited to bring their missions pledges for John and Kerri and place them in their hands. When all was said and done, nearly $10,000 in cash was raised, and approximately $6,000 of their total $6,500 monthly budget was pledged. The council celebrated this great victory together with the Fransiscos.

Tuesday 10:30 AM the "World Report" was given by Norm Correll. In spite of world trouble, God's church if moving forward, proclaiming the Gospel of Jesus Christ just before He returns. Examples he gave are:

1. God brought down the Iron Curtain

2. In China, the church has grown dramatically, even under intense persecution. Approximately 28,000 people per day are receiving Christ there.

3. World-wide, approximately 70,000 people per day are making decisions for Christ ...

3:00 PM – "Keeping Missions Exciting in the Local Church" – Spud [H. H.] DeMent. Spud began this session by congratulating the Nebraska District for having the highest percentage of churches who have an annual missions emphasis. He then told about the many promotional materials and ideas available from the Department of Foreign Missions for promoting mission in the local church ...

4:00 PM – "Unreached Peoples" – Norm Correll. Brother Correll noted that 25% of the world's population is Muslim (approximately one billion people). To help appreciate them and their beliefs more, he passed out a quiz on Muslims and the religion of Islam. After going over the answers to these questions, he then gave some encouraging news about how Muslims are coming to Christ in record numbers, often as a result of supernatural appearances from Jesus or angels....

In the Wednesday morning business session, Al Riskowski noted that the Ackerman Lodge was paid off and the funds that had been used for the mortgage were now freed up for the camp....

WHEREAS, The Scripture is very clear concerning the sanctity of life; and

WHEREAS, The partial birth abortion procedure particularly contravenes the upholding of life; and

WHEREAS, Believers have an obligation to voice their convictions concerning moral issues; therefore, be it

RESOLVED, That the sentiments of this District Council be conveyed to the President and other officials in our government, that we are adamantly opposed to this heinous practice. MSC.

1997 District Council Held in Hastings on April 14-16

... Superintendent Nazarenus invited any pastor with a praise report to come and share.

Gary Graesser came and shared about some financial miracles that the Lord was doing for their family.

Petey Tellez came and shared about a special outpouring of the Spirit in the Omaha area, and specifically at Bellevue Christian Center.

Mike Blatchley shared about some good things happening in Burwell. God has given him inroads into many mainline denominational churches, at the invitation of the churches.

Mark Rose shared about exciting things happening among Native Americans in Norfolk. Several have been saved over the last several weeks.

Terry Petty shared about more exciting things happening among Native Americans in Chadron....

Missionettes Retreats

Since 1983, there has been a Missionettes Retreat. In 1987 it was moved to May. Honor Star crowning services had been at District Council opening night for four years (1986-1989), then on WM Day during Family camp. In 1992, the Honor Star Crowning Service moved to the Missionettes Retreat and has remained there since then. In 1998, the retreat was the end of May with Honor Star Crowning on Saturday afternoon and a Reception following.

According to Caroline Deffenbaugh, who has been the District Missionettes Coordinator since October of 1985, there were 1138 girls enrolled in Nebraska Missionettes in 1997. This included Rainbows through Y's....

1998 District Council Held in Omaha on April 20-22

... In the Tuesday afternoon session, Resolution #2 was presented. WHEREAS, It is the intention of the Nebraska District to be sensitive to the direction being taken by the General Council in regard to Chi Alpha; therefore, be it RESOLVED, That Bylaw Article 12. College Ministry be rescinded, and that the Home Missions Committee be given oversight to develop a new structure for campus ministry that more accurately reflects the guidelines for campus ministry recommended by the National Chi Alpha office; and be it further RESOLVED, That an updated and completed structure be presented at the 1999 District Council. MSC

The council also approved the purchase of the 4.5 acre plot of land west of the Lexington Camp Grounds. The current offer was for $500 per acre. The final price and closing costs to be negotiated with the seller by the Officers of the Nebraska District Council of the Assemblies of God.

1999 District Council Held in North Platte on April 12-14

... Resolution #2 was presented regarding the building of a dining facility at the camp.

WHEREAS, The current dining facility at the Assemblies of God Camp and Conference Center in Lexington is unable to adequately service the larger groups that use the camp; and

WHEREAS, The current demand for sleeping space has already been exceeded by some of our camps and retreats; and

WHEREAS, Adding additional sleeping space and campers to accommodate this increased demand would only make food service in our current dining facility even more difficult; therefore be it

RESOLVED, That the 1999 District Council in session empower the Presbytery and Laymen's Council to pursue the building of a new camp dining facility, including all plans and financial arrangements.... MSC to pass Resolution #2

The Resolutions Chairman presented Resolution 3, regarding 2000 Celebration Sponsored by: The Assemblies of God General Presbytery:

WHEREAS, The 20th century began with an outpouring of the Holy Spirit, which has resulted in the worldwide Pentecostal Movement; and

WHEREAS, An integral part of the Pentecostal Movement is the Assemblies of God, formed in 1914 with 300 delegates and now encompassing a worldwide family of believers, numbered at approximately 30 million in 58 countries; and

... RESOLVED, That the General Superintendent and our leadership present fresh vision to the Assemblies of God for the future; and, be it further

RESOLVED, That in preparation for 2000 Celebration, the Assemblies of God engage in a grassroots process to assess what the Holy Spirit is saying to the Church in these hours, and that the vision presented by leadership reflect this assessment; and, be it further ...

RESOLVED, That strategic plans be developed to carry the Assemblies of God into the years ahead in fulfillment of the fresh vision; and, be it further

RESOLVED, That we ask the Lord of the Harvest to make 2000 Celebration on August 8 through 10 in Indianapolis, Indiana, an epicenter for the outpouring of His Spirit upon the Assemblies of God as we enter a new century and a new millennium; that we will indeed witness a new Pentecost as the Assemblies of God comes all together at one time in one place from the nations of this earth in the most international gathering ever witnessed by this Church.

The Resolutions Chairman moved its adoption. It was seconded and passed.

The following news items are from the 1999 Annual Report of the Nebraska District council of the Assemblies of God:

Youth & Christian Education by Rick Lorimer, Youth/CE Director

I thank God for a powerful year. God gracefully extended His mercy through out departments once again. We have witnessed continual growth in the Body of Christ and a renewed hunger for His Word. I anticipate great things in store for 2000!

"WE BUILD PEOPLE" is a philosophy of ministry and life that we in the Youth and Christian Education Department have embraced … Nebraska Youth Ministries is equally dedicated "We Build Students."

What a year for **Speed-the-Light** and our youth and churches!!! They gave $151,193.77 to God be all the glory! This was a 35% increase from 1998 … Our youth are learning to dream and sacrifice for missions … and this excites me.

Honor Bound by Steve Bowman, Director

As we enter the new millennium, we are looking forward to revival in men as we have never seen before.

It was another record year for **Light for the Lost**—The HonorBound Men's Missions Program. We had a record year with over $100,000 raised for literature for missionaries. It is estimated that for every dollar raised for gospel literature, we are able to reach approximately ten souls. With your pledges, we will be able to touch around one million people with the gospel this year. Praise God!!!

Many exciting new changes are coming to **Royal Rangers**. There is a fresh stirring of men who want to mentor young men for God. If there was ever a time we need men to mentor young men, it is now. Our Pow-wows are experiencing powerful moves of God. There are boys being saved, being slain and filled with the Holy Spirit. It is so awesome to see boys praying for boys at our altars.

We are excited about the renewed vision to ***Reach, Teach and Keep Boys for Christ***.

Women's Ministries Report by Nadine Sandoz, Director

This year has brought many changes for Women's Ministries. The changes have been exciting and challenging. One of these is a name change of *Dollars for Souls* or previously known as *Dimes for Souls.* We are now calling this LIFE or *Ladies Investing For Eternity.* We also have a name change in the Etta Calhoun Fund. It is now know as the *Women Touching the World Fund.*

The ladies from 38 churches gave over $25,000 to LIFE last year....

Missionettes Report by Caroline Deffenbaugh, Director

"Hitherto the Lord has brought us." Thanks be to God for His blessings this year in Missionettes. Our Love Gift Project for the year was "Project Rescue" for India. The girls from all over Nebraska raised over $6,000. This was a record for giving! PTL!

The following is our summary vision statement:

We are committed to a vibrant District Missionettes ministry in Nebraska where leaders are realizing their full potential; for girls to know and understand the treasure of Christ in us; the value of the Word of God; the desperate condition of the lost; and the call to active labor in the Kingdom of God. We will aggressively present Missionettes as an evangelism tool to pastors and churches. We envision an active Missionettes ministry in every church with positive leadership fulfilling the five-fold purposes of Missionettes. We are committed to world-wide missions both financially and by personal involvement.

Foreign Missions Report by Mark Rose, Director

"Who Should Give Nothing To Missions?" The question, and our response, is still pertinent as we close one millennium and enter a new one. Fortunately, Nebraska isn't a District that gives nothing. We have again shown our compassion for the world as churches have increased giving to foreign and home missions. In fact, every year since 1994 our District has increased its giving by at least 3% and 1998 was the greatest increase ever—almost 24% over 1997. For the first time, giving to foreign missions was over $1,000,000. The final numbers for 1999 are not yet in, but, based on giving through November, we have passed last year's numbers. As the youth would say, **"That's awesome."**

Chi Alpha Report, by Kirk Spain, District Chi Alpha Representative

Vision Statement: "Reconciling Students to Christ, Transforming the University, the Marketplace and the World."

We believe that, as we evangelize and disciple on campus, we will transform the university; after students graduate and assume leadership in the workplace, they will transform the marketplace; and they travel and locate around the world, they will transform the world.

It has been said that if you change the university, you can change the world. Chi Alpha Campus Ministries strives to be an instrument of change on the college and university campuses.

Nebraska currently has over 113,000 college and university students on 31 different campuses. Of this number, there are over 2,000 international students from numerous nations.

It is our belief that as we encounter a new millennium, the greatest days are yet ahead, Spiritual interest is very high on our college and university campuses and the question we must ask is, "If not us, then who will go and feed the TRUTH about Jesus Christ to a hungry generation???

Hispanic Ministries Report, by Robert Be Roos, Nebraska Hispanic Ministries

This last year of ministry has been a rewarding and challenging one. We have seen the churches we work with move into more of the vision we have for them. We have faced financial challenges and the resignation of one of the pastors. Overall, though, we have seen a number of life transformations in those who have accepted the Lord and also a growth in maturity among those who have been in the churches. It has been a good year, and has provided the basis for moving into the new millennium with hope for great fruitfulness.

Thank You! We are extremely grateful for you and your support of the ministry in this past year. You have made it possible for us to reach out to the ever-increasing number of Hispanics arriving in Nebraska. It is the fastest growing people group in Nebraska and in the USA. It is a mission at our doorstep, a people group in need of Christ, a culture that has begun to exert more and more influence on the general culture, and one which will continue to do so in the future. It is up to us whether that influence will be a positive, Christian one or not.

We thank you and pray for God's Best for you in 2000. ~ Dios Les Bendiga.

Honor of Recognition: 50 Years of Ministry

By 1999, the following men and women from the Nebraska District had received the Honor of Recognition for 50 years of ministry:

IN EXPRESSION of high esteem, and in gratitude of FIFTY years of continuous and dedicated service rendered as a minister in the FELLOWSHIP of the GENERAL COUNCIL OF THE ASSEMBLIES OF GOD, the Executive Presbytery confers this HONOR OF RECOGNITION.

This act recognizes with thankfulness the noble example and unselfish ministry that have helped to make the Assemblies of God one of the fastest growing religious movements in the world.

1978 — Albert M. Alber and Erwin V. Dunbar

1979 — Edward M. Herrmann

1982 — Harold James and Marie James

1983 — Victor C. Henry and Harry J. Blakkolb

1984 — Marjorie Brown, Robert O. Brown, J. Mervin Peck, and Lawrence E. Wilkins

1985 — Lester W. Dickinson and Dorcie B. Arnold

1986 — Herman Lebsack and Velma Lebsack

1988 — Harold E. Allen, Clarence Brotzman, Louise C. Gray, and Clyde O. King

1993 — Bernard F. Correll, Sr.

1994 — Hazel Lorene Hall, Clifford C. Sutton, and Herman W. Thiemann

1995 — Earl Larson

1996 — Ruth L. McKenney, and Lynn S. Nichols

Missionettes from Glad Tiding, Lincoln, Nebraska

Nativity scene at Columbus, NE

Unit 5: Nebraska District Camps

Chapter 22: Pentecostals Making Memories at Church Camps

"They devoted themselves to the apostles' teaching and to the fellowship, to the breaking of bread and to prayer. Everyone was filled with awe, and many wonders and miraculous signs were done by the apostles. All the believers were together and had everything in common." **(Acts 2:42-44 NIV)**

Of course this book would not be complete without the mention of the wonderful early camp meetings and later camp services, stories, and testimonies once the district established its own campground near Lexington. This section is divided into two chapters. The first covers camp meetings and camp memories prior to 1950. The second chapter tells about times of fun, fellowship, and testimony from the 1950s to the present.

Early Camp Meetings (1914-1918)

In the summer of 1914, (the same year the General Council of the Assemblies of God was organized) Johnny McConnell of Amarillo, Texas, went to Chappell to hold the first Full Gospel tent meeting. It was in 1915 that Harry Van Loon and a number of young people from Kansas went to Milford to conduct meetings in a Mennonite church of which Joe Rediger and Silas Miller were co-pastors. There was a definite outpouring of the Spirit at that time and many were filled with the Spirit. Among the number filled was Merle W. Roll. Another town visited by revival was Franklin.

Here and there across the state the revival began to spread. In the northeastern section, George Comstock (known to so many as Daddy Comstock) was used of the Lord to establish thirteen churches. Out in the panhandle, Merle Roll and Irl J. Walker were instrumental in establishing a number of churches. In the Ainsworth area, Herman L. Harvey, assisted by a Brother Timmons, was having meetings.

As more and more people were blessed, they began to feel the need of a closer bond of fellowship with others of like precious faith. It wasn‘t long until the first camp meeting was planned, a time for fellowship and also to consider how to work more effectively together. This camp meeting was held in 1917 at North Platte, with Fred Lohman of St. Louis, Missouri, as the speaker. In 1918 the Camp-Council was held on the south banks of the Republican River, a mile east of the river bridge at Franklin, Nebraska.

("Camp-Councils," *50th Anniversary Booklet of the Nebraska District.*)

Auburn Nebraska Camp, 1914

Praise God for the wonderful victory in the Camp here of 10 days, during which 20 were baptized in the Holy Ghost as in Acts 2:4, and many saved. A mighty work is going on still, and another week has brought seven more to the wonderful baptism and power still rests on the children of God. Bros. John Hastings, C. E. Foster, Gaskill and Fred E. Poole were with us and preached the word with signs following. I feel this is the beginning of a mighty work here for which we ask the prayers of the saints. ~ W. L. Short

(W. L. Short, "From Auburn, Nebraska," *Christian Evangel*, October 17, 1914, p. 3.)

From Auburn, Nebraska, 1914

Have had a wonderful victory. Nearly 40 have received the baptism since Sept. 4th and the work is still going on. Will go Omaha to hold a meeting with Bro. H. C. Gaskill, Pray for us. ~ Fred E. Poole

(Fred E. Poole, "From Auburn, Nebraska," *Christian Evangel*, October 24, 1914, p. 4.)

Nebraska State Camp, 1915

We are preparing for the Nebraska State Camp to be held here (Omaha) about the middle of June. God has been wonderfully working here lately, saving and baptizing several in the Holy Ghost and fire. One man, a backslider, was saved and baptized in his seat while the meeting was going on. The power of God fell like rain. Have also had a number of remarkable healings lately. A number of seekers. Pray that God will bring them through. Pastor Fred E. Poole, Omaha, Nebraska.

(Fred E. Poole, "Nebraska State Camp," *Weekly Evangel*, April 10, 1915, p. 3.)

Omaha Camp Meeting, 1915

The first annual camp meeting of the Pentecostal Assembly of Omaha, Nebraska, will be held from June 17th to July 17th and longer should the Lord so lead. On the Camp ground near the recently purchased Assembly House (formerly The Tinley Rescue Home) at 403-7 Bancroft St. Meals will be served. Please bring your own bedding.

We expect Brother T. K. Leonard of Findlay, Ohio, Brother Dieffenworth, Auburn, Neb., Brother Mills, Sioux City, Iowa and others whom the Lord shall send.

Take a Farnam or So. 10th car to Bancroft then east six blocks. The price of tents are as follows: 8 x 10 $1.50 for two weeks and $2.50 for 30 days; 8x 12 $2.00 for 2 weeks and $3.00 for 30 days; 10 x 12 $2.50 for 2 weeks and $3.50 for 30 days. Price of cots: 50 cents for two weeks and 75 cents for 30 days....

("Nebraska Camp Meeting," *Word and Witness*, May 1915, p. 4.)

Camp Councils, 1918-1920

... For many years the District Councils were held jointly with the Camps. The 1918 and 1919 Camp-Councils were held on the south banks of the Republican River, a mile east of the river bridge at Franklin, Nebraska. Both of these Camps were well attended from far and near. Many spirit-filled preachers were in attendance from Kansas, namely: Fred Vogler, Charles Sheall, Roy Farley. Many well-known preachers from various places were Edgar White, Willie Millsaps, C. E. Sims, Walter Nelson, Herbert and Mrs. Buffum, Walter Oliver, S. H. Patterson, William Burkett and Katy Udiger (who later became Mrs. McClure). John Goben, a well-known evangelist, was the Camp speaker. George Clopine was elected to serve as District Chairman at the 1918 Council.

(From the *50th Anniversary Booklet of the Nebraska District*.)

The 1920 Camp-Council was held in Red Cloud.

Franklin Camp Meeting, 1920

Goldsberry Grove, two miles southeast of Franklin, Nebr., Aug. 26 to Sept. 5. Bro. John Goben and other workers expected. Tents and cots for rent at reasonable rates. Bring your own bedding and toilet articles. Meals on free will offering plan at dining tent on the grounds. Write your orders before Aug. 5, stating clearly what you desire. Free will offerings will be appreciated. Write Pastor Henry Hoar, Franklin, Neb.

(Henry Hoar, "Nebraska Camp Meeting," *Word and Work*, August 1920, p 16.)

In 1921, Camp Council was at Milford and in 1922, the Camp-Council was held at

Franklin County Fair Grounds. J Logan Stuart was the speaker. In 1923, the Camp-Council was held at Franklin County Fair Grounds with Watt Walker, the Indian Evangelist, as the speaker.

From Omaha, Nebraska, 1923

Dear Bro. Brinkman and the Herald family: Peace and mercy be multiplied unto you. Owing to the fact that we have to build a tabernacle for our meeting and as it takes time and money we have found it necessary to announce that our second annual Campaign for God will begin Aug. 24th instead of Aug. 10th. The meeting will start with a shout of Victory and will continue as long as the Lord leads.

For those who want to come and Camp, tents and cots will be furnished at cost and meals and lunches can be had at reasonable rates. Ministers and Teachers will be entertained free. We cordially invite any full Gospel Minister to come and help in part of all of these Services.

It was estimated that from two to five thousand people attended our services every evening last year and the Lord gave us a wonderful time and we are expecting a still greater time this year. May every one that loves an old time Pentecost revival please pray for these meetings and every one that can come and help and enjoy these services you are cordially invited and we beg you to come.

Those that come to camp may bring your bedding and toilet articles. There will be two services each day. At 2 p.m. a teaching service and prayer for the sick, and at 8 p.m. a soul stirring evangelistic service backed up by the demonstrations and power of the Holy Ghost. Good songs sung by Spirit filled singers. If you like the old fashioned way, COME and enjoy it with us. For further information write to: Mrs. J. Z. Hyble, 1829 Colson Ave., Fremont, Nebr. Or to Pastor M. B. Long, 2214 S. 40th St. Omaha, Nebr.

("From Omaha, Nebraska," *The Pentecostal Herald*, August 1, 1923, p. 6.)

Hendley, Nebraska, 1924

The Nebraska District Council and Camp Meeting will be held at Hendley, Nebr., August 7 to 17, 1924. Elder T. K. Leonard of Findlay, Ohio, Evangelist and Bible Teacher, will be in charge. A mighty visitation of God's presence and power is expected. We especially urge all of our people in the Nebraska District to attend this meeting and let us cooperate in promoting and extending this work in our district. Bring your own bedding. Etc. Those desiring tents or further information, write Pastor A. R. Shaffer, Bambridge, Nebr.; G. W. Clopine, Chairman, Chappell, Nebr.

("Nebraska District Camp," *Pentecostal Evangel*, June 28, 1924, p. 14.)

Beaver City, Nebraska, 1924

We had a wonderful visitation of God's power at our camp, August 7 to 17. Brother Thomas K. Leonard was our evangelist. We thank God for his plain, deep, effective Bible teaching during the ten days.... The last night, the crowd was estimated at 2500 people. There was a wonderful demonstration of God's mighty power to heal. We covet the prayers of God's children. A. R. Shaffer, acting pastor, Cambridge, Nebr.

("From Beaver City, Nebraska," *Pentecostal Evangel*, September 20, 1924, p. 14.)

Report From Beaver City

Our annual District campmeeting was generally admitted to be one of the best District campmeetings we have ever had. Many of the saints came from far distant places. From the first the clean, straight Gospel of salvation was made a central theme. The ministry of Brother T. K. Leonard was very highly appreciated. He gave some practical teaching on deeply spiritual truths. The saints were edified, sinners convicted, and a goodly number saved, baptized in the Holy Spirit, and the sick were healed. One interesting feature of this meeting was the large crowds that came from night to night in this comparatively new field and listened attentively to the messages given.

Some very effective Council work was also done during our Council sessions. It should be said to the credit of the assembly at Beaver City, together with the one at Hendley, Nebr., that they entered heartily into their part of the meeting program in its varied details, whether work or worship and manifested a beautiful spirit of fellowship. One feature was an all-night altar service, crowned with a constant cloud of heavenly glory and the Holy Spirit's presence. It will be long remembered by all that were present. The farewell Morning Prayer meeting was another never-to-be-forgotten time wherein the heavenly presence and glory witnessed and such a sense of divine approbation and benediction pervaded the entire company as can only be understood or know by those of like precious faith. The meeting has passed on into history, but the results of victories won for the Lord, we believe will live and continue on and on.

~ G. W. Clopine, District Chairman.

(G. W. Clopine, "From Beaver City, Nebraska," *Pentecostal Evangel*, September 27, 1924, p. 12.)

1925 Camp was held at the Old City Park in McCook, Nebraska, August 7th to 16th.

1926 Camp was held at Riverton with William Faux, National Missions Treasurer, speaker. A. R. Shaffer was elected District Superintendent.

Memories from 1926-1927

During the summer months and the year of 1926, Lillie and I attended our first camp meeting, which was held at Riverton, Nebr. And My! How those young people could sing and play, after we went home it wasn't long until we purchased a guitar and mandolin, a violin and trombone. We learned it was quite another thing to be able to play those instruments, however Viola and I seemed to hang onto the guitar and mandolin. Lillie did pretty good on the violin also.

In the summer of 1927, we went to the camp meeting at Scottsbluff, Nebr. Did it ever rain and turn cold??? Those tents weren't very warm, we should have taken more quilts!!

(Rose Hallgrimson, "Rose Hallgrimson Remembers." In *Iceland to Nebraska: The Olafur Hallgrimson Family*, by Margaret L. Sybrant. N.p: N.p., the author, 1985, J-8.)

1927 Camp-Council was held at Scottsbluff. Ben Hardin was the speaker. Milton Smith was elected District Superintendent.

Evangelist Guy Shields

My first meeting in Nebraska was the State Camp meeting held in Lincoln at Bethany Park in 1928. I fell in love with the people of this state at once and was delighted when the opportunity came for me to return to Grand Island and hold a meeting for Bro. Foster who had formerly held meetings in Texas. This meeting further cemented my friendship for these people and I held a meeting later at Bayard, and again went to Grand Island for another meeting …

(From the "Camp Meeting Special," by Evangelist Guy Shields.)

Lincoln, Nebraska, 1928

Brother Merle W. Roll, Bethany Park, Lincoln, Nebr., writes: We want to sound a note of praise for the way the Lord was in our Annual District Convention. All the Assemblies of the District were well represented, and there was a sweet fellowship among the brethren. Brother Shields, of Amarillo, Texas, brought stirring messages, and the large tabernacle was well filled. It was, without a doubt, the best convention the Nebraska District has ever witnessed. Quite a few were saved, and numbers received their Baptism. The Lord also manifested His power to heal broken bodies. Lincoln was stirred, asking the question, 'What is This?' and we could truthfully say, 'This is That.'"

(Merle W. Roll, "Nebraska Council," *Pentecostal Evangel*, September 22, 1928, p. 13.)

At the 1929 Camp-Council, Edgar White was elected to serve as superintendent.

Under his supervisions the District adopted a constitution and by-laws at the 1930 Council which was held in Milford.

History of the Camp Meeting at Ord

As we pull into the camp ground, which is shaded by a large grove of beautiful trees, carpeted with blue grass, surrounded by large fields of corn and alfalfa, there is at first a little feeling of disappointment to find that the camp is so far from a city, but as we drive down through the main street of the 20 acre grove of trees, all beautifully marked off with streets and avenues, we were overjoyed to see the tents that were up....

... Friday morning I preached from the text of stirring up the fire or the gift within thee. God's seal was placed in a mighty way on this service and it seemed that from here on out the fire surely did fall. The number of campers increased each day. Brother White had to make arrangements for more tents, this he did by sending Brother [J. C.] Burkey to Lincoln for a truck load. The campers increased until the tents numbered 195 and several house cars and trucks on top of that. The estimation of the people camping is from 700 to 900 throughout the camp. The tide was rising higher and higher each service, and many more of the pastors came in each day.

Rev. Rake of Milford and the Anderson orchestra assisted by many other musicians constituted one of the greatest orchestras I have ever heard play in my life, and you can imagine just what a wonderful inspiration this body of about a 30 piece orchestra put into the meeting....

One very interesting service each evening was that of the children which was held in the dining room each evening at 7 P.M. They would sing choruses and we would give them a Bible story each evening. Sometimes Bro. [Walter] Evans, the colored preacher, would sing for them.

Rev. Rake of Milford and the Anderson orchestra assisted by many other musicians constituted one of the greatest orchestras I have ever heard play in my life, and you can imagine just what a wonderful inspiration this body of about a 30 piece orchestra put into the meeting. Each night they would play while the seekers were at the altar and it was just wonderful. I think Nebraska has more musician preachers than I have known elsewhere. The Christ Ambassadors under the direction of Rev. Lamar, their leader, were very faithful....

The night we prayed for the sick I witnessed the presence of God I believe more that I ever did in my life. We anointed 153 and many were greatly blessed and healed. A number fell under the hand of the Lord.

One of the most spiritual and inspiring parts of the meeting was dear old colored Bro. Evans of Colorado with his old guitar and he sang most every service. Other great singers were there all along and were enjoyed by all, but somehow he just seemed to lift everyone as he sang....

(Guy Shields, "History of the Camp Meeting at Ord, Nebraska, 1933: Camp Meeting Special," *Shield of Faith,* 1933, p. 15.)

Glenn Warriner Remembers the Camp at Ord

Glenn recalled being at this camp at Ord. He attended with his dad, George Warriner, and several other people from Franklin. For some of their meals, George cooked beans over an open camp fire. However, they were so busy enjoying the blessings of the Lord and the fellowship of God's people that food wasn't that important.

(Interview with Glenn Warriner, 1999.)

Early "North" Camp Meeting Memories, by Viola Hallgrimson

... Of course the first camp (North) was at Burton, then it was in a grove about two miles east of Bassett. People could hear the singing and no doubt the shouting here in town. One lady really enjoyed hearing it and later got saved.

Then they moved to a grove south of town (Bassett) on the highway but farther from town. Then it was moved to a grove out of Ainsworth. Later they used the High School Learning Center in Ainsworth and also the East City Park and the Assembly Church. I don't know the consecutive line of places nor the dates. They missed a few years then put up a tent (small) back of the Burton Church and ministers from the section ministered certain nights. Then this year (1995) it was here in Bassett for only four nights.

(Viola Hallgrimson, 1995.)

Camp Meeting Memories of Howard Dixon

... Camp meetings were very special in those days (mid 1930's). We would take turns during the meeting among our family for one to stay home and milk the cows. Brother Floyd Woodworth from Colorado was the speaker in 1936 at the camp grounds at Burton. In 1937 and 1938, camp was held east of Bassett and later years south of Bassett in the Walter Hazard Grove.

North Camp, always 10 days, concluding on July 4, was moved to Baker's Grove southwest of Ainsworth in 1939. Large crowds attended these services, coming from South Dakota and from as far east as Butte, Nebraska. Reverend Chat Anderson and family played many musical instruments and was a great blessing to the services. Church members from O'Neill, 60 miles east, and members from Valentine, 50 miles west, came often. Sunday afternoon and evening and the Fourth of July, one could count as many as 500 in attendance.

(From a letter written by Howard Dixon, 1997.)

Lexington Camp Facilities History up to 1967, by L. W. Dickinson

Prior to the year of 1940 the Nebraska District conducted its camp meetings in city parks or used other facilities which were available. There was a growing desire to obtain a camp site that could be developed which would meet the needs of district camp meetings.

During the District Council which convened here in Grand Island in 1939, a decision was made, after much discussion, to purchase a camp site. At the same time the present location of our camp came into focus. Authorization was given to the District Presbytery to acquire a district camp site. A brother in the Lexington church owned the property where our camp is now located. He was contacted concerning the possibility of purchasing some of his land for a camp site. Through the generosity of his heart he gave the district a deed to six acres without charge. This was a real boost to our camp program.

At this time land was being cleared in the basin which is now Johnson Lake, located south of Lexington. Farm buildings were being sold to make way for this large reservoir. Under the leadership of Brother A. M. Alber, District Superintendent, some of these buildings were purchased. With volunteer labor these buildings were torn down and hauled to the camp. From this material the tabernacle, dining hall, and the first units of cabins were constructed. These first buildings were constructed in 1940. Brother and Sister John Brinson who now reside in Lexington were the first caretakers and it was through their hard work that much of the camp building was done.

Trees were to be planted as the six acres were nothing but a cow pasture. Before the trees were planted it was of necessity to drive an irrigation well. This was done primarily by man power, but there was a camp to be built, so the work progressed. A tractor for light work was needed and there was no money with which to purchase one so Brother Alber made one. In this modern day it would hardly meet the specifications of a real tractor, but it was a great help in the early days of building a camp.

The first state camp was conducted on our own grounds, August 1941. Brother William McPherson was the speaker. The floor in the tabernacle was gravel. It was rather difficult to walk in and to say the least it was a little rough on a shoe shine and of course the children had fun playing in the gravel. These inconveniences were overlooked; this was camp meeting being conducted on our own District Camp Grounds.

Under the leadership of Brother M. F. Brandt, District Superintendent, the camp continued to grow and progress. More cabins were constructed and shower houses were built and other improvements were made.

In June of 1945 the first boys‘ camp was conducted. Brother Fred Lessten was the director. From that time the camps grew until within a short time we started boys‘ and girls‘ camps, then youth camp. A few years later we found we were over crowded so the district was divided into sections and there were two boys‘ and girls‘ camps and a youth and teen camp. For the past several years these camps have had almost 700 in attendance. As I travel from church to church I am made to realize more and more the true value of camp meetings. There are many who have been definitely influenced for God during camp meetings who are some of our most faithful members of our district fellowship.

By 1952 there was a feeling that our camp program was losing some of its enthusiasm. During district council that year a camp committee was appointed made up of laymen with Brother C. T. Beem as its chairman. This district council convened in Lexington. The committee went to the camp grounds and observed it as it was. They made a thorough study of the needs of the camp. Their report to the camp was quite extensive and many felt it was quite visionary. They made some recommendations which many felt was quite unrealistic. Among other recommendations they felt the starting place was to erect a new tabernacle and then remodel the old one into a dining hall and kitchen.

These recommendations kept coming to us from the camp committee from year to year until during the District Council in McCook in 1961 definite steps were taken and a resolution was passed by that council in session to begin construction on a new tabernacle. A loan of $30,000.00 was secured from the Home Federal Savings and Loan of Lexington and not only was a new tabernacle constructed, but a new sewer system was installed that connected to the Lexington sanitation sewer.

Ground was broken only a few weeks after that district council. The building was under construction. To say the least that was a busy summer. Every available man was put into the work and there were a lot of donated man hours that went into the building. The new tabernacle 80 X 112 made of concrete and steel was completed and in use for that August camp meeting. We ran very close on time, as we felt we must have the tabernacle for camp. We had advertised, “Come to District camp and worship in the new air conditioned tabernacle.” Completion was a must. The electrician tied the building into the electric power line late Thursday evening and in less than 24 hours the camp meeting was in progress.

The following year the old tabernacle was remodeled into a dining hall and kitchen. In 1966 the old dining hall was remodeled and named Alber Hall.

In 1953 during camp meeting the spirit of God moved upon the camp in a very marked way which was the means of re-vitalizing our entire World Missions Ministry.

It was in a ministers‘ meeting during that camp when Brother Loren Triplett offered himself for Foreign Missionary service. Like a great prairie fire this spirit of giving went through the ministers in that meeting. This spirit carried over into the morning service and on through the camp. By the end of that camp the Triplett‘s support and money for their outfit and fare was quite well taken care of. Since that time a number of couples have given themselves to missionary service and the camp has been a great factor in sending these fine young people to the field of their calling.

Home Missions has been greatly benefitted from the support that has come from the W.M.C.'s. This fine program had its inception and has been carried through the years during our camp meetings.

This is camp meeting in Nebraska. Without it we feel our entire District program would be greatly impaired.

(From the 50th Anniversary Nebraska District 1917-1967 Book, by L. W. Dickinson.)

Camp Memories of Carlyle Beebe

I attended camp at York, Nebraska in 1939. Guy Shields was one of the preachers. We lived in tents and ate at a common dining hall. P. C. Nelson was a Bible Teacher.

... I remember one evening service in which Brother [E. J.] Dewey jumped off the four (4) foot platform and ran down one aisle and across the back of the church and back up the other aisle. He was a large man but made the circle with no problem.

Due to haying in the Northern part of the state in August among the ranchers a camp meeting was conducted early June so the ranchers could attend. It was conducted in Bassett, Neb. and Bakers Grove in Ainsworth.... We had such speakers as Guy Shields, Jack Saunders, A. C. Bates (Texas) and [E. R.] Foster (Texas).

At the Gothenburg Camp, my mother took five ladies from Burton, Neb. with her. Those who went with her were Pearl White, Lucy Thiede, Florence Horton.... At this camp, my mother stopped by the kitchen and drank some tomato juice. It was spoiled and she got ptomaine poison and most of the camp was up all night praying for her.

The land for the camp was irrigated land, so trees were planted and irrigated so they grew very good.

The first year of camp a tent was used for the services. I had taken care of the Nebraska tent. It was rented to Gregory, South Dakota for a camp meeting. I slept in it to protect it from being vandalized. I drove the district truck and delivered the tent to Lexington for the first camp meeting. When I arrived at the grounds, Bro A. M. Alber was there running water on the trees. The first year at camp men from the camp tore down some buildings and the lumber was used to build the first Tabernacle....

(From Carylyle Beebe, 1997.)

Water for Trees at the Proposed Campsite

During an interview with Glenn Warriner (1999), he recalled his dad, George H. Warriner, Charles E. Blodgett (his pastor from Riverton), A. M. Alber (District Superintendent), and others going to Lexington to look at the proposed piece of ground for the new campsite. Glenn stayed home to do chores on the farm. When his dad came home, he excitedly told Glenn the following. By this time, at the end of the 1930s, the rains were becoming more frequent. However the affect from the "dust bowl years" was extremely evident as there was little green vegetation covering the sandy soil. Years of little moisture and insistent winds blowing across the plains left much of the prairie barren and brown. Some places were appearing to be waste lands. Apparently this was one of them.

Some of the men just looked at the area and shook their heads. One even said, "Well we can't have a campground without trees!" as they looked at the bare, sandy terrain. "Oh yes, we can have trees!" exclaimed Brother Blodgett. "But how?" they questioned. "Look," he stated, as he dug a hole. "Come back tomorrow and you'll see."

The next day the three foot hole Brother Blodgett dug had water from the underground water supply that Nebraska is so richly blessed with. A source of water to irrigate the trees and plenty to make a green, grass-covered campsite. Irrigation — this new method of watering the crops from underground sources could also make a green, campgrounds on the prairie. Now almost sixty years later, the campgrounds at Lexington still has trees, bushes, flowers and green grass (during the warm seasons) in abundance!

(Interview with Glenn Warriner, 1999.)

Memories of Retha Brandt Goss

Retha Brandt Goss in a letter of October 1997 writes that she and her brother, Eugene, remember the North Camp south of Ainsworth in a grove of trees with a big tent for the meetings and some people stayed on the ground living in tents. Bro. David Hastie was the speaker one year. During the war [World War II] the camp was dismissed. We also had camp at York, Nebraska. Was in a park, had a pavilion, and we lived in tents ... Eugene is an RV'er and he has been working in York all summer (1997) building a new church there and he said, "The park was still there and the creek but the pavilion was torn down and they had built tennis counts." One night at York we had rain and everything was wet, beds and clothes. What a mess!"

... In 1945, the first year M. F. Brandt was Superintendent, there was the first Boys Camp and Billie Davis was the speaker. In 1946, he had a Boys and Girls Camp. These were one of the first *children's* camps in the Assemblies.

Retha remembers her dad being a part of the officials that bought the property at Lexington. They built the tabernacle first, then the dining room and three cabins — for the Superintendent, Secretary/Treasurer, and Caretaker. She writes, "I remember working in the dining room. Eugene was saved at the camp in York. I do remember we went to camp every year....

(Letter from Retha Brandt Goss, October 1997.)

Leonard Herrmann's Memories of Kids Kamp

I remember well that first camp which I attended. At that time it was called Boy's Camp. The year was 1945 and I was 8 years old.... It was my first time to be away from home for a whole week. I only knew one other boy at camp; that was James Edwards, who now lives here in Springfield, Missouri and has been a teacher at Evangel College. Because Jim's parents had pastored the church in Maxwell, I met a friend of his from there, Leonard Guyers. We have remained friends since that camp.

That year it got real cold during camp and the directors set up a wood or fuel oil stove in the Tabernacle, which is now the Dining Hall, and that is how we were able to keep warm during the day.

It was either 1945 or 1946 when a tornado went through the north of Lexington during camp.... The caretaker had just mowed the grass before camp and when the wind came up it blew grass into our cabins and all over our bedding.

Several years later they changed the camp to Boys and Girls Camp. Because more campers came one of those years than were expected, they set up large tents for us boys and our counselors to sleep in. The counselors would set up their beds in the middle of the tent and we would make our beds on the ground around the edge of the tent. One night a rain storm came up and blew rain under the flaps of the tent and got our bedding all wet. I never could figure out why the counselors didn't warn us about this.

One of the things about Kids Kamp that I remember well is the good food and evening services we enjoyed, even the KP in the kitchen wasn't too bad.

It is my understanding the Nebraska District was the first District to have camps for Kids. Did it pay off in my life as a camper? Yes, I would say it has. After graduating from High School years later, I went to Bible College in Springfield, Missouri and came back to Nebraska to pastor churches for 29 years before moving to Kansas to pastor.

(Leonard Herrmann, "I Remember." *Book of Memories, 50 years 1945 to 1995 Nebraska Kids Kamps.)*

Camp group at Kearney, Nebraska, July 7, 1932

District ministers attending camp meeting at Ord, NE, July 27-Aug. 6, 1933

Camp meeting group at Ord, NE, July 27-Aug. 6, 1933

Chapter 23: Having Fun at Camp (1950s-present)

***"Then he said unto them, Go your way, eat the fat, and drink the sweet, and send portions unto them for whom nothing is prepared: for this day is holy unto our Lord: neither be ye sorry; for the joy of the Lord is your strength."* (Nehemiah 8:10 KJV)**

Kids Kamp Reminiscing, by Joyce DeMent

The first time I ever attended camp at Lexington, I was 11 years old, and it was 46 years ago (1949). I met friends there that year who are friends yet to this day.

I earned my money to attend camp (probably $8 for the week) by collecting pop bottles, selling grease to the grocer (it was just after the war and they bought used grease, for some reason) and cleaning a lady's house. Little did I know that year that someday I would return to camp as the wife of the Nebraska D-CAP, directing camps for other excited, impressionable kids kampers.

Camp made an indelible impression on me ... the outdoor bonfire services, meals in the old dining hall and fun around the tables (Remember singing "Get your elbows off the table"?), the smell of alfalfa, the roar of the trains which would periodically drown out the speaker in the old tabernacle, but most of all, the time spent around the altar seeking God. I always hated to leave and have to go home!

We were young, innocent, and unsophisticated in those days. Few had TV's and videos were unheard of. It didn't take much to entertain us and make us happy. I enjoyed the first camp so much, I didn't miss attending another camp from that year on until I went to college. And when we returned to Nebraska as pastors, we didn't miss any more camps until we moved to Springfield. That first Kids Kamp started a wonderful tradition in my life!

One of the funniest episodes I remember from directing Kids Kamp was a year the theme was Indians. We had a teepee set up on the platform and John Stocker was our daily mailman.... One day he tried to come popping out of the teepee, only to have the whole thing, (it was full size) come toppling over on him! We all got a laugh out of that ... and an unforgettable memory.

Our son, Doug (now a pastor), spent most of his summers through fifth grade at camps in Lexington. His memories include: catching ground squirrels together with Brent Wilkins on the camp grounds. (I remember them doing much more than that!) He also reminded me not to forget Paul Ackerman and Clyde King (and the horses) as two who contributed much to memories of kids kampers. I add to those two, Loretta and Bonnie, whose hard work and dedication helped make memories for many kids kampers.

(From Joyce DeMent, 1995.)

Memories of Kids Kamp, by Lebsack Blauvelt

We were introduced to Nebraska Boys and Girls Camp immediately after graduating from Southwestern College in the early 1950's. We (Bonni Roll and myself) served on the staff and saw the merit and tremendous work of this ministry. L. E. Wilkins and Clyde King were the directors. (There might have been one more, I don't remember.)

The camp, only one then, was crowded, understaffed and the facilities were in need of upgrading. Yet God did good things in young lives. These directors and the presbyters later asked if we would serve as directors. They requested the campers be kept busy, the staff be kept in control and that we try to reduce property damage. We agreed and requested they send us to camps in several districts to observe and learn. They were happy to do this.

At that time campers ranged from ages 7 to 12 with a few 13-year-olds sneaking in. We strongly suggested the age by 8 through 12 with few if any exceptions.

The tuition was $7.50. This we raised to $8.00 and later to $8.50 to provide operating expenses and supplies. Even at this low rate it was difficult for many families to send their children. At this time the name was changed to KIDS KAMPS.

Nutrition and good balanced meals were a must, (said we). Good roast beef fresh from Nebraska ranches, home style fried chicken, vegetables, salads, and desserts. The staff was thrilled and impressed, the campers were NOT! ...

LESSON: You don't change kids' eating habits in 5 days. They don't like foods requiring a lot of chewing! So, we went to hamburger dishes, hot dogs, etc. and would sneak in a well-liked vegetable and simple desserts. This idea was an instant success.

There was no Dickinson Dorm, no Roll Inn, no lots of things! The dining hall was where Alber Hall is now. All meals were served family style. We hurried the campers through by counselor groups to make room for those waiting in line outside. The present dining hall was the tabernacle. No buildings were air conditioned. Hot, windy, and humid were the norm. With windows wide open in the tabernacle, the frequent trains would disrupt services. We did have window water coolers which added to humidity but did stir the air. Fountains were a pipe with holes squirting water.

The pop stand was small and a very popular spot, open only at morning recess and from 2 to 4 p.m. This resulted in very hearty appetites at supper and fewer wet beds. Campers received a healthy snack in the dining room before bed time.

Showers and rest rooms were too few and inadequate.

THEN CAME STATE INSPECTIONS! Boy, did we hustle. In all areas we made corrections as the budget allowed. Water temperature in the army like dishwasher was carefully checked. Rest rooms and showers had to be updated but until then when leaving the showers we were required to step into pans with a Clorox solution to reduce spreading germs. Beds had to be a certain number of feet apart, fewer campers in each room and all double beds must go, etc., etc.

A diamond for softball, now and then the miniature golf was usable, and a few swings. We added hand pushed go-carts and archery, and ball teams playing tournaments. Various games and activities were tried: pantomimes, watermelon feeds, talent contests, tug of war, relays and whatever might fit into the program.

Of necessity the camp was quite regimented, lots of fun and enjoyable but all within boundaries of control, we hoped. The days began with simple things like gathering around the flag pole for pledges then calisthenics ...

Tabernacle services were also regimented: line up, come in with counselors, short preliminaries, the messages, to the altars in counselor groups no later than about 8 p.m.... Services didn't have as much splash and hoopla as today but with so many and so little time to make an imprint on their lives we felt every activity must count for eternity. God moved in mighty ways. Prayer times were wonderful.

DAY'S END. The first bell rang at 9 p.m., in bed and lights out by 9:30, counselors were on duty at all times. We had super staff members ... Thursday after the campers were asleep we had a thank you party for the staff.

Rows of old brown cabins, the old dorm out north which was unfinished, a few private cabins and a tent or two was the housing that we provided the campers. Rain and high winds brought their own emergencies. Storm shelters were needed. Under the old bell tower for the girls. In a culvert across the road for the boys. There were some scary moments. One evening the highway patrol came to inform us a tornado was close, coming down highway 30. There was not time to get to even these inadequate shelters. Believing prayers reached heaven. The storm divided and went around the camp!

Soon it was evident we needed two camps: DIVIDE! 240 campers plus staff were too many! Such wonderfully progressive leadership the District enjoyed! Soon there were two Kids Kamps as well as Teen and Youth Camps. Up went the new tabernacle, big and air conditioned, a big cheerful dining hall serving cafeteria style, classroom and craft space, more showers and rest rooms, big dorms and now even a pool. YEAH!!! Passing state inspection was a breeze now!

I can't remember for sure but it seems we directed camps 10 or 12 years and I carried on 2 or 3 years after Bonni went to Africa.

A vivid memory is of tears streaming down my face as buses and cars left Friday after the noon meal — many new believers, many filled with the Holy Spirit, happy kids, tired staff, singing "I'll Live for Jesus Day After Day" as they pulled out. JOY!! Yet the heartache of knowing many were returning to homes where they didn't have a chance unless the church surrounded, loved and nurtured them.

Even now we meet Nebraska Kids Kamp alumni who remember those "good ole days." How rewarding to know they are faithfully serving the Lord, good workers in their churches and raising their families to love Jesus and of course, go to NEBRASKA KIDS KAMP!

(Lebsack Blauvelt, "Memories of Kids Kamp," *Book of Memories, 50 years 1945 to 1995 Nebraska Kids Kamps*, 1995.)

Norman Correll Remembers Camp

Going through the pictures (of past camps) brought a flood of memories of grand camp days and wonderful friends: some of them now in heaven. Norma and I have always loved the Nebraska District and have always been "proud" to be a part of it. My ministerial credentials, to date, have always been with the Nebraska District.

I recall in my youth always looking forward to family camp: this was before youth camps started. It was the highlight of the whole year. I can't honestly say that it was always for spiritual reasons, because it was an opportunity to make new friends, see old friends, and socialize. Camp was always lots of fun.

Memories include the aroma (to some odious) of the Alfalfa Mills, and the roar of the trains roaring by almost constantly: sometimes so loud that the speakers had to wait until it had gone by. Speaking of trains — there was a joke in the early years, of the camp's development that centered on Brother A. M. Alber's snoring. This was when they had work weeks for the men, who slept dormitory style. They declared that Bro. Alber's snoring was so loud that the only time they could sleep was when the trains went by.

Only heaven knows how many romances concluding with marriage started at camp. I know ours did, and I can think of many more as well. But, after all, what better place to meet the person of your dreams and fall in love!

Of course nothing was air conditioned in those days. Everyone sat together and hoped that everyone's deodorant would hold out. Some didn't!!

The most wonderful camp days for us was when I was D-CAP. We had great camps mightily moved upon by the Holy Spirit. I'll never forget some of those powerful services.

Norma and I (she a bit later) received our call to Africa missions at camp. Two or three years later we were featured as Nebraska missionaries going to (then) Tanzanyike (now Tanzania). During that unforgettable service in 1957, they rolled a station wagon into the auditorium symbolic of our first Speed the Light vehicle. Money was raised that day to pay for it. We went to the field in 1958.

I could go on and on, but…!

~ The Corrells

(From Norman Correll, 1995.)

Norman Correll was D-CAP of the Nebraska District from 1954 to 1957. The Corrells then became missionaries to Tanzania, East Africa. After returning from Africa in 1966, Norman was the first National Representative for MAPS. He was National Youth Director from 1968 to 1974. Then in 1979 Norman became the National Secretary of Missionary Support, and in 1981 he became the Executive Administrator for the Division of Foreign Missions until his retirement. Norman Correll also was Director of International Relations for the Assemblies of God Congress in Seoul, Korea in 1994.

Don White's Kids Kamp Memories from 1959

My experiences started back in 1959 as an 8 year old camper. Two memorable experiences stand out in my mind from my initial camping experience. First, I was put in KP duty for pulling a girl's hair. It was not done maliciously, but was during a meal when many of us were laughing and teasing each other. I "gently" tugged at the young lady's pony tail, and later that day found myself crying before the camp tribunal. My punishment was to sweep the sidewalks and cement all around the pop stand. It was very humiliating, but the worst part was that I had to miss the annual camper baseball game.

The second experience was much better. It was at this camp that I gave my heart and life to the Lord Jesus Christ making Him my Savior. This commitment to Christ led to the surrendering of my life to His Lordship and eventual yielding to His calling on my life. Because of my gratefulness to God and the role the ministry of Kids Kamp had on my life I have tried to invest some of my time back into this ministry and involve my children and those of our congregation in this life-changing ministry ...

(Don. White, "Kids Kamp Memories from 1959: Memorable Experiences," *Book of Memories 50 years 1945 to 1995 Nebraska Kids Kamps*, 1995.)

Dedication of New Camp Tabernacle, 1961

On this, the 20th anniversary of Our District Camp Ground, it is a great and marvelous experience to dedicate a new Tabernacle to the service of God. It is an outward manifestation of what is in the hearts of the people. It is a sign of the Lord's blessing, because without that blessing, the building itself would not be possible. It is a reminder to others of the greatness, not of the people, but of Eternal God.

But the real importance is not in the building, not in the people, as such, that occupy it. The real importance of such an occasion is that it is a physical indication of the extension of God's Invisible Church — together with the facts and truths of such Church, and of God.

Our happiness on this occasion is based on statements from the Bible such as, "For God so loved the world that He gave His only begotten Son, that whosoever believeth in Him should not perish, but have everlasting life." John 3:16; "Not by might, nor by power, but by my spirit, saith the Lord of Hosts." Zechariah 4:6; and "Be thou faithful unto death and I will give thee a crown of life." Revelation 2:10.

When we look at our new tabernacle, we see more than a building; we see the greatness of God and of His promises to us. We see the holiness and purity of His Word. We see the suffering and death of our Savior and His glorious resurrection. And we know that this wonderful story as related in Holy Scripture, together with the above promises of God and many more, will be preached from the pulpit of this Tabernacle to many people in the years to come. This is why we are happy today. This is why we now give thanks to God for this building.

The heritage and traditions which lie before the building of this fine Tabernacle which we are dedicating to His service on this sixth day of August, 1961, find their beginning, so far as this District is concerned some forty-two years ago [1919].

(From the *Dedication and 20th Anniversary Nebraska District Council Assemblies of God Tabernacle and Conference Grounds, Lexington, Nebraska, 1941-1961.*)

Dedication of the Remodeled Suedberg Dorm

A number of years ago a man by the name of Frank Suedberg who lives in the southwest part of the state came to the camp meetings and showed a keen interest in the camp. For a number of years we lost track of him. But a little over a year ago, Brother Eden and I went to visit with Brother Suedberg and were able to renew his interest in the camp. He came to the camp meeting last year and while he was here he presented a check for $5,000 for the remodeling of the building that has been known as the little chapel. It is a barracks building that we moved in from the Kearney airport. From the gift of $5,000 we have remodeled the building with new windows and doors, paneled the walls and built an addition of 20 X 22 which has been equipped with rest room facilities for the building and that area of the camp. It has five rooms which will house ten to twelve campers in each room.

We now dedicate this dorm to the Lord and pray God‘s divine blessing upon Brother Frank Suedberg for this generous gift.

Dedication of Roll Dorm

During the last 31 years much has transpired on these grounds, many mile stones have been reached in the development of the camp facilities.

This past year has been no exception. Just a year ago we were in the planning stages in preparation to construct the two new housing facilities which are now in use.

Just a few months over one year ago the Floyd Rolls left word at the District office they wanted to visit with me. I drove to their home in Milford, Nebraska, at which time they told me they wanted to do something for the camp. Brother Roll had made the statement, “I want to do something tangible for the Lord‘s work so I can see that which is done while I am living.”

The decision to make the investment they made did not come over night, but extended over many years. Brother Floyd Roll was a member of the Laymen‘s committee from it‘s inception in 1952. To promote the boys and girls camps he visited the churches in his section and showed 35 mm colored slides of the camps in action.

Their daughter Bonni who is now our own Nebraska Missionary was a co-director of the Boy‘s and Girl‘s camps for many years. Through this close relationship with the camp through the years was the deciding factor that influenced the Rolls to contribute the sum of $20,000 for the construction of the new dorm which is named in honor of them. It is a unit 34 X 132. It has 14 rooms; each with its own rest room facilities and shower, and each room will accommodate eight campers. Brother Roll requested this building would be constructed with our youth in mind, be designed specifically for them.

So therefore we now dedicate this new dormitory to the Lord, and we also pray God‘s divine blessings upon Brother & Sister Roll for their contribution for without it this unit would not be here on the grounds.

(Taken from Nebraska District records.)

Kids Kamp Attendance

Attendance at Kids Kamp in 1962 was 355; 1963 was 362; 1964 was 342; 1965 was 392; and 1966 was 385.

Memories of Clyde King

The first Boys Camp that Clyde helped with was held at Lexington, Bob Nazarenus and Jim Wilkins were campers. I‘m not sure of the year. Clyde encouraged the district brethren to include the girls also in the camping program.... In the summer of 1965 Clyde took a Shetland pony team and a wagon to give the children rides. He was not long in learning the children would rather ride horses than ride behind them in a wagon. He borrowed some horses to give rides the next year. Before long he had his own horses for the trail rides. This meant taking care of the horses all year long. He had the responsibility of grooming the horses and getting the tack ready for the trail rides at Kids Kamp which usually involved three weeks each summer. All of this involved a lot of hard work but Clyde enjoyed doing it for the kids of Nebraska. Besides trail rides he had horsemanship classes and gave ribbons as rewards. There were games the kids played on horses. He conducted western pleasure classes and the winner would receive a belt buckle.

For several years Clyde gave a pony to the child who brought the most new kids to camp. He had horse and dog stories that were true put on tape and sold them to any of the kids that would like one. He was in charge of the horse program at camp twenty consecutive years. Some of his grandchildren were there each summer to help him.

Clyde also made some games for the camp grounds. One that has been used for many years is the hockey box. The carpet ball game is still a favorite of all campers no matter the age.

(Clyde King, "Memories of Clyde King," *Book of Memories, 50 years 1945 to 1995 Nebraska Kids Kamps*, 1995.)

(Editor's note: We will always be indebted to Brother Clyde King for all the unselfish hours he gave to make Kids Kamp an exciting place to go. I have heard from several people that the horses were the reason they came to camp, then they found that God was there too! Many kids never had an opportunity to be near horses and Kids Kamp will always be a special memory to them because of Clyde King and his horses.)

The Value of Boys and Girls Camps

The camping program of the Nebraska District has been one of the most outstanding projects of our entire district. Eternity alone will tell the value of these camps. Many of the boys and girls from across the entire State of Nebraska have been saved, filled with the Holy Spirit, received calls to the ministry and have been taught and blessed of God in these camps held on our camp ground in Lexington, Nebraska.

The Nebraska District was the first to inaugurate Boys and Girls Camps. The initial effort was a boys camp in 1945. Later the program was broadened to become a boys and girls camp. By 1953 the existing facilities were too small to accommodate the camp enrollment. Two camps were formed and they were under the supervision of our District Sunday School Directors, Bonni Roll and Loretta Lebsack. Former directors of our camps were: Ruth Fay, Church Wolstenholm, Frank Sabotka, L. E. Wilkins, R. D. Turner, Clyde King. From 1953 through 1963, Bonni Roll and Loretta Lebsack directed the camps; 1964, Loretta Lebsack; 1965, Rev. and Mrs. W. E. Reynolds and Rev. and Mrs. LeRoy Eichman; 1966 and 1967, Rev. and Mrs. Duane Palser

("The Value of Boys and Girls Camps," from the *50th Anniversary Book Nebraska District*, 1917 to 1967 p. 10.)

Remembering North Camp, by Howard and Patsy Rice

I am not aware if anyone had shared about the North Camp Tent Revivals that the Pastors and ranchers of the Niobrara section hosted for probably 50 years. From our years of pastoring at Burton, Nebraska in the 1970s, here is our experience.

The reason for the tent revival up in the sand hills … was the distance and road factors in early years. It was too great a distance to drive to the camp grounds in Lexington.

So every year the pastors and ranchers would rent a tent out of Norfolk that would seat some 300 people. A work day/days would be called by the sectional presbyter so all the men would converge on a grove … (first in Ainsworth area in early years) then to a grove south of Bassett. The tent would be pitched … lifted … then staked securely, for it was not uncommon to experience a summer thunder storm during the seven days of camp… Grass mowed… toilets cleaned … portable generator hooked up to sound system and strung up lights … camp sign placed out on the highway … and advertising sent out. We also had a spray plane buzz the area to discourage the mosquitoes and night bugs.

The men had designed metal brackets for the seats … lumber of 2 x 12's were borrowed from the local lumber yard … slid into the brackets … providing 12 foot pews … with backs, then lumber returned after camp use.

The camp convened last week of June and concluded on July 4th with a carry in lunch to finish … before cutting of the prairie hay season. Special speakers, evangelists, college choirs and local talent shared in nights of God's presence … souls saved … renewals … and revival blessings. Wonderful memories of fellowship and God's spirit out-poured.

Later years they moved the camp to an air-conditioned facility in Ainsworth, however it lost its intrigue … the appeal of the out of doors … the work days of fellowship and bonding among pastors and ranchers ... Ultimately died a graceful death. It ran its season, perhaps but OH! What divine encounters took place during those camp days.

(From Howard and Patsy Rice.)

Some Reminiscing, from H. H. "Spud" & Joyce DeMent

I (Joyce) grew up in Omaha Glad Tidings when it was located in downtown Omaha. We had moved to Omaha when I was in the 4th grade. Brother and Sister L. E. King were the only pastors I knew during those years. I remember attending Vacation Bible Schools each summer. I remember Loren Fox holding a tent meeting when I was in the 8th grade. Many people were saved and healed ... and then the "Latter Rain" movement hit, and some people who had come to the Lord lost out due to this erroneous doctrine.

One night during a midweek service, the Power fell and Merlin Wardrobe, one of the laymen in the church, was slain in the Spirit. He fell straight back, breaking the back of the chair, but it didn't hurt him. We used to spend hours praying at the altars, including Sunday mornings, Sunday evenings, and Wednesday evenings. When there was a revival on, my mom saw to it we were at church ... every night, even though we had to ride the bus to services. Norm Correll held a revival there, just after his son Brian was born. I remember a young missionary couple, Wes and June Hurst, holding meetings. I was saved in that church, at the age of 11, under the ministry of Christian Hild. A year later I was baptized in the Holy Spirit. We had a good youth group during my teen years. SAC Air Force Base also contributed young men to our congregation. The church never grew very big while I was there. I think the record attendance was only 97 when I went off to Central Bible Institute. It was later to become a large congregation.

Brother King took me to my first Kids Kamp in Lexington when I was 11 years old. I think Billie Davis, the "Hobo Kid", was the speaker that year. I was hooked, and never missed attending a camp afterwards. It was at camp that I made what were to be lifetime friends from around the district: Arlene Campbell, Darrell Herman, Leonard Hermann, Jim Wilkins, Verna Kisser, Joy Blakkolb, Jerry Spain, Jane Smith, Leland Lebsack, Ron Blauvelt, Nila and Sharon Cornwell, and many others. I collected pop bottles, cleaned houses, and sold grease (remember those days after the war?) to earn my way to camp. Loretta Lebsack and Bonnie Roll were the Kids Kamp directors in later years. My D-Caps were F. D. McClellan, Norm Correll, and Bud Leach. All were great! Little did I know how parallel my life would be to Norm and Norma's.

I remember sitting and fanning in the old tabernacle (now the dining hall). With the windows open, the passing trains would drown out the speaker, who would have to quit preaching till the train passed. It was one of those hot days in August during "State Camp," as it was called then, when Loren & Millie Triplett shared their missionary burden with the congregation ... and their entire missionary support was raised then and there! I count it a privilege to have been in that service. Again, little did I know how our paths were to cross later in missions.

At CBI, I met my future husband, Spud DeMent. We married in 1957 and he graduated in 1958. In October of 1959, after spending fifteen months as youth pastors in First Assembly in Baton Rouge, Louisiana (his home church), the Lord led us to pastor Decatur, a little church 60 miles north of Omaha. At that time we had one child, Doug, who was only a few months old. It truly was the Lord who led us there, for by then my family had moved to Texas and I had no desire to minister in Nebraska. I remembered how hard it had seemed to reach people in Omaha during my youthful years.

The little church in Decatur had been pioneered by Sister Eva Davis. We spent nine fruitful months there and saw a good growth in the congregation. The Congregation of about 19 grew to reach 86 on Easter Sunday. Years later, however, this church closed down and the congregation merged with Lyons and Walthill. Our presbyter, Brother B. F. Correll, was a real encouragement to us. The parsonage was a converted chicken coop, 16‘ x 24‘, covered with fake brown brick. It had concrete floors, no hot water heater, and no bathroom ... just an outhouse. The winter we were there it snowed 72”, and most of it stayed on the ground. Quite a welcome for the Southerner Spud was! However, he became a better winter driver than I ever was. And our young people loved the winter activities. After 15 months as youth and music directors across the state line at First Assembly in Sioux City, we were called to pastor Holdrege, where we stayed for five years. It was there that our first daughter, Joy, was born.

Holdrege had been pioneered by Ted Byars, whom we followed. We lived in the basement apartment for nearly four years, before we were approved to build a lovely parsonage just a few doors away. I think we built it for about $17,000. Out of that youth group came Rogene Christensen, who later married David Argue and returned to the district as our first Chi Alpha director, and of course later founders of Christ‘s Place. Other Christensen kids met their mates at Evangel College and returned to live in Holdrege, becoming strong supporters of the church and district activities. In fact, in 1980 (or thereabouts), our son Doug served his summer internship in that very church and returned after his graduation as the youth pastor, where he served for several years. [He is now serving as District Youth Director for the New York District (1999).]

While we were pastors in Holdrege, in February of 1962 the doctors discovered that Spud had diabetes. He was taking medicine 11 times a day and was on a very strict diet. That spring, April 12, when he was ordained in Lincoln First Assembly (along with Jerry Spain and Leland Lebsack), Bro. L. E. King also prayed for his healing as he prayed the ordination prayer. From that night on, Spud gradually began to get better. By August, he was totally healed, and has stayed that way to this day, all praise to the Lord!

During that time, being only 35 miles from the campground, we were involved every summer with camps. I remember the Minnesota D-CAP visiting one year to see how our program was run. He said in amazement, “I would never get any youth to come if this was all I had to offer them!” It‘s true that the campground wasn‘t beautiful ... there were no mountains, no lake, no creek. But it is holy ground to us because the Lord met us and countless other young people through the years in marvelous ways.

Many times we prayed till after midnight, rejoicing and weeping in His presence. (When I returned to spend the night this spring, I was saddened to see all the old cabins gone. Yes I loved those old, ugly cabins. Many memories…).

The older pastors took interest in we younger pastors, encouraging us along the way. They were wonderful examples of godly men before us.

Spud, who had been serving as assistant D-CAP to Jim Wilkins, was elected to follow Jim when he took the Milford pastorate. We moved into the “D-CAP” home, a large, old white house conveniently next to the district offices. Our youngest daughter, Jennifer, was born just a few months after we moved to Grand Island. L. W. Dickinson was superintendent. While in that office, the district voted to begin a Chi Alpha work, and began searching for a Chi Alpha Director. After praying, Spud felt impressed to tell Bro. Dickinson about David Argue, who had married Rogene from our Holdrege youth group. They were serving at that time in western Canada. After prayer, Dave and Rogene agreed to move to Nebraska and begin the first Chi Alpha work.

The AIM program was started while Spud was D-CAP, with several of our younger pastors taking C.A.'s to Panama and other countries. We took a bus load from Nebraska to join five other districts for a huge outreach in Monterrey, Mexico, where a total of 275 C.A.'s won hundreds of souls to the Lord.

One of the blessings of camp was Brother Clyde King, who maintained horses throughout the year and brought them every summer for the campers' enjoyment. It was especially meaningful to the city kids who never had seen a horse up close. Brother King used those times to work with problem kids. He took campers on daily trail rides. The miniature golf course was also developed during those years, giving campers another activity. So many pastors and their wives were faithful to help in the camping program, along with many faithful lay people who gave up weeks of their summer to come and work. I couldn't begin to name them all, and at the risk of forgetting to mention some — but the Blauvelts, Turners, Roggows (later to become involved with our family as their son Brian married our Joy), Campbells, Hermans, Cornwells, Mastens, Palsers, Tiedes, Frys, Harmons, ... some of those who weren't in the ministry later saw their children become ministers, or entered the ministry themselves! Some who helped us direct Kids Kamps were the Duane Palsers and Ella Marie Masten. The Halls certainly must be mentioned, as they had such a gift for praying people through to the Baptism in the Holy Spirit. One note here: any kids who ever came from the Hastings church never had to be prayed for the infilling.... Lebsacks had already seen to that!

As for the pastors we would have to list everyone on the roll, for all pitched in and worked to make the camps a success and the campgrounds beautiful. We often remarked on how much of a family all the pastors seemed. They were a joy to work with, and we spent many hilarious hours in the kitchen at the dining hall after service, or in cleaning the grounds together.

It seemed like every summer we had tornado warnings during camp. The plan was to take the youth to the ditches when a tornado warning came (the highway patrol usually warned our vigilantes), however one year it had rained so much that the ditches were full of water. Different pastors could tell stories of seeing tornados come along the land, lift up over the campground, and drop on the other side, while everyone else was in the tabernacle praying.

We also vividly remember going to North Camp one year and seeing a tornado drop down out of the sky just above the Ainsworth airport. It gathered speed and size and bore down on us. We pulled off the highway and watched it: Spud in wonder and awe, and Joy begging her daddy to get out and get in the ditch. I was pleading for him to back the car up. North Camp also holds memories; for it was there that our Joy gave her heart to the Lord as a young child.

It was also at camp that Jennifer was saved. After a particularly moving altar service, we were discussing those who had been saved that night. Jennifer, who was 4, asked, "Am I saved?" Her daddy assured her she was, but I took the opportunity to explain the way of salvation to her in her crib in the D-CAPS' cabin, and prayed with her. To this day, the camp is hallowed ground to Jennifer, too ... all of our kids, for that matter.

We served as D-CAPS and Sunday School Directors (after Bonnie Roll had gone to the mission field and Loretta had left to work in the national Sunday School Department) from 1966 to 1972, when we were called to Springfield by Norm Correll to work with him in the National Youth Department. Many years down the road, when we were on the mission field ourselves, Loren Triplett called us back to work with him in the Division of Foreign Missions. We have been so privileged to have worked with these men whom I, Joyce, admired as a young C.A. in good old Nebraska!

(From H. H. "Spud" & Joyce DeMent, 1999.)

Spud DeMent was D-CAP and Sunday School Director in Nebraska from 1966 to 1972. The DeMents later were missionaries to East Africa. Currently Spud is with the U. S. Relations Department of Foreign Missions, Springfield, Missouri [1999].

Kid's Kamps

The 1966 Kid's Kamp was directed by Rev. & Mrs. Duane Palser from Burwell. H. H. DeMent was director in 1968 and the cost to a camper was $9.50 if pre-registered.

Starting in 1967 the Nebraska District conducted three weeks of Kid's Kamp. The conducting of three camps helped to alleviate our housing problem and made our camps more enjoyable for the campers due to our over-crowded conditions. The campers do not have to wait now too long in any line. With our limited recreational program, most campers were able to participate in about any activity they desired.

In 1969, Rev. H. H. DeMent, Nebraska Director of Youth and Christian Education, was Coordinator for all three camps. However, the following were appointed as Directors for their respective camps:

1st Camp July 7-11, Rev. & Mrs. Robert McCown, Wayne: Attendance 148.

2nd Camp July 14-18, Rev. & Mrs. Melvin Johnson, Thedford: Attendance 135.

3rd Camp July 21-25, Rev. & Mrs. Perry C. Baublitz, Blair: Attendance 198.

1969 had an all time high in attendance of 481 campers!

Letter from Governor Norbert Tiemann to Mr. and Mrs. Joe Masten, 1970

Your work with the children of the Lexington area has been brought to my attention, and I wanted to take this opportunity to commend you for the efforts you have put forth on behalf of your church. I know your church is sincerely grateful and as you observe the 25th anniversary of the camp the Nebraska District of the Assembly of God Church will no doubt express its appreciation for all you have done.

May I add my best wishes to those of your church body and say a sincere thank you on behalf of all Nebraskans. The youth of our state are very important ... they are the future of our state ... they are the leaders of tomorrow. The training they are now receiving from God-fearing adults like you will chart the course of events for years to come.

(Letter from Governor Norbert Tiemann to Mr. and Mrs. Joe Masten, Directors, Nebraska Kids Camp (July 2, 1970)

The Nebraska State Camp and W.M.C.'s

The Nebraska District Council of the Assemblies of God conduct an annual Family camp at the Conference Grounds each year located one mile west of Lexington. This year's camp as in previous years was filled with special events. One featured day each year is the Thursday afternoon service conducted by the Women's Missionary Council. The attendance this year was around 750. The service consisted of a visual demonstration with a cast of 73 involved. The theme presented was "Go and Tell."

Each year the women present a Dime offering for the promotions of Home and Foreign Missions. This year they used a patriotic and worldwide presentation. A 5 x 9 foot American flag was used to feature the dime offering. Each star of the flag was lighted as one hundred dollars was presented. The goal was set for five thousand dollars. The goal was exceeded and reached a total of $5,371.83. Since 1953, the WMC's have brought in the total of $71,838.00 through this type of promotion....

("The Nebraska State Camp and W.M.C.'s," *Nebraska Fellowship*, September 1970, p. 3.)

Kids Kamp Memories of Ella Masten

One of my first memories of Kids Kamp was attending as a new Christian in 1958 with my 6 month old son, Joey, who slept in a dresser drawer in one of the old, red, row cabins. Things only got better from then on. Bonni and Loretta were the Kamp Directors and they were held in very high esteem for the great work they were doing with kids.

When I became Kids Kamp Director in 1971 Paul Ackerman was my co-worker. Paul was "Mr. Kids Kamp." He knew every one of the campers by name, even when we reached 709 in one camping season. Paul sent every camper a back-to-school letter, Christmas greeting, spring letter and back to camp information packet.

Paul worked at the University of Nebraska football games to earn money to send Kids to Kamp. He was a notary and when he signed documents he suggested the document holder may want to put a donation in a jar on his desk to help send a kid to kamp.

Paul would contact the County Sheriff Associations for the names of boys who were disadvantaged so he could contact them and ask them to attend our Kamps. Many young people had their first trip out of the city into a camping experience because of Paul.

Vigilantes have told me how at night after the boys were asleep, Paul would go to each room, lay hands on the boys and pray for them. Is it any wonder why we saw such great spiritual harvest....

Another GREAT in the camping program was Clyde King with his horses. He provided the horses each camping season to give the campers horseback rides. It's a fact he did as much counseling at the horse corral as many of the counselors did with their group.

Today Ackerman Lodge is in memory of Paul Ackerman and King Dorm is in memory of Clyde King. Things did get better.

One of the more outstanding years of Kids Kamp was when we had our own Nebraska Pastors, Mildred Larson and Linda Stiver, as Kamp speakers. Staff and speakers fasted the evening meal, spent afternoons in prayer, and prepared hearts for the evening service. I remember cancer being healed, calls to the mission field, calls to pastoring, adults getting right with God, grandchildren being healed who were not at camp, etc. Many adults said camp was for them and not just for the children.

A week at camp is intense and taxing for directors, counselors, cooks, recreation staff, vigilantes and etc., but when you see a young man come back from Viet Nam and walk around the grounds and tell you how one night at the altar got him through the war, or when you see a grown man shed tears as he enters the tabernacle because of all the memories he encountered, or when missionaries tell of how they received their call at camp or when young men felt the call to the ministry and find their life's mate at camp or when people who have been saved at camp and have a successful business and invest their time and money in the camping program, all at once the weariness of the week fades away.

We have a great heritage in being a part of the Nebraska Kamping program of the Assemblies of God.

(Ella Masten, "Kids Kamp Memories of Ella Masten," *Book of Memories, 50 years 1945 to 1995 Nebraska Kids Kamps Remembrances*, 1995.)

Silver Anniversary of Kids Kamp, 1970

This summer the Nebraska Kids Camp welcomed campers for the 26th consecutive year. This makes this camp one of the oldest — if not the oldest — kids camps in the Assemblies of God.

To celebrate the silver anniversary last summer, a banquet was held on the closing night of each camp. All former camp directors, as well as campers, teachers, and the dean of women at the first camp were invited.

Letters of congratulations were read from Nebraska Governor Norbert Tiemann, Congressman Carl Curtis, and United States Senator Robert Denney.

The city of Lexington sent two representatives to the last banquet to present a plaque congratulating them on their 25th anniversary.

1970 was a record year for the camp's attendance too. A total of 504 campers were there for the three weeks, and 78 youngsters received Christ as Saviour.

("Silver Anniversary of Kids Kamp Kids: Camp Marks Milestone," *Sunday School Counselor*. August 1971, p. 17.)

Kids Kamp Draws Crowds, 1972

Kids Kamp at the Assemblies of God Church Campground drew 460 youngsters age 9-12. It drew another 135 volunteer staffers. The two weekly sessions are but a part of the summertime activity at the 17 acre site to the west of this community.

John Stocker, state director of Youth and Christian education, said the 27 year old Kids Kamp features daily devotions, class time spent discussing biblical and religious problems in daily life, recreation and craft sessions....

Other sessions during the summer are for 13-18-year-olds, young couples and the last summer camp is for adults. At Thanksgiving time about 600 youthful members of the church return to the 31-year-old facility for a convention....

Free and recreation time is spent on the baseball diamonds, archery range, volleyball court (a real popular sport with the girls), and horseback riding and other activities....

The adult camp at the end of the summer will draw nearly 2,300 persons for part of all of the 10 day session. Up to 350 persons can stay at the camp at one time. Nearly 700 are expected for each of the two Sundays of the adult session.

("Facilities Drawing Over 3,000 Summer Youth, Adult Campers," *Dawson County Herald*, July 24, 1972, p. 5.)

Dedication of New Multi-Purpose Building, 1977

The New Multi-Purpose building at the Assembly of God camp will be completed soon. The building will house classrooms, a heated swimming pool and a gymnasium. Dedication ceremonies for the new structure will be August 6.

The building will contain three classrooms which can be converted into two larger classrooms or one large conference room, a basketball court, tennis court, two volleyball courts and a heated swimming pool ... $200,000 building was started in March of this year by Chief Building and Construction of Grand Island. Financing for the structure came from contributions from 75 churches and many individuals across the state.

("Church Camp to Dedicate New Building," *Dawson County Herald,* July 14, 1977.)

Nebraska Camp Hosts Lexington Chamber of Commerce, 1979

The Lexington Chamber of Commerce was the guest of the Nebraska District Council of Assemblies of God at their camp and conference center one mile west of Lexington for the Chamber's noon luncheon Monday.

The camp provided the Chamber a free meal at the camp dining hall and Jim Wilkins, District Supervisor, Assemblies of God Conferences of Nebraska, gave the Chamber a tour of the camp grounds and facilities.

Next year the camp, dedicated to physical, emotional and spiritual growth, will host its 35th annual kids camp, where children from throughout the state may attend the camp. The camp hosts three kids camps in the month of June and three youth camps in July. Family camps are held during August.

Wilkins, a native of Lexington, attended the first family camp held on the grounds and was present during the second kids camp. Although the camp is affiliated with the Nebraska Assembly of God churches, 18 different denominations have been represented so far this year and children from other states, including Texas and Colorado have traveled to Lexington to attend the camp.

Recently the camp has been opened up for year round activities. During the past year, the Evangelical Pastors, the Evangelical Freemen and Freewomen have rented the camp and conference grounds for their fall retreats. Campus Life, a Christian organization on college campuses through the country rented the camp for a retreat last year....

Dickinson Hall offers motel-type rooms and has a capacity for 62 campers while Roll Inn is a dormitory with accommodations for more than 100 campers. The auditorium seats 800.

The multi-purpose building includes a large meeting room, a pool and a gymnasium that has tennis, volleyball and basketball courts and is available during certain times of the year to churches and non-profit organizations on a rental basis. Wilkins said some family gatherings and birthday parties have been hosted at the pool in the past year.

Funding for the camp comes from donations by the Assembly of God churches throughout the state and from other donations. The camp staff is mostly volunteer labor from the state, only the cooks are full-time paid employees.

("Chamber Dines at Church Camp," *Dawson County Herald*, July 19, 1979.)

Paul Ackerman: Mr. Kids Kamp

Paul Ackerman had three loves: God, kids, and sports. "Paul is proof that God exists," declared Nebraska District Superintendent James Wilkins, at Paul's funeral service.

To many people, Paul Ackerman was "Mr. Kids Kamp." Nobody knows for certain the number of kids for whom he paid camp tuition and provided transportation every year, but a conservative estimate would be 20 to 40. Through the years Paul ministered to over 5,000 kids.

He would ask children's homes, welfare agencies, and the Sheriffs Peace Officers Association to help him find underprivileged kids. He then contacted the parents or guardians personally for permission to take the kids to camp.

In order to finance these children, Paul turned to his third love, sports. At every University of Nebraska home football game he sold tickets. During the winter he sold tickets at the Sports Center in Lincoln, and in the fall at the Nebraska State Fair. These earnings went into his special "Kids Camp Fund."

After spending his vacation time at the kids camps each summer, Paul would personally write to any young camper who was troubled or had problems. He sent all the campers (over 650) a back-to-school letter, Christmas greetings, a letter in the spring, and two more letters encouraging them to get ready for another great kids camp.

Mr. Kids Kamp knew each camper personally and by name. He not only worked with them at camp, but back home he was the local director of the Bible Memory Association. Many evenings and weekends he spent listening to the Scriptures kids and parents had memorized the week before.

A diligent student of God's Word, Paul incorporated it into his everyday life by helping others to love the Word. He utilized games, contests, and awards to encourage people to learn the Bible passages. He was also instrumental in getting kids started in hobbies like stamp collecting, and encouraging them in every good endeavor.

By being so active for about 25 years, Paul gave continuity and strength to the camping program that rotating directors could not maintain.

Paul Ackerman never married. He lived with his sister, Esther, who was a great asset to his children's ministry. For the past 35 years he was the accountant for the Southeast Community College at Milford, Nebraska. He loved people. He knew every teacher's name (over 100) and almost every student's name (over 900).

The Southeast Community College Student Council, in an unprecedented action, set up a scholarship fund in Paul Ackerman's name. Normally a scholarship is named in honor of a favorite teacher and not an office worker.

Paul gave many hours in service to his local church. He held positions of board member, teacher, Sunday School superintendent, and was past director of the Nebraska Men's Fellowship. He also printed letters for missionaries and sent them out to save the high cost of postage in foreign mailings.

Paul had a way with people, encouraging them and making them look good while he himself stayed in the background.

On December 7, 1980, Mr. Kids Kamp went to be with the Lord at age 59. This summer will not be the same without him. He was kind, gentle, and unselfish. Everyone — camp director, cooks, coaches, and counselors — found strength and encouragement from Paul's presence. His constant smile was a source of strength....

I am sure Paul has found all the kids campers who went on to heaven before him, and they are having a glorious reunion. He will have remembered them all by name.

(Ella Masten, "Paul Ackerman: Mr. Kids Kamp," *Pentecostal Evangel*, May 24, 1981, pp. 6, 7.)

Cowboy Smiley at Kids Kamp

Cowboy and Mrs. Smiley are appearing in special evening services at the Kids Camp at the Assemblies of God Campgrounds. His real name is Rev. Albert Hild and he and his wife currently live in Springfield Missouri ... and he lived in both Sutton and Lincoln, Nebraska, as a young child, where his father pastored German Lutheran Churches.

The programs conducted by the Smileys include happy sing times led by Mrs. Smiley and their exciting puppets. Smiley makes jumbo jigsaw pictures using rainbow colored lighting. He concludes the services with a talk geared to the young campers.

"An ounce of prevention in childhood is worth more than a ton of cure too late," Smiley said. The Smileys agree that they feel they are dedicated to do the work that "gave birth to the Sunday School 204 years ago, to round up boys and girls from the homes and streets who need to hear and know about the love of Jesus."

Camp director, Ella Masten said the theme for the 36th year of kids camp is "Camping on the Circle S Ranch." The three sessions for the youngest campers runs from June 7 to July 3. Mrs. Masten said they will have approximately 180 campers each week, with a total of about 700 anticipated. The children come from across Nebraska as well as several other states including Colorado, Kansas, South Dakota, Iowa, Missouri, Texas, California and Hawaii. Many of the children from other states were originally living in Nebraska when they started attending the sessions, Mrs. Masten said, and they continue to return to the camp even after their families have moved away.

The junior and senior high camps are held in July with family camping in August ... "The first family camp was conducted in 1941, with kids camp, youth and teen camps and retreats added soon after."

... The children also participate in Bible quiz competition, choir, organized athletics and horseback riding. The horses are provided by Clyde King of Elm Creek. They also learn to do some crafts. An all-camp ball game was planned for Thursday night. "I run a close program," said Mrs. Masten. The children are allowed one and one-fourth hours of free time during the day.

The campers are encouraged to write home and parents to write to the children. Mrs. Masten said 80 to 100 letters are delivered at mail call each day. She feels this helps alleviate the homesickness experienced by some children when they are away from home.

... The only paid staff includes the guest speaker and the cook. The rest of the staff is composed of volunteers and changes each week, along with the children ... Registered nurses are also on duty at the camp, to help with any emergencies or first aid. Mrs. Masten said the camp also has to pass health and fire inspections as well as a visit from the city inspector. The camp employs a full-time caretaker who actually lives on the grounds, although he is provided with an assistant during the summer months....

Smiling, Mrs. Masten said that each camper is given two homemade cookies and some milk before they go to bed at night. It sounds like a simple gesture, but the camp cook has to bake nearly 7,000 cookies to make that happen. This year it took about four days of work.

Seventeen different denominations were represented at last year's camp, she said....

("Cowboy Smiley Conducts Services At Assembly of God Camp," *Dawson County Herald*, Monday, June 14, 1982, p. 1.)

Answering the Call to Kids Kamp

The phone rang, I answered, and a voice at the other end asked, "Faith, would you consider being the Kids Kamp Director?" What a shock! Ella Masten, a dear friend, had been the Director and I knew that there would be no way I could fill her shoes. The Kids Kamping ministry was top notch and a wonderful opportunity for boys and girls to get away, have fun, and experience God. I prayed about it, talked to several people including Ella and decided that God wanted me to fill the position at that time.

The first camp I directed was in 1984, with Bob and Carol Albin as the speakers. I was very nervous about that first camp. However, Ella had left a well run program and had helped me so much and with God's help it went quite well. During the next eight years I found the ministry to be most fulfilling. The kids, staff and pastors were great and the Lord was so good to us.

A lot of changes were made on the grounds, during the time I was director. The addition of the Ackerman Lodge and later King Dorm was a big plus. One big change was to have meals prepared by PFM [Professional Food Management] instead of doing it all ourselves. What a blessing! Brother King was unable to bring horses after the third year so Joe Woodward helped to get go-carts for the kids to ride. The old playground equipment was removed for insurance purposes, but new playground equipment was built in its place. Changes come, old things go, but Kids Kamp has always stayed with its primary purpose of giving kids one week of fun, social experiences, and teaching on their level about God. In most correspondence and conversations about Kids Kamp, I hear the evening services and altar times were the highlight each year ...

We will never know the number of lives that have been impacted by a little extra effort, lots of love and hundreds praying for the Kids Kamp ministry. Kids Kamp was a highlight for my children for many years as campers and workers. It was an opportunity for us as a family to work together for the kingdom of God. I am very thankful that I was given the opportunity to have Nebraska in this way.

(Faith Tyson, "Who Me?" *Book of Memories, 50 years 1945 to 1995 Nebraska Kids Kamps*, 1995.)

Jeffery Tyson's Memories of Kids Kamp

I have many different memories of Kids Kamp both as a camper and a worker. As a camper I can remember looking forward to staying in Swedburg Dorm. I can remember getting up in the morning and going to morning exercises with Mr. Kids Kamp, Paul Ackerman. I also will never forget the prayer times up at the altars with my counselors.

My most memorable memory is my first night at Kids Kamp. I was staying in Swedburg Dorm and I was lucky enough to get a top bunk. When night came, I spread my nylon sleeping bag on the bunk and got into it. The next thing that I remember is lying on the cement floor. My counselor, Kenny Dickinson, picked me up and put me back in the bunk. I think he was more scared than I was. I switched bunks the next day and I have not cared for the top bunk since.

As a worker, I mainly remember all the friendships that I made. Because my mother was the camp director I worked over 20 camps. With all those camps I worked most every job possible. I did everything from being a counselor to cleaning toilets. My most touching memory was the only time I was a counselor. I had a boy in my group that had witnessed his father being murdered. I must admit that I had no idea what to do. I just tried to show him love and be his friend. I still think of Mark and pray for him.

The friendship that I will never forget was the friendship that I made with Renee Nazarenus now Renee Tyson. It was because of camp that I was able to spend so much time getting to know Renee. Because of camp Renee not only became my best friend, on June 9, 1990 she became my wife.

P.S. Special thanks to Leota Cornwell and Esther Brown for teaching me how to mop the dining hall floor.

(Jeffery Tyson, "Memories of Kids Kamp," *Book of Memories, 50 years 1945 to 1995 Nebraska Kids Kamps*, 1995.)

Kids Kamp Testimonies from 1993

Wow, what a year it has been! As the holiday season is coming upon us I am reminded to give thanks to God for all He has done. The Lord certainly did immeasurably more that I could ask or imagine this summer at Kids Kamp. I'm thankful for the six hundred and sixty-six campers that had an opportunity to experience the presence of the Lord in a very real way. I thank the Lord for the 115 campers that received salvation for the very first time, the 101 campers that rededicated their lives, the 140 that were baptized in the Holy Spirit along with the 72 that were refilled, and the 23 campers that felt called into ministry. Many things happened even beyond these numbers. God touched and did "the miraculous" in many lives.

One of these was a girl from Lincoln, Nebraska, who was healed of scoliosis. Here are some brief excerpts from a letter I received from Chaaron and her mother. Chaaron's mother, along with her aunt and cousin, have scoliosis. At the age of eight Chaaron was also diagnosed with this disease.

"During one of the evening services at camp I responded to an altar call for healing. I went with a group of friends from my church. We sat down and started to pray. We prayed for at least 25-30 minutes. One of my friends said to me, 'Your back's healed!' I had no doubt that was true. All the other girls had me bend over and touch my toes. They noticed that my back was straight, and we started to cry and jump up and down. God really is faithful and I'm glad I got healed instead of getting a back brace."

God moved in Chaaron's life at camp along with many other children.

As I reflect on this year I am grateful for all God has done. This holiday season we will be reminded of the Babe born in a manger who came to seek and save humanity. Many people have discovered the joy of this Christ at the altars of our Assemblies of God Campground. I'm thankful for that, and the lives that have been touched and molded in the last 48 years of our Kids Kamp history. As we go into this holiday season, will you join me in giving thanks to God for our camping programs and His faithfulness to meet us there time and time again? We do serve a loving God!

(S. Wertheimer, "Kids Kamp Testimonies from 1993," *Nebraska Fellowship*, November/December, 1993, p. 7.)

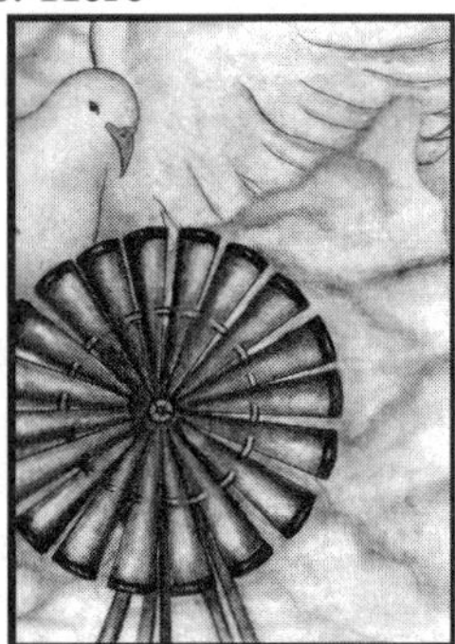

Chapter 24: Missionary Testimonies

"Go ye therefore, and teach all nations, baptizing them in the name of the Father, and of the Son, and of the Holy Ghost: Teaching them to observe all things whatsoever I have commanded you: and, lo, I am with you always, even unto the end of the world. Amen." **(Matthew 28:19-20 KJV)**

Next we have two chapters relating to missions and missionaries within the Nebraska District. The first chapter includes testimonies from missionaries from Nebraska who received their calling and went out into the mission field. These missionary testimonies start from the earliest years up to the present. The second chapter includes a fairly complete listing of missionaries with a Nebraska connection.

Lydia Rediger and Erma Miller: Early Missionaries

The first missionaries going forth from Nebraska were Lydia Rediger to India and Erma Miller to Brazil, both of whom were from the Milford church. Other missionaries who either went forth from Nebraska or who claimed it as their home district were the Murray Browns to Africa; the Herbert Griffins to Africa; the George Carmichaels to Egypt; the Cyle Davises to Chile; the Julius Olsons to Brazil; the Clarence Ollsens to Venezuela; the Elmer Niles to Nicaragua ...

(*50th Anniversary Booklet of the Nebraska District.*)

H. L. Griffin: Early Missionaries

In 1925, H. L. Griffin came to western Nebraska to a small town in the McCook area. He co-pastored there with George Carmichael. In 1930, his address was Scottsbluff. Both men were ordained at the 1930 Nebraska District Council. In 1931, Herbert L. Griffin went to the Belgian Congo, Central Africa as a single missionary. He was sent to Africa by the Nebraska District. In 1931, Brother Griffin was given a missionary offering of $65.00 from the district. The church board of the Maxwell Assembly of God Church decided to designate $4.00 per month to Missionary H. L. Griffin in Africa on September 8, 1936.

(A letter by Herb and JoAnn Griffin, 1996.)

Murray and Marjorie Brown

Early in 1935 revival services were held (*in Blair, Nebraska*) with Sister Marjorie Ball from Ord, Nebraska as the Evangelist. Miss Ball later became Mrs. Murray Brown and with her husband served as a missionary in Africa for many years.

The Tripletts' Call to the Mission Field: Loren Triplett Remembers

A message delivered at the Nebraska District Council — April 15, 1996:

.... Let me say it like this way, it was in 1949 a little bit before Thanksgiving, when Milly and I were driving a little Ford with a utility trailer behind it down a steep grade in the mountains of eastern Oregon, and I caught some movement out of the corner of my eye and saw a weird sight. We were the only car in sight, and I saw a wheel come up along side of me and go right on down the highway ahead of me and veer a little bit to the left and crash over the bank and disappear down toward the Snake River. Well, it was the wheel off of our trailer. A few days before, we had left our pastorate in Dayton, Oregon, and we had started out on that long trek to that distant land called Nebraska. We were from Oregon and the Lord had put a call upon our hearts, and we were coming to help to try to get an Assemblies of God work started in the great city of Syracuse. Now you all know that there is a great work there, so you probably pretty well have guessed that it was a slow start and got slower as the years went by. A couple of years ago, when Milly and I drove through Syracuse, we tried to find the corner it used to be on, because the building has been gone so long we had to guess between two corners. Anyway, we were on our way.

We left mother and father (both sides), sisters and one brother. I had six sisters, she had five, but we were on our way and came to this land. I rejoice to tell you that we landed in a friendly place. I have always said it again and again, we were strangers, and you took us in and you put your arms around us and you showed the kind of honesty and easy friendship that we were dying for. We were indeed people from a strange place, and we found ourselves among a people of integrity, insight and true fixed identity in the Kingdom of God. I have to tell you the truth, we still look back with awe and wonder at the grace and mercy of God and grace and mercy of His kingdom people in Nebraska, who gave us place and circumstance for four and a half formative years. We were just kids when we got here. I was 23 and Milly was 20. We had our first little one coming along but didn‘t say anything to our family. We figured half a continent away we could keep her pregnancy a secret until we wanted to tell it. We got here and found grace in the eyes of Lord and you people. I take this moment to thank you in these words: Thank you, Nebraska District. You gave us acceptance as though we were your own children, and we were just kids. You gave us a chance to put down enough roots to create indelible traces upon our lives and our identities. We bonded with Nebraska in many ways. After 46 years, we still find ourselves in debt to you. Burwell and the Sand Hills put it in my head that western boots are the world‘s most comfortable and practical footwear known to man. As a matter of fact, when I met Pastor Bob this morning over at the hotel, I had my Levi‘s and boots on and felt at home in Nebraska.

I have to make a confession, we have slipped just a little bit since we pastored in Burwell, because Milly and I both love a good rodeo. When we were pastors there, it was against the law, it was worldly. Can you imagine that we lived in Burwell without going to the rodeo? I don‘t know how far you have come; maybe I am out in dangerous territory. We only live about a mile and a quarter from the finest rodeos in Southern Missouri which are held twice a year. Milly is the one who always says, "Why don‘t we go to the rodeo?" So, I make that confession.

I have to tell you that I still root for Nebraska football. I greet strangers who have that kind of a license plate or that kind of coat, or that kind of a hat, or that kind of a tee-shirt with "Go Big Red." Sometimes they stare at me as if they are supposed to know me, but I guess that is just in our blood. I confess honestly that I still read USA Today by checking what it says on that page where all the states are listed. I look for what is happening in Oregon and Nebraska and in Missouri every time I do it. Let‘s see, I still remember my first battlefield experience with live ammunition. It happened right here in this state when Elmer Kirschmen, now district secretary for the Northwest District, pinned me down behind the brow of rise on the opposite side from me of a prairie dog town. I stayed there until his chamber was empty.

Thank you, Nebraska District. You also gave us opportunity to begin to develop our ministries. You let us pastor your churches. You let us fail at some things. You let us bring a young flaming evangelist and his musical wife to our congregation in Syracuse. Their names were Norm and Norma Correll. Later on, when we returned from the mission field on our first furlough, you let me find out what a real missionary was from the incisive and unflattering opinion of the young son of Spud and Joyce DeMent.

He asked me, “Are you a missionary?” and I replied, “Yes.”

I asked, “Do you know what a missionary is?” He replied, “Yes, it is a man who goes around showing pictures to churches.”

Thank you, Nebraska District. You honored me by ordaining me to the ministry in McCook in 1950, 46 years ago. Thank you, Nebraska. You gave us our two oldest children and later our youngest son, who are proud to be Cornhusker born. You gave us challenges big enough to form faith and trust. A fitting staging experience for Nicaragua, which was quite a bit farther from home than we had come thus far.

Thank you, Nebraska. You held a camp meeting in 1953 which changed our lives forever. It was there that you allowed the Spirit of God to perform a miracle. A miracle of spontaneous unanimity and that is a big miracle. That is a big miracle, isn‘t it, Bob? A spontaneous unanimity, it happened just like that. A miracle of sacrificial giving in unforgettable portions. A miracle of recognizing the will of God for a couple of adopted kids from Oregon. A miracle of recognition of what God wanted the Nebraska District to do about the Great Commission on the regions beyond in 1953. It was 43 years ago that District Council was cut out by the thrust of an idea born of God. He was the only one who knew when He went to that regular morning minister‘s meeting that day, God, I mean. No one was more surprised than we were. I simply stood up on that platform of the old tabernacle where the ministers gathered that morning and shared my long-term sense of call to Latin America, none of them knew anything about it: only my wife, and of my awareness that that morning seemed to be the time that God had asked me to ask for the prayers and the approval of my elders. I sat down and no one spoke until Brother Champion, Harold Champion, stood up and said that he would like to offer the first $75 to help us start toward the mission field.

In a few moments, the dam broke, and we all watched with awe as God took over. You know the story, if you know anything about that great camp meeting, great for us at least; I hope I am not boring you. It was a send-off like few people ever get, because we knew for the rest of our lives that God Almighty had called us to the mission field. You stood us up in the front and pinned money on us. People gave cattle. People gave tools. Jack Risner gave his shotgun, I never did get the gun. I hope he sold it, and I got the money. I am sure I did. There were things given that day, a fur coat. I don‘t know what all. All I know is that a great spirit of generosity and a great burden from the Lord of the harvest gripped this district, and you had done a favor for us kids, and I want to thank you for it. God bless you. The rest is history. Thank you for your faithful support during all the years of our missionary ministry before we were brought in the home office. Thank you for letting me tell this very personal story and being able to thank you, one more time, for blessing us and setting the stage for what God wants to do by His help even this evening.

... That wonderful camp that blessed our little family was so richly anointed in 1953. People brought money, people brought other things, people brought promises. My wife and I have talked again and again and again of the little lady who brought her five children to the altar of the old camp. She didn‘t have any money, but she set those kids on that altar. We went to the mission field after looking that in the face. She set those kids on the altar and gave what she had. She brought them to Jesus. I wish I knew where those kids are today. I just pray that somehow that kind of a liberty and that kind of sacrifice will be in our hearts forever. Hallelujah, hallelujah, hallelujah! ...

Loren and Milly Triplett served the Assembly of God in Nicaragua for twelve years. Loren was general manager for seven years of what later became Life Publishers. For sixteen years he was field director for Latin America and the Caribbean. In 1989 at the General Council, he was elected Executive Director of Foreign Missions where he served his Lord and the Assemblies of God until his retirement in 1997.

A Tribute to Loren and Milly Triplett

... The best thing I can say about them is that they have been "friends." The time I first met the Tripletts was a day in July 1953 on the campground in Lexington, Nebraska. It was that day the Lord catapulted this family into missions in an unprecedented way. I was 18 at the time, and had just finished my first year in Bible College. I was with my parents, Paul and Virginia Weidman, and Faith, my sister. They had just come home on furlough from Africa, and so drove up from Kansas to visit the Nebraska Camp.

It was a great Sunday. W. I. Evans was morning speaker, and I knew him. He was President of Central Bible College. That afternoon, the evangelist whose name was Robinson, if I recall correctly preached in the Missions Rally. It was awesome and the power and the presence of God was electric. At the conclusion of the message, Loren Triplett made his way to the front of the tabernacle, and said that God had called them to be missionaries.

Immediately, the Evangelist said "We must send them forth." People started streaming to the front and pinned money on Milly and Loren's clothes. Everyone was weeping, broken under the presence of the Lord. They were soon covered with bills of many denominations. People promised their automobiles, some gave their livestock. My friend, Phil Jones, gave every penny he had in the offering that followed. He was like me, just a Bible School student, and afterward when I invited him to go have a bite with me, he said he had given everything he had in the offering. I bought him "lunch" or "supper," or whatever it was. It was an amazing sum that was tallied up, and again, I am not sure of the exact figure but my recollection was something like $17,000 came in through cash and pledges. It was enough to cover their budget, their fare, and they were ready to go. For 1953, it was a HUGE offering. Word was sent to Springfield and the Foreign Missions Department---FMD, that "Nebraska had a missionary ready to go" and in days, the Tripletts were on the way to the field. I will never forget it.

Later, Betty and I as missionaries ourselves met up with Delta Kessler, Loren's sister in Ghana. The elder Tripletts visited Ghana during our sojourn there. We enjoyed their ministry. Years later, coming home to Springfield, Missouri we would see Milly's face at the reception desk at Headquarters. We had so much fun kidding around while waiting to get an appointment with the "powers that be" on the third floor ... Then Loren became one of those powers ... and made her "lose her job." Milly just smiled. She was always flexible.

Our kids and their kids went to school together. They helped each other out, played soccer, moved stuff in the pickup truck! We were at various camps and district meetings, like the Arizona Council together. It was always a warm and wonderful time ...

One day when I was in Graduate School, Loren spoke in the School Chapel time. It was at least twenty years ago. He preached on Samuel. He said, "I want to always be like a child, teachable. When God speaks, I want to answer. 'Speak Lord, your servant heareth ... '" And Loren Triplett showed that humility always.

One day, I don't even remember when or which missionary convention it was. I just know I was a rookie missionary about 29 years old. Loren was my roommate. The parsonage was small. We each had not much more than a cot. There was no room for a desk. One had to kind of lay across the bed to study or prepare. What I remember most was Loren praying. In the morning before the day began, and in the evening. On his knees, by the side of that bed, he'd pray aloud. And I heard him pray for me. The little 18 year old nobody who stood in awe that day in 1953 at Nebraska Camp when God sent forth this mighty veteran and his wife as warriors in missions. Loren and Milly. Inspiration, Faith, Love for God, HEART, they had it all. Nebraska can be proud.

(Written by John and Betty Weidman, missionaries to West Africa, in 1998.)

Sister Lester Dickinson Remembers the Memories of the 1953 District Camp

I remember the camp meeting in Lexington in 1953 when Loren Triplett shared their call to the mission field.

Camps were well attended in those days. Hundreds of people enjoyed the camps. During this summer people from all over Nebraska came to Lexington. (The camp grounds would have been only twelve years old.) This Sunday, I can still remember seeing the people come from the villages, towns, cities, farms and ranches. It was a wonderful day. I had never been in a service like that day, when the Spirit of God caused the people to give whatever they had to send the Loren Tripletts to Latin America. And never since that day, have I seen anything like it.

It was such a flow of the Spirit of God moving on the people to give unusual gifts, It was a powerful move of the Holy Spirit. Some brought money; some brought watches; some brought jewelry; some gave clothes; some said they would give cattle; someone even gave a gun. It was simply a unique service.

Children brought pennies, nickels and dimes to the altar. Whatever could be given, was! There was such an overpowering move of the Holy Spirit that day!

The district purchased a car in Lexington and had it delivered to the camp for the Triplett's Speed-the-Light vehicle.

(From a visit with Sister Dickinson on June 23, 1997.)

Wayne and Hazel Hall Remember the 1953 Camp and the Tripletts

The Halls also remember the Sunday when the Tripletts received the support to go to the mission field. Brother Hall closed his eyes and stated, "I can see Loren Triplett sitting on the platform even yet in my mind." He continued, "I can see the people bringing rings, watches, clothes and money! I'd never seen anything like it! And not since then either"!

Wayne remembers Brother Dickinson calling the Foreign Missions in Springfield and telling the missions department, "We have a missionary for you! And we didn't do it according to Hoyle"!!!

(From a visit with Wayne and Hazel Hall on June 23, 1997.)

Millie Triplett Remembers the 1953 Camp

We were in Burwell when we went to camp meeting in 1953. On Lexington campground, The Lord spoke to both of us. I had told Him I didn't know how in the world we could ever get to the mission field. It was in my heart, but I didn't know Loren was over there telling them that we were going: that we someday planned to go.

I had two little children so I had to step out. I was crying and didn't have a hanky. I went and laid on the bed and sobbed and said "Lord, if we wanted to go to the field, we couldn't go." Everything we had was home missions. We had a couch and a baby bed. But the Lord was talking to me in the same way. He just didn't reveal to me that on Sunday He was going to do an absolute miracle at the campgrounds.

People brought fur coats, money, jewelry, cattle, checks. Howard Cummings said he emptied his bank account, and he had just started it. He was a teenage at the time. He didn't have enough money to get home on.

Another couple I saw at Central (I didn't even recognize her) told me this story for the first time. She said, "You know we were at the camp meeting. We were newly married. The Lord told us to give money, and we only had our rent that we had to pay. I don't remember how we got the money for the rent, but we paid our rent on time." The Lord didn't just take from them, He gave too!

(Taken from Loren Triplett's missionary file, Division of Foreign Missions.)

Howard and Irene Dixon Remember the 1953 Camp

Every one on the camp grounds in 1953 was fully aware that God was calling the Tripletts to the mission field. This was in progress for a whole week.

They were living in the West room of the South row of dorms. Our house was North, and I would pass by their room on my way to the Tabernacle. The Tripletts were in their room--I knew they were praying--I wanted to walk softly as I passed their room. Of Course, Sunday was coming, and everyone, young and old, was being called to send the Tripletts to God's Mission Field!!

(Howard and Irene Dixon, letter, May 1999.)

A Historical Perspective from Jerry Spain, *Pastor, Evangelist and Missionary*

In a November 9, 1999 letter Jerry and Joy Spain recall the privilege of being part of the Nebraska Assemblies of God.

My earliest memories include going to a little white-sided Assembly of God at the corner of Fifth and Ray streets in Valentine, Nebraska. I was approximately three years old when my mother Roxie Spain gave her life to the Lord. That decision was made in the early 1940s and impacted our family for eternity. Reverend and Mrs. J.M. Peck were pastoring the church. The Nebraska District had contemplated closing the Valentine Assembly due to the lack of results. The Pecks were called of the Lord to "give it another try". The Sovereign Lord, who loves the lost, knew that a dysfunctional family was living within the sound of music from that church. Mom slipped into the back of the church to listen to songs she remembered from childhood. Life had been tough. At an early age she had married a Roman Catholic veterinarian who had done some work at her father's ranch near Cody, Nebraska. Three children were born to the Murphy family. He left her and the children, destitute and without a source of income. She met my father, Charles Spain. They were married and rented a house near the Assembly of God in Valentine. She was told that the few people who attended the church were "holy rollers." She should stay away from the place. The Holy Spirit told her otherwise.

Mom was committed to her Lord and His church. When the doors were open for a service of any kind, we were present. No questions needed to be asked. If it was time for Sunday school or church, everything else became secondary in importance. Dad refused to attend and even ridiculed those who did. Mom persevered.

In 1943, the church changed pastors. H.W. and Velma Lebsack along with their son, Leland assumed responsibilities. Lee and I were the same age. The first Sunday, the Lebsacks made Lee sit on the platform. Since both Reverend and Mrs. Lebsack participated in the service, they wanted to keep a good eye on their lively son. We were in the same Sunday school class and started kindergarten the same day. We formed a friendship, which has lasted for more than 50 years. To this day, we communicate regularly and neither of us would make a major decision without consulting the other. Other lasting friendships were formed. In a brief historical perspective, it would be impossible to name all of them.

Under the Lebsack's leadership, the church experienced rapid growth. Evangelistic services were conducted in country schoolhouses. Many people were saved. For example, I vividly recall going with Lee and his parents to Litteberg a community just across the South Dakota border. The Holy Spirit was outpoured and many lives were changed. Entire families were swept into the Kingdom and became a part of the Valentine Assembly. Some ranchers would drive as much as fifty miles to attend Sunday services.

Meanwhile the Valentine community was experiencing Pentecostal revival. Evangelists would be scheduled for meetings conducted nightly for weeks. We would erect a tent on a vacant lot near the town center or conduct services on a street corner near the main grocery store. One would never know when Pastor Lebsack would call upon you to give a testimony at one of these services. I still see an African American by the name of Brother Evans who would often come by to visit and play his guitar and sing.

Memories of the Assemblies of God during these times included trips to Lexington Camp. In the beginning, the children and youth would meet at the same time. It seemed like we traveled to another world. Some of the road was not paved, and it was a long journey from Valentine to Lexington. A highlight of the trip was to stop at Thedford or Broken Bow and spend a nickel for a soft drink. The rich could also afford a candy bar. There were also exciting trips to C.A. Conventions. North Camp near Ainsworth/Basset was a normal event during the week of July 4.

Some time around 1950, I was in a missionary service in the old Valentine church. Murray and Majory Brown had returned from Upper Volta and were showing slides and telling about the work in that part of the world. At the end of the service, Brother Brown called for people to respond to the missionary call. There were thousands of people waiting for the Gospel and they needed more workers. I responded. Sister Brown prayed for me. Later, I told my cousin that I was called to be a missionary to Africa. I must have been about 12 years old.

In 1951, the Lebsacks resigned to accept a pastorate in Madison, South Dakota. I was devastated. My best friend was moving to a "far country". Little did I realize how providential this change would be for me. The new pastors were Reverend and Mrs. Harry Blakkolb, Nolan and Norma Joy. By this time, my hormones were humming, and the very first time I saw Norma Joy, I thought she was the most beautiful girl these eyes had ever seen. We were both in the seventh grade. By the time we graduated from Valentine High School in May of 1956, we were considering spending our lives together.

Shortly after graduation, I attended the annual youth camp at the Lexington Camp Grounds. A few weeks prior to this camp, the University of Nebraska had offered me a track scholarship. During the altar services the Lord seem to be reminding me about the commitment I had made to missions. I was not certain about the missionary business, but told the Lord I would follow Him into the ministry, and if that included going overseas, I was ready. I refused the track grant and enrolled as a freshman at Central Bible College in September of 1956. Joy (she chose to drop the name Norma and go by her middle name) decided to stay in Valentine and work for a local dentist.

Bible College was okay. But I was lonely and homesick and I especially missed my girl friend. I could not wait for the Thanksgiving break and a chance to return to the C.A. Convention in Nebraska. It was to be held in North Platte. I do not remember much about the convention. I do remember asking Joy to ride back to Valentine with me. Somewhere between North Platte and Valentine, we talked about making a long-term commitment. We were formally engaged the following year and married in 1958. Her father performed the ceremony. We have now celebrated more than 40 years of marriage and ministry.

Joy assisted me in completing Bible College and we accepted our first pastorate at Chadron during the summer of 1959. The Chadron church was 10 years old. There had only been two previous pastors. We followed Carlyle and Betty Beebe. Our daughter, Kerri was born at Chadron in 1960. We saw some growth in the church and built a new parsonage.

At District Minister‘s Institute at McCook in 1961, Missionary Murray Brown was asked to minister. When he concluded his message, he gave his usual appeal; was there anyone who would be willing to go to Africa? I remember saying to myself, "Lord, you want me to keep that commitment I made ten years ago." I went to the altar again to be prayed for by the same dedicated Nebraska missionaries. I was informed that the first step to going to the mission field was to be ordained by one‘s home District. I was ordained in 1962. I knew that missionary ministry was somewhere on the distant horizon, but we decided to travel as evangelists for a couple years. In 1964, we met with District officials and asked for missionary approval. We were told the District had already approved several missionaries and were asked if we would accept a home missions' position. Lincoln Glad Tidings had built a new building at 12 and D. Due to heavy mortgage payments, the church was unable to pay a pastor an adequate salary. We accepted, and I sold clothes at Miller and Payne for a part time job. After about a year, the church had grown in number and finances and we could give full time to the church. One morning during my prayer time at the altar in the church I heard the Lord say, "what about that matter of my wanting to send you to Africa?"

I left the altar and went where Joy was taking care of a new baby. Kirk was born in May of 1965. I asked, "Are you ready to go to Africa?"

I can still hear her say, "But we just got to Lincoln!" In addition to that, Africa was in terrible turmoil. J. W. Tucker, an A/G missionary was killed in Congo in November 1965. In some of my quiet time the enemy would whisper something like, "That is where they will send you!" I would look at a beautiful wife and two lovely children and say "Spain, what in the wide world are you doing?" The Holy Spirit gave calm assurance. The Lord promised to go with us always. District Superintendent L.W. Dickinson announced to the District Council held at Grand Island in 1966 that we would represent the Nebraska District in Tanzania East Africa. Due to health problems, Norm and Norma Correll and family had just returned from Tanzania to take a job at the Assemblies of God Headquarters in Springfield, Missouri. Brother Dickinson graciously asked the pastors and churches to transfer support from the Corrells to the Spains. The timing of the Lord is marvelous.

A blessed year was spent visiting churches soliciting prayer and financial support. In August, 1967, we said good bye to family at the Omaha airport and headed for Africa. Our first major layover was in Holland to visit missionaries Bud and Lena Mae Leach. After a few days in Europe, we proceeded to our first assignment in Arusha Tanzania.

That was over thirty years ago. These have been glorious, golden days of missionary expansion. Our third child, a lovely daughter named Krisit was born in Nairobi. She is a Kenyan. We speak the language of Swahili and love the people and their culture. We have seen the church grow from about 100 Assemblies in Tanzania to more than 1200. We have had a part in pioneering the work in Kenya. There are more than 1800 churches in that country.

At the time of this writing, Joy and I are serving as Area Directors for 17 countries from Sudan to Madagascar. To put that in geographical perspective, that is larger than the 48 contiguous United States. It includes challenges like Rwanda and Somalia.

Like Missionary Murray Brown, when I am visiting the USA I still ask if there are others who will answer the missionary call to go to Nations of this world with His message.

In a few words of historical perspective, how can one adequately express appreciation to his home District for such a rich heritage. Thanks for sending home missionaries to the Sandhills. Thanks for fellowship and friendships. We will share rewards in heaven.

A Record of the Spains' Trip to Africa (Written October 4, 1967)

Greetings from Kenya!!!! After several delays, we finally arrived! We left Valentine after Sunday night services on August 10, 1967 ... Our plane left from Epply Field at 4 o'clock, needless to say it was a sad parting, but we all survived. We flew non-stop to Chicago ... then on to Cleveland where Leland Lebsack met us, had a lovely time ...

We flew from Kennedy International. We arrived in Amsterdam and the air terminal there was the most modern we have seen, just newly opened in May. The Bud Leaches, former Nebraska District Youth President met us there, and they were a welcome sight! David, their youngest and Kerri's age, presented me with a beautiful bouquet of flowers, a Dutch custom ... We literally fell in love with Holland; it is so quaint, clean, fascinating and the bicycles! You never saw anything like it. Everyone rides and I mean everyone! There is a special lane for the cyclers in the country as well as in town.

Sunday we attended services at the English Protestant Church, a lovely building which had originally been at the Brussels World's Fair, the minister gave a very good message ... We spent two days seeing sights around the Hague, then left from the Amsterdam Airport for Zurich, Switzerland.

In Zurich, Jerry met the Bob Crabtrees from Ohio, who live in Munich, Germany and were new missionaries. They were Bible School classmates of ours. We spent two days with the Williams, Bible School Classmates, who are studying French in Lausanne for a year, then will go to work in France.

We arrived in Rome Saturday evening, September 2nd ... We arrived in Athens shortly after noon on Monday, the 4th, and then to Nairobi. Never once was our luggage checked on our trip. That was a relief, as the suitcases were crammed to the very limit.

We woke up to beautiful Nairobi. Norms (Correll) had prepared us somewhat, but seeing is believing ... The foliage is simply breathtaking. Everything seems to bloom. Even the trees have all colors and kinds of blossoms. Poinsettias grow the size of Lilac Bushes and Germaniums grow like trees.

We are living at a guest house during our three months language study here in Nairobi ... We rented a car and drove to Arusha the first weekend we were here. We really saw Africa that day, thatched roofs and all. Saw quite a bit of wildlife too, the 100 miles or more that weren't black topped were rather rough ... Arusha is a progressive little town.

Jerry preaches through an interpreter. Another of our new couples from Texas drove back from Arusha on Sunday afternoon. They were also in language school and live here at the guest house, we surely enjoy their fellowship.

We now have been in language school for a month. I would hate to state our progress at this point, maybe after a month or so. Sometimes I feel like I haven't learned a thing, and then I know I've a lot more in my Swahili vocabulary than I had when we came, just one word then ... Must close, time to study Swahili ...

(Joy Spain, "Record of Spains Trip to Africa." In *Iceland to Nebraska: The Olafur Hallgrimson Family*, by Margaret L. Sybrant. N.p: N.p., the author, 1985, I-8 to I-13.)

Speed-The-Light Vehicle Helps Jerry and Joy Spain

The Spains sent the following note:

A few weeks ago I was invited to preach at one of our very fine Maasai churches in rural Kenya. The pastor and his lovely wife are both graduates of the East Africa School of Theology where we ministered for 13 years. The church is located at Kajiado, which is on the road to Tanzania. It was a bright, sunny morning and I decided to take advantage of the one hour drive to praise the Lord. As I counted my blessings, I thanked the Lord for calling me to be a missionary. Among other things, I recalled that for most of my missionary career I had traveled over that road in STL vehicles. In fact, one vehicle is still in the mission with more than 200,000 kilometers of "wear and tear."

I preached my message in Kiswahili. People responded to the invitation. We enjoyed a great time of fellowship over an African meal, and I returned home rejoicing. It would have been difficult for any of these things to happen without STL. Please express our Asante Sana (thanks) to our friends in Nebraska *for the Misubishi Lancer.*

("Speed-The-Light Vehicle Helps Jerry and Joy Spain, Area Director for East Africa and the Indian Ocean Basin," *Youth & Christian Education Update*, September 14, 1988.)

Note: the following examples of AIM and MAPS events by Nebraska people are only a very small sample of what God's people are involved in to further the gospel of Jesus Christ. Through the years, God has used Nebraska men and women around the world for Him.

A I M TO Jamaica Report

"Jamaica '88 is history, but the memories will last a lifetime," reports trip coordinator, Jim Byh, Youth Pastor at Lincoln First Assembly. He shares that the trip was a "life-changing experience to each of the 17 members. God's Spirit was evident in a powerful way as our young people were involved in sharing Christ with the nations."

Ocho Rios, the Jamaican city being impacted, is a tourist city where drugs and immoral living are widespread. During the week, Christ was shared with 700 people and more than 50 individuals made decisions to follow Jesus.

From the Youth & Christian Education Update by John Francisco, Director, August 23, 1990

Over the last few weeks several Nebraska A.I.M. teams have been involved in special ministry throughout the world. I am rejoicing in the great things God is doing through our youth.

West Germany – Our young people were involved in nightly crusade services, street ministry and one-on-one witnessing. Eight people received Christ as their savior.

Lima, Peru – Our young people were involved in daily children's services, nightly adult services, as well as street services. Thousands of tracts were passed out. Around 100 adults and children received Christ in the street services; 46 people rededicated their lives to the Lord in the adult services; and literally hundreds of children prayed the prayer of Salvation during the children's services.

Chicago, Illinois – City Limits Urban Camp – Our young people did everything from counseling to washing dishes as 160 inner city kids spent a week at camp getting to know God. Many lives were changed around the altars.

In addition to these highly publicized trips we had one youth group participate in the Annual Chicago Outreach and two youth groups participated in the Denver Outreach. Bellevue Assembly of God also sent A.I.M. teams to Mexico and Paraguay. All in all a tremendous summer of ministry!

Missions Giving Through 1997

From the 1997 annual Report of the Assemblies of God Foreign Missions 88 Nebraska churches participated. This was 98% of the churches giving $1,147,440 to total Division of Foreign Missions. A total World Ministries giving from Nebraska was $1,971,150. Nebraska was among the leading 10 Districts in Foreign Missions Conventions. From the total of 88 churches 86% held missionary services and 57% held missions conventions.

MAPS (Mission America Placement Service) History and Activities of the Chappell Church from Shirley L. Leopold (1998)

Rich Ingersoll writes: "On March 8, 1997 some ninety plus people met in Juarez, Mexico. The mappers came from Nebraska, Colorado, Kansas, and South Dakota, all meeting to minister to the people of Mexico, not only with construction but in many areas.

We were to add a building to the school that we have done construction work for two years. The Lord just keeps blessing Pastor Padilla's ministry with the children of Juarez. They have had to turn down 125 students because of lack of facilities.

Because of our large number of workers, we were able to help build another large building consisting of several classrooms. This is such a special project and always touches the heart and lives of not only the school but those going on the mission trip. I recall on our first meeting with the school they had 36 students and were using pallet buildings. We were just there in December and they now have 465 students and have had to turn away approximately 145 again because of lack of classrooms. We plan to help again in 1999.

Along with the construction we try to meet many other needs that exist. The physical needs of the people were met by our own Dr. Brown and the rest of the medical team. We also had a Kids Crusade with puppets and teaching that touched hundreds of children. And we also had an evangelistic team that prayed and passed out over 300 Spanish Bibles. The times of worship both in the morning and in the evenings are always a special time with the Lord and lives are touched in very special ways.

What a joy it is to be a part of such a giving team of Christian people. We were blessed financially, by the giving of our church MAPS team and the other churches of $18,000.00 for the project, and $2,000.00 for medicine and Bibles.

We are once again going to Mexico in March to work on an orphanage in Chihuahua. This too will be an exciting project as there is much that needs to be done for the forty-eight children. We will be adding a second floor and enlarging the kitchen along with many repairs to the existing buildings. What a place to touch the lives of so many little ones for Christ. Thank you for your support in both finances and prayer."

MAPS has been a big part of the Chappell Church since 1987 when Pastor Al Riskowski was our pastor and started it. Rich Ingersoll helped head it up since 1987. In February of 1998, Rich and Milton Peterson from the Chappell Church are going to Benin, Africa to build two churches.

Almost without exception, the people that have gone on MAPS trips say it is a life changing experience!

1987--Rich and Al went to Kenya to help build a church

1988--Colulacon, Mexico to build a church

1989--Colulacon, Mexico to build a church

1990--Camargo, Mexico to build a church and school

1991--Camargo, Mexico to build a church and school

1992--LaCruz, Mexico to build a church and school

1993--Juarez, Mexico to build a church and school

1994--Juarez, Mexico to build a church and school

1995--Two trips this year, one to Juarez and the other to Taramara Indians

1996--Juarez, Mexico

1997--Chihuahua, Mexico

People from the Chappell Church and surrounding churches built eighteen (18) churches, four (4) school buildings, three (3) orphanages at a cost of $150,000.00 in expenses. The money came from all the different churches. They gave out 1,500 Bibles. Twenty eight Bibles sent to Russia. In the evenings, the mappers had church services and saw many people come to know Jesus as their Lord and Saviourwo of the building project saw the completion of the new sanctuary and the remodeling of the former sanctuary into offices, nursery, and overflow area. This project was accomplished under the capable leadership of Rev. Al Rishowski.

Herbert Griffin, Sr., 1950s

Loren Triplett

Loren and Millie Triplett at the 47th General Council in 1997

Chapter 25: Listing of Nebraska Missionaries

***"How beautiful upon the mountains are the feet of him that bringeth good tidings, that publisheth peace; that bringeth good tidings of good, that publisheth salvation; that saith unto Zion, Thy God reigneth!"* (Isaiah 52:7 NIV)**

Nebraska Missionaries (through 1999)

Some Missionaries From the Early Years:

Elsie Hedges, North India
5/30/19-9/1/22
Lydia Rediger, India
5/30/19-1942 (died 5/1/68)
Erma Miller, Brazil
H. L. Griffin, Belgian Congo, Central Africa
Murray & Marjorie Brown, Africa
Cyle Davises, Chile
Elmer Niles, Nicaragua, Venezuela
Clarence Ollsens, Venezuela

Missionaries in Alphabetical Order (with years of service)

Derik Buescher HM
Chi Alpha, Wyoming

Jim & Kristi Byh AG
7/23/91–
Book of Hope West Africa

George & Christine Carmichael (both deceased) AG
(both) 8/20/46-1/7/49
(George) 7/56-1/60
Jordan, Egypt

Sandy Clopine AG
Africa

Brian Correll AG
12/23/82-12/31/97
Kenya

Norm & Norma Correll (Norma died 4/2008) AG
7/3/58-12/31/66
8/8/75-4/17/2001
East Africa, Kenya & Global University, U. S. Relations

Charles & Nada Dates AG
5/14/86-10/31/2005
Indonesia

Bryan & Laura Davis AG
3/12/2002-
Senegal W Africa

Spud & Joyce DeMent (Joyce died 7/2007) AG
8/26/81-12/31/2007
Kenya, U. S. Relations, Europe

John & Kerrie Fransisco AG
1/1/97-
Peru

Steve & Anna Groseclose AG
1/11/72-7/31/81
Suriname

Wendy Heuvelmann AG
1/13/2002-
North Africa

Jeff Haase MA
Sudan, Africa

Lyndsey Humston, MA
Philippines

Matt & Kristi Kling AG
8/31/2004-
Venezuela, Royal Rangers International

John & Lucille Mazurek (John died 8/13/2005)
8/13/62-7/31/97
Chile

Trent Mettenbrink MA
Mexico

Harold & Bea Mintle AG
Ecuador

Wayne & Diann Nestor (Diann died 10/21/97
5/28/93-10/31/2000
Germany, IMM Europe

Julius & Bertha Olson (Julius died 11/12/84)
8/1/68-3/10/82
Brazil

Vino Rodriguez MA
IMM, Spain

Bonnibel Roll (died 5/7/2003) AG
8/20/63-1/31/90
Ghana, Thailand, Philippines

Jimmy & Jean Root
8/10/87-1/31/93
Colombia

Gene & Karen Schachterle AG
8/6/73-
Thailand, Global University,Life Publishers International, Northern Asia

Jerry & Joy Spain AG
8/1/67-
Tanzania, Kenya, East Africa Africa's Hope

Solomon Wang AG
Southern Asia

Michael Schwebach MA
Northern Asia

Tim Thomas HM
Chicago Inner City

Ellis & Roberta Townsend AG
6/24/70-5/30/74
Panama

Loren & Mildred Triplett AG
10/15/53-11/13/97
Nicaragua, Life Publishers International, Regional Director for Latin America, Executive Director of Assemblies of God World Missions

David & Pauline Wineinger
5/25/83-5/30/87
Nigeria

Missionaries with Nebraska Ties:

Wanda & Ron Sommers AG
Belgium

Missionary Codes

AG = career appointed and general or special appointed Assemblies of God world missionaries
HM = U.S. home missionaries: Chi Alpha, Inner City, Chaplaincy, etc.
MA = missionary associates — 2-year assignments working with career missionaries

Chapter 26: Sketches of the District Superintendents

***"The elders who direct the affairs of the church well are worthy of double honor, especially those whose work is preaching and teaching."* (1 Timothy 5:17 NIV)**

To wrap up this narrative are two chapters on the Nebraska District Council officers. One chapter includes sketches on each of the Nebraska District Superintendents. The second chapter gives a listing of Nebraska District Council officers.

J. C. Rediger (1919-1920)

Joseph C. (Joe) Rediger was the first superintendent of the Nebraska District Assemblies of God from 1919 to 1920.

I can truly join with David of old and cry out, "Bless the Lord, O, my soul and all that is within me, Bless His holy name." As a boy I was reckless, thoughtless and indifferent toward religion. My parents belonged to a formal church, having a form of godliness but denying the power thereof. In this church it was not preached that we had to be born again, and I thinking by having my name connected with the church I was saved, but after studying God's word, I found it was necessary to have our names written in heaven. I was finally led to a meeting which was held in the neighborhood where the word of God was preached and where it was said that we could be saved from sin. I attended and was marvelously saved from sin at the age of sixteen and from that time on I commenced to walk in the light, and the blood of Jesus Christ. His Son, cleansed me from all sin. I was the only one in the family that knew God. My relatives and friends opposed me and even my parents couldn't understand the attitude I took toward God. They thought it strange of me to leave their church and obey the Spirit, but never the less in spite of the opposition God wonderfully blessed my soul, and I became rooted and grounded in God. I walked in all the light I had and as God was thus dealing with me and leading me on I soon became convinced that He was calling me into His service. I tried to hide this so that no one should find it out but in prayer, and testimony meetings, God would give me wonderful liberty, so it soon became known that I was called to the ministry. This was at the age of twenty-three. I then labored under an older minister for a while but was soon left alone as pastor of that church.

Not long after that, trouble arose with the so-called second work of grace people. I being the only minister of the church felt my responsibility and being upright and honest in heart I sought His face to know His will. I soon came to the place where I was misunderstood and fought against and had no fellowship in the Spirit even with those that professed to be sanctified. I soon learned that their lives and dealings did not harmonize with the word of God, neither with the way the Lord was dealing with me. Finally God gathered a small company and we being hungry continued to seek God's face and received wonderful blessings. God led us on step by step until the full light came then we humbled our hearts and tarried before God. He baptized me and many others with the Holy Ghost and every one received the Bible evidence and spoke with other tongues as the Spirit gave utterance. Glory to His name.

Now the question arises what are you going to do with your first blessings--throw them away? God forbid. That was all good in its place but now the fullness has come. I am therefore settled once for all. The thirst is quenched as far as seeking the Holy Spirit is concerned. But it means to go on with God and walk in the light as He gives it and thus be ready at His appearing. Glory to His precious name. ~ J. C. Rediger.

(J. C. Rediger, "Personal Testimony of Pastor J. C. Rediger," *Gospel Witness*, Vol. I, No. IV, [1915?], p. 3.)

George W. Clopine (1920-1926)

George W. Clopine served as second superintendent of the Nebraska Assemblies of God from 1920 to 1926.

George Washington Clopine, the son of George A. and Elizabeth Clopine, was born on April 19, 1875, in Cortland, Nebraska. He was the fourth child of a family of five.

On March 28, 1905, he married Emma Pearl Kleinkemper, who was his loyal helpmate through all his years of ministry. God blessed their home with two sons, Mervin E., Oshkosh, Nebraska, and Fay D. of Chanute, Kansas.

In 1913, G. W. Clopine was ordained an elder in the Baptist church, and two years later, after having pastored a church in Dallas, Texas, for a year, he was ordained with the General Council of the Assemblies of God on March 20, 1915.

From Dallas, Texas, Clopine returned to Nebraska in 1917, where he evangelized and helped to establish the Chappell Assembly of God. Rev. Irl J. Walker was his coworker in these meetings.

Soon after Chappell Assembly was founded, the Nebraska District was organized. J. W. Rediger was elected as the first chairman, and Clopine served as district secretary-treasurer. The following year he was elected to the office of chairman, which position he held for six consecutive years.

These were difficult years. He traveled across the state in an open touring car in all kinds of weather over roads that were but trails across the prairie. He served not for the money he received, but because the love of God constrained him as is clearly shown by the fact that the remuneration for his entire eight years of district service was less than $1,000. He was acquainted with hardships, but never distressed by them.

Though Brother Clopine led a very active public life, his first thoughts were for his family.

In addition to serving as an officer with the Nebraska District, Clopine also pastored the following Assemblies of God congregations: Chappell, Nebraska; North Platte, Nebraska; Pleasant Green, Kansas; Sunol, Nebraska; and the Miller Assembly, Hill City, Kansas.

He continued preaching until 1943 when failing health forced his retirement. The rest of his days, he spent in study and advisory ministry.

George W. Clopine lived a rich and full life, passing away on March 5, 1954, at his home, 220 North Highland, in Chanute, Kansas.

(Information compiled from his eulogy, March 10, 1954; letters and personal papers supplied by his descendants.)

Allen R. Shaffer (1926-1927)

Allen Shaffer was the third superintendent of the Nebraska District.

Allen R. Shaffer was ordained September 2, 1923 by the Nebraska District Council. He was issued national credentials on November 13, 1923. He was recommended by G. W. Clopine, the Nebraska District Chairman. At that time he was 50 years old, which would indicate that he was born in 1873. He was married and had 5 children at the time and lived in Franklin, Nebraska. His ministerial application showed he had a common education [probably 8th grade].

After serving as district chairman for approximately one year, he became an evangelist, living at Beaver City and Riverton, Nebraska. He moved to Canton, Oklahoma, in the fall of 1934 and from there he moved to Bridgeport, Washington. He moved back to Nebraska in 1938 and ministered as an evangelist at Guide Rock and Red Cloud, Nebraska. His final years were spent at Twin Falls, Idaho. He was on the evangelistic field for twenty years and ministered in all of the states west of the Missouri River. He passed away on January 23, 1956 at Twin Falls, Idaho.

(The above information comes from Allen Shaffer's ministerial file and other resources at the Flower Pentecostal Heritage Center.)

Milton Smith (1927-1929)

Milton Smith was ordained by the Nebraska District council on August 16, 1925 as an evangelist while living at Milford, Nebraska. At that time he was 28 years old, married, and had 3 children. His birth year would have been 1897. His ministerial application showed he had a seventh grade education. He was recommended by G. W. Clopine and ordained on the national level on August 27, 1925.

Smith was a pastor and evangelist at Bayard, Nebraska from 1926-1927. Then while living at Milford, he served as Nebraska District Superintendent from 1927 to 1929. He later lived in California.

(The above information comes from Milton Smith's ministerial file and other resources at the Flower Pentecostal Heritage Center.)

E. W. White (1929-1934)

Edgar W. White was superintendent for the Nebraska District of the Assemblies of God from 1929 to 1934. Here is a report he delivered as superintendent in 1932.

To all the brethren and especially to the Churches of Nebraska. Greetings; Grace be unto you and peace from God our Father, and from our Lord Jesus Christ. Who gave himself for our sins, that he might deliver us from this present evil world according to the will of God and our Father: To whom be glory forever and ever, Amen.

It is indeed a pleasure to write to you thru the pages of our Nebraska Pentecostal Fellowship, for it is of our Magazine that I wish to write. The brethren have long felt the need of a medium through which we could keep in closer touch one with the other, and through which we would be able to get the Gospel into homes that heretofore have not been reached. And as we contemplate the possibilities of such a paper (as we trust this shall be). Reports from the field, testimonies, sermons by our own Nebraska brethren: in fact a panoramic view of the work of the Lord in Nebraska coming into your home every month, to inspire your faith and to keep you in touch with your sister Assembly in the other part of the state; a report of revivals. Fellowship meetings, etc., etc.: our hearts are filled with gratitude that God has made it possible, for of a truth we feel that God has had his hand upon this part of the District work, and is working it out in His own time--and NOW is working time.

This paper will be largely what we make it by the help of the Lord. Much prayer is needed, and your co-operation will be greatly appreciated; a testimony, a report or sermon sent in will go a long way toward making it a success. Also much patience and forbearance will need to be exercised. Always remember the Editor is doing his best and will get your article in if possible. It is by no means a small job to glean from all the material sent in and get the variety that will make up the best reading material possible to offer to the public.

We thank you in advance for your hearty cooperation in getting this initial copy before the public. We feel sure that once we get it into the hands of (especially our Pentecostal people) we will experience no further trouble in disposing of every copy. We therefore suggest that you ascertain just how many copies you will be able to make use of, and send your orders in, and when your papers come, appoint one of your Pentecostal boys. "A Pentecostal News Boy." Let him take his bike and deliver the papers, collecting ten cents per copy; thus he can feel that he is doing something for his Lord; or let the Christ Ambassadors take the responsibility of delivery and collection, for the Nebraska Pentecostal Fellowship, thus increasing their activities and proving a greater blessing in the Assembly.

Trusting you will catch the vision of this wonderful opportunity to strengthen the fellowship for the work of the ministry, and to spreading the Pentecostal message into every town and city in Nebraska, I am Yours for, The Nebraska Pentecostal Fellowship. Edgar W. White.

THE OPEN DOOR: In the eighth verse of the third chapter of Revelation we find the words of our Lord, "I have set before thee an open door." Oh, the possibilities that are set before us! An open door set before us by our Lord, and He has said that "by me" if any man will enter in he shall go in and out and find pasture. As we venture in through the open door it is so new, so strange and wonderful, we are barely able to realize its reality--but it is real. Hallelujah!

... And to those who will obey, a great door and effectual is opened; but remember there are many adversaries. But there is no victory without a battle; no crown without a cross, an effective door is opened to us--let us enter in.

... Jesus saith. "I am the door, by me if any man enter in, he shall be saved." Dear Soul, let us enter in, while it is yet day, and the Door stands open.

(E. W. White, "Superintendent's Report," *Nebraska Pentecostal Fellowship,* Vol. 1:1, March, 1932.)

Edgar Wayne White was born March 24, 1897. He was ordained by the Nebraska Disrict on August 3, 1914. White passed away on September 22, 1960 at Cottage Grove, Oregon.

Albert M. Alber (1934-1945)

A.M. Alber was superintendent of the Nebraska District from 1934 to 1945. He received a certificate for 50 Years of ministry in 1978.

A. M. Alber was born on October 7, 1896 and attended Mennonite public prade school in Reno County, Kansas. He was married in 1917.

Brother Alber said, "He went to the altar for salvation twice, once in 1912 and the other time in 1914. It was in 1914 that I really broke through to a real experience, and God met my life for a lifetime, you might say. I soon went into the ministry and preached for all these years."

"In 1914," Brother Alber continued, "my father fell sick. The doctors said he had hardening of the arteries and heart trouble and gave little hope. I was very upset. I couldn't reconcile myself to my father dying. I would go into the field and drive my team up and down the furrows and pray. 'Oh God, save my father, and I will serve you.'

"A preacher from Tennessee came to our community to hold revival. He and some of the men gathered around my father's bed and prayed for him. My father got up and knelt on the other side of the bed. Then he walked out into the dining room, and we looked at him and wondered if it would last. We were full of doubts, in spite of the faith we had. He sat in a chair, a straight chair for a while. Then we ate supper; he ate a good supper. He hadn't been eating solid foods for quite a while. I remember very well the morning when he called us. It was the same old voice that used to ring up the stairs, 'Boys get up!' Of course, we piled down very quickly, because we wanted to see how dad was getting along. There was no disturbance through the night, and we slept so solidly. He also ate breakfast with us that morning. From then on, he grew steadily stronger and lived with us another six years.

"As a result of my father's healing, it gave acceleration to the revival that was going on, and it grew to such proportions that we had to move into a conference tent to hold the people. The conference tent held several hundred people ... People came from far and near. The interest just increased and increased, the preaching increased, and the singing increased. It was a gloriously powerful meeting. 150 people were saved in that revival.

"After that revival, two men came from California and brought the message of the baptism of the Holy Ghost. They preached that when you receive the baptism of the Holy Spirit you speak in tongues as the Spirit gives utterance as in the early church."

In an interview, Albert Alber told about his personal experience in receiving the baptism of the Holy Spirit:

"Well, I fell under the power like many people in those days. The glory of God came down and filled my life. I say life because it isn't enough to say He filled my heart. He has done so much for me, and I want to be faithful to the end."

Alber went to Chicago and worked in a mission from 1915 to 1918. It was there he felt God dealing with his soul, whether he was going to be true to his commitment of serving God. He then went back to Sterling, Kansas, worked in a lumberyard, farmed, and also did evangelistic and pastoral work while there. He was ordained in 1918 and came into the Assemblies of God in the 1920s.

In about 1926 he went to Chappell and took a church there. Because he was surrounded by Assemblies of God people he joined the Assemblies. Alber served as assistant superintendent from 1930 to 1932; secretary/treasurer from 1932 to 1934; and superintendent of the Nebraska District from 1934 to 1945.

Brother Alber also told about the beginnings of the Lexington camp:

"It wasn't easy going in those days. It happens that the government was selling homes and buildings in an area where they were going to make a dam. We went out there before they started and bought our buildings, took them down, and hauled them into Lexington to the camp ground. The work was done mostly by the preachers. Those were the days when you rolled up your sleeves and worked, and you got as dirty and black as the rest of them.

"Preaching didn't just involve being behind the pulpit, it meant many things. Your adaptation to the kind of work that presented itself was tremendous."

A. M. Alber pastored at Sioux City, Iowa and Des Moines, Iowa. He also ministered in conventions and camp meetings across the Midwest throughout the years. He said, "Instead of going on vacation, I took camp meetings."

In a June 19, 1981 interview, Albert Alber shared a charge:

"As I look back over the years, over 60 years, I realize the work of the Lord has gone forward. We preached the Word in season and out of season, with all long suffering, as Paul says. I am sure God is with us even in the nursing home. So I want to give my precious wife credit for all she did through the years. She reared the family, and I preached the gospel. That is a pretty good combination. I conclude by saying let every man be faithful, be honest, be upright, and God will see you through."

He passed away on June 4, 1984.

(Personal information about Albert M. Alber is taken from an interview by Larry Matwichuk, June 19, 1981; personal data sheet; and *The Shepherd's Staff*, edited by R. D. E. Smith. Minneapolis, MN: Northern Gospel Publishing House, 1946.)

Melvin Frank Brandt (1945-1951)

Melvin Brandt was superintendent of the Nebraska District from 1945 to 1951.

Melvin Frank Brank was born in the small community of Brandt, South Dakota March 23, 1904. He attended school in South Dakota. M. F. Brandt came to know the Lord Jesus Christ as his personal Savior at the age of 15 in Watertown, South Dakota. This city was also where he and Ruth Hale were united in marriage on February 26, 1926. Shortly after marriage they embarked on a trip to San Jose, California, in their Model T Ford. They made their church home in San Jose at The Upper Room Mission where he served as a deacon. He engaged in an automobile repair business, working on Pierce Arrow and Essex automobiles, and in addition, a fleet of trucks.

In 1929, the couple and new baby daughter, Retha Louise, moved back to Watertown, South Dakota where they established an Assemblies of God Church. While in Watertown their son, Eugene was born. In 1933, they moved to Nebraska where they undertook to pioneer a number of churches. He was ordained by the Nebraska District on April 12, 1934.

Their first Nebraska church was in the town of Ainsworth. They welcomed their third child, a daughter, Velda Ruth in Ainsworth. While in Ainsworth, he was also selected by the Nebraska District Council to become the District's Christ's Ambassadors President, now known as the District Youth Director.

Other new churches established by him, following Ainsworth, were Bassett and Woodlake. He evangelized throughout Northern Nebraska. The church at Milford called him to be their pastor in 1936, and in 1939 he established a new church in Beatrice. The church at Lincoln called him as pastor in 1939. While there in 1945, the Nebraska District Council of the Assemblies of God called him to accept the office of district superintendent, which gave him the oversight of 95 Assemblies of God churches throughout the state.

Scottsbluff called him to be their pastor in 1952. In addition to pastoring, he opened a religious book store there. In 1954, he was requested by the denomination's headquarters in Springfield, Missouri, to come and open a bookstore for the Gospel Publishing House.

In his younger days, his fiery preaching would "bring the house down." "I'm glad I'm a Christian, and not a Republican or Democrat," he would sometimes voice. When he entered a room, his presence was made known by his shouting a loud "Hallelujah," with that accent that made you know it was M. F. Brandt who had arrived.

Romans 1:15-16 "I am ready to preach the gospel. For I am not ashamed of the Gospel of Christ, for it is the power of God unto salvation to everyone that believeth!"

Brandt passed away on March 19, 1995 at Omaha, Nebraska. No doubt the example of M. F. and Ruth Brandt, as faithful ministers of the gospel, had its influence!

(Information for Melvin Frank Brandt was taken from his eulogy, March 23, 1995, by Taylor Holden, and submitted by his daughter Retha Goss, and from his ministerial file.)

Lester W. Dickinson (1951-1975)

Lester Dickinson was superintendent of the Nebraska District from 1951 to 1975. He was honored for 50 years of ministry in 1985.

During Family Camp of 1951 the Ministers and Delegates in a special District Council meeting, asked me to be their District Superintendent. Brother M. F. Brandt had resigned this position. I was elected on the nominating ballot. Again this was a very frustrating experience, as I felt so completely overcome with the vastness of the position. This position I felt was far above my qualifications and it was, but again we found God's requirements are always met with His wisdom and strength working through us to complete the task He asks us to do. To be the President of this large Corporation, manage the business of the Corporation, lead the church and all else that was required of the District Superintendent was overwhelming to say the least.

We moved into the District Home in Grand Island September 1, 1951. This was to change our family lifestyle as I would be away from home most of the time, leaving Gary and his mother at home alone. Again we found God and His provision all sufficient ...

The years following were very interesting and challenging to say the least. We both loved pastoring and wanted to get back into fulltime pastoral work, but it seemed the Lord had other plans, and we found ourselves involved in the District work for almost 24 years, as the District Superintendent of the Nebraska District Council of the Assemblies of God, 1951 to 1975 ...

I participated or ministered in 91 dedications, one type or another, ministered 1,400 times in churches, attended and spoke in approximately 500 Fellowship meetings, conducted approximately 200 business meetings.

The Camp program possibly was the major involvement through the years. The family camp of 1952 was not up to what we thought it should be, so we knew something had to be done to pump new life into it or the camping program that had been a blessing to so many would go as others across the country had gone.

The District Council in 1953 was conducted in the Lexington church. We appointed a Camp Committee made up of seven laymen and C. T. Beem as their chairman. The committee met at the camp ground, went over the facilities, came back to the district council with their committee recommendations. They made an observation, "We have added to some of the buildings until there is no place to go." They recommended a number of things in the way of improvements, but one was a New Air Conditioned Tabernacle and the old tabernacle to be remodeled into a kitchen and dining hall.

In 1961 the district council in session voted to proceed with the building of the new tabernacle as per the plans that had been drawn and submitted to the council. Immediately wheels begin to turn toward this project and by August of that same year we moved the camp meeting into the new air conditioned tabernacle.

Along with this updating we laid a sewer line one half mile east and connected it to the Lexington City Sewer. Other improvements were also carried through. The vision of those laymen, such as Floyd Roll, Bill Kaighan, John Pierney, Mervin Clopine and others were carried through.

The following year the old tabernacle was remodeled into a nice kitchen and dining hall. Many other improvements were realized during those years.

(Information on Lester W. Dickinson compiled from Nebraska District records and Lester W. Dickinson personal writings.)

Lester W. Dickinson was born October 6, 1910. He was ordained on April 8, 1937. Dickinson passed away on January 28, 1989.

James Wilkins (1975-1987)

James D. Wilkins was Nebraska District Superintendent from 1975 to 1987. He also served as assistant district superintendent for Nebraska for one year. He has been a member of the general presbytery of the General Council of the Assemblies of God since April of 1974. Jim pastored in Nebraska and California. While in California, he served as a district presbyter and executive presbyter for the Northern California/Nevada District Council.

During the twelve years Jim was Superintendent a new gym and indoor swimming pool was built on the campgrounds at Lexington. His real desire was to see a combination motel and dorm constructed there. That undertaking got underway during the last couple of years when he was in office. The building was named after Mr. Kids Kamp, Paul Ackerman. Though it was not quite completed when the Wilkins resigned and moved to California, it was finished soon after, and they were able to come back for the dedication.

It was under the direction of Brother Wilkins that the district office was brought into the computer age. During that time the staff grew. In addition to the Superintendent and D-CAP there were three secretaries and an administrative assistant to the superintendent in the office building at 1503 West 2nd Street.

Brother Jim Wilkins‘ main burden was for church planting. In 1975, there were 66 churches in the District. At the time of Wilkins‘ resignation in 1987, there were 85.

(Jim Wilkins supplied the above report in 1997.)

Robert L. Nazarenus (1987-2005)

Robert L. Nazarenus served as Nebraska District Secretary/Treasurer and then as Nebraska District Superintendent from 1987 to 2005.

Highlights of the past years include the times we have had with our ministry team and churches. It is a very special blessing to see an increasing hunger for God among us. This makes the thousands of miles and hundreds of hours behind the steering wheel more than tolerable.

1992 was seventy-five years since the first Nebraska Camp Meeting in Auburn, Nebraska. The outpouring of the Holy Spirit was having a definite impact on the Midlands.

Since those days, God has been gracious to allow wonderful growth in Our Fellowship. To date (1992) we have 85 churches in the Nebraska District and 208 ministers on our roster. Our number of Members and Adherents reaches toward 18,000. The Decade of Harvest is well into the third year.

We have been blessed with a marvelous heritage. Great men and women of God have ministered faithfully as lay persons, ministers, missionaries, and evangelists.

Ministry in our local churches is always a joy filled experience. As we travel the district, we are sensitive to a fresh wind of the Holy Spirit blowing in many churches and communities. It is so refreshing to see people who have a heart for God. As we unite our hearts in prayer and faith, we will see unprecedented revival.

As superintendent, I am privileged to be part of the General Presbytery, North Central Bible College Board of Regents and the board of directors for Highlands Child Placement Service.

By the close of 1994 we anticipate that our Camp and Conference facilities will be on a regular preventive maintenance schedule, which hopefully will help us avoid unexpected expenditures.

In the mid-90's the Nebraska District Council and Sandhills' Section Churches sponsored *The Rural Evangelism Conference* at Thedford. Speaker, "Rev. Robert Nazarenus is a great supporter of evangelism in general. His understanding and love for small towns and rural people is evident in the leadership he gives to each of us. His heartbeat is for revival."

Looking back at the final year of the 1900's there are many things for which to be thankful. God's faithfulness, mercies and love have certainly been evidenced.

The rapid changes in technology have been the catalyst to effect several changes to our office. Enhancements in computer software and hardware have been made in order to keep us as close to the cutting edge of service as resources will allow.

The positive reports coming to the District Office are filled with excitement and new direction for ministry. Special thanks to all of you who make our ministry a wonderful delight. You are a special blessing to both Mary and me.

(This information is extracted from the *Nebraska District Council of the Assemblies of God Year-End Reports.)*

Dwight A. Sandoz (2005-present)

Dwight Sandoz is the current Nebraska District Superintendent, having taken office in 2005.

Chapter 27: Officers of the Nebraska District

"And when they had ordained them elders in every church, and had prayed with fasting, they commended them to the Lord, on whom they believed." (Acts 14:23 KJV)

A Partial listing of the Officers of theNebraska District

Chairmen/Superintendents:

1919-1920	J. C. Rediger
1920-1926	George W. Clopine
1926-1927	A. R. Shafer
1927-1929	Milton Smith
1929-1934	E. W. White
1934-1945	Albert M. Alber
1945-1951	Melvin Frank Brandt
1951-1975	Lester W. Dickinson
1975-1987	James Wilkins
1987-2005	Robert L. Nazarenus
2005-present	Dwight A. Sandoz

From the 50th Anniversary Book comes a list of the early Secretary/Treasurers:

George Clopine	1919
Merle Roll	1930
A. M. Alber	1931-33
Glen Millard	1934-35
R. S. Barnes	1939-42
L. W. Dickinson	1943-50
Clyde King	1951-52; 1956-58
Erwin Rohde	1962-66
L. E. Wilkens	1968-74
S. K. Biffle, Jr.	1975
Howard Rice	1976-81; 1987-92
David Argue	1982-84
Robert Nazarenus,	1985, 86
K. Mel Johnson	1993-99

Early Christ's Ambassadors — D-CAPS

W. M. Lamar	1931-33
M. F. Brandt	1938
Lester Dickinson	1939
Charles Blair	1942
Clyde King	1943-44
J. M. Peck	1945
Carlyle Beebe	1947-48
Forest McClellan	1949
Delbert Turner	1952-55
Norman Correll	1955-56
Roscoe Leach	1957-60

Now called Director of Youth and Christian Education

James Wilkins	1963-66
Spud DeMent	1966-72
John Stocker	1973-76
Ted Brust	1979-82
David Graves	1983-88
John Fransisco	1989-95
Rick Lorimer	1996-99

Appendix 1: Significant Events of the Assemblies of God

Compiled by Glenn W. Gohr

The following events provide a background for understanding the role of the Nebraska District of the Assemblies of God in church history. They are adapted from time lines which originally appeared in the *Pentecostal Evangel*, April 2, 1989; April 10, 1994, and September 29, 1996, and in *Enrichment*, Fall 1999.

1901—Agnes N. Ozman and others speak in tongues at Charles Parham's Bible school in Topeka, Kansas.

1906—Azusa Street revival begins in Los Angeles under William J. Seymour.

1910—Lillian Trasher goes to Egypt to found the Assiout Orphanage (now Lillian Trasher Orphanage).

1912—The Tri-State (Interstate) Camp Meeting held at Eureka Springs, Arkansas was instrumental in the formation of the Assemblies of God. That year also, Maria B. Woodworth-Etter preaches a campaign in Dallas, Texas, gaining a large Pentecostal following.

1913—*Word and Witness* paper issued a call for Pentecostals to meet at Hot Springs, Arkansas to organize.

1914—Some 300 people gathered in Hot Springs, Arkansas, April 2-12, for the organizational meeting of the Assemblies of God. E. N Bell elected first chairman; J. Roswell Flower elected secretary. The *Christian Evangel* and *Word and Witness* became the official publications of the new fellowship. First headquarters was at Findlay, Ohio, on the campus of T. K. Leonard's Gospel School and printing facilities.

Second General Council held in Chicago, November 15-29, authorized raising $5,000 for additional printing equipment. A. P. Collins elected chairman.

1915—AG headquarters moved to St. Louis, Missouri. J. W. Welch elected chairman.

1916—Statement of Fundamental Truths adopted which included the Trinitarian position.

1917—Foreign Missions Committee organized. Missionary offerings for the year — $10,223.98.

1918—AG headquarters relocated to Springfield, Missouri.

1919—Name of the official magazine changed to the *Pentecostal Evangel*. Foreign Missions Department established with J. Roswell Flower as the first missionary secretary. Gospel Publishing House offered new periodicals.

1920—E. N. Bell followed J. W. Welch as chairman. Midwest Bible School at Auburn, Nebraska, became the first AG Bible school; later that year Southern California Bible Institute started in Pasadena.

1921—Stanley H. Frodsham elected editor of the *Pentecostal Evangel*.

1922—Central Bible Institute (now Central Bible College) started in the basement of Central Assembly of God in Springfield, Missouri.

1923—E. N. Bell died in office; J. W. Welch succeeded him.

1924—Gospel Publishing House produced its first songbook, *Songs of Pentecostal Fellowship*.

1925—W. T. Gaston elected chairman. Etta Calhoun organized the first Women‘s Missionary Council.

1926—Latin American Bible Institute in California and Latin American Bible Institute in Texas, were both founded to minister to Hispanics.

1927—Constitution and bylaws adopted by the growing Fellowship. Noel Perkin became missionary secretary. Southwestern Bible School founded in Enid, Oklahoma (now Southwestern Assemblies of God University in Waxahachie, TX). Youth officially recognized as "Christ‘s Ambassadors."

1929—E. S. Williams elected general superintendent; North Central Bible Institute (now North Central University) opened in Minneapolis.

1935—A benefit fund established for retired ministers (basis for the present-day Aged Ministers Assistance). Marcus Grable named head of the Sunday School Department. Three Bible schools opened — Northwest in Washington; Peniel in Kentucky; and South-Eastern in Alabama (now Southeastern University in Lakeland, FL).

1936—First radio broadcast from AG headquarters is aired in Springfield, Missouri on KWTO radio.

1937—Education Department established. Home Missions Department organized with Fred Vogler as first executive.

1938—*C. A. Herald* magazine started for youth. Eastern Bible Institute (now Valley Forge Christian College) opened in Pennsylvania.

1939—*Sunday School Counselor* first printed as a monthly magazine for workers. Lillian Trasher is hailed as "the greatest woman in Egypt."

1940—First national youth conference and first national Sunday school convention held in Springfield, Missouri.

1941—Chaplaincy Department developed as a ministry to military personnel. *Reveille* magazine introduced for military personnel.

1943—National Christ‘s Ambassadors Department established with Ralph Harris as secretary. AG became a charter member of the National Association of Evangelicals.

1943—A missionary conference set goals for Assemblies of God missions, including the appointment of field secretaries for all major areas.

1944—Speed-the-Light began to raise funds for vehicles for missionaries. Hillcrest Children‘s Home in Hot Springs, Arkansas, endorsed by the AG. Minister‘s Benefit Association established as a retirement and savings program for AG ministers.

1945—Radio Department started with Thomas F. Zimmerman as director.

1946—*Sermons in Song* radio broadcast introduced. Spanish Literature Department founded.

1947—Publications Department created to supervise printing plant operations and editorial staffs. Berean School of the Bible established as a correspondence program. Dead Sea Scrolls are discovered.

1948—Benevolence Department created. Children‘s program, *The Gospel Rocket*, broadcast. Assemblies of God became charter member of Pentecostal Fellowship of North America. Lakewood Park Bible School (now Trinity Bible College) started.

1949—Wesley R. Steelberg succeeded E. S. Williams as general superintendent. New printing plant built on Boonville Avenue in Springfield. Boys and Girls Missionary Crusade began. Robert C. Cunningham succeeds Stanley H. Frodsham as editor of the *Pentecostal Evangel*.

1950—The Assemblies of God radio program lengthened to 30 minutes and was renamed *Revivaltime* with Wesley Steelberg as speaker.

1951—Women‘s Missionary Council (now Women‘s Ministries Department) established.

1952—Gayle F. Lewis filled unexpired term of W. R. Steelberg, who died while on a trip to Europe. The Men‘s Fellowship Department (now Men‘s Ministries) organized.

1953—Ralph Riggs elected general superintendent. *Revivaltime* gained first full-time speaker, C. M. Ward, and aired on the ABC radio network.

1955—Evangel College (now Evangel University), a liberal arts college, started in Springfield, Missouri on the site of the former O‘Reilly Hospital. Missionettes (now Girls Ministries) launched for girls.

1956—Music Department established.

1957—*Melodies of Praise* hymnal published. Global Conquest (later called Good News Crusades) started to evangelize world‘s urban areas.

1959—Thomas F. Zimmerman elected general superintendent. Noel Perkin succeeded by J. Philip Hogan as executive director of Foreign Missions. Teen Challenge program instituted by David Wilkerson.

1960—Bethany Retirement Home in Lakeland, Florida, dedicated.

1961—A four story administration building is built adjoining the printing plant on Boonville Avenue in Springfield, Missouri. Light-for-the-Lost founded to provide literature for overseas.

1962—Royal Rangers started for boys ages 5-17. Bible Quiz and Teen Talent Search (later renamed Fine Arts Festival) program launched.

1963—Mobilization and Placement Service (MAPS) started to provide short-term missions assignments. David Wilkerson publishes *The Cross and the Switchblade*.

1964—50th Anniversary Convention for the Assemblies of God held in Springfield, April 20-23. Missionary J. W. Tucker martyred in Congo (Zaire).

1965—*Advance* magazine first published for ministers. Disaster Relief established. The Young Women‘s Auxiliary (Y‘s) started.

1966—Ambassadors in Mission (AIM) developed to encourage overseas evangelism. Action Crusades begun to train for witnessing. Highlands Child Placement Center opened in Kansas City, Missouri.

1967—International Correspondence Institute (ICI) launched.

1968—The Council on Evangelism in St. Louis was a significant turning point as the church redefined its goals. A 10-acre tract in Phoenix, Arizona, dedicated as campus for American Indian Bible Institute (now American Indian College).

1969—*Hymns of Glorious Praise* published.

1971—AG Headquarters departments regrouped into divisions of Christian Education, Church Ministries, Communications,

Foreign Missions, Home Missions, Publication, and Treasury.

1972—A six story distribution center was added to the AG headquarters complex in Springfield. Council on Spiritual Life held in Minneapolis.

1973—Assemblies of God Graduate School (now Assemblies of God Theological Seminary) established in Springfield, Missouri. Maranatha Village retirement center opened in Springfield.

1974—*Turning Point*, a television ministry, released.

1976—Gloria Orengo became first woman military chaplain appointed by the Assemblies of God.

1977—Church Loans Department created. Deferred Giving and Trusts Department authorized. Assemblies of God Archives (now Flower Pentecostal Heritage Center) established.

1979—Dan Betzer succeeded C. M. Ward as speaker of the *Revivaltime* radio program.

1981—International Media Ministries established. Center for Ministry to Muslims founded.

1982—A national Conference on the Holy Spirit held in Springfield. Kingsmen developed by Men's Ministries Department.

1983—Mission America is launched by the Division of Home Missions.

1984—Richard G. Champion named editor of *Pentecostal Evangel*. Health-Care Ministries started by Division of Foreign Missions.

1985—Berean School became Berean College of the Assemblies of God.

1986—G. Raymond Carlson succeeded Thomas F. Zimmerman as general superintendent. National Royal Rangers Training Center established in southwest Missouri.

1987—General Superintendent G. Raymond Carlson and executive presbyters signed a declaration proclaiming "Decade of Harvest" with the strategy to reach 5 million for Christ.

1988—Plans for the Decade of Harvest were officially announced.

1989—75th anniversary of the Assemblies of God. The AG reported more than 11,000 churches in the U.S. with a constituency of more than 2 million members. Overseas ministry had grown to include some 16 million people in 120 countries. Youth carried a torch from Hot Springs, Arkansas, to remember the revival fire from which the Assemblies of God emerged. Terry Raburn, then national Youth Department secretary, completed the run and presented the torch to General Superintendent G. Raymond Carlson at the General Council in Indianapolis.

Michael Cardone Media Center built in Springfield.

1992—First national Student Youth Alive Congress held in conjunction with National Sunday School Conference. *On Course*, a discipleship magazine for youth, was started.

1993—G. Raymond Carlson retired as general superintendent. Thomas E. Trask was elected general superintendent at General Council in Minneapolis, Minnesota.

1994—World Assemblies of God Congress convened in Seoul, South Korea. AG National Prayer Center established. Ministerial Enrichment Office established. AG participates in forming Pentecostal/Charismatic Churches of North America. Speed the Light giving reached $6 million.

1995—Senior Adult Ministries established. Jeffrey Brawner named *Revivaltime* speaker and initiates *MasterPlan* as the new weekly radio program. The Brownsville Revival began in Pensacola, Florida, on Father's Day.

1996—90th anniversary of Azusa Street revival. Cooperative Fellowship Agreement signed between the U.S. Assemblies of God and the Belarussian/Ukrainian Pentecostal Union.

1996—Pentecostal movement had spread around the world, represented by some 430 million people.

1997—Assemblies of God Theological Seminary moved to a beautiful new facility adjacent to the Evangel University campus in Springfield, Missouri.

1998— Missionettes curriculum rewritten and two new clubs, Friends and Girls Only, introduced; 40,000th Honor Star crowned.

1999—85th Anniversary of the founding of the Assemblies of God. Boys and Girls Missionary Crusade marked its 50th anniversary. A new radio program premiered called *From This Day Forward*, with hosts Dr. Richard Dobbins and Jerry Qualls. Berean University and ICI University began merger to form Global University.

2000—The close of the 20th century and the beginning of the 21st century.

Appendix 2: Churches of the Nebraska District *(as of March 2010)*

1. Ainsworth — Assembly of God — Gary D. Graesser
2. Albion — New Life Assembly of God — Donald L. Dennison
3. Alliance — Calvary Assembly of God — Steve A. Hahn
4. Atkinson — Abundant Grace Assembly of God — Loran R. Epp
5. Auburn — Calvary Christian Center Assembly of God — Tiger Moses
6. Aurora — Assembly of God — James A. Garfield
7. Bassett — Assembly of God — Gary D. Graesser
8. Bayard — Cornerstone Fellowship — Paul B. West
9. Beatrice — First Assembly of God — David A. Cramer
10. Bellevue — Bellevue Christian Center — Gary L. Hoyt
11. Big Springs — Assembly of God — Chris A. Wadle
12. Blair — Living Hope Christian Center — Andrew J. Korenak, III
13. Bridgeport — New Life Assembly — Scott A. Mans
14. Broken Bow — Assembly of God — Rick D. Johnson
15. Burton — Burton Assembly of God — Jesse Lee Meduna
16. Burwell — Assembly of God — David L. Garrett
17. Butte — Butte Full Gospel Church — Timothy L. Hazen
18. Chadron — Chadron Community Church — Dominick D. Warne
19. Chappell — Assembly of God — Richard L. Graeff
20. Coleridge — Coleridge Family Church
21. Columbus — Word of Life Church — Donald I. Owen
22. Cozad — Living Hope Assembly of God — Blake E. Armstrong
23. Crawford — Christ Community Church Assembly of God — Stephen A. Mallery
24. Crete — Radiant Springs Church — Victor H. Corrales
25. Dalton — Assembly of God
26. Ewing — Full Gospel Church — Wayne C. Smith
27. Fairbury — Fairbury Assembly of God — Randy J. Novotny
28. Falls City — Good News Assembly of God — Brian A. Thomas
29. Fremont — Full Life Assembly of God — Michael J. Washburn
30. Geneva — Assembly of God Family Worship Center — Hugh E. Campbell
31. Gering — Northfield Assembly of God — Phillip R. Parker
32. Gordon — Victory Hill Assembly of God — Danny L. Floyd
33. Gothenburg — Victory Assembly of God — Mark A. Borchardt
34. Grand Island — Abundant Life Christian Center — Stephen G. Warriner
35. Grand Island — Northridge Assembly of God — Mark K. Oberbeck
36. Grand Island — Vida Nueva — Carlos A. Barcenas
37. Hastings — North Shore Assembly — Anthony W. Anderson
38. Hebron — New Life Assembly of God — Timothy R. Boatright
39. Holdrege — North Park Assembly of God — Alexander S. Brodine
40. Kearney — New Life Assembly — Robert A. Wine
41. Kimball — Kimball Assembly of God Church — Scott R. Bailey
42. Lexington — Calvary Assembly of God — Marvin J. Masten, Jr.
43. Lexington — Emmanuel Assembly of God — Maria Celia Merino
44. Lincoln — Christ's Place — Richard S. Lorimer, II
45. Lincoln — Glad Tidings Assembly of God — Christopher Anderson
46. Lincoln — Lincoln Family Church — Sydney J. Maness
47. Lyons — New Life Assembly of God — Jeffrey L. Clark
48. Maxwell — Assembly of God — R. Mark Hoffman
49. Mc Cook — First Assembly of God
50. Milford — Assembly of God — David A. Geary
51. Minatare — Lighthouse Community Assembly of God — Paul D. Maunu

52. Mitchell — New Hope Assembly of God — Randall M. Brotzman and Brad Staman
53. Mullen — Mullen Assembly of God Church — Van Kelly Berry
54. Nebraska City — Cornerstone Church — Robert D. Conner
55. Norfolk — Victory Road Assembly of God — Mark D. Rose
56. North Platte — Calvary Assembly of God — Dennis K. Leitner
57. North Platte — First Assembly of God — Gary L. Goodwin
58. Ogallala — Radiant Life Assembly of God — David F. Gill
59. Omaha — Flatland Church — Bartley K. Wilkins
60. Omaha — Flatland24 — Jeffery S. Baker
61. Omaha — Freedom Church — Teran Anderson
62. Omaha — Glad Tidings Assembly of God — Walter J. DeVries
63. Omaha — Iglesia Cristiana Bendicion — Luis S. Gonzalez
64. Omaha — New Creation Community Church — Samuel J. Newland, II
65. Omaha — Omaha Christian Center — Ronald E. Helmick
66. Omaha — Omaha Hope Community Church — Petey K. Tellez
67. Omaha — Pacific Springs Assembly of God — Kelvin L. Nygren
68. Omaha — Rios De Alabanza
69. Omaha — South Side Assembly of God — Charles A. Davis
70. Omaha — The Market Church — Gregory S. Wallace
71. Omaha — The River
72. Oneill — Assembly of God — Michael D. Durre
73. Oneill — Word of Life Assembly — James Loutzenhiser, Jr.
74. Ord — Heartland Assembly of God — Thomas L. Burkholder
75. Oshkosh — Assembly of God — Maynard McCarthy
76. Papillion — Southridge Church — Troy E. Vandament
77. Pender — Cornerstone Assembly of God — Jonathan O. Olson
78. Plattsmouth — New Life Assembly of God — James R. Nielsen
79. Red Cloud — Cornerstone Assembly of God — Stephen Wilson
80. Saint Paul — River of Life Community Church — Timothy M. Rust
81. Scottsbluff — First Assembly of God — Leroy Z. Wyre
82. Scottsbluff — River of Life — Jose M. Menendez
83. Sidney — Christian Life Center Assembly of God — Arthur J. Gerhold
84. South Sioux City — River Hills Church of the Assemblies of God — Kevin W. Roach
85. South Sioux City — River Hills Hispanic Church — Omar Macias
86. Taylor — Assembly of God — Michael Sullivan, Sr.
87. Thedford — Bethel Assembly of God — William J. Trumblee
88. Valentine — Valentine Assembly of God Church — Dale E. Williams
89. Walthill — Assembly of God — Harold D. Ross, Jr.
90. Wayne — Praise Assembly of God — Richard D. Snodgrass
91. West Point — Elkhorn Valley Assembly of God — Raymond M. Libby
92. York — New Heights Assembly of God — Thomas L. James

Bibliography

"At Fremont and Omaha, Nebraska." In *Marvels and Miracles God Wrought in The Ministry for Forty-five Years,* by Mrs. M. B. Woodworth-Etter. Indianapolis: the author, 1922. pp. 411-414.

Blair, Charles E., with John and Elizabeth Sherrill. *The Man Who Could Do No Wrong*. Lincoln, VA: Chosen Books Publishing Company, 1981.

Burgess, Stanley M., Gary B. McGee, and Patrick H. Alexander, eds. *Dictionary of Pentecostal and Charismatic Movements.* Grand Rapids, MI: Zondervan, 1988.

Clark, Earl W. "Healed of Tumor on Brain Through Anointed Cloth." *The Need of the Hour: Healing for the Body.* Springfield, MO: Gospel Publishing House, 1924. pp. 60-61.

Correll, Norma. "Norma (Shoff) Correll." In *Iceland to Nebraska: The Olafur Hallgrimson Family*, by Margaret L. Sybrant. N.p: N.p., the author, 1985. p. H-15.

DeMent , Joyce. "Kids Kamp Reminiscing." In *Book of Memories, 50 Years: Nebraska Kid's Kamps, 1945 to 1995.* [Grand Island, NE: Nebraska District], 1995.

Hallgrimson, Rose. "Rose Hallgrimson Remembers." In *Iceland to Nebraska: The Olafur Hallgrimson Family*, by Margaret L. Sybrant. N.p: N.p., the author, 1985. p. J-8.

Hastie, Eugene N. "Growth and Spread of the Work." *History of The West Central District Council of the Assemblies of God.* Fort Dodge, IA: Walterick Printing Co., 1948. pp. 105-107.

Herrmann, Leonard. "I Remember…" In *Book of Memories, 50 Years: Nebraska Kid's Kamps, 1945 to 1995.* [Grand Island, NE: Nebraska District], 1995.

LaBerge, Agnes N. O. "History of the Pentecostal Movement from January 1, 1901." In *What God Hath Wrought: Life and Work of Mrs. Agnes N. O. LaBerge*. Chicago: Herald Publishing Co., [1920?].

Nebraska District Council. *Book of Memories, 50 Years: Nebraska Kid's Kamps, 1945 to 1995.* [Grand Island, NE: Nebraska District], 1995.

Ozman, Agnes. "Where the Latter Rain First Fell: The First One to Speak in Tongues." *Latter Rain Evangel*, January 1909. p. 2

Ramirez, Y. "Ministering Among Hispanics." In *Reflections of Faith: Assemblies of God Pioneers Sharing Memories Reflecting on Their Spiritual Heritage*. Springfield, MO: Benevolences Department, General Council of the A/G, 1983.

Spain, Joy. "Record of Spains Trip to Africa." In *Iceland to Nebraska: The Olafur Hallgrimson Family*, by Margaret L. Sybrant. N.p: N.p., the author, 1985. pp. I-8 to I-13.

Walker, David and Kathy Walker. *Spanning The Tide: Dedicated to All the Pioneers of Faith.* Mt. Jackson, VA: Bible Missions, [197?]. pp. 39, 44-49.

"Revivals at Ainsworth, Nebr. And Muncie, Indiana." In *Marvels and Miracles God Wrought in The Ministry for Forty-five Years,* by Mrs. M. B. Woodworth-Etter. Indianapolis: the author, 1922. pp. 366-367.

The Shepherd's Staff, edited by R. D. E. Smith. Minneapolis, MN: Northern Gospel Publishing House, 1946.

Timmons, J. C. "Report by Evangelist." In *Marvels and Miracles God Wrought in The Ministry for Forty-five Years,* by Mrs. M. B. Woodworth-Etter. Indianapolis: the author, 1922. p. 367

"Winnebago, Nebr. Indian Reservation." In *Marvels and Miracles God Wrought in The Ministry for Forty-five Years,* by Mrs. M. B. Woodworth-Etter. Indianapolis: the author, 1922. pp. 407-409.

Personal Papers

Anderson, I. "A Glimpse into Past Years." February 1962.

Palmer, L. "A Brief History of the Beginnings of the Franklin, NE Assembly of God Church." [199?]

Strom, Clarence L. "Our Family Story: A Bit of Yesterday and Today." N.p.: N.p., the author, [1975].

Articles from the *Pentecostal Evangel*

Aug. 30, 1913 Reif, Fannie. "Auburn, Neb.," p. 8.
Oct. 17, 1914 Short, W. L. "Auburn, Neb.," p. 3.
Oct. 24, 1914 Poole, Fred E. "Auburn, Nebraska," p. 4.
Oct. 31, 1914 Poole, Fred E. "Omaha, Nebraska," p. 4.
Dec. 19, 1914 Poole, Fred E. "Omaha, Nebraska," p. 3.
Jan. 9, 1915 Mills, Ralph L. "Omaha, Nebraska," p. 3.
Jan. 16, 1915 Poole, Fred E. "Omaha, Neb.," p. 3.
April 10, 1915 Dieffenwierth, L. A. "Auburn, Neb.," p. 2
April 10, 1915 Poole, Fred E. "Nebraska State Camp," p. 3.
April 17, 1915 Poole, Fred E. "Nebraska State Camp," p. 2.
May 29, 1915 "Workers Home and Assembly Room," p. 1.
Sept. 2, 1916 Stephens, J. F. and Emma. "Chappell, Neb.," p. 11.
Nov. 16, 1918 Harvey, Hermon L. "Report of Sister Etter's Meeting at Ainsworth, Nebraska," p. 13.
Junc 14, 1919 "State Camp Meeting at North Platte, Nebraska," p. 15.
Sept. 6, 1919 "Nebraska District Council," p. 14.
Nov. 15, 1919 Harvey, Hermon L. "McPherson Campaign in Nebraska," p. 10.
May 1, 1920 Bell, E. N. "Mid-West Convention," p. 10.
May 1, 1920 Rediger, J. C. "Helping the New Bible School," p. 10.
Oct. 30, 1920 "Omaha, Nebr.," p. 14.
Aug. 1, 1923 Smith, Mrs. H. G. "Healing at Chappell, Nebraska," p. 4.

June 28, 1924 Brown, W. H. [Mr and Mrs.] "Reports from the Field: South Sioux City, Nebr.," p. 12.
Nov. 5, 1927 Steinle, Hannah Mae. "New Nebraska Field," p. 12.
Sept. 22, 1928 Roll, Merle W. "Nebraska District Council," p. 13.
March 26, 1932 Foster, E. R. "Heavy Gains in Nebraska District," p. 13.
May 12, 1934 Millard, Glenn. "Nebraska District Council, Hastings, Nebr.," p. 13.
Nov. 30, 1946 Honderick, Loine C. "A Thrilling Home Missions Project" [Broken Bow, NE], p. 14.
Aug. 5, 1950 "Assembly of God, North Platte, Nebraska," pp. 1-2.
Nov. 1, 1953 "Glad Tidings Assembly, Omaha, Nebraska," pp. 1, 11.
Aug. 26, 1956 "New Church Dedicated at Alma, Nebraska," p. 23.
Dec. 8, 1957 "Church Dedicated in Nebraska" [Holdrege, NE], 28.
Feb. 23, 1958 "New Church Dedicated in Riverton, Nebraska," p. p. 19.
Nov. 9, 1958 "Men's Fellowship Day Observed at Nebraska Camp Meeting," p. 9.
Nov. 23, 1958 Leach, Roscoe L. "Thanksgiving C.A. Convention To Be Held in New Church at Grand Island, Nebraska," p. 25.
Dec. 21, 1958 Wilkins, L. E. "New Church in Nebraska" [Kearney, NE], p. 9.
Sept. 3, 1961 Dickinson, Lester W. "Nebraska Assemblies Release Revivaltime on Lexington Station," p. 24.
Sept. 3, 1961 "Omaha Church 25 Years Old" [Glad Tidings Assembly], p. 27.
April 18, 1965 "Breakthrough in Nebraska" [Cozad, NE], p. 22.
June 5, 1966 Foster, E. R. "The Converted Chicken House" [Aurora, NE], p. 7.
May 26, 1968 "Congregation Dedicates New Facilities" [Hastings, NE], p. 29.
Oct. 18, 1970 "Nebraska Church Notes Progress" [Glad Tidings Assembly, Omaha, NE], p. 29.
Feb. 17, 1974 "Nebraska Congregation Dedicates New Church" [Big Springs, NE], p. 29.
Aug. 18, 1974 "Three Days of Celebration Mark Dedication of New Building" [South Side Assembly, Omaha, NE], p. 24.
Nov. 24, 1974 "Nebraska Church Celebrates 50 Years; Dedicates New Building to the Lord" [First Assembly, Scottsbluff, NE], p. 27.
March 30, 1975 Wilkins, James D. "God Uses BankAmericard" [Bellevue Assembly, Bellevue, NE], pp. 18-19.
Jan. 29, 1978 "New Church Started in Nebraska" [Ord, NE], p. 28.
April 23, 1978 Altman, Larry. "Air Force Personnel Build a Church" [Bellevue Christian Center, Bellevue, NE], p. 10.
April 23, 1978 "Bellevue Assembly Adds Ministry to the Deaf," p. 11.
Aug. 20, 1978 "National Camp Leadership Institute To Meet in Nebraska Next Month" [North Platte, NE], p. 25.
Dec. 21, 1980 "Nebraska Assembly Outgrows New Sanctuary in First Year" [Glad Tidings Assembly, Omaha, NE], p. 28.
March 22, 1981 Nebraska Assembly Occupies New Facilities [Cornerstone Assembly, Pender, NE], p. 26.
Dec. 19, 1982 "Nebraska Church Observes 50th Year" [South Sioux City, NE], p. 27.
July 22, 1984 "Nebraska Pastor is Senior Police Chaplain" [J. Robert Birdwell of Christian Life Fellowship, Lincoln, NE], p. 27.
Nov. 25, 1984 "Nebraska Assembly Commemorates 50th Year" [First Assembly, Norfolk, NE], p. 25.
Nov. 24, 1985 "New Church Planted in Omaha, Nebr., Suburb" [Millard, NE], p. 28.
Dec. 14, 1986 "Prayer, a Bus Ministry, and a Jar of Pennies" [on Dale Campbell, a staff member at Bellevue Assembly, Bellevue, NE], p. 18.
Nov. 15, 1987 "Nebraska District Elects Two Officials" [Robert Nazarenus, superintendent; Howard Rice, secretary-treasurer], p. 27.

Aug. 12, 1990 Warriner, Stephen. "One Church Helping Another" [Calvary Assembly, Grand Island, NE], pp. 10-11.
Oct. 7, 1990 Robarge, Kim. "The Harvest As Close As Our Doorstep" [New Life Fellowship, Plattsmouth, NE], pp. 24-25.
Oct. 13, 1991 Blauvelt, Ronald. "Reaching Rural America" [Bethel Assembly of God, Thedford, NE]. pp. 19, 30.
Oct. 11, 1992 Edgerly, George. "We Have to Check the Figures" [Good News Assembly, Falls City, NE], pp. 8-9.
Nov. 10, 1996 "Outdoor Nativity," p. 22.
Feb. 22, 1998 "Revival Begins After House Burns," p. 24.
Aug. 16, 1998 Baker, Dana. "Why I Serve," p. 5.
Aug. 29, 1999 Noonan, Kirk. "Pastors Unite in Omaha, Nebraska," p. 23.
July 16, 2000 Kirpatrick, Joel. "Unity fans revival in Omaha," p. 24.
Aug. 13, 2000 "Court Invalidates Restrictions on Late-term Abortions," p. 23.
Nov. 19, 2000 Smith, Fred. "Why We Serve," p. 5.
Feb. 18, 2001 "Judge Upholds Praise Music," p. 26.
Sept. 30, 2001 "Husker Finds the Meaning of Life," p. 10.
Aug. 18, 2002 Matty, Danette. "Pastor Keeps Preaching After Accident," p. 7.
Nov. 24, 2002 "Christians Gather for Prayer After Bank Shootings," p. 11.
Oct. 19, 2003 "Nebraska Church Has 'Amaizing' Fund-raiser, p. 10.

Other Articles

Blumenthal, H. H. "Reports from Hershey and Carns, Nebraska." *The Pentecostal Advocate,* June 1930.

Boddy A. A. "A Nebraska Homestead on the Plains." *Confidence* [Sunderland, England], September 1914, pp. 165-167.

Eckley, Mrs. Edwin. "My Experience." *Word and Work* [Framingham, MA], July 1920, p. 5.

Forester, Mrs. J. J. "Letter from Mrs. J. J. Forster." *The Pentecostal Herald,* January 1, 1922, p. 3.

Gohr, Glenn. "The Midwest Bible School: Remembered on its 70th Anniversary." *Assemblies of God Heritage* (Summer 1990), pp. 13-16.

Gohr, Glenn. "The Midwest Bible School: Remembered on its 70th Anniversary, Part 2." *Assemblies of God Heritage* (Fall 1990), pp. 11-13.

Guth, A. D. "A Life of Victory and Power." *The Gospel Witness* [Los Angeles, CA], Vol. I, No. IV [1915?], p. 6

Hybl, Mrs. J. Z. "Letter from Mrs. James Z. Hybl." *The Pentecostal Herald,* January 1922, p. 3.

Hybl, Mrs. J. Z. "Letter from Mrs. James Z. Hybl." *The Pentecostal Herald,* August 1923, pp. 4-5.

Long, M. B. "Personal Letter." *The Pentecostal Herald*, February 1921, p. 1.

Long, M. G. "Letter of Praise." *The Pentecostal Herald,* May 15, 1922, p. 4.

Miller, John S., "Nine in One Family Baptized in the Holy Ghost," *The Gospel Witness* [Los Angeles, CA], Vol. I, No. IV, [1915?], pp. 2-3.

Miller, Silas J. "Personal Testimony of Pastor Silas J. Miller." *The Gospel Witness* [Los Angeles, CA], Vol. I, No. IV [1915?], 2.

Nicholson, J. "Evangelizing in Nebraska and Iowa: Remembering George and Katie Comstock." *Assemblies of God Heritage* (Spring 1998), 9-10.

Ozman, Agnes. "The First One to Speak in Tongues." *Latter Rain Evangel*, January 1909, 2.

Pike, J. M. "Testimony from B. H. Irwin." *The Way of Faith,* November 4, 1896.

Rake, G. H. "Dorchester Revival." *Nebraska Pentecostal Fellowship* 1:1 (March 1932).

Rediger, J. C. "Personal Testimony of Pastor J. C. Rediger," *Gospel Witness*, Vol. I, No. IV, [1915?]. p. 3.

Thurmond, C. E. *Nebraska Pentecostal Fellowship* 1:1 (March 1932).

Miscellaneous Photographs

Azusa Street Mission, Los Angeles, California, circa 1906

1st General Council of A/G at Hot Springs, AR, April 2-12, 1914

Horse transportation in the early years

Ministers on bank of Republican River, Franklin, NE, circa 1915

Lillie Hallgrimson Blakkolb with the Lena Mae Wilson team

Herbert Buffum

Union Pacific Train

SALT LAKE, ASHTON, YELLOWSTONE AND BUTTE

Butte Express No. 31 Day		Butte Special No. 29 Day		Table No. 6 Mountain Time	Salt Lake Special, No. 30 Day		Butte Express No. 32 Day	
				Union Pacific System				
Sun	11.30	Sun	1.15	Lv. Salt Lake Ar.	10.30	Sun	8.30	Mon
Mon	1.05	"	2.30	Lv. Ogden Ar.	9.20	"	7.20	"
				Mountain Time				
"	5.45	"	8.20	Ar. Pocatello Lv.	5.05	"	2.40	"
				Pacific Time				
"	6.50	"	8.50	Lv. Pocatello Ar.	4.55	"	3.30	"
"	8.55	"	8.45	Ar. Idaho Falls Lv	3.00	"	1.40	"
"	9.25	"		Lv. Idaho Falls Ar.	8.50	"	8.10	Sun
"	11.35	"		Ar. Ashton Lv.	6.45	"	6.05	"
				Ar. Yellowstone Lv.				
Mon	9.10	Sun	8.45	Lv. Idaho Falls Ar.	3.00	Sun	1.40	Mon
"	1.54	Mon	1.30	Lv. Armstead Lv.	10.35	"	9.10	Sun
"	4.05	"	3.45	Lv. Silver Bow Lv.	7.35	"	4.55	"
"	4.25	"	4.05	Ar. Butte Lv.	6.15	"	4.35	"

PORTLAND, WALLA WALLA AND SPOKANE

P'rtland-Sp'kane Limited No. 12 Day		Table No. 7 Pacific Time	Sp'kane-P'rtland Limited No. 11 Daily	
		Union Pacific System		
Sun.	7.00	Lv. Portland Ar.	8.15	Mon.
"	9.30	Lv. The Dalles Lv.	5.30	"
Mon.	12.10	Lv. Umatilla Lv.	2.35	"
"	12.55	Ar. Wallula Lv.	1.35	"
"	2.30	Lv. Wallula Ar.	12.30	"
"	4.00	Ar. Walla Walla Lv.	11.00	Sun.
"	1.05	Lv. Wallula Ar.	1.25	Mon.
"	3.10	Ar. Ayer Junction Lv.	11.45	Sun.
"	3.35	Lv. Ayer Junction Ar.	11.15	"
"	4.25	Ar. Riparia Lv.	10.25	"
"	7.00	Ar. Lewiston Lv.	7.00	"
"	3.15	Lv. Ayer Junction Ar.	11.40	"
"	7.15	Ar. Spokane Lv.	8.40	"

SALT LAKE, BUHL, BOISE AND PORTLAND

Butte Express No. 31-19 Day		Portland Special No. 29-17 Day		Table No. 5 Mountain Time	Oregon-Washington Limited No. 6-32 Day		Oregon-Washington Express No. 18-42 Day	
				Union Pacific System				
Sun	11.30	Sun	1.15	Lv. Salt Lake Ar.	8.30	Tue	5.20	Mon
Mon	1.05	"	2.30	Lv. Ogden Ar.	7.20	"	4.10	"
				Mountain Time				
"	5.45	"	6.20	Ar. Pocatello Lv.	3.40	"	12.01	"
				Pacific Time				
"	11.20	"	5.35	Lv. Pocatello Ar.	3.00	"	10.30	"
"	1.15	"	7.25	Ar. Minidoka Lv.	1.10	"	8.50	"
"	1.30	Mon	9.00	Lv. Minidoka Ar	7.00	Mon	8.30	"
"	3.45		11.35	Ar. Twin Falls Lv.	4.45	"	6.25	"
"	4.25	"	12.20	Ar. Buhl Lv.	4.00	"	5.45	"
"	1.15	Sun	7.25	Lv. Minidoka Ar.	1.10	Tue	8.50	"
"	2.45	"	8.50	Lv. Shoshone Lv.	11.45	Mon	7.25	"
"	3.40	"	9.40	Lv. Bliss Lv.	10.45	"	f 6.30	"
"	7.45	Mon	1.25	Ar. Nampa Lv.	7.00	"	3.00	"
"	7.50	"	3.10	Lv. Nampa Ar.	7.30	"	12.50	"
"	8.35	"	3.55	Ar. Boise Lv.	6.45	"	12.05	"
"	7.45	"	1.25	Lv. Nampa Ar.	7.00	"	3.00	"
Tue	3.15	"	8.15	Lv. La Grande Lv.	11.35	"	8.20	Sun
"	3.30	"	7.00	Ar. Portland Lv.	11.00	Sun	9.30	"

SPOKANE-BOISE

Sp'kane-P'rtland Limited No. 11-6 Day		Table No. 8 Pacific Time	Fast Mail No. 5-8 Day	
		Union Pacific System		
Sun.	8.40	Lv. Spokane Ar.	8.45	Mon.
Mon.	2.30	Ar. Umatilla Lv.		
"	5.15	Lv. Umatilla Ar.		
"	7.30	Lv. Pendleton Lv.	8.00	Mon.
"	11.35	Lv. La Grande Lv.	2.20	"
"	5.25	Lv. Ontario Lv.		
"	7.00	Ar. Nampa Lv.	8.20	Sun.
"	8.35	Ar. Boise Lv.	6.45	"

EQUIPMENT

For condensed schedules see preceding tables indicated by numbers shown below.

WESTBOUND

No. 1 Overland Limited. Daily. Table 1

Club Car................Chicago to San Francisco.
Observation Sleeping Car. Chicago to San Francisco—Drawing-room and Compartment.
Ogden to Los Angeles, Ten-section.
Standard Sleeping Cars...Chicago to San Francisco—10 Sections, Drawing-room and Compartment.
Chicago to Los Angeles—10 Sections, Drawing-room and Compartment.
Chair Car................Ogden to Los Angeles.
Dining Cars..............Serving all meals.

No. 5 Fast Mail. Daily. Table 8

EASTBOUND

No. 2 Overland Limited. Daily. Table 1

Club Car................San Francisco to Chicago.
Observation Sleeping Cars. San Francisco to Chicago—Drawing-room and Compartment.
Los Angeles to Ogden, Ten-section.
Standard Sleeping Cars...San Francisco to Chicago—10 Sections, Drawing-room and Compartment.
Los Angeles to Chicago—10 Sections, Drawing-room and Compartment.
Tourist Sleeping Car......Los Angeles to Chicago—Sixteen-section (Ogden to Chicago in No. 20).
Chair Car................Los Angeles to Ogden.
Dining Car...............Serving all meals.

No. 4 Atlantic Express. Daily. Table 4

Union Pacific Railroad Schedules

Aimee Semple McPherson meeting at Holdrege, NE, Oct. 1919. Front row, starting in the center (l-r): Minnie Kennedy (in fur coat), Aimee Semple McPherson, Hermon L. Harvey, A. P. Collins, 5 unidentified.

Maria Woodworth-Etter , June 1, 1922

George & Katie Comstock in Salvation Army uniforms with children, Lula (front, center) and Leroy & Howard (in back), circa 1910

Midwest Bible School with S. A. Jamieson, principal, standing in front, 1920

E. R. Foster revival poster

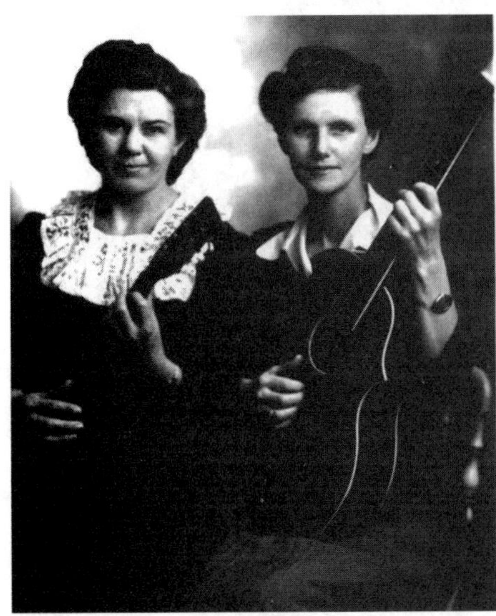

Rose and Viola Hallgrimson

Harold and LoRee Allen

Chester Anderson family musicians and evangelists with bus Chester used to transport people during World War II.

Rev. and Mrs. Allen Shaffer

Irl J. Walker

Rev. G. A. Comstock

Hasting Pavilion at Prospect Park, circa 1937

The B. C. Heinze family in the 1930s

Southwestern Bible School students at York, NE camp, 1937. W. B. McCafferty (front, center); Catharine McCafferty (back row, dark dress).

P. C. Nelson, 1930s

Camp meeting at Gothenburg, NE, 1936. (L-r): Hugh Cadwalder & Myer Pearlman, speaker; A. M. Alber, NE District Superintendent.

E. M. and Estella Clark's wedding, 1938

Tents at York camp, 1937

Baptismal Service and cars

J. M. Peck

M. F. and Ruth Brandt

Congregation in front of new parsonage at Westerville, NE. Harold James is standing on the far left.

1946 map of Nebraska District

Clyde King family in the 1950s

Kids Kamp directors and camp speaker in the 1950s. (L-r): Bonnie Roll, Phil Wannenmacher (speaker), Loretta Lebsack.

Loyalty campaign

Lena Mae (James) Leach playing for *Revivaltime* in the early 1950s

Roscoe (Bud) and Lena Mae Leach, 1958

Norman Correll family in the 1950s

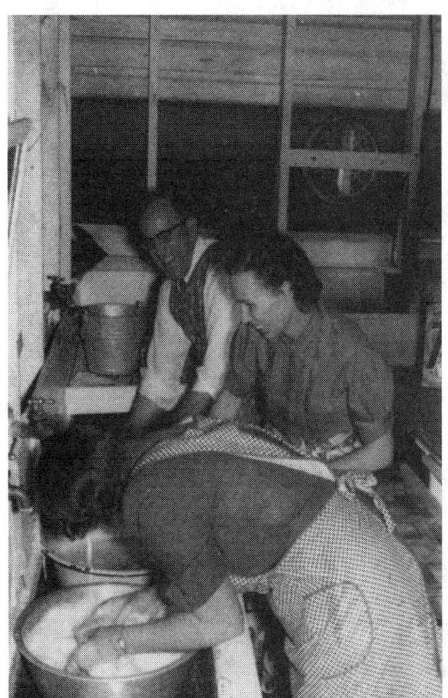

Lester Dickinson doing dishes in the old dining hall

Bonnie Roll

Ministers at McCook for 1956 District Council

Men's day in the old tabernacle

Loren and Millie Triplett at camp with money pinned to them

Lynn Nichols

Joyce DeMent at Camp

Supt. Lester Dickinson at his desk

Spud DeMent

The Herman W. Lebsacks

1970 Kids Kamp

Camp Observes 25th Anniversary

. . . Was 1st in U. S.

LEXINGTON CHAMBER OF COMMERCE gave a plaque to Joe Masten, camp director, in observance of the Camp's 25 years. Melvin Brown made presentation.

Nebraska Assemblies of God Kids Kamp, the very first one ever held in the United States, Friday, observed its 25th anniversary of founding at the Assemblies conference grounds in west Lexington.

At a banquet in the dining hall, 260 people were present, including 185 Kampers along with a staff of workers, teachers, counselors and special guests.

Melvin Brown of Lexington Chamber of Commerce presented the camp director, Joe Masten, with a plaque commemorating the 25th anniversary. Nebraska has the distinctive honor of having the first Kids Kamp in the nation. The Rev. Fred Lessten, who was at the time chaplain of the penitentiary in Lincoln, served as director of the first Kamp in 1945. More than 8,000 boys and girls have been registered during the 25-year period.

Several men, who were enrolled in the first Kamp in 1945, were present for the 25th anniversary and each spoke briefly. They were Eugene Brandt, administrator of the nursing homes in Gering and Minatare, the Rev. Nolan Blakkolb of Lincoln, the Rev. Leonard Herrmann of York, and the Rev. Dale Lesher of Norfolk. Each of these fathers had a son or daughter enrolled in the 1970 Kamps.

Among the guests were two instructors of the 1945 Kamp, the district superintendent Lester W. Dickinson of Grand Island and the Rev. Clyde King of Elm Creek. Several former directors were present and extended greetings.

Mr. Masten was master of ceremonies and introduced the guests. Superintendent of the schools at Winside, he and his wife, Ellen, were directors of the three 1970 Kids Kamps held July 6-25, with a record registration of 504 children. Lynn and Becky Wickstrom of Loveland, Colo., were speakers for the Kamp.

Letters of congratulations were read from Governor Norbert Tiemann, Senator Carl Curtis, and Congressman Robert Denney.

25th YEAR FOR KID'S KAMP IN NEBRASKA

One-hundred eighty-eight boys and girls from the lower Pan-Handle, the Republican Valley and the Siouxland sections registered for the final week of 1970 Nebraska Kids Kamp at the Assemblies of God Conference Grounds near Lexington, Nebra., last Monday.

"Mr. Kids Kamp", Paul Anderson, State Director of Milford, Nebr., and Mr. and Mrs. Joe Masten of Winside, Nebr., who directed this year's camps were pleased with the record-breaking total enrollment of 505 for the three camps.

Rev. and Mrs. Wickstrom and Joey (dummy), the guest speakers, the Mastens and a staff of about 50-60 workers, counselors, and teachers helped make it a great time for all the campers including those attending from this area: were Jeff and Jay Bellar, Jeannie and Cheryl Rose, Debby Arnold, Kathy Kramer, Regina and Reva Watson, Tami Kunzie and Rick Fahrenholz, all of Walthill, Theresa and Bruce Smith from Rosalie, and Kevin Kellogg of Decatur.

Joe Masten , Sr. receives a 25-year camp award

Horsemanship Class, 1967

Clyde King and Horsemanship Class, 1970

Completed multi-purpose building at Camp

Enjoying the pool at the multi-purpose building

Page 5
DAWSON COUNTY HERALD

Lexington, Nebraska
Monday, July 24, 1972

BOX HOCKEY is one of the popular sports at the Assembly of God Kids Kamp. Wednesday, Dwight Stubbs of the Lexington Chamber Diplomats played one game with a Kamper. The Diplomats were on hand for a goodwill tour of the facilities.

Facilities Drawing Over 3,000 Summer Youth, Adult Campers

Kids Kamp at the Assemblies of God Church Campground drew 460 youngsters age 9-12.

It drew another 135 volunteer staffers.

The two weekly sessions are but a part of the summertime activity at the 17 acre site to the west of this community.

sion and a 30 minute session.

Free and recreation time is spent on the baseball diamonds, archery range, volleyball court (a real popular sport with the girls), horseback riding and other activities.

Stocker, a seven year veteran of the ministry and a college degree holder, was elected to the post he now holds in April by the state district. He lives in Grand Island, church district headquarters, and spends most of his summer at the camps.

Mrs. Stocker spent much of her summer here with her husband but, is now back in the Third City for a short rest.

"With the exception of myself, District Director Rev. L. W. Dickenson, Campground Director Mrs. Joe Masten of Lexington, the caretaker and cooks;" Stocker said, "everyone is working on a volunteer basis. A number of leaders for Kids Kamp are high schoolers."

Caretaker Lowell Young has been at the campground for four months. His is a permanent position.

The adult camp at the end of the summer will draw nearly 2,300 persons for part or all of the 10 day session. Up to 350 persons can stay at the camp at one time. Nearly 700 are expected for each of the two Sundays of the adult session.

"Working with Christian education means I have duties at adult camp, too," said Stocker. "But soon after the end of the last session I will take off for a few days fishing and to relax before the fall and winter work begins."

W.M.C. Day at camp in 1970 (newspaper)

Playing basketball in the multi-purpose building

Paul Ackerman, "Mr. Kids Kamp"

1987 D-CAPS Dave and Laura Graves

Rev. Charles Blair and Rev. & Mrs. L. W. Dickinson at reception for Leota Eigsti's retirement as secretary for district office, January 1984.

1987 officers: Howard Rice, Sec/Treas., Robert Nazarenus, Supt. and Sam Mayo, Asst. Supt.

1986 Family Camp. On the left: Jeanne and Dwain Jones, speaker, and Spud and Joyce DeMent One the right: Verna and Jim Wilkins, Jennifer DeMent (in back)

Susan Wortheimer

Kevin Wehrli family, Feb. 1996

Having fun at Camp

Bellevue Christian Center Master's Commission